A
FIGHTING
CHANCE

A
FIGHTING
CHANCE

Elizabeth Warren

METROPOLITAN BOOKS   HENRY HOLT AND COMPANY   NEW YORK

Metropolitan Books
Henry Holt and Company, LLC
Publishers since 1866
175 Fifth Avenue
New York, New York 10010
www.henryholt.com

Metropolitan Books® and ® are registered trademarks of Henry Holt and Company, LLC.

Library of Congress Cataloging-in-Publication Data

Warren, Elizabeth.
  A fighting chance / Elizabeth Warren. — First edition.
     pages   cm
  Includes bibliographical references and index.
  ISBN 978-1-62779-052-9 (hard cover) — ISBN 978-1-62779-053-6 (electronic book)
 1. Warren, Elizabeth.   2. Women legislators—United States—Biography.   3. Legislators—
United States—Biography.   4. United States. Congress. Senate—Biography.   5. United States—
Politics and government—2009–   I. Title.
  E901.1.W37A3 2014
  328.73'092—dc23
  [B]   2014000776

Henry Holt books are available for special promotions and premiums.
For details contact: Director, Special Markets.

First Edition 2014

Designed by Meryl Sussman Levavi

Printed in the United States of America

10 9 8 7 6 5 4 3 2 1

For Octavia, Lavinia, Atticus, and all our children

Contents

Prologue: A Fighting Chance   1

1 | Choosing Battles   5

2 | The Bankruptcy Wars   48

3 | Bailing Out the Wrong People   83

4 | What $1 Million a Day Can Buy   127

5 | An Agency for the People   164

6 | The Battle for the Senate   208

Epilogue: Fighting Again . . . and Again   273

Notes   279

Acknowledgments   337

Index   347

A
FIGHTING
CHANCE

Prologue | A Fighting Chance

I'M ELIZABETH WARREN. I'm a wife, a mother, and a grandmother. For nearly all my life, I would have said I'm a teacher, but I guess I really can't say that anymore. Now I'd have to introduce myself as a United States senator, though I still feel a small jolt of surprise whenever I say that.

This is my story, and it's a story born of gratitude.

My daddy was a maintenance man and my mother worked the phones at Sears. More than anything, my parents wanted to give my three older brothers and me a future. And all four of us have lived good lives. My oldest brother, Don Reed, served twenty years in the military, with 288 combat missions in Vietnam to his credit. In good years, my brother John had a union job operating a crane, and in leaner years he took whatever construction work he could get. My brother David had a special spark; he started his own business, and when that didn't work out, he started another business, because he couldn't imagine a world where he wasn't living by his wits every day. I went to college and became a teacher, first for special-needs kids and then for law students; only much later did I get involved in politics. My brothers and I all married and had children, and my parents plastered their walls, their refrigerator, and their tabletops with pictures of their much-loved grandchildren.

I will be grateful to my mother and daddy until the day I die. They worked hard—really hard—to help my brothers and me along. But we also succeeded, at least in part, because we were lucky enough to grow up in an America that invested in kids like us and helped build a future where we could flourish.

Here's the hard truth: America isn't building that kind of future any longer.

Today the game is rigged—rigged to work for those who have money and power. Big corporations hire armies of lobbyists to get billion-dollar loopholes into the tax system and persuade their friends in Congress to support laws that keep the playing field tilted in their favor. Meanwhile, hardworking families are told that they'll just have to live with smaller dreams for their children.

Over the past generation, America's determination to give every kid access to affordable college or technical training has faded. The basic infrastructure that helps us build thriving businesses and jobs—the roads, bridges, and power grids—has crumbled. The scientific and medical research that has sparked miraculous cures and inventions from the Internet to nanotechnology is starved for funding, and the research pipeline is shrinking. The optimism that defines us as a people has been beaten and bruised.

It doesn't have to be this way.

I am determined—fiercely determined—to do everything I can to help us once again be the America that creates opportunities for anyone who works hard and plays by the rules. An America of accountability and fair play. An America that builds a future for not just some of our children but for *all* of our children. An America where everyone gets what I got: a fighting chance.

My story seems pretty unlikely, even to me. I never expected to run for office—but then again, I never expected to do a lot of things in my life. I never expected to climb a mountain. I never expected to meet the president of the United States. I never expected to be a blonde. But here I am.

The story starts in Oklahoma, where I grew up, and it tumbles through a life built around husbands and babies and setting the kitchen on fire. I made my way to a commuter college, a teaching job, a public law school, and, eventually, a professorship. As I started weaving in academic research, I became more and more worried about what was happening to America's families, and the story shifted to Washington, where I picked my first public fight. In 1995, I agreed to take on what I thought would be some part-time public service for a couple of years, and I quickly got caught up in a battle over our nation's bankruptcy law. I know that sounds a little obscure, but underneath it was a clash about whether our government exists to serve giant banks or struggling families.

The battle lasted much longer than I'd expected—a full ten years, in fact. My own life threaded through, of course, with graduations and funerals and grandchildren of my own. When that battle ended, I picked up another, and then another and another—a total of five big fights in all. They ranged from fighting for a fresh start for families who had suffered a job loss or a serious illness, to trying to force the government to be transparent about what was really going on with the bank bailout, to tangling with the big banks over dishonest mortgages. But the way I see it, even as they took me this way and that, all five battles were about a single, deeper threat: America's middle class is under attack. Worse, it's not under attack by some unstoppable force of nature. It's in trouble because the game is deliberately rigged.

This book tells a very public story about fraud and bailouts and elections. It also tells a very personal story about mothers and daughters, day care and dogs, aging parents and cranky toddlers. It's not meant to be a definitive account of any historical event—it's just what I saw and what I lived. It's also a story about losing, learning, and getting stronger along the way. It's a story about what's worth fighting for, and how sometimes, even when we fight against very powerful opponents, we *can* win.

I never expected to go to Washington. Heck, for the most part I never even *wanted* to go. But I'm here to fight for something that I believe is worth absolutely everything: to give each one of our kids a fighting chance to build a future full of promise and discovery.

1 | Choosing Battles

I KNOW THE DAY I grew up. I know the minute I grew up. I know why I grew up.

I was twelve, tall for my age and self-conscious about how thin I was. My bones stood out in my wrists, my knees, my elbows. I had crooked teeth and wore glasses for reading. I had straight-as-string dark brown hair that my aunt Bert cut twice a year. I already knew that I would never be beautiful like my much older cousin Candy, who was a sorority girl and had married the son of a successful car dealer.

I was standing in my mother's bedroom on a warm spring day. Mother had pulled a black dress out of her closet and laid it on the bed. She was crying. My mother cried a lot after my daddy got sick.

A few months earlier, on a cold, gray Sunday, my daddy had been working on our car. Near evening, he came in and sat down at the kitchen table. He just sat there. Daddy was always on the move, so it was odd to see him sit still, looking down, as if he was concentrating on something. His skin looked splotchy and his hands shook.

I was at the table reading, and Mother was at the stove, frying something for dinner. She asked him what was wrong. When he didn't say anything, she accused him of being sick, and he denied it. I closed my book and went upstairs to my bedroom.

After a while, Mother called up the stairs, "Betsy, we're going to the hospital. You stay here. Eat your dinner." By then my three brothers had all grown up and moved out, so it was just me and my little dog, Missy.

After dinner, Missy got the scraps and I waited for someone to come home.

For the next week, Aunt Bee and Uncle Stanley picked me up from school. Every afternoon, they took me to the hospital, where Mother sat by Daddy's bed. Daddy was slim, with close-cropped gray hair. He had light blue eyes and fair skin that was always slightly sunburned, but now he looked gray and tired.

All week, people from our church came by our house with casseroles and thick, sweet desserts. I remember how they used the words *heart attack*. Everyone paused before they said it. "When your father had his, uh, heart attack, was he working outside?" "I heard your daddy had, um, a heart attack. I hope he's going to be all right." The pauses scared me.

After Daddy got out of the hospital, he stayed home for a long time.

He ate poached eggs with the yolks taken out, and when he lifted a bag of groceries out of the car, Mother would yell, "Don, stop! Stop that!" I could hear a thread of panic in her voice.

We lived in Oklahoma City. My parents had bought this particular house because it was right inside the boundary line of what my mother believed was the best school district around. The house had wiring that sparked and plaster that fell off the ceiling, but Daddy was handy, and it had a big yard where my mother grew irises and roses. That spring, Daddy didn't work around the house. Mostly, he sat by himself on an old wooden chair in the garage, smoking and staring somewhere far away.

My mother usually picked me up from school in our bronze-toned station wagon. One day she showed up driving the old, off-white Studebaker that Daddy had been driving back and forth to work. As I climbed in the car, I asked where the station wagon was.

"It's gone."

"Gone where?"

"Gone."

I kept pushing. My mother was staring straight ahead, fingers tight on the steering wheel.

After one more "Where?" she answered in a low voice, "We couldn't pay. They took it."

I never should have asked.

Eventually, Daddy's doctor said he could go back to work, but somehow his old job—selling carpeting at Montgomery Ward—was gone.

The store gave him a different job selling lawn mowers and fences, only he didn't get a regular paycheck anymore. Now he depended on commissions. Daddy was naturally quiet, not the kind who usually thrives in sales.

One night at dinner, I asked him why he didn't work in the carpet department anymore. My mother cut in with something about his hours and his insurance. I didn't understand it, but I understood the bitter tone. In her view, his company had robbed him of something he'd worked for. And now, she said, "They think he's going to die."

I needed to stop asking questions.

After school one day, I went with Mother and Aunt Bee to look at a little house with a FOR RENT sign in the front yard. It was small, white, and up on blocks, which meant dogs or raccoons could hide under it. I still remember that it smelled funny, like dust and old cooking.

I didn't ask why we had to move.

Sometimes that spring I would overhear my parents arguing. I guess I shouldn't describe it as arguing; my father never said much of anything, while my mother yelled louder. They drank more, a lot more. No one told me, but I knew, the way kids always know. I knew we were about to lose our house, pretty much the same way we lost the car. I knew that my mother blamed my daddy for not doing "what a man is supposed to do" and taking care of us.

A few days later I was upstairs, standing in my mother's bedroom. Mother's face was puffy, and she had rubbed her eyes to a fierce red color. About a dozen wadded-up tissues were on the bedspread next to the black dress.

I remembered the dress from years earlier, when we still lived in Norman. It was the dress she wore to funerals and graduations. It was a stiff black fabric, with short sleeves and an insert panel in the front, and it had a short black tie at the neck. The dress zipped on the side.

At first I was confused. I wondered if someone had died. But then I understood that she had an important appointment. She had heard that they were hiring at the Sears, Roebuck near our house, and she was interviewing for a job. She was fifty.

Mother barely acknowledged my presence. But as she wrestled her way into her girdle and fastened her hose, she began talking. She wasn't going to lose this house. She would walk to Sears. She would make only minimum wage, but that was a whole lot better than commission. Betsy could take care of herself. I wasn't sure if she was talking to me or just to herself, so I didn't say anything.

She tugged the dress over her head, struggling to get it over her shoulders, across her belly, and pulled down over her hips. Sometime during her forties, after giving birth to four children, the slim beauty my daddy married had given way to a thicker version of herself.

I stood looking at her while she tugged on the zipper. She held her breath. She worked the zipper. The tears dropped off her chin and onto the floor. At last, she got the zipper all the way to the top. She rubbed her eyes with another Kleenex and blew her nose. She stood still for a while.

Finally, she lifted her head and looked straight at me. "How do I look? Is it too tight?"

The dress *was* too tight—way too tight. It pulled and puckered. I thought it might explode if she moved. But I knew there wasn't another nice dress in the closet.

And that was the moment I crossed the threshold. I wasn't a little girl anymore.

I stood there, as tall as she was. I looked her right in the eye and said: "You look great. Really."

I stood on the front porch and watched her walk down the street. It was quiet at that time of day. The sun was hot, and she was wobbly in her high heels, but she walked straight ahead.

She got the job answering phones at Sears. Later, Daddy left his job as a salesman at Montgomery Ward—or maybe he was let go, I don't really know. He got work as a maintenance man cleaning up around an apartment building. My parents held on to the house until after I graduated from high school, and then they gave it up and moved to an apartment.

My mother never had it easy. She fought for everything she and my daddy ever had. And when things got really tough, she did what needed to be done.

Dreams of Flying

My family stories set the direction of my life long before I was born.

In the 1920s, my daddy had big dreams. He wanted to fly airplanes. I grew up hearing about how he was barely out of high school when he rebuilt a little two-passenger, open-cockpit airplane and taught himself to fly above the prairies of eastern Oklahoma. I always pictured him landing and taking off in vast wheat fields, a tiny plane in an immense blue sky.

But there was something he loved even more than an airplane: he loved my mother. She was fifteen when he noticed her, a whisper-thin, dark-haired beauty who was lively and funny and whose beautiful low voice made her a favorite to sing at weddings and funerals. She would sit for hours in an empty room and play the piano and sing. My daddy fell completely in love with her. His parents bitterly opposed the match because my mother's family was part Native American and that was a big dividing line in those days. But that didn't stop my parents. They eloped in 1932, when Mother was nineteen and Daddy had just turned twenty.

They survived the double blows of the Dust Bowl and the Great Depression in the small town where they had grown up. Half a century later, both my parents still talked of bank failures and families who lost their farms.

By the time World War II came along, they already had three young boys. Daddy tried to enlist to be a fighter pilot in the war, but the Army Air Forces (as it was known then) said he was too old, or at least that's the explanation I heard. Instead, they took him on as a flight instructor, so the family moved from the little town of Wetumka, Oklahoma, to the bigger town of Muskogee. When the war finally ended, Daddy desperately wanted a job flying the new passenger planes for one of the fast-growing airlines like TWA or American. But that didn't work out either. My mother told me that those jobs also went to the younger men.

After the war, my parents wanted to go back to Wetumka, where they had grown up. But now that my mother and daddy had been away, my grandfather said that my daddy no longer had a job in the family store. He would have to find work somewhere else.

So my daddy scraped together what cash he could and joined up with a partner to start a new business selling cars in Seminole, another small town in Oklahoma. Daddy had always been handy, so he did the car repairs, while his partner worked the front office and handled sales. But the partner ran off with the money, or so the family story went—maybe he just ran the business into the ground. My parents had to start over again.

After that, Daddy moved from one job to another and my parents moved from one little rental house to another. My three brothers grew up, and I was the late-in-life surprise, born in 1949. Daddy used to say that after three boys, I was "the cherry on the whipped cream." Mother used to say that she was a member of the PTA "longer than any woman on God's green earth."

By the early 1950s, our family landed in Norman, and my parents put a down payment on a tiny tract house on a gravel street at the edge of town. It had two bedrooms and one bath, with a converted garage where my three brothers slept. One by one, each of my brothers headed off to the military—the air force for the oldest two, Don Reed and John, and the army for David.

The summer I turned eleven, we moved the twenty miles to Oklahoma City. Mother had lobbied Daddy to move to the city in the hope that I'd be able to go to a really good school. By then, Daddy was selling carpet at Montgomery Ward, and eventually my parents found a house that they liked. Daddy kept his tired old Studebaker, but he bought a used station wagon for Mother. To me, that station wagon was luxury itself: it was a glowing bronze color, with leatherette seats and an automatic transmission. It even had air-conditioning.

Book of Colleges

Like a zillion other families, we got by.

My family had been through plenty of ups and downs over the years, and after Daddy's heart attack, it took both my parents' paychecks to manage. But things steadied out over time and we regained our footing. They kept the house and I got to stay in the same public school. I took on babysitting jobs, waitressed in my aunt Alice's restaurant, and made money by sewing dresses for my aunts. I even sold puppies: Daddy borrowed the neighbor's little black poodle and introduced him to Missy, and the result was a litter of adorable puppies that I sold in a single weekend.

Like a million other teenagers, I hated high school. Classes were okay, and I liked my teachers. I tried hard to fit in, joining the Cygnets Pep Club and the Courtesy Club, but I wasn't good at *high school*—friends, parties, football games. We still had the old Studebaker, now pocked with rust, and my daddy used to drop me off a block away from the school. We both said it was to avoid the traffic, but the traffic was an endless stream of shiny new cars. At the time, I was sure I was the only kid in the entire school whose parents struggled with money. By now I'm just as sure that wasn't true, but the teenage me didn't have much perspective.

My senior year, I checked out a book about colleges from the high school counselor's office. When my mother saw the book, she gave me a hard look. "You aren't thinking about going away to college, are you?" Maybe that had once been her plan for me, before Daddy's heart attack changed everything, but now it was out of the question. She pointed out that we couldn't afford it, that she and Daddy just didn't make enough money. Besides, she argued, I needed to set my sights realistically. It was harder for a woman with a college education to find a husband. "Find a husband" was clearly the goal for any young girl, and I was a pretty iffy candidate.

But later she came back to the topic. If I really wanted to go to college, I could live at home, get a job, and go to school part-time somewhere close. She knew I wanted to be a teacher, and she figured that kind of ambition would probably get pushed aside once I got married and real life set in, but maybe I could go to college until I snagged a husband.

I had a different plan.

Girl with a Plan

It was the fall of 1965, and I was only sixteen, but because I'd skipped a grade, I was now a senior in high school. The way I looked at it, I wasn't pretty and I didn't have the highest grades in my school. I didn't play a sport, couldn't sing, and didn't play a musical instrument. But I did have one talent. I could fight—not with my fists, but with my words. I was the anchor on the debate team.

Debate let me stretch as far as I could go. We researched hard topics— free trade, collective bargaining, nuclear disarmament, Medicare—and I started to understand that I could tackle things I didn't know and teach myself a lot. But most of all, debate was about self-discipline and never giving up. I might get battered, but not beaten.

I figured that debating was my shot at college. So I sat in my room with the door closed, and I read every description in the college book, looking for schools that bragged about their debate teams. I hoped I could find one that would offer me a scholarship. I found only one school—Northwestern— that featured debate in its description. Then I got another lead from a boy who was a year ahead of me on the debate team. After graduation, he had gone to George Washington University. He told me GW had a great debate team—and a debate scholarship.

Two possibilities. The way I figured it, two was a lot more than none. This plan could work.

I sent away to both colleges for applications, then raced home from debate practice every afternoon a few minutes ahead of my mother to intercept any mail. When the forms arrived, I filled them out, bought money orders at the 7-Eleven, mailed them off, and then settled in to wait.

I had the idea that I would get a great scholarship and then present it to my parents as an accomplished fact. If I could go to college for free, how could they say no?

But the plan hit a snag. As I filled out the college applications, I realized that to be eligible for a scholarship, I also needed a financial disclosure form from my parents. I'd applied to college, but there was no way to get the help I needed without telling them what I was up to.

I waited until dinner one night. As the three of us sat quietly at the kitchen table, I suddenly said very cheerfully, "There are lots of scholarships for people who want to go to college." I probably had the same forced merriment of the woman selling floor wax on a television commercial. When no one said anything, I said in a quieter voice, "I want to try for one." I didn't mention that I'd already sent off applications to two faraway colleges.

My mother repeated that we couldn't afford college, but I was ready. I argued. I pleaded. There are scholarships that make college free. Why couldn't I try to get into one of those?

My mother kept saying no, but then Daddy surprised both of us, saying: "Let her try, Polly."

And that was how I ended up with my parents' tax returns. As I filled in the financial aid forms, I was surprised by the numbers. I divided their income by 52 and saw how little money they earned each week. I knew money was tight, but were we *poor*? My mother had always claimed that we weren't poor, but I felt very unsteady.

I gave Daddy the forms to sign and handed back the tax returns. No one talked about the forms again.

One afternoon in the spring, two letters arrived on the same day: both schools had accepted me, but the money wasn't the same. Northwestern offered some help, but George Washington went all the way—a full scholarship and a federal student loan. If I was careful with the money they were offering, I could afford to go. I was thrilled. Good-bye, Oklahoma City—GW, here I come!

My mother responded to my news with equal parts pride and worry. She would say to friends: "Well, she figured out how to go to college for free, so what could I say? But I don't know if she'll ever get married."

First Comes Marriage

College was a whole new world for me. I had never been north or east of Pryor, Oklahoma. I had never seen a ballet, never been to a museum, and never ridden in a taxi. I'd never had a debate partner who was black, never known anyone from Asia, and never had a roommate of any kind. But the most remarkable part was that in college I wasn't poor. I had sold my parents on the idea of college being free, and although it turned out I was a little too optimistic, I had my loans and a part-time job, and I worked all summer. I still kept cash in a white sock tucked in the back of a drawer, but now I knew I had enough to get me through each term. I had a taste of security, and it felt like heaven.

Two years into college, Jim Warren popped back into my life. He was the first boy I'd ever dated—and the first to dump me. He was seventeen and I was thirteen when we began dating; he was a high school junior on the advanced debate team and I was a freshman just beginning debate. Now he had graduated from college. He had landed a good job with IBM in Houston and was ready to get married. He told me I was cute and fun. Best of all, the guy who had dumped me said he wanted to marry *me*. He seemed so sure of himself, so confident about what life should look like.

I was amazed—amazed and grateful—that he had chosen me. I said yes in a nanosecond.

Less than eight weeks after Jim proposed, I gave up my scholarship, dropped out of college, sewed a wedding gown, and walked down the aisle of Oklahoma City's May Avenue United Methodist Church on Daddy's arm. It was the fall of 1968. I was nineteen.

Jim and I packed up his little sky-blue Mustang and moved into a small apartment in Houston. I got a temp job the first week. The money was good, but I wanted to go back to school. I still dreamed of being a teacher, and that meant I needed a college degree.

I now had what Jim jokingly called a "reverse dowry"—I owed money on my student loans from GW, even though I hadn't gotten a diploma. But I had a plan. If I could finish college and get a teaching job, I could make a steady salary *and* the government would forgive some of those loans every year. The University of Houston was about forty minutes away, and tuition was only $50 a semester. I persuaded Jim that it would make sense for me to go back to school.

In 1970, just after I finished college in Houston, Jim was transferred to IBM's office in New Jersey. Soon after we moved, I got my first real job, as a speech therapist for special-needs kids at a nearby public school. I was twenty-one, but I looked about fourteen. By the end of the school year, I was pretty obviously pregnant. The principal did what I think a lot of principals did back then—wished me good luck, didn't ask me back for the next school year, and hired someone else for the job.

We had a beautiful baby girl and named her Amelia Louise, after Aunt Bee (Bessie Amelia) and my mother (Pauline Louise).

Jim thought life was just fine. He could support us, and we both assumed I would stay home.

I tried. I really tried.

For a while, I dedicated myself to making a home. We bought a converted summer house, slightly damp in the summer and freezing cold in the winter (my first lesson in the importance of insulation). But it was in our price range, and it had a magnificent rhododendron bush that made spring feel like a celebration. I bought a home-repair book, and with Amelia safely deposited nearby in her playpen, I set about changing my little corner of the world. I rebuilt bookshelves and taught myself how to refinish the floors and lay bathroom tile (only a little crookedly). At one point, I decided I could cover up the cracks in the bathroom ceiling by wallpapering over them. I learned the hard way that wallpapering a ceiling is entirely different from doing the walls; days later, I was *still* washing wallpaper paste out of my hair.

I sewed, and I tried to cook. In high school, I'd won the Betty Crocker Homemaker of Tomorrow Award, but the prize was based on a written test, not a taste test. (Ask me the butterfat content of heavy cream or how to tie off a lazy daisy stitch and I was golden.) For a wedding present, my mother had bought me a Betty Crocker cookbook, but cooking up those recipes day after day made me feel numb, and my attention often wandered. I gave us all food poisoning twice and set the kitchen on fire maybe four or five times. My daddy bought me a fire extinguisher for Christmas.

Amelia and I went everywhere together. She was an adventuresome baby—willing to eat anything, willing to nap anywhere. I loved her until my chest hurt and my eyes filled with tears. I wanted everything for her. But no matter how hard I tried, I felt I was failing her.

The women's movement was exploding around the country, but not in our quiet New Jersey suburb and certainly not in our little family. I wanted to be a good wife and mother, but I wanted to do something more. I felt deeply ashamed that I didn't want to stay home full-time with my cheerful, adorable daughter.

My first choice was to go back to teaching, but I never even asked Jim. I knew he would say that a demanding full-time job was out of the question. So somewhere between diapers and breast-feeding, I hatched the idea of going to school. At first Jim resisted, but finally he agreed. School would be okay.

Suddenly the world opened up. It was kid-in-the-candy-store time. At first I thought about graduate school in speech pathology. I also got the applications for engineering school. And then I thought of law school. I knew next to nothing about being a lawyer, but on television lawyers were always fighting to defend good people who needed help. Besides, there was just a little wonderment in the notion that I could actually earn a law degree. I loved the thought that someday Amelia would be able to say that her mommy was a lawyer.

Telling my mother about my plan to go to law school was worse than telling her about college. She was sure something was wrong with me. I should stay home. I should have more children. I should count on Jim to support me. She cautioned me against becoming "one of those crazy women's libbers" and warned me that they weren't happy and never could be.

I loved my mother. I wanted her to smile, to believe that I was doing the right thing. But that wasn't going to happen. So I ducked my head and kept on going.

Law School

For three years, Amelia and I bundled up in the mornings, strapped ourselves into our bright blue Volkswagen Beetle, and made our way in the world. Amelia stayed with a lady who looked after half a dozen other kids, and I went to classes at Rutgers Law School. Every afternoon, when I picked up Amelia, just after lunchtime, we'd tell each other stories about our days—about the boy who smeared pudding in his hair (Amelia) or the professor who couldn't see very well and called on a coat hanging on a rack in the back of the room (me). We laughed and laughed.

I loved law school. I loved the intensity, the sharp interactions as teachers grilled us and we cross-examined one another. I loved the optimism of it all, the idea that we could argue our way to a better world.

About three weeks into law school, one of the professors was setting up a hypothetical problem, and he referred to "the guy's secretary, a typical dumb blonde." A woman a few seats over immediately started booing. For an instant she was by herself, but then the entire class picked it up. We booed and hissed. Someone hollered something. The professor looked up quickly and then actually staggered back as if he had been hit. One tiny collective action and his world had just shifted a bit. So had mine.

During my second year, I interviewed for jobs as a summer associate at Wall Street law firms. Women were relatively rare in law; only about one in ten lawyers was a woman. Stories still circulated about women who graduated and were offered jobs as legal secretaries or assistants—not as real lawyers.

My first interview was with one of the many firms that had plenty of women secretaries and clerks but hardly any women lawyers. I borrowed a dress, a black-and-red wool number that I thought looked very professional. I took the train from New Jersey to Wall Street and made my way to the towering building where the firm was located. The first couple of interviews went well, but the third partner to interview me leaned back in his chair, scowled at my résumé, and looked up at me with barely concealed contempt. "There's a typographical error on your résumé. Should I take that as a sign of the quality of the work you do?"

I didn't flinch. "You should take it as a sign that you'd better not hire me to type."

He jumped. Then he leaned back and laughed. "You'll do just fine."

On the train on the way home, I went over every word on my résumé. There was no typo. I thought the guy was a jerk, but I smiled politely when I got the job offer.

I lined up ten weeks of babysitting by getting help from the teenage girl down the street, the lady across the street, and another mom with a little girl the same age as Amelia. The Wall Street money that summer was astonishing—enough to buy us a second car and for me to get my teeth straightened. I headed back to my last year of law school with a mouthful of wires and a four-year-old who was settled in preschool, as well as the faintest hint that I might actually be able to have a career as a lawyer.

By graduation day, the world looked very different. It was June 1976, and on the morning of the ceremony I had the worst headache of my life. I was wearing an ugly maternity dress, panty hose that were way too tight, and stiff shoes that felt too small. The whole outfit was shrouded in a heavy wool graduation gown and a too-big mortarboard that slipped if I shifted my head even a fraction. I was eight months pregnant, and I felt like an enormous water balloon that might roll off my folding chair and explode on the ground. Instead of listening to the speaker, I counted my breaths, partly so I wouldn't faint and partly so I wouldn't cry.

For me, law school had been all about possibilities. But now, sitting at graduation, those possibilities seemed to have evaporated. Once I had gotten pregnant, my efforts to find a job with a law firm had been politely but firmly turned aside. Everyone smiled, but no one invited me for a second interview.

My friends were heading off to real jobs. Not me: I was twenty-six, I would soon have two children, and I was heading home. I believed the working world was now closed to me forever.

Several weeks later, Alex was born. He was a cranky baby who cried for hours at a time. I rocked and jiggled and sometimes cried with him. But I loved him dearly, and I knew that my family was now perfect: a steady husband, a clever daughter, a healthy son. I had done everything I was supposed to do. Over and over, I told myself that Fortune had smiled on me. Be grateful; count your blessings.

I tried to settle my heart, but in the quiet spaces early in the morning or late at night, I wondered why I felt as if I had run as fast as I could and just missed the train.

Hire Me—Please!

After a few months, I bounced back a bit and put together another plan. First I would take the bar exam; then maybe I could figure out a way to practice law part-time. When I called the licensing board to say I needed to bring a nursing baby to the exam, the man on the phone seemed flustered. (What on earth were these women up to?) But I got my license, and I hung out a shingle—literally. I had a sign painted up, a classy number with a black background and white printing: ELIZABETH WARREN, ATTORNEY-AT-LAW. I hung it from a little arm on the light post by the front steps of our house. I figured if I got any clients, I could meet them in the living room and kick the toys under the couch.

In early 1977, I got a call from one of my old professors at Rutgers. The spring semester was starting, and the school had hired a local judge to teach a section of legal writing. But the judge hadn't shown up, so they were casting about for someone to teach one night a week. Would I be interested?

I started the next night.

My neighbor watched Amelia and Alex, and I got another chance. I was a teacher again: Wow. Babies and classrooms, getting dinner on the table and writing an academic article—my life bubbled over, and it was thrilling. As the term came to a close, the school asked if I wanted to come back the next semester for another part-time gig. You bet.

I'd been teaching nearly a year when Jim announced that IBM would be transferring him again. The company gave him some choices about where he might go, but the mix of possibilities seemed bizarre: Houston, Texas; Vandenberg, California; Concrete, North Dakota.

I went out to our car and got the big map from the glove compartment. Vandenberg was about halfway between Los Angeles and San Francisco. Concrete wasn't even listed, but Jim said it was somewhere near the Canadian border. I stared at the map, frozen.

My teaching career at Rutgers was over. For days I felt as if I couldn't breathe. Then I thought: This is stupid. Do something.

One afternoon, I pulled out my Smith Corona portable typewriter and ginned up a résumé. I knew the University of Houston had a law school; I didn't know whether they had any openings, but what could it hurt to write them a letter? I gave my typewriter a nice big smile and started in. I was now an experienced law teacher (sort of) and I'd be interested in teaching legal writing at the University of Houston (or anything else they needed), and so on. I finished just as Alex woke up from his nap, and I carried him in my arms and walked my letter to the mailbox.

Nothing happened.

Jim talked about the great work the guys in Concrete were doing. He called some friends to find out more about Vandenberg. I smiled and said it all sounded promising. I was determined not to panic.

In the spring of 1978, shortly before Jim had to decide where to go, the phone rang. It was early evening, the cranky time of day. I was jostling Alex on my hip and frying pork chops. Amelia was on the floor with crayons scattered all around. I kept an eye on the clock, knowing Jim would come through the door in about twenty minutes.

The white phone was on the wall in the kitchen, and it had a long spiral cord. I said hello, tucked the phone expertly between my ear and my shoulder, and walked back over to the stove.

"This is Eugene Smith from the University of Houston," said the man on the phone. "We got your letter and I'd like to ask you some questions." And off he went. Subject areas? Scholarly interests? Teaching philosophy? Holy cow. I'd never had a job interview as probing as this one, and I was completely unprepared. I tried to sound smooth and relaxed, even as I jiggled Alex furiously in the hope that he wouldn't start crying. And I kept looking at those damn pork chops and thinking, If you burn, I'll throw you through the window.

Somehow, it never occurred to me that I could offer to call Professor Smith back later. I figured it was now or never. It also didn't occur to me to turn off the heat under the pan. At least this time I didn't set the kitchen on fire.

Finally, Professor Smith stopped asking questions and said good-bye. I put the pork chops on a plate, then sat on the kitchen floor and put my head in my hands. That interview had been my golden opportunity, and I had blown it. I wasn't ready, I hadn't worked hard enough, and now my one chance at a good job was gone.

About a week later, Professor Smith called back. Would I fly to Houston to meet the faculty?

I got the job—a full-time, tenure-track, all-the-bells-and-whistles teaching job. I would teach contract law and run the legal writing program.

I'd have an office (wow!), and, unlike at Rutgers, I'd be called "Professor." When I called my parents, my mother reminded me how hard this would be—two little children to care for, a house to manage, a husband to keep happy. I shouldn't jeopardize all I had by reaching too far. But my daddy gave me no such warnings. He just said, "That's my Betsy."

Jim agreed to ask IBM for the Houston transfer, and by late spring we were heading off again on a new life. We bought a nice house in the Houston suburbs. We had two adorable little children, and at twenty-eight, I was about to become a real live law professor. I wished I knew how to do cartwheels, because I would have flipped over and over.

The best I could do was say my prayers every night, always starting with a heartfelt, "Thank you, Lord, for these Thy blessings."

Smacked Down by Child Care

There was only one other full-time woman on the faculty at UH Law School, and she had landed the job a year after her husband had been hired. In that first year of teaching, I was mistaken for a secretary, a student, the wife of a student, a lost undergrad who had wandered into the law school by mistake, and a nurse (blood drive day).

I headed straight for the money courses. I started with contract law and over time added business and finance courses. I loved the idea of mastery over money. Besides, these were some of the most technical, complex areas of law. I figured that if I could manage this, no one could question whether a young woman with two little children belonged here, even if I looked like someone's idea of a school nurse.

That first year of teaching law school took my breath away. I loved the classroom. I watched faces, and it felt like a victory every time I saw the *click!* as a student grasped a really hard idea. I was doing my best to stay just one step ahead of the students, and new ideas seemed to race through my head a million times a second. We were making something happen in the classroom. We were growing brains. We were growing futures.

But the new job was hard, and at home my world was stretched to the breaking point. I traded car-pool duties, took my turn as a Girl Scout leader, taught Sunday school for the fifth graders, and made cookies for bake sales, but I could never catch up. I kept a calendar in the kitchen, and I hated to look at it. I felt as though I had this giant pile of duties balanced on my head as I rode a wobbly bicycle on a high wire stretched across a canyon. The slightest mishap—the dog got loose or the car wouldn't start—and we would all go crashing down.

Jim and I never argued. He didn't say much about my job, but he always looked at his watch when dinner wasn't served on time or when I sat up late at night grading exams. I thought he felt I had reneged on our unspoken deal that he would work and I would take care of the house and children. I also thought he was right.

I kept pedaling faster, but child care brought me down.

It was a Tuesday, winter in much of the country but warm and sunny in Houston. My classes were over for the day, and I hurried to the car. I needed to get to the child care center in the strip mall to pick up Alex. It was a little past five, but the center was still full. Alex was sitting on a small cot. When I saw him, he didn't run over to me. He just sat and looked at me. I felt my chest tighten.

He was a beautiful child. Big for his age, sturdy, with blond hair, dimpled knees, and huge brown eyes.

I picked him up. His diaper was soggy, and I tried to lay him down on the cot to change him, but he clung to me and cried. I gave up and carried him to the car. By now, he was going full force, crying louder and kicking. I had tears, pee, and baby snot on my blouse.

By the time we got home, he was exhausted and so was I. I called our neighbor Sue and asked her to send Amelia home. I gave Alex a bath and started crumbling up hamburger in a skillet as I made dinner. I put in a load of laundry.

When I was in law school, Amelia and I had been buddies. She allowed me to believe that a life that combined inside and outside—family and not family—could actually work. But Alex cried for hours at a time, turning red and sweating and seeming to be furious at my inability to fix whatever was wrong. Once I started teaching, mornings were torture. Alex knocked his cereal bowl across the room and cried when I dressed him. He kicked me while I tried to fasten him in his car seat and clung to me when I needed to leave. He was heavy and strong for a toddler. I was outmatched.

I was so tired that my bones hurt. Alex still woke up about three every morning. I'd stumble out of bed when he cried, afraid he'd wake Amelia or Jim. I'd feel around in the dark, wrap us together in a blanket, and then rock him back and forth in an old rocking chair I'd had since I was a kid. We held each other, and for a while each night while I drifted in and out of sleep, I prayed that he forgave me for my many shortcomings.

But on that Tuesday night, I couldn't forgive myself. I knew the day care place wasn't good. Alex had been there only a couple of weeks, but it wasn't working. I couldn't quite say why. Maybe it smelled funny. Maybe the people weren't friendly. I wasn't sure what was wrong, but I knew it wasn't working.

I'd been teaching only a short time, but I had cycled through one child care arrangement after another. The pain of each transition was intense. Each represented a failure. A sitter who never showed up. A neighbor who changed her mind. A child care center that left Alex in dirty diapers all day. I knew I was failing my son.

One night after I had put both kids to bed, Aunt Bee called. By now, she was in her late seventies. She asked how I was doing. I said, "Fine," and then abruptly started to cry. "I can't do this. I can't teach and take care of Amy and Alex. I'm doing a terrible job. I'm going to have to quit."

I hadn't even thought of it until I said it: Quit. Once I started to cry, it was as if something inside me broke. I cried harder.

Aunt Bee, one of my mother's older sisters, had been born in 1901 in Indian Territory, before it became the state of Oklahoma. She was short, with an ample bosom and small, arthritic hands. From her teens, she had worked variously as a secretary, a typist, and a clerk. She had lived with my grandparents on and off, pitching in her paycheck to the household budget. She was a highly independent woman in every way except one: she never learned to drive. As a young woman, she'd gotten a driving lesson in my grandfather's old Model T, and she had run over a wild turkey. Fifty years later, she still teared up when she told the story. After that, she swore she'd never drive again—and she hadn't.

"Bee" was short for Bessie Amelia, and when my parents had a baby girl, my mother said she would be named Bessie. Aunt Bee was tickled, but she asked my mother to name me "Elizabeth" and use "Betsy" for short. Aunt Bee carried me home from the hospital, wrapped in a pink blanket with a pink satin ribbon tied in my dark hair. She bought me two new dresses each year—one for Easter and one for the first day of school. She never had children of her own. In her fifties, she had married Uncle Stanley, a butcher at the meat packing plant. Now she was a widow.

That night on the phone, Aunt Bee listened to me fall apart. She didn't try to soothe me or tell me it would be all right. Instead, she let me cry and cry.

After a while, I wound down. I blew my nose and got a drink of water. Aunt Bee said calmly, "I can't get there tomorrow, but I can come on Thursday."

It took me a moment to understand what she was saying. She never even asked. She just walked away from her life so she could come fix mine.

Two days later, I drove to the Houston airport to meet the late afternoon flight from Oklahoma City. Aunt Bee had arrived with a Pekingese named Buddy and seven suitcases. She and Buddy lived with us for several months, both of them sleeping on a pull-out couch.

At last I was able to breathe again. It was as if someone turned off the Tilt-A-Whirl we had been riding, and life stopped spinning.

A Marriage Fails

But it didn't fix things between Jim and me. I had failed him. He had married a nineteen-year-old girl, and she hadn't grown into the woman we had both expected. I was very, very sorry, but I couldn't change what I had become. I was supposed to be the Betty Crocker award winner, but I set things on fire. I was supposed to be 100 percent focused on our home and our children, but I was making a life outside that neither of us expected. I loved every new adventure I took on—and he didn't.

One night I'd left the dishes until after I'd put both kids to bed, and I was cleaning up in the kitchen. Jim was standing in the doorway, smoking a cigarette, just looking at me.

I asked him if he wanted a divorce. I'm not sure why I asked. It was as if the question just fell out of my mouth. I was shocked that I'd said it.

Jim looked back at me and said, "Yes." No hesitation, just yes. He moved out the next weekend.

Of course, no divorce is that simple. There were reconsiderations and some attempts at one-more-try-to-make-it-work. No one ever yelled or hurled nasty accusations, but once we had opened the door to divorce, we both knew what was coming.

After Jim moved out, I had to confront the hard truth: I had failed at the one thing by which I believed my life would be measured. And now my failure was out in the open.

I was determined to keep everything the same for Amelia and Alex. The children and I stayed in the same house, the same school, the same church. I still taught Sunday school and Aunt Bee made mashed potatoes.

Daddy was still working as a maintenance man, mowing lawns and keeping the heating and air-conditioning running in an apartment complex in Oklahoma City. He was sixty-seven, and the work was getting harder. But the job came with a free apartment, and he and Mother planned to hang on there as long as they could.

At some point during the back-and-forth of separating with Jim, I hatched a new idea: they could move to Houston. We could all pitch in— Mother, Daddy, and Aunt Bee could help take care of Amelia and Alex. With the money I would save on child care, I could help them with their expenses. They would have to leave Oklahoma, where they had spent their whole lives. But they could have a home of their own and be woven into my little family's life. And I needed them.

So they came.

Jim paid child support faithfully, and I had a regular paycheck from teaching, but I was deeply worried about money. Mother and Daddy offered to move in with me, and I was grateful for the offer but terrified by the thought. I started balancing my checkbook obsessively, almost every night.

I had told Jim that he could take all the furniture in our bedroom, and I slept on a makeshift twin bed in a big, empty room. I gave him the pictures off the walls. I had a garage sale and got rid of the dining room table. I wallpapered Amelia's room and painted a big rainbow on the wall in Alex's room. It was an odd, herky-jerky sort of stripping down and rebuilding.

While I carefully put one foot in front of the other, determined to keep my life more or less the same, Jim went in a different direction. He quit smoking, lost thirty pounds, and took dancing lessons. Eventually, he met a very nice woman and remarried. We didn't see him often.

New Lives

Unlike a lot of single mothers, I was lucky enough to have my family nearby. I still worried about money, but we managed the other day-to-day challenges more or less okay. Aunt Bee made peach cobblers and cheese grits, Mother took care of short trips to the grocery store, and Daddy picked up Amelia from piano lessons. Child care was finally under control—a kid with a fever no longer turned life upside down. Daddy was always tinkering with something, so we could even handle a car that wouldn't start or a busted pipe.

My life hadn't worked out exactly the way I'd expected, but I could breathe. The children were flourishing. My parents were happy. Aunt Bee told me that it was a blessing to be "nearly eighty years old and *so needed*." I loved teaching. I thought I knew now what my life would look like forever: family and teaching. And that sounded just fine to me.

That summer, Mother and Daddy kept the kids so I could go to an intensive course for law professors who wanted to learn more about economics. Enrolled in the course were about two dozen professors from around the country, including one named Bruce Mann.

A lot of people might think that two young law professors would be drawn together because they wanted to talk about law all the time. Nope: I fell in love with Bruce because he had great legs. Really. The weather was hot, and people were wearing knit shirts and shorts. I spotted Bruce on the first morning. He was sitting in the row in front of me, with his chair turned sideways and his legs stretched out. Bruce is six feet three inches, most of that in his legs. Those legs seemed a mile long. Through college and part of graduate school, he had spent his summers teaching tennis. He was gorgeous.

By lunch on that first day, I'd found out who he was and what he had done before becoming a professor. I bounced up to him and cheerfully asked if he would give me tennis lessons. Long after our first meeting, Bruce admitted that he was appalled. "I was sick of giving lessons, especially to beginners. I wanted to teach legal history—not how to hit a tennis ball." But he was polite, so I set up a time to meet him on the courts after that day's last session, never noticing his lack of enthusiasm.

Mixed in with the tennis lesson, I learned all the basics: Bruce had both a law degree and a PhD in history, and his specialty was legal history, law in the age of the American Revolution. He was Yankee to the bone, the descendant of tough, quiet, hardworking people who had lived and died in Massachusetts for generations. Like me, he had gone to college on a mix of scholarships, loans, and part-time jobs. It didn't take me long to figure out that we were very different people. If I was a hard-charging, go-to-the-mat-for-whatever-you-believe kind of professor, he was more of a scholarly, camping-out-in-the-archives-poring-over-an-old-legal-manuscript kind. I asked him if he'd give me another tennis lesson the following day.

Years later, over a great deal of beer, Bruce confessed that I wasn't just pretty bad at tennis, I was terrible. I was his Worst Student Ever. I hit balls everywhere: over fences, over hedges, over buildings. Once I had a weapon in my hand, I gave it everything I had.

But Bruce loved me anyway. And when I proposed to him, he said yes.

Bruce tells his own version of how he fell in love with me, but I figure the details don't really matter. I was completely crazy about him, and I still am. Even though I'm sure I'm hard to live with, he says he is crazy about me, too—he just says it more quietly than I do.

We faced only one problem back then: getting married made no sense at all. Bruce was a single guy finishing his second year as a junior professor at the University of Connecticut Law School. I had all the things that weren't on his to-do list—two children, a red station wagon, and an extended family of Okies who popped in and out of my kitchen every single day. I loved what I had built, and I had no plans to leave Houston—ever.

Soon after we met, Bruce came to visit me in Houston. One morning, we went to the grocery store together. I stood beside him as he gazed at a big display of fresh strawberries.

"We can get those if you want," I said.

He smiled, and as he picked up a couple of cartons, he said he was thinking about his mother and how embarrassed she was whenever she borrowed money from him to pay for groceries. "We didn't eat things like fresh strawberries."

I knew we would be bound to each other forever.

In short order, I had my thirty-first birthday, bought a white cotton sundress that could double as a wedding gown, and married Bruce Mann. I kept Jim's last name because I thought it would help make life a little easier for the kids.

In an act of recklessness that still startles me a little, Bruce left his job at the University of Connecticut. He moved to Houston to build a family with the children and me (and Mother, Daddy, Aunt Bee, and Buddy the Pekingese). Fortunately, the University of Houston gave him a one-year temporary job. But UH also made it clear they didn't plan to keep him on, so we started our married life with a big problem. Bruce could stay in Houston and end his career before it ever really started, or I could give up my teaching job and my life in Houston and follow him somewhere else.

Our first year together was tough, but not because of the usual challenges faced by new families. I knew I wanted to build a future with him, even if it meant upending everything I'd built in Houston. So from the first day, we were desperately looking for teaching jobs that would keep us in the same city. For months we got no bites at all, not even nibbles. Then lightning struck. We were both invited to teach the following academic year at the University of Texas at Austin. This wasn't just any law school; it was one of the best law schools in the country. UT made it clear that for both of us, this would be a "visit," a sort of nail-biting, year-long tryout for a permanent job, but we didn't care. It was the big time—and a chance to be together.

We were alive for one more year, with Bruce teaching legal history and property classes while I taught courses about money and finance. We sold the house in Houston, loaded a U-Haul with our stuff, packed up the kids, and rented a house in Austin. Mother, Daddy, and Aunt Bee would stand by, waiting 160 miles away in Houston to see if we got lucky as we all anxiously hoped for the best—two steady jobs in the same city.

Teaching Without a Textbook

If I'd been smart, I would have kept teaching the classes I already knew how to teach. But my curiosity got the better of me, so before we moved to Austin, I called the dean at the University of Texas and offered to teach a course I'd never taught before: bankruptcy.

Why the interest in people who go bankrupt? When a family files for bankruptcy, they are essentially admitting that they're dead broke and unable to pay their bills. There are a few twists and turns in the law, but basically a family keeps a small stake and then gives up pretty much everything else they own—their savings, their stocks and bonds, sometimes their home or their car. In return, the family's old debts are wiped out and they get what they most need: a fresh start, a chance to start over without a pile of debts pulling them down.

When a family goes bankrupt, it is a moment of great defeat and, often, personal shame. For many, it is like going before a judge and declaring to the world that they are losers in the Great American Economic Game. I wanted to know what drove them to the edge of disaster and why they had tumbled over. I wanted to know who those people were, what they did, and exactly what had gone wrong.

I think I was looking for an answer to a question I couldn't quite ask out loud, maybe because it was a little too personal.

I felt like my family was mostly safe now. Bruce and I didn't have secure jobs yet, and sharing the responsibility for two children, three old people, and an aging dog required patience and some creativity, but I knew Bruce had my back and I had his. But I also knew what it was like to be afraid, to fear that whatever you had built could be taken away. Bankruptcy was a terrible admission of failure, and I wanted to believe that everyone who filed had done something terrible or stupid or had lazed about and never tried to make anything of themselves. I wanted to know that the work-hard-and-play-by-the-rules people might not get rich, but they didn't need to be afraid. And I wanted to know that they never, ever went bankrupt.

Teaching bankruptcy in the early 1980s presented a special challenge. A new bankruptcy law had recently gone into effect, the first major reform since the Great Depression. The new law did a lot to strengthen bankruptcy protection for families in trouble, and help them get back on their feet.

The difficulty was how to teach this new law. I thought it was pointless to teach the old law, but nobody had yet published any good textbooks that addressed the new one. When the dean at UT took me up on my offer, I faced a little panic over the corner I'd put myself in: for the next year, while trying out for a job, I'd be teaching a class I'd never taught before, with no textbook to show me the way. Not smart. Exciting, but not smart.

My solution was to teach the bankruptcy class by turning it into something like a giant game of *Jeopardy!* I gave everyone a copy of the new law, and I took the class through each section, teeing up the issue: If [a phrase in the law] was the answer, then what was the question? In other words, what problems did the lawyers and senators think they were solving when they wrote these new laws? It wasn't the standard way to teach a class, but I'm pretty sure that everyone learned the statute inside and out.

Not long after I started my new course at UT, one of the world-famous professors who had advised Congress about the revised code happened to visit the university, and he agreed to talk to my bankruptcy class about the new law. Dr. Stefan Riesenfeld was in his seventies, bent and small, with wispy gray hair circling his balding head. He was a learned man—he spoke four languages, had written or edited about thirty books, and still had a thick German accent that made him seem like a perfect copy of the brilliant scientist from every 1950s sci-fi movie. He was tough and direct, famous for yelling at students, "You have mashed potatoes for brains!" and other forms of encouragement.

Dr. Riesenfeld gave a few opening remarks to my class, talking about his work on the new laws and describing conversations with well-known members of Congress. When a student asked about the families in bankruptcy, he explained that the people who filed were mostly day laborers and housemaids who lived at the economic margins and always would. He seemed to suggest that a lifetime of poor choices had landed these folks in bankruptcy courts, and these people had little in common with my students and their friends and neighbors.

Then I asked the obvious follow-up question: How did he know that people in bankruptcy existed mostly at the economic margins and would always be there?

I smiled at my students with a confident, wait-till-you-hear-this look. I figured he would give us some inside information about some giant study that Congress had commissioned or the reams of research his fellow professors had done.

No dice. Instead, Professor Riesenfeld (I couldn't possibly call him "Stefan") dismissed the question with something along the lines of, "Because everyone knows that." Then he added an afterthought: "Vell, every *expert* knows that."

I missed the barb. Even so, I probably should have shut up at that point. This was my first bankruptcy class, and he had thirty or more years of experience. I was trying out for a job, and he was a famous professor with a long list of honors. But I just couldn't stop myself—I wanted to know.

"Uh, *how* does everyone know that?"

Now he was clearly irritated. He took a deep breath. Everyone just *knew*. That was it. According to the professor, at least, that had been the basis for the new law.

My God. I felt like Dorothy in *The Wizard of Oz*. Professor Riesenfeld was a giant in the field, a man of deep learning and vast experience, and he really didn't know what was happening on the ground. And if he didn't know, then I figured no one else did, either.

How could anyone be sure that what had gone wrong in these families' lives was the result of their own bad choices? Were they not willing to work hard? Were they wild spenders? Were they any different from me and from my family?

And there was one more question I'd never thought about before: What the heck was Congress doing passing laws if they didn't actually know what was going on?

I don't remember anything else Professor Riesenfeld said during the class that day. At the end, I thanked him for coming, and my students applauded politely. But I do remember that as he walked out of the classroom, my teeth hurt. Here I was, teaching the bankruptcy code to a classroom of future lawyers, yet I couldn't answer the most obvious question: *Why* were these people broke?

Sore Points

The year of visiting ended, but we didn't get the job offers we had been hoping for, so we packed up and moved back to Houston, where I started teaching again. Then, a year later, UT law school reconsidered and offered me a permanent job as a tenured professor. So we packed up a U-Haul yet again and moved back to Austin. This time Mother, Daddy, and Aunt Bee came too, and they settled in a duplex with Mother and Daddy on one side, Aunt Bee on the other. Buddy the Pekingese died, and Bonnie the cocker spaniel moved in. The kids switched schools for the fourth time in four years, and we added a golden retriever puppy named Trover to our family. Gradually, Bruce and the kids and I settled into Austin. Bruce coached soccer. Daddy helped me plant roses. Amelia joined the church youth group, Alex was an acolyte, and I was a substitute Sunday school teacher and a reliable source for chocolate-oatmeal bake-sale cookies. Jim was still in Houston, and the kids went to visit him from time to time.

We had a new house, with a sunny kitchen on the back. Over time, Bruce quietly took over most of the cooking, and I pitched in with what I did best—mostly cakes and pies, and the occasional pot of mac-and-cheese.

I loved working alongside him, with music on the stereo and Trover sprawled out in front of the refrigerator and the kids thumping around upstairs. There were moments when the sun would slant in and Bruce would smile, and I would think my heart might burst with gratitude for all the good things that had come to me.

We might have stayed in Austin forever if not for one thing: Bruce didn't land a permanent position at UT. Instead, he got a job at Washington University in St. Louis—also a terrific law school, but it was 825 miles away. Barely missing a beat, he set up a tiny apartment in St. Louis and began flying back and forth every week. He continued to coach Alex's soccer team, and we all showed up to cheer on the junior high orchestra, listening hard to catch Amelia's clarinet. We pieced together lives that were as nearly normal as possible, but everything turned on his making the connecting flight at the Dallas airport. Meanwhile, we kept job hunting, but finding two professorships in one city was tough.

Not long after we moved to Austin, my oldest brother, Don Reed, received terrible news: his wife, Nancy, was diagnosed with leukemia. For twenty years, Don Reed had lived the life our father had always dreamed of—he was an air force pilot, eventually rising to the rank of lieutenant colonel. After moving around for all those years to wherever the air force sent them, including six years when he was sent back and forth to Vietnam, Don Reed and Nancy had finally bought a home and settled down in Grapevine, Texas. Now Nancy was sick—really sick.

Mother, Daddy, Bruce, and I drove to San Antonio every few days to visit her at the military hospital, and I doubled down on my prayers. Nancy was determinedly cheerful, but one day she grabbed Bruce's sleeve and spoke to him in hushed tones, asking him to write her a will. She wanted Don Reed and the boys to know how her possessions—her wedding ring, her piano, her share in her daddy's farm—should be divided up and where she wanted to be buried. She told Bruce not to worry about her. She just wanted to take care of my brother and their boys, leaving them with no questions and no doubts. A few days after she signed the will, she died.

My brother John had his own health troubles. He had worked construction nearly all his life, and as he approached fifty, the wear and tear on his body was starting to add up. Then the oil bust of the early 1980s wiped out a lot of new construction projects in Oklahoma, so jobs were much harder to come by.

David had also been hit hard when the market for oil collapsed. Over the years, he had built a business that delivered various supplies to oil rigs dotted across the state. The oil boom had made him rich, but the bust brought his business crashing down. He always said that he'd be fine if his customers could pay him, but they were out of money, too. He still got up at four thirty in the morning and worked himself into the ground, but he couldn't save his business. The forces that swept away billions of dollars in wealth around the globe wiped out my brother as well.

We knitted our multigenerational, multicity family together. Mother, Daddy, and Aunt Bee still helped out with the kids, although they did less babysitting and more driving here and there. We cooked together a couple of times a week. Now that Don Reed was a widower, he visited us more often, and holidays involved all three brothers and their families. David's daughter was just a little older than Amelia, so she came to stay during summer vacations. We helped one another in whatever ways we could.

Mother worried about my brothers and me—that was always her way. But Daddy enjoyed watching my career begin to take wing. Unlike Mother, Daddy never seemed to worry that I would ruin my children because I was a Working Mother or that I would end up single and miserable. In truth, I think he found it pretty miraculous that his baby girl had ended up in the world of colleges, libraries, and tree-lined campuses. He was glad to tell people I was a law professor and, if given half a chance, happy to tell them that I wrote articles and gave speeches and won teaching awards. He was proud that I made good money and nearly busted his buttons the first time I was quoted in the newspaper.

But the part Daddy had a hard time with was talking about money and, especially, bankruptcy. For years after I first began teaching that part of the law, I don't think my daddy ever spoke the word *bankruptcy,* at least not when I was around. Whenever one of my uncles or the guy at the hardware store asked what my speeches were about, I noticed that Daddy would look off and say something like "Oh, she's special, that one. We never had to worry about her." And then he would move on to something else.

Maybe it was personal. My daddy and I were both afraid of being poor, really poor. His response was never to talk about money or what might happen if it ran out—never ever ever. My response was to study contracts, finance, and, most of all, economic failure, to learn everything I could.

My daddy stayed away from big sores that hurt. I poked at them.

When "Dead Broke" Is a Step Up

As I dug deeper into my study of bankruptcy and the new law, I kept bumping into the same question over and over: Why were people going bankrupt? I couldn't find solid answers anywhere. In those days, almost all young law professors specialized in theory. They wrote articles and books about the theory of this and the philosophy of that. But theory wouldn't provide answers that anyone could count on, answers that would explain what had gone wrong. I clung to the idea that the people in bankruptcy were different and everyone else would be safe. I might not have said so at the time, but I think I was on the lookout for cheaters and deadbeats as a way to explain who was filing for bankruptcy.

As my search got under way, I found two terrific partners. Terry Sullivan, a newly minted PhD, was a bright young star in the Sociology Department at UT. (Terry went on to an amazing career, winding up as the first female president of the University of Virginia.) Jay Westbrook was already a bankruptcy expert, and by the time we met he had practiced law for eleven years. (Jay has also had a remarkable career; he is a renowned bankruptcy scholar and the hands-down expert on international business law.) But back then we were just three young professors who were excited about putting together the kind of study that legal experts almost never did. We decided to collect hard data about families that went broke.

Terry led the way as we developed a sampling protocol, drew up a list of the data we wanted to get, copied cases, recorded numbers, and began to create a database. I'd never been involved in a project like this—a careful, systematic collection of information that would form a picture of the people who filed for bankruptcy. It was the statistical equivalent of building a giant mosaic, one tile at a time.

During the data collection phase, I visited an old paneled courtroom in San Antonio. It was summer, and the air-conditioning was cranked down to freeze-your-toes-in-one-minute-or-less. Back then, people still had to come before a judge to get a decree forgiving their debts. (Nowadays, the process usually happens by mail.) I sat in the back, shivering.

The judge sat higher than everyone else, although I barely noticed him and he didn't pay any attention to me. My eyes were on the people who moved in and out of the courtroom. I guess I had so completely absorbed the prevailing wisdom that I expected people in bankruptcy to look scruffy or shifty or generally disreputable. But what struck me was that they looked so *normal.*

The people appearing before that judge came in all colors, sizes, and ages. A number of men wore ill-fitting suits, two or three of them with bolero ties, and nearly everyone had dressed up for the day. They looked like they were on their way to church. An older couple held on to each other as they walked carefully down the aisle and found a seat. A young mother gently jiggled her keys for the baby on her lap. Everyone was quiet, speaking in hushed tones or not at all. Lawyers—at least I thought they were lawyers—seemed to herd people from one place to another.

I didn't stay long. I felt as if I knew everyone in that courtroom, and I wanted out of there. It was like staring at a car crash, a car crash involving people you knew.

Later, our data would confirm what I had seen in San Antonio that day. The people seeking the judge's decree were once solidly middle-class. They had gone to college, found good jobs, gotten married, and bought homes. Now they were flat busted, standing in front of that judge and all the world, ready to give up nearly everything they owned just to get some relief from the bill collectors.

As the data continued to come in, the story got scarier. San Antonio was no exception: all around the country, the overwhelming majority of people filing for bankruptcy were regular families who had hit hard times. Over time, we learned that nearly 90 percent were declaring bankruptcy for one of three reasons: a job loss, a medical problem, or a family breakup (typically divorce, sometimes the death of a husband or wife). By the time these families arrived in the bankruptcy court, they had pretty much run out of options. Dad had lost his job or Mom had gotten cancer, and they had been battling for financial survival for a year or longer. They had no savings, no pension plan, and no homes or cars that weren't already smothered by mortgages. Many owed at least a full year's income in credit card debt alone. They owed so much that even if they never bought another thing—even if Dad got his job back tomorrow and Mom had a miraculous recovery—the mountain of debt would keep growing on its own, fueled by penalties and compounding interest rates that doubled their debts every few years. By the time they came before a bankruptcy judge, they were so deep in debt that being flat broke—owning nothing, but free from debt— looked like a huge step up and worth deep personal embarrassment.

Worse yet, the number of bankrupt families was climbing. In the early 1980s, when my partners and I first started collecting data, the number of families annually filing for bankruptcy topped a quarter of a million. True, a recession had hobbled the nation's economy and squeezed a lot of families, but as the 1980s wore on and the economy recovered, the number of bankruptcies unexpectedly doubled. Suddenly, there was a lot of talk about how Americans had lost their sense of right and wrong, how people were buying piles of stuff they didn't actually need and then running away when the bills came due. Banks complained loudly about unpaid credit card bills. The word *deadbeat* got tossed around a lot. It seemed that people filing for bankruptcy weren't just financial failures—they had also committed an unforgivable sin.

Part of me still wanted to buy the deadbeat story because it was so comforting. But somewhere along the way, while collecting all those bits of data, I came to know who these people were.

In one of our studies, we asked people to explain in their own words why they filed for bankruptcy. I figured that most of them would probably tell stories that made them look good or that relieved them of guilt.

I still remember sitting down with the first stack of questionnaires. As I started reading, I'm sure I wore my most jaded, squinty-eyed expression.

The comments hit me like a physical blow. They were filled with self-loathing. One man had written just three words to explain why he was in bankruptcy:

Stupid.
Stupid.
Stupid.

When writing about their lives, people blamed themselves for taking out a mortgage they didn't understand. They blamed themselves for their failure to realize their jobs weren't secure. They blamed themselves for their misplaced trust in no-good husbands and cheating wives. It was blindingly obvious to me that most people saw bankruptcy as a profound personal failure, a sign that they were losers through and through.

Some of the stories were detailed and sad, describing the death of a child or what it meant to be laid off after thirty-three years with the same company. Others stripped a world of pain down to the bare facts:

> Wife died of cancer. Left $65,000 in medical bills after insurance.
> Lack of full-time work—worked five part-time jobs to meet rent, utilities, phone, food, and insurance.

They thought they were safe—safe in their jobs and their lives and their love—but they weren't.

I ran my fingers over one of the papers, thinking about a woman who had tried to explain how her life had become such a disaster. A turn here, a turn there, and her life might have been very different.

Divorce, an unhappy second marriage, a serious illness, no job. A turn here, a turn there, and my life might have been very different, too.

You're Not That Funny

One early spring morning in the mid-1980s, a shocking rumor floated around the UT faculty lounge: There had been a total of seven failing grades handed out in the preceding term, and they had all come from one professor. I didn't say anything, but I knew who the professor was. I'd taught two large classes, and a few knuckleheads had thought they could skate through without working hard. They had miscalculated. In fact, exactly seven of them had miscalculated.

I took teaching seriously. The students who showed up in my classroom would soon graduate and go out in the world with incredible power, perhaps more than they realized. They would handle other people's money, other people's businesses, other people's lives. On the first day of class, I always made the same promise: If the students worked hard, I would bust my tail to teach them the material. And though I never doubted for a moment that they could learn it, I was dead serious about the "students work hard" part.

By now I had been teaching at UT for a while, and I thought it was going pretty well. I was starting to feel more confident. When the public schools were closed one day, I decided to take seven-year-old Alex with me to my class. I settled him in the back row with a new *Star Wars* sticker book, and then I taught a great class—hard work, but plenty of lively exchanges and some jokes to keep everyone engaged.

After class, Alex and I were walking hand in hand down an empty hallway back to my office. The afternoon sun was slanting in through the windows, and I thought it was a perfect mother-son moment. I was smiling and relaxed. "So, sweetie, what did you think of my class?"

Alex paused a long time, clearly considering his words. Finally he said, "Mom, you aren't that funny."

I felt stabbed in the heart. Before I could think, I cried out, "But, sweetie, they laughed."

This time he didn't hesitate. "They had to, Mom."

Huh. I guess I still had a lot to learn.

Punch Back

Over time, I started wrangling with a number of academics and others about banks and bankruptcies. Whenever I heard someone claim that the bankruptcy courts were loaded with cheaters and lazy slugs who wanted the easy way out, I started fighting back. This was not a good way to make friends, but to me that didn't seem especially important.

I started giving more speeches. I was invited to participate in a panel discussion at a gathering of bankruptcy judges in Chicago to talk about how the courts should treat small businesses that go bankrupt. One of the other panelists was a well-known judge who essentially declared that when small-business owners hit financial trouble, they should just turn their businesses over to the bank.

This seemed deeply unfair. Did he have any idea how hard people worked when starting a business? Big businesses that fell on hard times were given lots of special protections by the bankruptcy courts so that they could restructure and keep going. Why shouldn't little businesses have the same chance to survive?

The judge and I were seated at a table on a small stage, and we got into such an intense back-and-forth that the other panelists started inching away, leaving the two of us to jockey for a single microphone placed between us. The judge probably had a hundred pounds on me, and he started shifting himself closer to the microphone and edging me out of his way. I grabbed the table for leverage and pushed my way to the microphone, going shoulder to shoulder with the judge as I hit back with arguments about giving everyone the same chance to rebuild. As we escalated the fight, we leaned harder and harder into each other. The scene was rapidly becoming more than a little ridiculous, but for me this didn't feel like just another theoretical debate. I felt I knew the people he was dismissing so easily. I thought they were worth fighting for.

I glanced over and noticed with satisfaction that the veins in his neck were throbbing and his face was red and sweating. I wondered briefly whether he might have a stroke right there on the small stage.

It was not a nice thought for a suburban mom who tended roses and dutifully brought chocolate-oatmeal cookies to every church bake sale.

Leaving Texas

In 1985, the University of Pennsylvania called to ask if I would be willing to interview for a job opening. The next year, independently, they called to ask Bruce if he would consider interviewing for a different job opening. It took a while for us to work it all out, but the law school needed two professors—someone to teach contract law and bankruptcy and someone to teach legal history. Two good jobs in the same city—finally!

I should have been thrilled, but I wasn't. Penn was a great school, but Philadelphia felt like a million miles away from my brothers and all my assorted nieces, nephews, and cousins. And the prospect of moving two kids, my parents, Aunt Bee, and two dogs seemed overwhelming. But Penn was a great place for a legal historian, and they promised to support my bankruptcy research. And Bruce's commute to St. Louis was hard on all of us. So after a lot of discussion, we decided it was time: Bruce and I took jobs at U Penn in the fall of 1987. We bought an old stone house about five miles from the U Penn campus. It hadn't been updated in decades, but it was big and roomy.

Aunt Bee was packed and ready. She was eighty-six now, and she and Bonnie the cocker spaniel were eager to come live with us. But as we started preparing for the big move, Daddy said he and Mother had decided to stay in Austin a while longer.

Mother and Daddy came to visit us in Philadelphia soon after the move. Mother sat by herself in the living room, playing the piano and singing for hours at a time. She talked more about when she was a little girl, about growing up out on the prairie, and about when she and Daddy were first married.

My parents visited us two or three more times over the next few months. Each time, I pressed them on when they would move to Philadelphia. Finally Daddy said, "Betsy, we aren't moving up here. We need to go back to Oklahoma."

The kids were older now, and I didn't need as much help as before, but I very much wanted Mother and Daddy close by. We were kin; we were part of each other's lives. I couldn't understand why they wouldn't agree to come, and I wheedled and pleaded and even cried. But Daddy was quiet and calm and immovable. "We need to go back to Oklahoma."

Bruce and I helped them buy a house in Oklahoma City, which Daddy promptly named "Old Blue" because of its offbeat color. It was just a few blocks from my brother David, and my brother John was a short drive away. A few weeks after they moved, David called me. "Talk to Mother," he said. "She says she won't get a new driver's license." In a place as spread out as Oklahoma City, that seemed crazy. Besides, she was only seventy-eight.

I called her, but she wouldn't change her mind. "I'm through driving."

I remembered Mother behind the wheel of our old Studebaker. When the car stalled at a stoplight, she would put it in neutral, set the brake, pop the hood, grab the huge screwdriver from under the front seat, jump out of the car, hold the screwdriver by the blade, and pound on some part of the engine while she shouted at me to push down on the gas pedal with my hand. She couldn't name a single part of the engine and didn't know why this worked, but it was what Daddy told her to do and we always made it home.

Now my mother would never drive again.

Changes were everywhere. Amelia was no longer my buddy. Now a teenage girl with a mane of long, curly hair, she regarded me as a complete pain in the rear—her rear. Bruce played referee, and he blew the whistle on both of us plenty of times. Still, even if she didn't want my opinion on one single thing, I could see that she was turning into a pretty sensible young woman.

Alex was changing, too. He was still a cranky kid who butted his way through life, but by seventh grade he was taller than I was. He was also whip smart and very funny. We had bought him a rudimentary Texas Instruments computer when he was five, and by now he was a full-fledged computer geek. At his prodding, the four of us—Bruce, Alex, Trover, and I—watched every episode of *Star Trek: The Next Generation* and loved almost every minute of it. Meanwhile, Alex went about the tough business of growing up.

Amelia headed off to college. Alex read stacks of books. For the first time in more than a decade, the knot in my stomach began to ease. Maybe I hadn't ruined my kids after all. I was making peace with being a Working Mother.

Banking Isn't Boring

I kept teaching bankruptcy, but the world outside my classroom was changing, too. The numbers of people going bankrupt kept climbing, in good times and bad. By 1990, more than seven hundred thousand families filed for bankruptcy in a single year—the number had more than doubled in the decade since I had started teaching. That shocked me.

Early one spring semester, a student came by. She settled herself in and made some small talk, looking everywhere but at me. Finally, she asked if she could close the door. She wasn't the first—I knew what was coming.

"My parents are bankrupt." She started to cry. I pushed a box of tissues across the desk and waited.

They had a small business. It went under, but not until after her parents had cashed out their retirement savings and lost the house.

She gave a strangled sob. I came around the desk and pulled up a chair next to her. I rubbed her forearms and patted her hands. She didn't care that her parents couldn't help her with school—she'd been on her own for a while. She cried because the world was imploding for people she loved.

And it spilled out beyond classes. At school, I heard from secretaries and cafeteria workers. I heard from other professors whose children or old friends were in trouble. Sometimes someone would stop me in the mailroom or while I was waiting in line for a sandwich. Most people didn't ask for help. They just seemed to want me to know. I think they hoped to hear me say, "There are a lot of good people who end up bankrupt." At least, that's what I believed, so that's what I always said.

In the early 1990s, the big banks stepped up their efforts to change the bankruptcy laws.

They got in the fight through an odd twist in an old law. Ever since the days of the Founding Fathers, the United States had had laws in place that made it illegal to lend money at extraordinarily high interest rates, a practice known as usury. Later, during the Great Depression, the United States created more regulations to ensure that banking would be safe and dependable. From that time on, banking became a pretty boring business. Banks weren't allowed to speculate in crazy, risky ventures. Banks had to keep plenty of money in reserve in case anything went wrong. FDIC insurance promised to protect the deposits entrusted to the banks by their customers. And, since the usury laws put caps on interest rates, the only way for a bank to make a profit was to go to a lot of trouble to make sure that nearly all of their loans would be repaid—in full and on time. Bankers put plenty of safeguards in place so they wouldn't lend money to people who couldn't pay them back.

With usury laws and the 1930s banking regulations as a backdrop, banks played a really important role in helping America's economy grow. They lent the money for families to buy homes, and those monthly payments became a sort of giant savings plan, so that by the time people retired they owned a valuable asset—and a place where they could live without paying rent. Over time, banks financed cars and college educations. They helped small businesses get a start. A handful of larger banks served the biggest corporate clients, giving them access to the money they needed to expand and create jobs. Banking was all about evaluating customers, making sure that they would be able to repay loans, and keeping interest rates competitive with the bank across the street.

It all worked pretty well. Until the 1980s, that is.

At that point, with scant notice and very little public discussion, a momentous event occurred: thanks to a Supreme Court ruling about a century-old banking law and an amendment quietly passed by Congress, the cap on interest rates was effectively eliminated. Suddenly, banking was changed forever. The usury ban for large American banks disappeared, and deregulation became the new watchword. The bigger banks were now unleashed, and they started loading up credit cards with fees and escalating interest rates—tactics that would have been illegal just a few years earlier. Once the banks began to figure out just how lucrative these cards could be, they started juicing their profits by lending money at super-high interest rates to people who were a lot less likely to repay all those loans. By the 1990s, they were targeting people who were barely hanging on—those with modest or erratic income, those who had lost their jobs and were scrambling. In other words, the banks were targeting people just like the folks who ended up in the bankruptcy courts.

But for all their enticing new opportunities to make big profits, the bankers faced a new problem. As the number of bankruptcy filings continued to skyrocket, the megabanks had to write off more and more bankruptcy losses.

One spring, an executive at Citibank called me. He had read some of my bankruptcy work, and he invited me to come do a day-long seminar to help them think through how to cut their bankruptcy losses.

I took the train from Philadelphia to New York and arrived at the Citibank building in Manhattan just as hundreds of employees were streaming into the building. I was ushered into a brightly lit conference room with about forty men, all outfitted in expensive suits. I pulled out my graphs and charts, the Citibank people pulled out their data, and we got under way.

As we discussed the bank's bankruptcy numbers, I wasn't surprised. Most people struggled with debt for a long, long time before they went bankrupt. People didn't suddenly run up credit card bills on Tuesday and then dash to the bankruptcy courts on Wednesday. People who ended up in bankruptcy court put up lots of red flags ahead of time. My advice to Citibank was pretty simple: If you want to lose less money, stop lending to families who are in financial trouble and can't afford to take on more high-interest debt.

After finishing my pitch, I heard lots of interested murmurs, and hands went up around the room. But before anyone took the floor, a slightly older man spoke up. He had been quiet, watching the discussion with a faintly bemused smile.

"Professor Warren," he said firmly.

The room went immediately silent, signaling that the Head Honcho was now speaking.

"We appreciate your presentation. We really do. But we have no interest in cutting back on our lending to these people. They are the ones who provide most of our profits."

He got up, and the meeting was over. I never heard from Citibank again.

So there it was. The banks were losing money when people filed for bankruptcy, and even though they knew they could cut their losses with a quick credit check on their customers, they didn't want to stop. In fact, they did the opposite. Even as a family got more and more behind on their bills, the banks made more offers: Consolidate your bills with our new credit card! (At a mere 29 percent interest . . .) Take a home equity line of credit! (And the bank takes your home if you get too far behind . . .) Get a second mortgage—and a third!

Why would the big banks do this? Here was the trick: Even with the bankruptcy losses, the banks could make *more* money if they kept giving credit to people who were in trouble. Yes, the banks had to absorb bigger losses when people went bankrupt. But in the meantime, they could make a *lot* more money from all those people on the edge who didn't file for bankruptcy protection, or at least didn't file for another year or so. Interest rates and fees were so high that, in the end, the banks came out ahead—way ahead.

Even with profits breaking records every year, the banks weren't satisfied. They thought of more fees to tack on, more ways to escalate interest rates, and more aggressive ways to market their cards. Credit card vendors started showing up on college campuses, targeting kids with promises that there would be no credit checks and no need for their parents to sign. Children were preapproved. And occasionally even a dog would get his fifteen minutes of fame, when a local newspaper heard about some cute little pooch who had just been offered a credit card.

To pump up their returns even more, the banks tried a new tactic: What if they could persuade the government to limit bankruptcy protections? Sure, a lot of families were broke, but maybe some of them could be pressed to pay just a little more. If they couldn't file for bankruptcy, maybe more families would decide to move in with their in-laws, or borrow from the neighbors, or hock their wedding rings, or cancel their health insurance—who knows? If several hundred thousand families a year could be squeezed just a little harder, maybe the banks could add yet more profit to their bottom lines.

The bankers might not have said it in so many words, but gradually their strategy emerged: Target families who were already in a little trouble, lend them more money, get them entangled in high fees and astronomical interest rates, and then block the doors to the bankruptcy exit if they really got in over their heads.

If you knew anything about bankruptcy law—and by now I knew a lot—you could see exactly what the big banks were up to. I was just a law school professor, so I didn't have the power to change anything, but the deep cynicism behind these new tactics infuriated me. For the banks, a change in the bankruptcy laws was just one more opportunity to try to boost profits. For the families—the moms, dads, kids, grandparents, aunts, uncles, and cousins—who would lose their last chance to recover from the financial blow of a layoff or a frightening medical diagnosis, the pain could never be measured.

Bruce and I would walk Trover, and I would start talking about the damage the big banks were doing to families all across the country. One night my voice started rising as I told Bruce how vile I thought this was. Did the banks have any idea how many people were getting hurt?

I chopped the air with my hands. I clenched my teeth. I talked louder and faster, until finally I ran out of words. And then Bruce asked the question that has gnawed at me ever since:

"So what are you going to do about it?"

A Visit to Harvard

In 1992, Harvard Law School invited Bruce and me to come teach for a year.

Jay, Terry, and I had published our bankruptcy findings in a book called *As We Forgive Our Debtors* a few years earlier. It had caused a mild stir, at least in academic circles, and snagged a national prize. Jay and I were now working on the second edition of a textbook we'd written on bankruptcy law, and another professor, Lynn LoPucki, and I were writing a book on secured financing. I also had a new study on business bankruptcies in the works and another on families in financial trouble. And I had won four awards for outstanding teaching. I loved what I was doing, and I wasn't looking for a change.

But Bruce thought that a year in Massachusetts sounded like fun, and we could be near his family. Alex thought this was his big chance to see a Celtics game live. And besides, who could resist trying out Harvard for a while? After all, I'd never even seen the place. So I said sure.

By now Amelia was off at college, and Aunt Bee said she and Bonnie the cocker spaniel would rather spend the year back in Oklahoma with Mother and Daddy. So Bruce, Alex, Trover, and I headed off to Cambridge, Massachusetts. Once again, Bruce and I agreed to undertake one of those year-long job tryouts—but this time we had good jobs waiting for us in the same city, back at Penn, so there was no nail-biting. This was more of a fun adventure. Amelia missed most of it, but Alex took the opportunity to reinvent himself at a new high school as a football player and stage crew handyman. Trover was getting old, but she was still eager to chase the ball every afternoon.

When Mother and Daddy came to visit at Thanksgiving, I thought they would be pleased to see the famous Harvard, but they didn't seem all that interested. At dinner the first night, Mother looked around the table and asked, "When will we see Amelia?"

I had already told them both that Amelia would be home from college in a couple of days. Daddy said, "Wednesday."

The conversation picked up again, and about a minute later, Mother asked, "When will we see Amelia?"

Daddy said, "Wednesday," as if he had never heard the question before.

When she asked a third time a few minutes later, Daddy answered pleasantly, "Wednesday." But his head was bowed, and when he looked up, the pain was unmistakable.

When Daddy and I made a run to the hardware store the next day, I asked him about Mother. He said she was just tired, that we all get forgetful when we're tired. But it began to hit home that my mother and daddy—now eighty and eighty-one—wouldn't be with me forever. I felt like I was living on borrowed time.

Late in the school year, Harvard offered me a tenured job, but there wasn't a place for Bruce. I wasn't interested in living in two cities again, so I said no thanks. On the last day of classes, my students gave me a golden retriever puppy. They named her Good Faith and asked me to come back.

Two days after we took Faith home, Trover died of sudden liver failure. I called Daddy, crying so hard that he couldn't make out what I was saying. So he went through this list: Are you hurt? Is it Alex? Amelia? Bruce? When he named Trover, I managed to choke out a yes, and he started to cry, too. What can I say? Dogs are part of our family. Twenty years later, Bruce still has Trover's picture on his desk.

After Bruce and I went back to Penn, the Harvard dean would call every now and then. They were keeping the offer open. Perhaps I'd like to reconsider?

No, not really. We had a good life in Philadelphia. Amelia was nearby, Aunt Bee and Bonnie were back from Oklahoma and living upstairs, and Alex was still in school. After so many moves over the past dozen years, it felt good to know that we were finally settled in.

Harvard Again

But maybe I wasn't so settled after all. Bruce's question—"What are you going to do about it?"—kept tugging at me. I began working longer hours. I expanded my research. I wrote more articles, worked on my next book, and made plans for the one after that. I gave speeches, trying to tell anyone who would listen to me about the importance of bankruptcy protection and the families who needed it.

A year or so after we moved back to Philadelphia, Bruce and I were driving somewhere one spring day when an interview with a bank spokesman came on the radio. The guy was railing about deadbeats who took advantage of everyone else by filing for bankruptcy. I was furious. After the interview ended, I railed right back, rebutting everything the spokesman had said. The farther we drove, the more I argued into the empty air.

I was glaring out the window when Bruce glanced over from his driving. His voice was firm. "Take the Harvard job."

Bruce doesn't catch me by surprise very often. I'm usually the one with the wild schemes, and he's usually the voice of reason, calmly explaining why it isn't a great idea to paint the ceiling dark purple or rip all those unknown vines out of the overgrown flower bed by hand. (The purple ceiling worked out great, but I paid dearly for the gardening mistake—the vines were poison ivy and I found out that I'm wildly allergic.)

But Bruce usually thought very carefully about things before he said them, and he had been thinking about the Harvard offer for a while. Penn was a terrific school, but Bruce argued that if I wanted people to listen to my ideas, I might as well shout from the highest mountain I could find. He thought working at Harvard might improve my chances of making a difference.

By now, our lives had changed again. I wasn't a Working Mother anymore; I was a forty-five-year-old professor, and our kids had grown up. Alex was in college, and Amelia was getting her MBA. At ninety-three, Aunt Bee didn't get out much, and she was lonesome with no one at home all day. She said she didn't want to hurt our feelings, but she and Bonnie the cocker spaniel wanted to go back to Oklahoma City, so we started working to set her up in a tidy little apartment in the middle of the sprawling Baptist Retirement Center. Now that we were pretty much on our own, Bruce declared that he and I and Faith could manage a two-city life. And a move to Massachusetts would mean that we would see a lot more of Bruce's parents, his brother and sister, his niece and nephew. We would be close to family again.

Meanwhile, those bankruptcy numbers kept climbing, in good times and bad. More than eight hundred thousand families—husbands, wives, children—were going bankrupt every year. Across the country, another person declared bankruptcy every twenty-six seconds—twenty-four hours a day, seven days a week. The numbers were staggering.

Something was terribly wrong in America, and it seemed to be getting worse. I was worried—worried, angry, and ready to fight for every one of these families. I didn't have an organized plan, but I knew that fighting meant throwing everything I had into the battle. I was going to take the best shot I could.

So I called the Harvard dean and said I was coming.

2 | The Bankruptcy Wars

F AIR WARNING: THIS story doesn't have a happy ending. It's a David versus Goliath story, but this time David gets his slingshot shoved down his throat—sideways. It's also the story of my long and painful baptism into national politics.

How I got into this fight takes a little explanation. It started when I said no.

In 1995, Congress launched a blue-ribbon commission to review the bankruptcy laws. President Bill Clinton appointed former Oklahoma congressman Mike Synar to head a nine-person nonpartisan commission. The commission would spend two years completing its review and then deliver a report to Congress. Now the congressman was on the phone, calling me. Would I join him in working on the National Bankruptcy Review Commission?

In one of those little twists that makes me wonder about divine intervention, Mike and I had crossed paths when we were teenagers. Mike had been a high school debater from Muskogee when I was debating for my Oklahoma City high school. We hadn't seen each other in the intervening decades, but fourteen-year-old boys seem to remember fifteen-year-old girls who once beat them in tournament play.

I told him no. I was deep in my research, and I thought the way I could make a difference was by writing books and doing more research about who was filing for bankruptcy and what had gone wrong in their lives. I didn't know anything about Washington, but the bits I picked up from the press made it sound pretty awful.

So Mike asked me to come to DC for lunch. Just lunch.

It was fun to see him. Mike had been a political wunderkind. He had been elected to Congress at twenty-eight, in the wake of a report that mentioned that his opponent slept in a heart-shaped water bed, a revelation that didn't sit well with a lot of folks back in Oklahoma. While in Congress, Mike had battled Big Tobacco and the National Rifle Association. But after sixteen years in the House, he had just lost his seat.

Mike still looked boyish, with dark hair and bright eyes and a sort of goofy smile that reminded me of Opie on the old *Andy Griffith Show*. He was always in a hurry, the kind of guy who waves his hands a lot and interrupts—cheerfully, of course. We met in Mike's Washington office, but he quickly gathered up a few young staffers and we all walked over to a noisy restaurant nearby.

Over lunch, we mostly swapped stories about our high school debate days. Mike talked about beer and poker. I talked about the kid who got left behind at the Turner Turnpike rest stop. He told stories about the times we had debated each other, regaling the young staffers with comic blow-by-blow descriptions of our early meetings.

We didn't talk much about the commission at lunch. Mike knew why I was skeptical. Sure, the commission was supposed to be neutral, but I'd heard that the banks had already started lobbying to cut back on bankruptcy protection. I didn't want any part of a process that would probably just make life harder for people who were already struggling to get by.

Besides, Mike and I weren't exactly friends. I'd barely known him back in high school, and we hadn't stayed in touch. Before our lunch, I'd checked him out, and each person I called had suggested that during his time in Congress, Mike had a pretty friendly relationship with some of the big banks.

When I stood up to leave, Mike walked me out of the restaurant. Once we were alone, he turned serious. He'd read one of my books, and he knew where I stood. Then Mike made his pitch: Think about the families the new commission would affect, the people who file for bankruptcy every year. Here's an opportunity for you to make a real difference.

Then Mike offered me a deal. If I would work with him to come up with three good changes—changes in the law that could help the folks who were struggling with debt—then he would work hard to get them turned into law. The way he saw it, I would develop the ideas about how to change the bankruptcy law, and he would use his political savvy to try to get those changes enacted.

The whole idea was deliciously subversive—and not what I expected. Here was the guy a lot of people thought would carry water for the industry, and instead he was trying to figure out how to expand bankruptcy protection for families who needed it. Wow.

Even so, I hesitated. I believed Mike's intentions were good, but I wasn't sure he could deliver. Besides, I'd never worked in a political setting before. Heck, I'd never done anything more political than voting. But he had sunk the hook. If we worked together, we might be able to help some of those families that were going bankrupt every single day. Just think of the difference we could make with three good changes in the law. Here was a chance to *do* something about all those people getting hurt.

And that's what I thought about, all the way home. My office was stacked with piles of questionnaires from people in bankruptcy, and many of them told personal stories about what had gone wrong in their lives and described the sense of defeat that they carried to the bankruptcy court. I thought about the family that finally got a shot at their lifelong dream to launch a new restaurant—and it went belly-up. The young and very tired woman who described how she finally managed to leave her abusive ex-husband, but now she was alone with a pack of small children and a pile of bills. The elderly couple who had cashed out everything they owned and then went into debt to bail out their son and put him through rehab again and again.

Two days later, I called Mike and said yes.

The job with the commission was part-time, so I kept teaching at Harvard and started flying down to Washington for a day or two at a time. I was the commission's senior advisor, and it was my responsibility to make proposals, manage the research, and write first drafts of the recommendations for the commissioners to approve.

Over the next few months, I began digging in. I met with the other commissioners. I went about gathering research and hiring good people, setting up a schedule, and organizing our agenda. Mike started pulling in people to talk about our plans. It was exciting—like drawing up blueprints and beginning to build something new. But the best part was lying in bed at night thinking about the three good changes. It felt better than Christmas. Three changes that could make a difference for working families. Three wishes.

Two Funerals

And then it all broke apart. Before the commission could really get under way, before we had even agreed on those three good ideas, Mike was diagnosed with a brain tumor. He stopped working and hunkered down for radiation therapy. The last time I saw him, Mike was bony and bald and his hands shook. Just talking seemed to exhaust him.

On January 9, 1996, Mike died. He was forty-five.

The day of his memorial service was cold and rainy. We gathered at historic St. John's Episcopal Church, on Lafayette Square, across from the White House. President Clinton spoke, along with then-congressman Dick Durbin. It was a huge affair, packed with the politically powerful. There were lots of handshakes and hugs, but I kept pretty much to myself. I'd never met these people.

I left the church believing that I was leaving Washington for the last time. Mike and I had a deal. Now Mike was gone, and I wasn't coming back.

Mike's funeral was the second in six months. The first was a much harder good-bye, smaller and more personal.

Daddy had called in the summer of 1995 to say that Mother needed to have an operation—a cancerous polyp, but nothing serious. The doctors had promised a noninvasive surgery. She'd need to be in the hospital for a few days.

Nothing serious, Daddy insisted, but he seemed rattled. Bruce and I decided to go back to Oklahoma City for a little family gathering. We wanted to be there when Mother went into the hospital.

I'd been home only a few hours when my brother David took me aside to say that not long ago he had found Mother wandering near their house, apparently lost. I tried to ask Daddy about it, but he said she was just tired or a little confused by the odd layout of the nearby streets.

Daddy held Mother's hand whenever there were people around. He talked more now, and he would start nearly every sentence with "Polly, you remember . . ." and then fill in the story or the name of whoever was in the room.

After the operation, the doctors told us it had gone well, and Mother seemed to be recovering just fine. The day after her surgery, we gathered in her room, telling stories and laughing. Mercy Hospital was pretty relaxed, and they let some of my teenage and twenty-something nieces and nephews take Mother on wheelchair races up and down the hallways. Everyone laughed, and we ate cookies and drank juice from the nurses' station.

Mother was due to go home the next morning, and Daddy thought we were tiring her out. So on her last night in the hospital, Daddy sent us all home and sat quietly holding her hand.

Late that evening, she sat up in bed and said, "Don, there's that gas pain again." Then she fell back dead.

The doctors arrived in less than a minute and tried to revive her, but she'd had a massive heart attack. The autopsy showed that she had advanced coronary disease—never diagnosed, never treated. And now she was gone.

John's wife, Barbara, called. "Oh, sweetie, I'm so sorry." I didn't cry—I just didn't believe her. I couldn't believe her. My mother was eighty-three, maybe old by some standards, but Aunt Bee was ninety-three and spry as ever. And my grandmother had been energetic and active until she died at ninety-four. I knew Mother was fading a little, but I thought she was strong and healthy.

That was the hardest part for me: my mother was always strong—and in the blink of an eye she was gone.

Family poured in from everywhere for her funeral. I felt dazed.

A few days later, I was back in the spare bedroom at my parents' house. I was lying on the twin bed on my back, crying. My daddy came in, and I got up and held out my arms. I thought he would hold me and tell me that we were very sad but we still had each other.

But he just stood there and said, "I want to die."

I held him while he cried. I rubbed his shoulders, but he kept on crying. I told him what I'd hoped he would say to me: that our hearts were broken but we still had each other and everything would be all right. But I wasn't sure it was true.

Stacking Sandbags

Two months after Mike Synar died, President Clinton appointed a lawyer from Madison, Wisconsin, to head the National Bankruptcy Review Commission. Brady Williamson was a quietly remarkable guy. He maintained an active law practice, but he had represented Bill Clinton in negotiations involving the presidential debates and in setting up various trips to meet with foreign leaders. In legal circles, he was known for his work on the First Amendment and for a bankruptcy case he had won in the United States Supreme Court. He'd done great work on the case, but I didn't know him. Now the commission was his problem.

Officially, I was still the senior advisor for the commission, although we hadn't done much work since Mike's death. When Brady called, I was blunt: Mike and I had a deal, but that was then. Mike is gone, and I'm out of here.

Brady asked me to wait to resign until he could come to meet me and talk with me about his plans. I said okay.

Brady is cute. Not movie-star handsome—just cute. He's short, with glasses, a mustache, bright eyes, and a quick sense of humor. When he came to the house a few days later, we sat on the enclosed porch, enjoying an unexpectedly warm day. I offered him iced tea, and Faith put her head in his lap. Unlike most goldens, Faith was a little picky about people, so I took this as a sign that maybe Brady was a good guy. More than anything, though, I felt a little sorry for him. By now I knew that most of the other commissioners didn't share Mike's vision, and leading this group was going to be tough. But this wasn't my problem. I was going back to my books and my classes.

Like the superb lawyer he is, Brady had done his homework and knew what the commission was up against. Once he got past the preliminaries, he didn't sugarcoat the situation. President Clinton was facing a Republican-controlled Congress bent on fighting him at every turn, and Washington was still reeling from two government shutdowns. Besides, the big banks were pushing harder than ever to change the bankruptcy laws. Brady didn't think President Clinton would pick a fight with the big banks right now. And if the president didn't want to push back, who would?

I was starting to understand. Despite the huge numbers of people in bankruptcy, it's almost impossible to form a political coalition around them. They come into the bankruptcy system and exit as soon as they can, a big, fast-moving river of people who lose a job or face some terrible health crisis. Our research had shown that they aren't especially old or young, northern or southern, black or white, male or female. Instead, they're a cross section of pretty much everyone who has reached the end of their rope. They spend most of their waking hours scrambling to sell off a car or hold down a second job. They barely have time to fend off calls from angry creditors, let alone write letters to Congress. And most are profoundly, desperately ashamed of their situation. For many, the decision to file for bankruptcy proves to be the darkest secret of their entire lives.

Politically speaking, they are almost invisible. And yet these families were up against what was already one of the best-organized, best-funded lobbies in America. (It would get even better organized and better funded in the years to come.)

The situation looked pretty hopeless. Mike had died, and the committee's work had stalled. Now the banking industry would get what it wanted, and the families who needed some relief would get rolled. If ever a game was rigged, this was it.

Brady's pitch was different from the one Mike had made a year earlier. The way Brady saw it, millions of middle-class families were sinking, and the banks were moving fast to make a bad situation worse. He admitted that the commission might not be able to make much progress and that we probably couldn't achieve Mike's ambition of improving the bankruptcy laws. But Brady thought we had a good chance of holding off the banks—at least for a while. If we stood our ground and started fighting right now, we might be able to deny them the opportunity to use the commission as a rubber stamp for everything they wanted. And if we could do that, maybe we could do more.

My three wishes were gone. Now it was about hanging on to whatever we could salvage from the existing law. Besides, as Brady pointed out, every day the current bankruptcy protections stayed strong was a day that another five thousand families would get the fresh start they so desperately needed.

Lord, this was discouraging. But I signed on, and we started stacking sandbags as fast as we could. Maybe we'd lose in the end, but every day we held on was a better day for struggling families.

The Slow Kind of Cancer

There was nothing fun about the National Bankruptcy Review Commission. Nothing.

Our job was to produce a report for Congress that would recommend changes to the bankruptcy code. The battle lines were drawn early. Thanks to my books and speeches, my views about families in trouble were pretty well known by then, and they sharply contradicted the views of the commission's most outspoken member: Judge Edith Jones.

Jones, a federal judge from Texas, was a very big deal in conservative circles. Her name had been on the short list for the Supreme Court under both George H. W. Bush and George W. Bush, and one of my Texas buddies once told me that George W. Bush called her "Auntie Edith." I think Judge Jones saw bankruptcy as a world of opportunists, one in which many people would take advantage whenever they could. As she once wrote, "Nobody is holding a gun to consumers' heads and forcing them to send in credit card applications." She worried about "widespread gaming of the system," and she said she thought it was a "matter of personal integrity and honor not to take on obligations beyond one's means." Judge Jones talked of economic failure as akin to moral failure.

I thought the research showed something very different. Medical problems, job losses, and family breakups had laid these families low. Most had hung on and tried to repay long past any reasonable chance of doing so. As I saw it, the families in bankruptcy were mostly good people caught in a bad situation—a point of view that did not put me high on Judge Jones's list of favorite people.

Neither Judge Jones nor I had any money at stake in this debate. Neither of us was being paid by bankers to advance our positions. We simply saw the world very differently. She probably thought I was too optimistic about human nature, and I was sure she was too cynical. (Or maybe she thought I was too cynical about the nature of giant banks, and I thought she was too optimistic.) Judge Jones consistently sided with industry-friendly changes in the law—and I fought her at every turn.

The back-and-forth with Judge Jones was relentless and wearing. Not long after starting my work on the commission, I bought a fax machine, which I put in my office at Harvard. When anyone sent me a fax, the machine made a funny warming-up noise. Judge Jones faxed me so many painful memos that at one point I realized that I felt like one of Pavlov's dogs: whenever I heard the machine revving up, my stomach clenched and I felt sick.

I was also fighting hard to hang on to my daddy. After Mother died, he seemed lost. I called him every night. I told him about things that had happened during the day: about Alex, who loved his computer classes but seemed bored by his other course work at college; about Amelia, who had moved to California after getting her MBA and seemed to be seriously involved with her boyfriend; about the pansies that were starting to bloom or the leaves that were changing color. Most weekends we watched sports together, with Daddy in Oklahoma and me in Massachusetts, and we called back and forth on the phone after a really good (or bad) play. I tried everything I could think of to help fill the gaping, dark loneliness that seemed to be swallowing him whole.

I begged him to come live with us. He made a couple of short trips to Boston but said he felt my mother back in their house, and that's where he wanted to be. Every few days he drove to Wetumka to visit her grave.

I could tell that I was losing him. He had always been thin, but now he looked translucent and his pale blue eyes were watery. His doctors did some tests and told him he had prostate cancer, although Daddy assured me it was "the slow kind." He admitted that he couldn't sleep.

The worst was when he cried. Daddy had always been quiet—quiet and proud. I had almost never seen him cry, but now it was different. We'd be on the phone, talking about gardening, and I'd cheerfully say something about roses and he'd say that Mother loved roses, and then he would get quiet. I could hear him making choking sounds, and occasionally he'd let out a strangled sob. I felt helpless. He wasn't dying of cancer. He was dying of a broken heart.

The People No One Heard

For two years, I traveled. Back and forth to Washington, back and forth to Oklahoma. Then I'd fly off to various cities where the commission held hearings. Detroit. Seattle. San Antonio. Santa Fe.

The commission's most visible work was to hold public hearings. The staff and I worked hard to create a balanced list of witnesses—some banking industry advocates and some consumer advocates, some conservative economists and some liberal ones—but that doesn't capture how these hearings actually worked. When we started, I thought the real point of the hearings would be to let people from different parts of the country participate in a public conversation about our bankruptcy laws. Gradually, I came to realize that even though the commission's staff tried to be evenhanded, the playing field was sharply tilted.

Many of the same people showed up at the hearings, no matter where we held them. After a while, Brady clued me in: A bunch of bank lobbyists were being paid to follow us from town to town.

By contrast, relatively few bankrupt families attended those hearings. The commission's chief counsel, Melissa Jacoby, worked hard to seek them out, but most people didn't want to draw attention to their own financial failure. Even if they wanted to come, most bankrupt families couldn't take a day off work or afford any travel expenses—and they had no lobbying group to put them up in a nice hotel and foot the bill.

To most of the people who attended those hearings, the families in bankruptcy were little more than abstract numbers. There was hardly anyone to talk firsthand about what it was like to lose a job or face overwhelming medical bills and how the bankruptcy system had given them a chance to get back on their feet. Commissioners might talk about debtors "gaming the system," but they almost never had to look at a real person and make that accusation.

The whole process made me gag.

By law, the National Bankruptcy Review Commission's report was due in October 1997. The final vote on our list of recommendations was a nail-biter. Judge Jones pushed hard for a series of recommendations that Congress should make it harder for families to file for bankruptcy, but in the end, she mustered only four votes. Five commissioners, led by Brady, recommended keeping the safety net intact and making just a few modest adjustments to the law. It wasn't the three wishes that Mike Synar had once promised me, but the official commission report stood with the families in trouble.

The day arrived to deliver the report to Congress, and ceremonies were planned in Washington. All the commissioners and the staff showed up. I didn't go. The good guys had won, by a one-vote margin, but I was sick of politics. I'd had enough of Washington.

Another Death

A few days after the final commission report was delivered, I flew to Oklahoma. My daddy's slow cancer, it turned out, wasn't so slow.

Daddy was eighty-six, and he wanted to die at home. In my whole life, I couldn't remember that he had ever asked me for anything, but he asked for this: Let me die at home.

My brothers and I pulled in closer. We called a hospice. We split up what needed to be done. John and David were there every day, and I came whenever I could.

In a catalogue I came across a video series about the airplanes of World War II. I bought all the videotapes and took them to Daddy. I was sure he would love seeing the old planes, that he would point out this or that plane he remembered from the war. But he had no interest in those memories anymore. The only thing he wanted to talk about was Mother.

Daddy never spoke about it, but I could see that he was in a lot of pain. His breathing was often jagged. When someone moved him to change a sheet or adjust his pillow, he would often cry out involuntarily. Then he would quickly reassure us: "It's fine. It's fine."

In December, Don Reed and I were both back for the weekend. With all four children nearby, Daddy seemed to let go. He was suddenly much worse. He held my hand and told me how much he loved me and that I was strong and I was going to be fine. The last thing he said to me was, "It's time for me to be with your mother." He closed his eyes and he never opened them again. Within the hour, he died.

After we buried Daddy, I grieved for a long time. For months—for years, actually—I would see or hear something and think, Oh, I'll tell Daddy about that. And then I'd get a little jolt all over again.

I stopped watching sports as often. Without Daddy, the games weren't the same.

Two years later, Aunt Bee died in her sleep. She was ninety-eight. A few days after that, I stood in the cemetery in Wetumka. Aunt Bee was way over on my left, in what had once been the northern edge of the cemetery, in the same family plot as my grandparents and various aunts and uncles. Far off to my right, near the southern edge of the cemetery, were my daddy's parents and his side of the family. My mother and daddy were buried together, in a single plot right in between the two families. They had picked this spot many years earlier, and I wondered if all the angry words that had been traded back and forth about their defiant elopement mattered anymore.

Bruce and I seemed more alone. Bruce's family—his mom and dad, his sister and her family, his brother—were all nearby, and every few weeks it seemed like someone had a birthday or we had a holiday to celebrate. But our house—which once hummed with slamming doors and buzzing voices—was quiet. Our kids were grown, and Mother, Daddy, and Aunt Bee were all gone. Bruce and I went hiking more often, and Faith stayed closer by my side. The hours I spent working—teaching, writing, researching—grew longer and longer.

A Thousand Cuts

The commission's vote may have made it seem that the country's families had won, but our side wasn't celebrating. The banking industry had already found another way to push for what it wanted.

Months earlier, as it was becoming increasingly clear that Judge Jones and her allies might not get a majority vote to recommend overhauling the bankruptcy code, the banks opened a second front in the war. Instead of waiting for the commission's report, the industry wrote its own version of a bankruptcy bill and then shopped it around to some friendly members of Congress. The bill was introduced in September 1997—one month before the commission's deadline. By the time the commission delivered its report, the industry-backed bill was already in play.

The strategy was very effective. By beating us to the battlefield, the banking industry had more success at defining the terms of the fight. In their version of the world, Congress could support either "honest people who pay their bills" or "people who skip out on their debts." There wasn't any room to talk about rising health care costs or lost jobs. There was just a black-and-white question about people in financial trouble—do you pay your bills or don't you?

The industry didn't propose to eliminate bankruptcy protection altogether. After all, the Founding Fathers had called for bankruptcy protection in the Constitution itself, and surely even the banking lobby wouldn't pick a fight with them. But they did propose changes—stacks and stacks of changes. Most of the proposed revisions were exceedingly complicated, and those complications worked to their advantage. The complex twists and turns of the recommended changes made it hard for the press or the public to follow, which provided great cover for what the banking industry was really trying to do. (Years later, I saw this move during the bank bailout: banks hid behind jargon and gibberish, deliberately making everything sound more complicated than necessary so they could avoid public scrutiny.)

The ultimate impact of those hundreds of changes in the industry-backed bill would be to make it harder for struggling families to get bankruptcy relief. It would become more difficult to discharge debts and more expensive to get help from a lawyer. There would be more paperwork, more hoops to jump through. It would become harder for people who were struggling to get relief from student loans. The bill also made it tougher for single parents to collect back child support from an ex who was buried in debt. (For decades, the bankruptcy laws had given special consideration to the needs of single parents, but now the credit card companies wanted to elbow them aside to get whatever money their ex had left. That one *still* makes me grind my teeth.) Meanwhile, the new legislation would make it easier for bill collectors to harass people forever.

In so many ways, the industry-supported bankruptcy bill would make life worse for families in trouble. It stunk like a pile of manure.

A Champion for the People

The National Bankruptcy Review Commission's work was over, and I went back to spending most of my time on teaching and research and going back to Oklahoma to be with my brothers. The commission's report seemed forgotten within weeks, and the banking lobbyists looked unstoppable.

But I couldn't just walk away. *More than a million families* were now seeking bankruptcy protection every year. So I stayed in the fight however I could. I started new research projects. I talked with consumer advocates. I gave speeches to judges and lawyers. Sometimes I got a call from the press, and I tried to explain what was at stake.

A few heart-of-gold allies took up the fight. Nonprofit advocacy groups like Consumer Federation of America and Consumers Union joined the cause. A group of lawyers built a small advocacy group, and the National

Partnership for Women & Families pitched in, as did the AFL-CIO. But resources were already stretched thin, and each of these groups had a host of other battles they were fighting on behalf of their members. As far as I know, there wasn't even one full-time paid staffer on our side in the bankruptcy fight.

For months, we were so outgunned that we seemed to have no chance. It was as if we were shouting in the wind and no one could hear us. And then, just when it seemed like it was all over, we found a champion.

It was Friday afternoon, April 17, 1998, not far from Boston Harbor, only a few miles and across the river from where I live. I was about to sit down with a man I'd never met, Senator Ted Kennedy. The senator's brilliant young chief counsel, Melody Barnes, had heard me give a speech about bankruptcy. She thought I should meet her boss, so here I was.

A few minutes earlier, I had entered the lobby of the John F. Kennedy Federal Building, accompanied by Melissa Jacoby, my smart young chief counsel from the National Bankruptcy Review Commission. As we rode up to the twenty-fourth floor, I couldn't help wondering what it must be like to work in a building named for your assassinated brother. Then, when I looked around the senator's waiting room, I realized that he lived with a lot more than his brother's name on the building. Hanging on the walls were family photos of the three brothers he had lost—John, Bobby, and Joe.

We were scheduled to meet with Senator Kennedy for only fifteen minutes, so I knew I needed to talk fast. But as soon as we were ushered into his office, the senator stood up, greeted me warmly, and swept me across the room to his windows. The views were amazing—the neighborhoods, the harbor, the ocean beyond. He wanted to show me where his grandparents had once lived or something—I didn't quite catch it. But he was cheerful and enthusiastic, saying, "Right there—right there!" as he tapped hard on the glass. He pointed out other buildings and projects and noted how great it was that the harbor was now cleaned up.

I'm sure he had won over a zillion visitors with his good humor and plain old Irish charm. But when he laughed, he seemed to take genuine delight in looking out the window at this place he loved.

Finally we settled in, and the senator picked up a small bound notebook. The friendly patter was over, and it was time to get down to business. Bankruptcy is a tough subject for a whole lot of reasons—and it didn't help that I was sitting there with a lap full of graphs and charts. He looked uncomfortable, as if he were about to take some bitter-tasting medicine. He would do it, of course, but he knew it wasn't going to be pleasant.

Seeing his expression, I left the graphs and charts on my lap and just started talking. I talked about medical bills, layoffs, predatory lending. I talked about families broken apart by a cascade of financial problems and crushing debt. Melissa and Melody joined in, and we talked about how bankruptcy served as a last safety net for so many.

The senator took careful notes, and he asked questions. At first he was hesitant to say much, but as I told stories about some of the people I'd met while doing our research, he jumped in more frequently, talking faster and asking more questions. Sometimes he skipped ahead, and sometimes he took off in another direction. But no matter where the conversation went, he always got back to what was happening to working people. Eventually he asked to see the charts.

At some point during the meeting, the senator's assistant came in from the outer office to say that it was time for him to leave. He waved her off, and we kept digging into the issues.

A while later, Senator Kennedy's wife, Vicki, stepped in. The senator introduced us and explained what we were talking about. She asked some very thoughtful questions, and he promised that he would be finished soon. Another half hour or so went by, and she reappeared with a gentle reminder that they were already late.

When that didn't work, Vicki came back in again. And again. She was very sweet about it each time, but they clearly had plans and the senator was way over schedule.

We had talked for about an hour and a half when the senator finally said: "Well, Professor, you've done it. I see why we need to stop this bankruptcy bill." He paused to give it extra emphasis: "You've got my vote."

He smiled broadly. He and I both knew that people asked for his support every day, and his commitment to vote no was a big deal.

I paused for a moment and gazed out at the grand view. Then I said: "Thank you, Senator, but we don't need your vote. We need your leadership. We need someone to lead the charge."

Taking the lead on an issue in the Senate is very different from agreeing to lend support. It's a little like the difference between throwing a party and stopping by to have a drink. The leader needs to rally the troops, lay out a strategy, swap favors here, and apply pressure there. Serious leadership requires an enormous effort, and it takes an enormous amount of time. The bankers had already lined up a lot of powerful Democrats and Republicans to support their bill, which meant this would be an even tougher undertaking.

Senator Kennedy stared at me for what seemed like forever. His enthusiasm was real, but he looked tired. His eyes were puffy, and he was a little stooped. By then he was sixty-six years old, and he suffered from constant back pain. He had been representing Massachusetts in the Senate for thirty-five years and had probably fought more battles than just about any senator in American history.

He glanced over at an old, battered satchel that was stuffed with files and loose papers that involved all the battles he was already fighting. This was the famous bag—the bag that had all of his homework in it, the bag he took with him each evening so that he could read late into the night. He looked back at me, then back at the bag. The silence stretched.

Finally he spoke. "Lead?" he asked.

"These families need you." I said it quietly, and the silence stretched some more. I tried to steady my breathing.

He paused again, then gave a deep sigh and said, "All right. I'll do it. I'll do what I can."

I thanked him, and as we stood up he gave me a pat on the shoulder. Vicki Kennedy came back into the office. She was gracious about the delay, and she nodded when the senator explained that he was going to fight against the bankruptcy bill. She said she knew it was important but her expression made it clear that she worried about her husband. Melissa and I gathered ourselves up and hustled out of the office.

After pushing the button for an elevator, I put my forehead against the cool, stainless-steel wall in the twenty-fourth-floor lobby. And then I started to cry.

No high fives with Melissa. No hallelujahs or hurrahs about a big win. More than anything, I felt a deep sense of relief and gratitude.

Politics so often felt dirty to me—all the lobbyists and the cozy dealings and the special favors for those who could buy access. But as I stood in the lobby outside Ted Kennedy's office, I felt as if I'd been washed clean.

We had been so outnumbered for so long, and now we had Ted Kennedy. *Ted Kennedy.* I'd come to his office without political connections of any kind. I didn't offer a nickel of campaign contributions. Improving the bankruptcy system wasn't going to help him the next time he ran for reelection. But he had promised us that not only would he join our effort to stop the industry-backed bill, he would lead the fight against it in Congress.

For me, this was a defining moment. Ted Kennedy agreed to take on the big banks and the credit card companies and then fight back against a terrible bill—and he did it only because he thought it was the right thing to do for hardworking people who had run out of options.

A $550 Lie

Senator Kennedy was true to his word. He strategized. He planned. He cajoled other senators. And when the time came, he fought the bill on the Senate floor.

Soon we picked up some other terrific allies in the Senate. Dick Durbin of Illinois and Chuck Schumer of New York were both in their first terms, but they jumped in for leadership roles. Russ Feingold of Wisconsin and Paul Wellstone of Minnesota were barely into their second terms, and they were also ready to help. I imagine each one of them could have used some hefty campaign contributions from the banking industry, but that didn't matter. They joined the fight with energy and enthusiasm—and I will be forever grateful.

During the bankruptcy battles, Senator Wellstone—a former professor and an unapologetic liberal—and I got to know each other pretty well. He used to call my office at Harvard after a long day at work. Now that Bruce was commuting to Philadelphia, Faith and I had fallen into the habit of staying in the office later and later into the evening. When I'd pick up the phone, he would always ask the same question in a mock-stern voice:

"*Professor,* what are you doing working at this hour?"

And my standard response was: "*Senator,* what are *you* doing working at this hour?"

We'd both laugh, and then we'd start talking about the fight. He was passionate and funny, and his energy never flagged. But he couldn't change the fact that the deck was still stacked against us. All the lobbyists, all the press flacks, all the campaign contributions—it seemed as though the banks had it all, and nothing we did could prevent them from gaining a little more ground every month.

The banking industry bought everything; they even bought their own facts. The industry commissioned three different studies, each of which was touted as "independent." Each explained the urgent need to change the law—exactly the way the banking industry wanted it changed. One particularly damaging result of these bogus studies was a claim that bankruptcy cost every hardworking, bill-paying American family a $550 "hidden tax." The number was entirely made up, fabricated out of thin air, but the press reported it as "fact" for years.

This one hit me hard. I'd spent nearly twenty years sweating over every detail in a string of serious academic studies, agonizing over sample sizes and statistical significance to make certain that whatever I reported was exactly right. Now the banks just wrote a check, commissioned a friendly study, and purchased their own facts. Then they had their press people distribute the facts and lobbyists hand the facts to congressional staffers. From the halls of Congress to the front pages of newspapers all over the country, these new "facts" became reality.

This strategy—and the cynicism behind it—made me furious. It also scared me. If the facts about bankruptcy could be purchased, then who knew what they would claim next?

The commission report had been delivered in October 1997, and for the next three years we fought off the industry as best we could. But in 2000, we were running out of ways to counter the relentless campaign. The industry-supported bankruptcy bill passed the House and the Senate by sizable margins. Fortunately, one last warrior held out against the banks and the credit card companies: President Clinton. In 1998 I had met with First Lady Hillary Clinton to discuss the proposed bankruptcy legislation, and after our meeting she had declared that she would fight on behalf of working families, against "that awful bill." Now the president was under enormous pressure from the banks to sign the bill, but in the last days of his presidency, urged on by his wife, President Clinton stood strong with struggling families. With no public fanfare, he vetoed the industry's bill.

We were still stacking sandbags, and working people would be protected a little longer.

An Obscene Phone Call

The banks lost in 2000, but they didn't quit—they just spent more money on lobbying and campaign contributions. Soon the banking industry was outspending everybody else—tobacco, pharmaceuticals, even Big Oil. Credit card companies lined up to boost George W. Bush's presidential campaign.

In 2001, the bill looked sure to pass Congress again, and now George W. Bush was in the White House, promising to sign it into law. The recent election kept the House in Republican control, and every single Republican was ready to support the bill. The Senate was evenly split between the two parties, but one of the bill's lead sponsors was Democratic powerhouse Joe Biden, and right behind him were plenty of other Democrats offering to help.

Never mind that the country was sunk in an ugly recession and millions of families were struggling—the banking industry pressed forward and Congress obliged. Eventually, versions of the bill were passed by both the House and the Senate, and in late 2002, a final version of the bill emerged from conference. A few weeks earlier, we had lost a friend and key champion when Senator Paul Wellstone was killed in a plane crash. Now it seemed that our epic battle was all but over.

By that point, I was resigned to the outcome. We had rallied some great organizations and terrific people to our cause: since 1997, we had protected a lot of families from disaster. We had fought the good fight, but now we would lose.

One day in mid-November, I sat in my office writing the final exam for the term.

When the phone rang, I jumped. I picked it up and answered with my usual, "Elizabeth Warren." My mind was still on the exam.

I heard a man shouting. He was struggling to catch his breath, and mixed into his shouted words was a jumble, including what sounded like some surprising epithets. "We showed those #*&!!s. They shouldn't mess with us!"

I thought: Wow, my first obscene phone call—and it's happening at Harvard. Who knew?

I had taken the phone away from my ear and was about to hang up when I realized that the voice sounded oddly familiar. There was something about the accent.

I pulled the phone back to my ear and listened for another few seconds. Then I said: "Senator Kennedy?"

"Yes, yes!" he yelled into the phone. "We're here. We're in the cloakroom. We did it! We pushed back—and we won! Here, talk to Dick."

Senator Durbin came on the line and told the whole story. The politics were fierce, he said, and they revolved around . . . abortion.

Recently, a handful of pro-choice groups had won some big lawsuits against a few super-aggressive abortion clinic protesters. The judgments levied by the courts against the protesters added up to more than $1 million, but the victories by the pro-choice groups evaporated when the protesters filed for bankruptcy and dumped the court orders to pay. A fight erupted over whether this was a fair use of bankruptcy. Pro-life advocates argued that it was, but Senator Schumer pushed back hard, adding an amendment to the Senate version of the bankruptcy bill that would block such actions. His amendment inflicted chaos on the credit industry's well-laid plans.

When the House and Senate bills went to conference, negotiators worked out a compromise. At the last minute, however, House Republicans rejected the compromise language. Now all the pressure was on the Senate to accept the House version and give up on any limits on abortion protesters. But the Senate held firm. Schumer, Kennedy, and Durbin worked the phones, and they picked up enough allies to kill the bill without a vote.

After explaining what had happened, Senator Durbin handed the phone back to Senator Kennedy. He had stopped yelling, and now he was laughing. We did it, he said. We did it! He sounded as if he'd just scored the winning touchdown.

So we had won, at least for another day. The victory was the result of some pretty tangled politics, but the families who needed bankruptcy protection were safe behind our sandbags for a little while longer.

Wanted: A Real Live Banker

The banking industry had lost for a second time, but it came back once again, bringing even more money and more lobbyists. It was like fighting some kind of mythical creature—cut off one head and two grow back.

One morning, I got a call from the producer for a national television news program. I had talked to the media from time to time, sometimes on the record and sometimes on background. My hope was always that they might help bring attention to the important safety net that bank-ruptcy provides families in trouble. I could tell from the producer's breathless tone that he thought he had a great offer for me: he asked if I'd agree to come on their show and debate the bankruptcy issue with some-one from the banking industry. No interruptions, enough time to talk, a conversation that went straight to the issues.

My stomach knotted up with tension. National television. I might really mess up. On the other hand, I might be able to reach a lot of people.

I was in. "Who will the banker be?"

The producer said he didn't know, but once they had someone lined up, he would call back. A couple of days later, he telephoned to say that the debate was all set, and he named the other person they would invite.

I asked which bank he worked for.

He checked his notes and then answered: The other guest would be an "industry representative."

I felt like my balloon had just popped. I told the guy I wouldn't debate a lobbyist. I said that if he could find a *real* banker who was willing to go on television and explain his company's lending practices and their posi-tion on this law, I'd be happy to debate him all night long—but not a lob-byist.

He was pretty cheerful. "Okay," he said, "I'll call you back."

Several days went by before he telephoned again. This time he seemed a little more subdued. He told me that he had called bank after bank, and none of them would allow a representative to participate in the debate. The giant banks employed countless executives, but not a single one would appear on television to defend their lending practices or explain all their lobbying in Washington. Not one.

And there it was, the industry's strategy made plain: Take no respon-sibility, don't show your face, just keep spending millions of dollars behind the scenes. Let the "industry representatives" working at trade associa-tions all over Washington talk to the media and keep pushing the $550 lie.

So I turned down that interview, and I didn't get any other offers to debate bankers. I talked to the press when I could, and occasionally I went to Washington to testify before a congressional committee about the intricacies of bankruptcy law. But mostly I taught my classes and wrote my books.

The Two-Income Trap

In the early 2000s, Terry Sullivan, Jay Westbrook, and I launched another bankruptcy research study. This was our fifth time gathering this kind of data, so I assumed our new findings wouldn't generate much interest. Boy, was I wrong.

By 2001, the number of families in financial collapse was shocking:

- More children would live through their parents' bankruptcy than their parents' divorce.
- More women would file for bankruptcy than would graduate from college.
- More people would file for bankruptcy than would be diagnosed with cancer.

To say the numbers were huge—or enormous or gigantic—didn't even begin to cut it. Pick an adjective, and the problem was bigger than that.

And it was no longer "just anyone" who was going bankrupt. It was families with kids. To be sure, older folks and childless people were going broke in record numbers, but our newest finding knocked me back: The single best predictor that a family would go bankrupt was if they had a child. And this didn't apply just to poor, single mothers with limited education and no opportunities. Bankruptcies were exploding among solidly middle-class families, families with Mom and Dad both working full-time—or working full-time right up until something went horribly wrong.

So I set out to pick at the sore yet again, but this time the sore was a lot bigger. Instead of asking why people went bankrupt, now I had a different question: What on earth was wrong in our country? How could we have *that* much distress? And what made having children so dangerous to a family's financial security?

By now Alex and Amelia were grown. Alex was twenty-five and a full-fledged computer expert, designing databases or taking on software troubleshooting jobs that I didn't know existed. He was on his way to Los Angeles to live near his sister and enjoy the sunshine.

Amelia was thirty. She had married her boyfriend, Sushil Tyagi, a brilliant young man from a village in northern India, who had come to the United States for graduate school. Now they had a baby, a beautiful little girl they named Octavia. My relationship with Amelia had changed completely. Now my daughter was the Working Mother. And somehow I was no longer the meddlesome mom who was trying to keep her from having any fun. I had been promoted to "Wise Person Who Knows How Babies Work."

In 2001, I went to California to help Amelia during my summer break at Harvard. Little Octavia was a fretful baby, and I rocked and rocked her. And then, at some point during all that rocking, *bam!* I fell in love. And this was the real deal: hit-on-the-head, knock-me-over, stars-in-the-eyes love. It was a lot like the way I had loved my own babies, but much better. This was all the love without any of the scary responsibility or the guilt over whether I was making the right choices. Amelia could be the anxious Working Mother. I just got to love-love-love the baby. Octavia gave me the chance to experience some of the purest joy I'd ever felt in my life.

When it came time to go back home, I could barely stand it. My arms ached for that little person. So I came back—and came back again. And somewhere along the way, I made a promise that I would find a way to be a part—a real, in-the-trenches, regular part—of this little girl's life.

Amelia and I had lots of long, rambling conversations during my visits, and sometimes the talk spilled over to my research. During one of those early trips, I asked her to help me dig into some government data about bankruptcy. Amelia had worked for consulting giant McKinsey and then cofounded a start-up business. A self-avowed "quant jock" (which just meant she liked to work with numbers), she jumped right in and soon began to offer up some intriguing insights. One day, between fretting over a bad rash under the baby's chin (it was really gross) and poring over the data, we hatched a plan: Let's write a book together.

Bruce thought this idea was nuts. He remembered the days when Amelia and I could barely make it through dinner without one of us yelling at the other. What was I thinking? Besides, a mother-daughter collaboration just isn't something professors *do*. Professors are supposed to coauthor books with other professors, and the books ought to be really dull and have a million footnotes that almost no one ever reads.

But Amelia brought something important to the new work. I was now the old generation, and she was the new. We framed the book around our lives. We compared the middle-class family of 1971—the year I had started out as a young mother with a new baby—with the middle-class family of 2001—the year Amelia was starting out as a young mother with a new baby. Thirty years, one generation—and in that snippet of time the middle class had turned upside down. This was the story we would tell.

Amelia brought a second value to the table: she was the only person who had the nerve to look me straight in the eye and say calmly, "Mom, you are boring." She still does that. I learned the hard way that collaborating with my daughter is not for sissies.

Our minds made up, we set about launching our unconventional version of a family business, and that's how our book, *The Two-Income Trap*, was born. We started with a familiar question: Why are so many families going broke? Ask almost any pundit, and the response would likely have been: Families are going broke because they buy too much stuff! All those name-brand running shoes, closets full of clothes, and microwave ovens were pushing the middle class deep into debt. The "urge to splurge" was overtaking us.

Amelia tackled the conventional wisdom head-on. As it happens, for decades the government has been collecting data on how much families spend on pretty much everything—from frozen fish to pet food to boys' pajamas. When Amelia dug into this trove of information, she found that the numbers simply didn't support the story. Consider clothing, a favorite target for the pundits. Even when we accounted for all the Nike sneakers and name-brand sunglasses, the average family of four spent *less* on clothing in 2001 than they did a generation earlier (adjusted for inflation). What about food? Even including all the restaurant meals, Starbucks coffee, and fresh-squeezed smoothies, the average family spent *less* on food than they did thirty years earlier.

That's not to say that families never frittered away any money. Americans spent more than they used to on such things as televisions, premium channels, and home computers. But they spent less on furniture and home appliances (microwaves included), and the savings just about balanced out. The balancing act held in other places, too. Families spent more on airplane travel, less on dry cleaning. More on cell phones, less on tobacco. More on pets, less on carpets. And when we added it all up, we realized that the hollowed-out middle class of Amelia's generation wasn't any more frivolous in its spending than the solid, comfortable, growing middle class of my generation.

So what had gone wrong? Wages were flat; that was part of the story. For most of the twentieth century, wages had risen steadily. But that stopped happening in the 1970s. For the middle class, wages (adjusted for inflation) had remained stagnant for an entire generation.

Other things being equal, the middle class might have made it through—no richer than their parents, but no poorer either. But other things *weren't* equal, because costs went up for stuff that was a lot harder to live without, like health care and education.

And then there was housing. Millions of families did exactly what my parents had done two generations earlier—they stretched to buy homes in good school districts. But now the stretch was different. Thanks to a newly deregulated banking industry, the strict lending standards that my parents faced had gone the way of the dinosaur. Teaser rates, interest-only loans, and no-down-payment loans appeared, and families grabbed hold. Many figured this was their best chance for their kids to get a good education or to live in a nice neighborhood. The rush to buy homes seemed so hopeful at the beginning. But with all that money flowing into the housing market, prices were starting to climb fast, so even families who wanted to play it safe didn't have much choice—take on a giant mortgage or get shut out. Much was said about fancy new "McMansions," but that proved to be another myth, at least among the middle class. Most middle-class families lived in a house only slightly larger—and often quite a bit older—than the one their parents owned, and the huge, new homes remained the domain of the wealthy.

As the family budget got tighter and tighter, women all across the country made the same move I had made a generation earlier: they took a job. But I had gone to work because I wanted to, while a lot of these women didn't have much choice.

Single-income families found themselves falling further and further behind. Even for those lucky enough to have two incomes, it often wasn't enough. On average, once the basic bills were covered—the mortgage, the health insurance, day care, the cost of preschool or college tuition—the modern two-income family had *less* money left over each month than the one-income family of a generation earlier. Amelia and I called this "the two-income trap," and middle-class families everywhere were caught in it and could see no way out.

Once families got caught in this trap, they had to make some hard choices. First to go was savings. Back when I was a young mother, a typi-cal one-income family put away 11 percent of their take-home pay in savings. By 2001, even though many families now had two incomes, the savings rate for the average family was approaching zero.

For some families, working hard and pinching pennies allowed them to get by. If a married couple could somehow get their kids off to college (which now cost three times what it cost when they were young), they might pay down the mortgage on the house and still have a little left over to retire on.

But if anything went wrong—anything at all—they were out of luck. A job layoff, a long stretch of unemployment, or a serious illness, and the family careened off a financial cliff. They had no savings to fall back on. And because so many of the costs that ate up every paycheck were fixed, there wasn't much room to "cut back." They couldn't just lop off the fourth bedroom for a few months or buy half a health insurance policy until Dad found a new job. They were stuck, and now the trap's teeth cut a lot deeper.

Amelia and I turned in the first few chapters of our manuscript for *The Two-Income Trap*, and the publisher seemed to like it, except for one thing. It's so depressing! Who wants to read such a bleak book? Make it happy! Make it hopeful!

We tried, we really did. But I felt as if someone were asking me to deliver stand-up jokes at a funeral.

Worse, we hadn't even come to the really tough stuff. The remaining chapters of the book told the hardest part of the story: Once families ran out of money, they turned to debt. Credit card debt piled up—and up and up. Payday loans popped up everywhere and sucked in people who were in a crunch. And when someone missed a payment or fell behind on the debt treadmill, they got socked with staggering increases in their bills. The result? *Fifteen million* families filed for bankruptcy in a single decade and uncounted millions more were hanging on to the cliff by their fingernails. Home foreclosures were also starting to climb, even back in the 1990s and early 2000s. All we needed was the music from *Jaws* to signal that this debt monster was going to hurt a lot of people.

During the months when I pored over the research and carefully wrote that book, I came to some painful conclusions. America's middle class was under attack. The nation's broad prosperity had been forged by people like my parents—people who knew hardship and conflict and who kept on fighting, determined to pass on something better to their children. But the strength of the middle class was not unlimited. I felt as though I were looking at a once sturdy house that was crumbling: the windows were broken and the roof was caving in.

It wasn't a happy story. Instead, the book was an alarm, a warning that our country was headed in a terrible direction. As we finished the book, I felt deeply, deeply worried.

Tell Someone Who Could Do Something

Apparently, I wasn't the only person who was worried. Amelia and I had written a book that was aimed at the policy crowd (after all, I was still a professor at Harvard and the book had fifty pages of footnotes). But when it came out, in September 2003, *The Two-Income Trap* struck a nerve. *Newsweek* ran a three-page spread about the book, complete with a picture of Amelia in her backyard. The *Today* show brought me on to talk about the trap. Within days, the book was covered by CBS News, the *Boston Globe,* NPR, and CNN. In its first two weeks of publication, the book focused more attention on the economic security of America's families than I'd been able to generate in nearly a decade of fighting the bankruptcy wars.

I figured we were onto something, and the optimistic part of my brain believed that suddenly I had a chance to make a bigger difference. So I tried reaching out to several of the men who were running for president in 2004: Howard Dean, John Edwards, General Wesley Clark, John Kerry. I also asked a favor from a well-connected Republican friend from Harvard. Could he get me a meeting with someone on the staff of President Bush?

My plan was to give each of them a copy of the book, tell them some key facts, lay out some policy ideas, and hope for the best. I had visions of long, thoughtful policy discussions, not unlike the first conversation I'd had with Senator Kennedy. Only now the conversation had to go beyond bankruptcy. Now I wanted to talk about a seismic shift in the middle-class family balance sheet, and I wanted our leaders to know that America's middle class was in big trouble—and the trouble was growing.

In those days, I didn't have the faintest clue about the pressures on someone running for public office. First they'd spend hours reading my book, and then we'd have long policy talks? Clearly I didn't know squat.

Then one day in early 2004, I was walking through an airport when my cell phone rang. My caller identified himself as John—John Edwards. He said he had read *The Two-Income Trap* and wanted to talk about it. I was so surprised that as I wrestled with my roller bag, my phone, and my iced tea, I dropped my backpack on the floor. The zipper on the outer pocket wasn't closed, so even as I was talking to Senator Edwards, I was scrambling to pick up the thousand things that had spilled everywhere. But the ideas in the *Two-Income Trap* clearly interested the senator, and he seemed to be thinking hard about them.

Not a relaxed, detailed conversation, but not bad. And over the next several months, Edwards called a few more times, and I was also able to talk with staff members from some of the other presidential campaigns.

Months later, at a rally in April 2004, John Kerry spoke about the transformation of the American family and said *The Two-Income Trap* was "one of the best books that actually describes the transformation that has taken place in America." For me, that was a "wow" moment. Kerry was the presumptive Democratic nominee. Maybe he would become president. Maybe he would put a big focus on rebuilding the middle class. Maybe.

But Kerry lost. Meanwhile, I never got a meeting with anyone from the Bush White House, not even an aide. After the election, the industry-supported bankruptcy bill was back again, and it kept moving right along in Congress. Campaign money rolled in. MBNA, the country's biggest credit card lender, through its executives and PACs and "soft money" pledges, had been the single biggest contributor to President Bush's first campaign, and in 2004 they stepped up to the plate again. And all over the country, middle-class families were still getting hammered.

Dr. Phil

Once *The Two-Income Trap* started to get some mainstream attention, I decided to take one more swing at sounding the alarm and trying to get the book's ideas into wider circulation. When Dr. Phil McGraw agreed to have Amelia and me come on the show, I wasn't sure what we'd be in for, but I thought I should give it a shot.

At the studio, people rushed about, talking, carrying clothes, calling out to aides. Amelia and I were tucked into a tiny room with a huge mirror and enough lights around the mirror to cover the landing strip at the

Los Angeles airport. Someone came by to pronounce Amelia's shirt "the wrong color" and thrust a new blouse into her hands with the command "Change!" She never got her original shirt back. We figure it's probably still hanging in some wardrobe room somewhere.

About an hour later, a young woman knocked on the door and said urgently, "You're up! You're up! Let's go! Let's go!" She clapped her hands at us, and I wondered if she said everything in twos.

She brought us backstage, where it was freezing cold. I could hear loud music and an even louder announcer revving up the crowd. "Do you *love* it here? *Do you?*" someone shouted into the microphone.

A few minutes later, I joined the audience and took a seat in the front row next to Amelia. When Dr. Phil came onstage, I jumped to my feet and clapped wildly along with everyone else.

Dr. Phil interviewed a couple who had gotten in financial trouble and had tried to bail themselves out by cashing out their home equity. Eventually, Dr. Phil called my name and asked what I thought about their decision. Suddenly everyone shifted toward me, the camera bore down, and I knew this was it—the chance to say something useful to a big audience. My heart started banging in my chest and I felt blinded by the lights, but I already knew what I wanted to say. I said that taking out a second mortgage to pay a debt was like "playing roulette with your house" and that it was "the single worst move that homeowners can make."

Dr. Phil pressed on. What about the push from the giant banks to get people to consolidate their bills through a second mortgage? I answered:

> Dr. Phil, that's how they make money. They make money by getting families like this to get into debt. *They* don't make money unless *you* borrow more money. The whole idea is to tell you how smart, clever, and safe you'd be if you took your house and placed it on the roulette wheel.

A moment later, the camera swung back to the stage and the audience once again stared intently at Dr. Phil and the couple on the stage. I blinked.

As the show went on, I got to say a few more things, but the gist was the same. Although piling on debt might seem to be a solution to a family's financial problems, too often it led to disaster.

As Amelia and I stood up at the end of the show, I couldn't help smiling. I had been working on family economic issues for more than twenty years. Year in and year out, I'd been fighting as hard as I could—doing research, writing papers, giving interviews. I'd even tried to advise presidential candidates (or at least I'd tried to advise the advisors to presidential candidates). But by spending a few minutes talking to that family on Dr. Phil's show—and to about six million other people who were looking on—I might have done more good than in an entire year as a professor. And although I was still fighting hard in the battles over bankruptcy laws in Washington, it was pretty clear that we were losing the war. Families were getting sucked down every day, and too many people in Washington were fighting on the side of the rich and powerful. But now I had just given the best advice I could to six million people. Maybe *that* was a better way to make a difference.

After the show, Dr. Phil sent someone to fetch me back to his office. Phil said he liked *The Two-Income Trap,* and he thought the argument was right: hardworking people really were getting hammered. I smiled. But the compliments about the book stopped after about five seconds. He didn't quite come out and say it, but he made it clear that he thought the book was for policy wonks, and he doubted that it would do much to help regular people fix their financial problems. So much for my smile.

Then he gave me some advice: Write another book, and this time write it for people who can use it.

So I did.

The Rules of the Game Have Changed

Amelia and I set to work right away. Life intervened, of course—and so did death. In 2003, Jim Warren developed lung cancer; within months he was gone. He was only fifty-eight. I hadn't seen him more than a dozen or so times in the many years since our divorce, but I felt truly awful that he had died so young. For Amelia and Alex, the loss of their father hit hard.

Much happier news came the next year, when Amelia announced that another baby was on the way. That motivated both of us to get cracking on the new book, and we completed a draft ahead of Amelia's due date.

All Your Worth was a pretty cheery book, full of optimistic advice about how to take charge of your finances and secure your future. But, truth be told, it was born from a fairly dark place. Families were still falling off the financial cliff, and Washington seemed hell-bent on serving the rich and powerful. As far as I could tell, nothing much was going to change that.

Our first book together had described many things Washington could do to strengthen the middle class. But *All Your Worth* started with a very different premise: In a world where no help is coming from Washington, what can you do to protect yourself? A generation ago, people who worked hard and played by the rules usually came out okay, as long as they didn't go too crazy with spending. That just wasn't true anymore. Now the rules of the game had changed, and people needed to learn these rules—and fast—so they could protect themselves and their families. The way I saw it, hard-working people were scrambling just to survive, and a giant credit industry had drawn a bull's-eye on the back of every struggling family. I wanted to show them how to stay low, fight smarter, and take care of their families.

To that end, we created a formula to help people budget their "Must-Have" expenditures (mortgage, child care, utilities, and the like), their "Wants" (an extra pair of sneakers, a latte at Starbucks, or a vacation), and their "Savings." We called this strategy "financial balance." We didn't push people to go on a starvation budget that left no room for fun—life is just too short! Instead, we helped people evaluate whether they were on a sustainable financial path and offered strategies for managing some significant downsizing if they weren't. We also argued that anyone with a debt problem should cut up their credit cards and pay with good old-fashioned cash. I had seen the giant banks in action, and I knew how dangerous debt could be. I hoped this book would help at least a few people get out of debt once and for all.

The book didn't turn me into the next Suze Orman. But I loved writing it, and I still get an occasional letter from someone who says the book made a real difference.

> Up to this point in my life, I have always relied upon the BOMD [Bank of Mom and Dad]. I not only used my parents as a source of money, but I more importantly also used them as an excuse to continuously ignore my own financial situation. . . . [Now] I feel empowered.

> This month we were able to make our loan payment four days early and we have money left over each month to pay our credit card debt off more quickly.

[Achieving financial balance] won't happen overnight and that's probably the hardest thing to accept, but it will happen.

The people who wrote me sometimes told tragic stories, but most of their letters showed determination and threw off sparks of optimism.

All Your Worth hit the bookstores in March 2005, just before the arrival of a beautiful little sprite Amelia and Sushil named Lavinia. This new addition to our family was a cuddler, and I put the California rocking chair to good use. Sometimes, late at night, when the house was quiet, I'd scoop Lavinia out of her crib and hold her. We'd rock back and forth in the dark—not because she needed it, but because I did.

We got more good news that year when Harvard offered Bruce a professorship. He loved Penn, but it was time to stop commuting and at last come home to Massachusetts. By now we were thoroughly settled in our home a few blocks from the law school, close enough that Bruce, Faith, and I could walk there every day, even in the blizzards.

And my work at Harvard? I kept launching new research projects and publishing papers in academic journals, but my energy was now spilling in lots of different directions. I didn't know if *All Your Worth* would spur any big changes, but at least I'd found another way to help more people.

We Lost

In the late spring of 2005, the families who needed help from strong bankruptcy laws finally ran out of luck. The House and the Senate passed the industry-backed bankruptcy bill by lopsided majorities, and President Bush signed it into law.

A few months before the vote, Faith, who had been a gift from my students so many years earlier, died. After that I said to Bruce, "No more dogs. It hurts too much when they die." Bruce hugged me and didn't say much. But that summer, he came home with Otis, a golden retriever puppy with huge feet whose first act was to stagger into the house, find an air-conditioning vent, and flop down on top of it. Otis was born ready for a nap.

Okay, so Bruce was getting a dog. I announced that I was fine with this, but I would *not* fall in love. (Yeah, right.)

The changes to the bankruptcy law were set to go into effect in the fall of 2005. That year, more than two million families raced to the bankruptcy courthouse, afraid they would lose their last, best chance at protection. Sure enough, the minute the amendments to the law kicked in, bankruptcy filings dropped sharply. And the credit industry got what it wanted—less help for families in trouble.

No single change made the difference. Instead, it was death by a thousand cuts. The law got more complicated. The paperwork multiplied. Single mothers got less help, and they had a harder time collecting past due child support. Filing fees went up. Some people were still eligible for relief, some people weren't. Some debts could be discharged, some could not. Some lawyers quit the practice of bankruptcy altogether, and those who stayed in the business often charged more—sometimes a lot more—to navigate the more complex law. There were hundreds of changes, some big and some small, but every change tilted in the same direction: Squeeze the families in trouble and increase the profits for big banks, credit card companies, car lenders, and a slew of other very successful businesses.

The banks also won an important public relations coup. After the changes to the law went into effect, a lot of people thought bankruptcy protection had been eliminated altogether. Many families figured there wasn't any help for them, no matter how much trouble they were in. Debt collectors advanced this notion, telling people that bankruptcy was now "illegal" or that they would be audited by the IRS if they tried to use bankruptcy to clear their debts. It was a lie, but to someone who wasn't an expert in the law and who was getting harassed by debt collectors, it probably sounded like the truth.

So what happened to the hundreds of thousands of people who might have filed bankruptcy each year but didn't? No one knows for sure. Some may have regained their footing, although with their huge debts it's hard to see how. Some pulled the belt even tighter, gave up health insurance, or stopped taking their kids to the doctor. Some disconnected their phones in a desperate attempt to avoid harassing calls from debt collectors. Some people moved to the underground economy, working for cash so their wages couldn't be garnished. Some missed the chance to catch up on mortgage payments and lost their homes. Some gave up their dream of getting a college degree. Some single mothers lost hope of receiving their past due child support from their bankrupt ex-husbands and moved in with family or fell into bankruptcy themselves. And some people shut down their small business, because without a fresh start the business no longer had a chance to survive.

On good days, I reminded myself that our fight to protect America's middle class had held off the banking industry for nearly a decade. From the day President Clinton appointed Mike Synar to launch the National Bankruptcy Review Commission to the final passage of the bill, millions of families had gotten some relief from their debts. On bad days, I admitted that right from the beginning, the game was so rigged that working families never had a fighting chance. The big banks would eventually win. They simply had too much power.

Even with help from great senators like Ted Kennedy, Dick Durbin, Chuck Schumer, Russ Feingold, and Paul Wellstone, we didn't win. Even with careful research and numerous studies showing the damage being done to America's families, we didn't win. Even with the AARP, the NAACP, and dozens of other great organizations on our side, we didn't win. Even in a democracy, with millions of people pushed to the breaking point, we didn't win. We didn't win? Heck, we didn't even come close. In the end, the vote in favor of the industry-supported bill was 74–25 in the Senate and 302–126 in the House.

David really did get the slingshot shoved down his throat sideways. It hurt then, and it still hurts now.

The bankruptcy wars changed me forever. Even before this grinding battle, I had begun to understand the terrible squeeze on the middle class. But it was this fight that showed me how badly the playing field was tilted and taught me that the squeeze wasn't accidental.

We had lost the bankruptcy battle, but this war wasn't over. People were getting pounded, debts were mounting, and the squeeze was getting more intense than ever.

I spent the next few years looking for more ways to fight back. I joined forces with several professors and we launched another study, this one designed to gauge the impact of the change in the bankruptcy law. (The news was bad.) I updated all of the research from *The Two-Income Trap*. (The news was worse.) This time I had to work the data without Amelia, who had headed off to start another new business and was busier than ever taking care of her two little girls. I helped out on some big lawsuits, and I eventually got to go to the US Supreme Court (as second chair—not the one who actually stands up and speaks to the Justices) on a case to try to get more money for asbestos victims. I wrote more about the crumbling foundations of America's middle class. I started blogging, posting my own pieces and inviting my students to get involved. I joined a commission set up by FDIC chairman Sheila Bair that was dedicated to helping low-income families gain access to more affordable banking services.

The hard part was figuring out what might actually have some impact. I was restless—restless and anxious. I could see warning signs of a coming catastrophe everywhere, but I couldn't stop it.

3 | Bailing Out the Wrong People

IT WAS EARLY evening on Thursday, November 13, 2008, and the financial crisis was battering the country like a storm whose winds gathered strength every day. No one was sure what wreckage might wash up next.

In about ten minutes, thirty or so hungry law students were going to show up on our doorstep, ready for an informal discussion over dinner about what life after law school might look like. The doorbell rang, and I let in a delivery guy who was juggling several aluminum pans of barbecue. I'd already made four trays of peach cobbler, and the iced tea was steeping. Otis, now a glorious one hundred pounds, had just settled down for yet another nap when the doorbell roused him and the smell of the barbecue gave him a newfound energy. He was slobbering and running in circles around the delivery guy, who was a little uneasy about the oversize dog. I was trying to write a check and get the fellow on his way when the phone rang. My caller was a soft-spoken man who identified himself as "Harry Reid."

I could barely hear him. "Who?" I asked.

"Um, Harry Reid." Pause. "Majority leader, US Senate."

"Oh." (Great start!)

Senator Reid got right to the point—no "how are you," no small talk. The country was in a crisis, and he wanted me to come to Washington to help provide some oversight of the Treasury Department's handling of the bank bailout. I didn't know what that meant or what I could do, but everyone I knew was scared about what was happening to the economy and to the nation. I don't think I'd ever met Senator Reid, and I really didn't know why he believed that I was the right person for this job. But if he was calling, it meant he thought I could help. So I said yes. No questions, no negotiations. Just yes.

It had been thirteen years since Mike Synar had called and asked me to help him with the National Bankruptcy Review Commission, and it had been three years since Congress had ripped gaping holes in the bankruptcy safety net. My time in Washington had left me fed up with the whole place. But this was an emergency. The financial system had melted down, and millions of middle-class families were getting crushed, so if Senator Reid asked me to help by mopping the floors or licking envelopes, I would say yes. Besides, I thought that in an emergency, surely people in Washington would dial back on political maneuvering and focus on finding ways to help struggling people. So if Senator Reid thought I could make a difference, it was time for me to go back to Washington.

As soon as the barbecue was eaten and the last student had left, I called Bruce. He was out of town at a conference with a bunch of other history professors. Otis was sprawled across the floor, his belly bulging from the bits of meat and cornbread that the students had slipped his way. I put on my telephone headset and my long white apron and cleaned up the dishes while we talked.

I told Bruce that Senator Reid had asked me to join a five-person Congressional Oversight Panel. COP: what a great name! I wondered if I might actually get a badge and a set of handcuffs—okay, no handcuffs, but maybe a badge?

Six weeks earlier, in near panic, Congress had agreed to authorize a $700 billion fund to bail out the financial system—the Troubled Asset Relief Program, or TARP. The bill that set up TARP also created COP, which was assigned the task of monitoring how Treasury handed out the bailout money.

"This is really amazing," I said to Bruce. "I can't wait to meet the Treasury people, to talk about how they plan to use the money. Maybe I should cancel office hours tomorrow and fly to Washington." I was revved up and ready to go; it felt good to think about helping out.

Bruce was Bruce—happy that I was excited, but a lot calmer than I was. "I haven't read anything in the paper about a cop." (Bruce is a traditional guy; he still gets his news from old-fashioned printed newspapers.) "What exactly will you be doing, babe?"

I paused. "Oh. Well. Hmmm. I haven't seen anything about a cop either, but I guess I'll get to do cop stuff. You know, check out how things are working, investigate, and tell them if things are wrong. At least I think so." It occurred to me that Senator Reid hadn't said exactly what my role would be, so I didn't have a clue.

It was after midnight when we hung up and I pulled out my laptop. I located the law authorizing the gigantic fund that would go to the Treasury Department to deal with the country's "troubled assets." Eventually I found the section dealing with COP. My optimism about how I could help sank a little.

The new law spelled out how a five-member panel would be chosen, how we'd get paid, and how expenses would be reimbursed. But the section describing the duties of COP had essentially one entry: "Submit reports." COP was supposed to give Congress a report every thirty days. That was pretty much it. Huh: no arrests, no handcuffs, no perp walks.

And what tools would we be given so that we could oversee the distribution of all that money? The statute said we could "take testimony," but the lawyer in me instantly noticed that COP would have no subpoena powers. We could politely invite people to testify . . . and they could politely decline. (Or impolitely, if they preferred.) We could also ask agencies for "official data," and the agencies "shall furnish it." But if we wanted something the agencies deemed "unofficial," well, we could be out of luck.

Okay, so our authorities were limited. No ability to subpoena witnesses. No power to blow a whistle to stop the flow of money if we thought something shady was going on. And there was no requirement that the secretary of the Treasury explain his strategy to us.

Nope, none of that. It looked like the law setting up COP envisioned that its role would be to write boring reports that would gather dust while the economy tumbled over a cliff. In other words, this new adventure in Washington might not be nearly as productive as I had hoped.

But when Harry Reid had asked, I'd said yes—so I was going, like it or not.

How a Downturn Becomes a Meltdown

Whenever I think of the meltdown, I still think of Flora. (I've changed her name to protect her privacy.) She was probably in her eighties by the time we spoke with her in 2007 while conducting interviews for more bankruptcy research. She explained that she and her husband had retired and moved to a small town in the South a few decades earlier to be near family. They bought a modest house. ("That's all we needed.") Flora's husband had passed on, and she was on her own now. Flora said that until recently she had been doing fine, getting by on her Social Security check each month.

Flora explained that she'd gotten a call a few years ago from "a nice man from the bank." She said he'd told her that because interest rates were low, he could give her a mortgage with a lower payment. She'd asked him what would happen to the payment if interest rates went back up. According to Flora, he'd assured her that "the banks know about these things in advance" and that he would "call her and put her back in her old mortgage."

She had taken the deal, and before long, her payments had shot up. She paused, then said quietly, "He never called." The new monthly payment swallowed nearly every penny of her Social Security check. She had tried delaying her payments, borrowing on credit cards, going to a payday lender, but it had all come crashing down.

The Bankruptcy Project, which my co-researchers and I had developed to find out more about families who filed for bankruptcy after the laws were changed, had promised her $50 in return for participating in an hour-long interview. She knew we planned to send the money to the address she'd given us and understood that it would take a few weeks. She explained that next week she would have to leave her home.

"I'll be living in my car," she said, "at least for a while. I don't know how I'll get mail, so can you tell me how to get my fifty-dollar check? I really need it."

That's the real story behind the meltdown: the mortgage market sank, one Flora at a time. Some homeowners made bad decisions or tried to game the system, but many others got trapped by lousy mortgages sold to them by sophisticated financial institutions that should have known better.

By the early 2000s, the mortgage companies could see how much money the credit card lenders were racking up with deceptively low "teaser" rates, and a lot of them wanted to get their turn at the trough.

And boy, did they get it. With interest rates effectively deregulated, there was no longer any limit on what these banks could charge, so the sub-prime lending spree was born.

New "mortgage products" popped up like weeds. Families were offered loan agreements that used unfamiliar terms like "balloon payments" and "option ARMs" and "prepayment penalties." A lot of people didn't look too closely at the deals—and like Flora, many relied on the word of a salesman who gave a slick description of the arrangements. As the mort-gages got more complicated, lenders found plenty of new opportunities to slip in an extra trick here or a little trap there.

Many lenders made a mad dash for quick profits, abandoning their time-honored practice of carefully investigating job histories and pay stubs before approving a mortgage. Down payments shrank. Penalties and fees shot through the roof. Mortgage lending became so profitable that salesmen went door-to-door, often targeting African American and Latino neighborhoods for their highest-cost, most deceptive products. Other lenders pursued seniors like Flora.

Sometimes they pitched a lower monthly payment, and sometimes they pitched immediate cash. Millions of families had already run up tens of thousands of dollars in credit card debt, and these loans sounded like a lifeline. A lot of TV pundits were telling people that they were fools to pay the high interest rates associated with credit cards. Even Federal Reserve chairman Alan Greenspan urged Americans to "tap" their home equity. The math seemed compelling: Why pay 19 percent on your debt to a credit card company if you could pay 3 percent on a subprime mort-gage? Of course, 3 percent was just the low introductory rate. And those glossy ads never showed how your rates might skyrocket over time, as the interest rate adjusted or if you missed a payment or two. And the ads never, ever showed pretty homes with red FORECLOSURE signs out front.

Fueled by all that new mortgage money, home prices caught fire. As the prices shot up, speculators jumped into the game. Everyone seemed to have a story about someone they knew who was getting rich by flipping houses. And as long as home prices kept rising, it was easy to overlook the danger signs. After all, anyone who couldn't pay the mortgage could always sell their house for a profit—or they could as long as the happy music kept playing.

And then the music stopped. When the market finally collapsed, millions of people were caught in a trap. They couldn't pay their mortgages, they couldn't refinance, and they couldn't sell their homes. By late 2008, one out of every five mortgage holders owed more than their homes were worth. The banks called in the loans, and the foreclosure notices piled up.

The housing crash ripped a huge hole right through the middle class. A home isn't just a place to live; for most families, it's their most valuable asset. It's the savings plan, the retirement plan, and the inheritance all wrapped up in one big, bright package. Pay off the mortgage, and a family has a comfortable life raft, come what may. But if the mortgage is "underwater" and a family owes more than their house is worth, that life raft is made of cement.

When the housing market sank, so did America's middle class.

Oversight in the Dark

The week after Senator Reid called, I went down to Washington to meet some of the other panel members and start figuring out the business of oversight. We needed to get organized, and we needed to do it fast.

TARP had been passed with an odd mix of Democrats and Republicans, but the effort had been spearheaded by President Bush's secretary of the treasury, Henry Paulson. When the COP panelists arrived in Washington for the first time, TARP had been law for only seven weeks, but already the Treasury had committed a whopping $172 billion. We were deeply concerned that a lot of money was flying out the door with little oversight in place, so we had asked for a brief meeting with Secretary Paulson and other Treasury officials.

On Friday, November 21, I stood at the big gates in front of the Treasury Building and tried to catch my breath. I met up with two of my fellow panelists: Damon Silvers and Richard Neiman. The three of us were the Democratic appointees; Speaker Nancy Pelosi had appointed Richard, Senator Reid had appointed me, and the two lawmakers jointly had appointed Damon.

Damon Silvers is a big guy—tall, with big hands and big feet. He wears loose-fitting black suits and white wash-and-wear shirts, and he talks with the kind of speed that suggests his brain is full of ideas that are elbowing to get out all at once. After getting three degrees from Harvard—undergraduate, MBA, and law—he could have gone for the big bucks, but that wasn't Damon. Instead, he organized strawberry pickers in California and shipyard workers in New Orleans, and eventually he became associate general counsel of the AFL-CIO. I knew him a little from the bankruptcy wars, when the AFL had weighed in on our side against the big banks, and I figured I was in good company.

The other panelist, Richard Neiman, had started as a banking regulator, then spent much of his career in the banking industry before becoming New York's chief banking supervisor. I didn't know Richard before that day, but I hoped his extensive experience would be helpful.

The Treasury Building is a National Historic Landmark that looks a lot like the White House—only much bigger and more fortress-like. It's 120,000 square feet of stately columns and white marble, all of it carefully guarded behind iron gates, with no public access. Its security is run by the Secret Service. Behind the gates is the first guard station, where visitors must be cleared; the second security check—including a walk-through metal detector and a full screen of all packages—is located just inside the building. Visitors must be checked twice to make certain they are on pre-cleared lists. After we were allowed to pass, we were met by an escort who walked us quickly to the meeting room.

This was my first visit to the Treasury Building, but there was no time to look around. We were told that Secretary Paulson was not available, but we would be spending a few minutes with other officials, including Neel Kashkari, Paulson's assistant secretary, who had been named to administer TARP.

We knew time was tight, so as soon as Kashkari appeared we jumped straight to the point of our visit. We pressed him on the status of the big financial institutions: Did Treasury anticipate additional bailout assistance to the giant banks? Could we see the terms of the arrangements that had been worked out so far? Kashkari objected to the word *bailout,* so we wrangled about that for a couple of minutes. But he was very clear on one point: The big cash injections were done, and Treasury would now concentrate on getting assistance to smaller banks.

The meeting was short, and we were soon back out on the street, outside the heavy iron gates.

Our meeting was on Friday. Less than forty-eight hours later, the news broke that Treasury had just made a huge new commitment to Citibank, a giant bank that had already received $25 billion in TARP money. Now

Treasury was giving $20 billion in *additional* TARP bailout funds to Citibank, *plus* a $306 billion taxpayer guarantee. The numbers were staggering—and the timing was even more staggering. As best we could piece together from the news reports, at the same time we were receiving reassurances from the head of TARP that the big bailouts were finished, his colleagues were down the hall negotiating this gargantuan deal to bail out Citibank for a second time. In fact, the special inspector general for TARP would later report that this weekend was known in the halls of Treasury as "Citi-weekend."

I was stunned—and furious. I understood that this was a crisis, and I knew that sensitive information might need to be closely held. I also understood that we might be asked to keep something confidential for a period of time or even that some official might say, "I can't tell you that right now" and explain why. But that wasn't what had happened. During our meeting, the team at Treasury didn't hesitate and didn't hedge. They sent us out of the room knowing we believed that the big bailouts were over and knowing exactly how wrong that belief was.

Our panel hadn't even had our first organizational meeting, but whatever vision I'd had of cooperation and candor had vanished. If we wanted any transparency in this process, we would have to fight for it every inch of the way.

What Is a TARP?

As I thought about COP's mission, I kept coming back to one number: $700 billion. That number kept me awake at night. Heck, it still keeps me up from time to time. It's hard to put in perspective just how gigantic that number was.

Sure, there were crazy comparisons. We could have bought seven laptops for every child in America. We could have sent thirteen million kids to a private university. We could have put a large colony of badgers on Mars. (Well, maybe not.)

But it was the real "could haves" that tore at me. We could have fixed our roads and bridges and public transportation. We could have launched universal preschool and made state universities affordable again. We could have doubled our federal investments in medical research and scientific research for the next twenty years.

The responsibility for exercising oversight on how the Treasury Department spent all that money weighed heavily on me, even if we weren't expected to do anything besides write reports.

Over and over, Congress had declared that there was no money for bridges or preschool or more medical research, but now the American taxpayer was on the hook for a $700 billion bank bailout. How did that happen? Yes, TARP was designed as an investment and Treasury would work to get the money back, but infrastructure, education, and research are investments, too—investments that deliver enormous economic payoffs but are shamefully underfunded.

The mortgage crisis—when millions of families suddenly couldn't pay their mortgage—was only the first layer of the problem. There was a second layer, one that elevated "shock" to "crisis."

With so much money to be made selling the jazzy new mortgages, Boring Bankers gave way to Hotdog Wall Street Traders. As Washington increasingly deregulated the banking industry—starting in the 1980s and picking up steam in the 1990s—the big banks were on the lookout for new investment opportunities that had previously been closed off to them. Over time, a lot of them decided they could make more money if they resold their mortgages on Wall Street instead of holding on to them as borrowers paid them back over the years. At first, reselling the mortgages brought in more cash, which made it easier for more people to get loans and made our housing system work better. But as the big banks figured out that they could make a lot more money on the jazzy new mortgages, they started buying and selling packages of very-high-profit, very-high-risk products. Many of the big banks quickly became more like the speculators and house flippers who were buying these houses—out to make a quick buck.

The traders soon figured that if they could make a little money bundling and trading a few mortgages, then why not make a mountain of money selling a mountain of mortgages? Soon the mortgages were bundled into giant packages, and then the bundles were sold and resold, repackaged and resliced. As time went on, the deals and the packages got more and more complicated.

Eventually, these bundles of mortgages were sold everywhere, and many were like time bombs just ticking down to the moment they would explode.

Nobody sold packages labeled "Warning: Grenades Inside!" Instead, those packages were all graded for risk, with AAA, BBB, and so on. The problem was that the grading was done by private rating agencies that got paid by the bundlers for those grades and, incidentally, were also trying to sell the banks millions of dollars of other services. The federal regulators could have supervised these rating agencies, but "deregulation" was the mantra of the day, so they looked the other way, leaving the rating agencies free to make up their own standards. Surprise, surprise—the private rating agencies gave most mortgage bundles AAA ratings.

Brokers used those AAA ratings and sold the "safe" bundles to investors everywhere. Pension funds invested in them. So did city governments, insurance companies, nonprofit charities—you name it, if a company or an organization was big enough to attract Wall Street's attention, it probably owned some "AAA-rated mortgage-backed securities."

When the housing bubble popped and families couldn't make their mortgage payments, the bombs started going off. The effect was entirely predictable—a catastrophic meltdown.

The financial giants stumbled and started to fall. First Bear Stearns, then Lehman Brothers and Merrill Lynch. It looked like the whole financial system might crumble to nothing.

In the fall of 2008, the banking system went into lockdown mode. Large and small businesses struggled to get credit, which meant that many companies couldn't buy inventory or even make payroll. Home buyers struggled to get mortgages. Car buyers struggled to get car loans. It was as if someone had thrown truckloads of sand into the giant gears that drove the entire economy.

Treasury secretary Henry Paulson went before Congress and explained that the financial system had stalled. He insisted that only a government rescue could get things moving again and prevent a complete financial collapse. And thus was born the Troubled Asset Relief Program—TARP.

In theory, TARP had two goals aimed at getting the economy back on track. First, it was supposed to stabilize the banking system. The idea was that if the banks had more cash, they would start lending again, and that would mean that large and small companies could all get back to business. The other goal was that TARP would bring the mortgage crisis under control. The details of the plan were sketchy, but the general idea was that a lot of the TARP money would eventually be used to clean up the terrible mortgages that had been sold to a lot of hardworking American homeowners, so that they wouldn't be forced into the streets. This second goal was reflected in COP's statutory mandate: we were specifically instructed to report to Congress on the "effectiveness of foreclosure mitigation efforts."

As soon as TARP was set up, tens of billions of dollars started flowing to the giant banks. Although a couple of huge financial institutions had already fallen, it soon became clear that Treasury would make sure the other giant banks would survive the crisis. But that didn't keep credit flowing to the small businesses, and more and more of them were shutting down. At the same time, the tide of foreclosures just kept rising. In those early, terrifying days, TARP seemed to be doing precious little for small businesses or families in trouble.

Ten Questions

So when would our new oversight panel issue its first report? We knew that once we sent out the first one, we would be running on a treadmill we couldn't get off. By law, we would have thirty days until the second report was due, thirty days until the third report, and so on, for the next two years. We would have no chance to pause and catch our breath—we would have to go all out.

If Congress had set up a panel like this in ordinary times, the date for the first report might have been far into the future, allowing plenty of time for everyone on the panel to get to know each other, conduct research, hire staff, and map out a strategy. But these weren't ordinary times. The country was in a crisis, and Congress wanted a report now. We could either stand on the sidelines or wade in and do whatever we could to help.

The day before Thanksgiving, we had our first official meeting, which was held by conference call. The new COP still didn't have an office or any staff. We didn't even have a coffeemaker. In fact, the last two panelists had just been chosen only the week before. The Republicans had named Jeb Hensarling, a congressman from Texas, and Judd Gregg, a senator from New Hampshire. Representative Hensarling joined our call that day, but Senator Gregg wasn't available. (He soon resigned, temporarily leaving us with only four members.)

The panel voted to name me chairman, and we agreed to get a report out as soon as we could. We settled on December 10 as our first due date, which meant we had exactly two weeks to decide which issues to address, conduct research, write the report, review it, vote on it, and send it out. Ooh boy.

With the clock ticking, I offered to write a first draft of the report and send it around to the other panelists.

So there I was on Thanksgiving morning, baking a cake. Bruce and I usually celebrate Thanksgiving in Plymouth, just a few miles from Plymouth Rock, where the Pilgrims landed. The Plymouth locale is just a coincidence. Bruce's sister Gretchen and her family live there, and the relatives all gather at their house. Her husband, Steve, makes homemade pastas and lays out an amazing feast, Italian American style. I offer my thanks by making his favorite dessert, apricot upside-down cake. This year Bruce and Otis would take the cake without me, and they promised to bring back some leftovers.

After I put the cake in the oven, I stared at my computer screen and wondered: What did it mean to conduct oversight in the middle of a raging storm? And what could we actually accomplish?

I figured we were supposed to serve as a kind of watchdog. A watchdog's job was to bark so that everyone would look up to see a threat. Our economy was collapsing, millions of people were out of work, families were losing their homes, retirement funds were disappearing, and right now one of the very few tools granted to the government to deal with this crash was $700 billion given to Treasury through TARP. How Treasury spent that money could determine whether the economy pulled out of its tailspin and how the recovery would be forged. Treasury had made it clear in our first meeting that they weren't planning to cooperate with the COP watchdog, so if oversight was going to mean anything, these reports might be all we had.

Meanwhile, if we were going to get this report done in just two weeks, we needed help, and we needed it fast. In time, we would reach out to experts and hire a full staff. But right now, we didn't have a second to lose.

In those early days, I turned to some of my former students for help. They were young and smart, and, most of all, they were willing to lend a hand on short notice. At that moment, before we had staff or infrastructure, they were more valuable than diamonds.

Ganesh Sitaraman was an American success story. His parents had emigrated from India before he was born. As a kid, he was an Eagle Scout, and eventually he made his way to Harvard Law. In my 1L class, he had his hand up every day, raring to go. Most of my students move on once class is over, but not Ganesh. He kept showing up every week or so to talk about economics and social policy. By the time the crisis hit, Ganesh had graduated, but he was still at Harvard on a fellowship.

Dan Geldon was Ganesh's near opposite. In a big class, Dan was quiet to the point of invisibility. But it would be a mistake to underestimate Dan: he has an iron will. His older brother once told me that when Dan was seven, the family was eating a meal at McDonald's. Dan was halfway through a cheeseburger when he put it down and announced that he had decided to become a vegetarian because eating meat wasn't right. His mom and dad smiled indulgently, and his older brother rolled his eyes. But twenty-five years later, Dan still doesn't eat meat.

The minute I asked for their help, Ganesh and Dan jumped in. We talked for hours and wrote furiously. Nearly every day, with help from Ganesh, I finished a draft of the report and shot it off to the other panelists. They edited and flagged questions and added pieces and sent it back. Each night at about ten, I sent the latest version to Dan. He worked on it all night, filling in the research and answering panelists' questions. Each morning, I picked up the draft again, and we started the process all over.

The final report was only thirty-seven pages, which is unusually short for a government report. But we really wanted something that was concise and clear, and that's a lot harder than it looks.

The country was awash in news programs featuring financial experts who spoke about the crisis using language that to most people sounded like gibberish. Collateralized debt obligations, special-purpose entities, synthetic derivatives—whatever the topic, the explanations offered by the talking heads all had the same subtext: *Only the insiders are smart enough to understand what's really going on, so just trust us.*

I didn't buy that. In fact, I thought it was the oversight panel's job to make sure that *everyone* could understand what was going on. The issues swirling around the financial crisis were important—too important to be hidden away. I remembered the early conversation with Mr. Kashkari and the rest of the TARP team at Treasury: instead of going along with the idea that we should "trust the insiders," I thought oversight ought to mean holding the insiders accountable and making them earn that trust.

Our report started with a grim update on where the country stood. In the preceding three months, 1.2 million people had lost their jobs. Millions more were on the verge of losing their homes. The stock market had lost 40 percent of its value. All three auto companies reported that they were on the verge of bankruptcy. And there was no end in sight; the economy was getting worse by the day.

At this point, a typical report would have kept pumping out more data, but we decided to focus not on what people already knew, but on what they didn't know. So we asked questions.

Our questions—ten of them in all—became the centerpiece of the report. They were fairly simple, and we wrote them using good old plain English. For example, we asked the Treasury Department:

- Is your strategy helping to reduce foreclosures?
- What have financial institutions done with the taxpayers' money received so far?
- Is the public receiving a fair deal?

I loved the simple language of the report. Cutting through the jargon and tangled verbiage made it possible for everyone to join the inquiry. Plain language was also about blowing the Bullshit Whistle. (Sorry about the dirty word, but I can't think of another way to say it.) Yes, the crisis involved complicated financial dealings, but a lot of the supposed complication was nothing more than BS designed to cover up what was going on. And Treasury had already made it clear that they had no plans to be especially forthcoming with COP. The only way to know what was really happening was to ask some plain questions and get some plain answers—no wiggling around, no hiding away.

We submitted the report, and then we made it public.

Another of my former students, Caleb Weaver, discovered that the Senate had a full setup for making video recordings. (It came complete with fake backgrounds—the first question I was asked on the set was, "Do you want the fake plant or the fake window?") I made a four-minute recording (fake window included) that introduced our panel's mission and provided an overview of the report. We uploaded it to YouTube. We also set up a website, posted the report so that anyone could read it, and created a portal that would allow people to share their stories with the panel.

YouTube and an interactive website didn't sound much like a Congressional Oversight Panel, or at least that wasn't how most people thought a panel ought to operate in 2008. But we figured that if our goal was to be a watchdog for the American people, then we should involve the American people as much as possible.

Once we set up the website, e-mails started pouring in. We heard from people who had lost their homes, people who were desperate for financial help, people who were frustrated about what was happening to our country. I was a little surprised by the outpouring—after all, we started out as a pretty obscure government panel. But this crisis was personal. People felt like their whole world was unraveling. Maybe our report gave them a voice. Maybe it asked some of the same questions they would have asked if they had the chance.

I had hoped our report wouldn't get caught up in any kind of political crosswind, but that's not how it worked out. In the two weeks our panel had to write the report, we circulated drafts, had conference calls, swapped e-mails, and agreed to compromises—all in the hope that we could deliver a unanimous report. But it wasn't to be. Congressman Hensarling voted against it.

So our first report was signed by all three Democratic appointees, with no Republican support.

I started to understand that oversight was going to be hard, every step of the way.

Shirts and Skins

On December 10, the day the first COP report came out, I had an appointment with our dissenter, Congressman Hensarling. I figured he had invited me to his office on Capitol Hill to discuss what he thought COP should be doing differently.

Early that morning, I got lost—again—this time in the basement of the Capitol. Michael Negron, another of my former students, was with me. He had been a navy officer before law school, and he was a lot less likely to get rattled by a little thing like getting lost.

The congressional office buildings are linked by big underground tunnels and small shuttle trains that curve in odd directions, and the offices are numbered in ways that make no sense to me. We turned one way and then another, and finally Michael announced that we were almost there. Go, Navy!

Hensarling's office was already open for business, and the congressman came out quickly to greet us. Handshakes all around, and Michael and I joined Hensarling and one of his staffers in his private office. I perched on the edge of a sofa, with my coat across my lap.

After Hensarling's dissent on the first report, I hoped I could find out what he wanted to do differently. Maybe he had strong views about what we should investigate. Maybe he had an idea for how we could monitor where the TARP money went. Maybe he wanted to put more pressure on Treasury to show progress in slowing foreclosures. Maybe he wanted to talk about the second, staggering bailout for Citibank—and Treasury's willingness to lie to us. The list of issues our panel might work on was growing by the day, and I didn't know what priorities the congressman wanted to address.

After giving me a big smile, Hensarling dived right in. He said something along the lines of "I want to know your plans for dividing up the budget."

Dividing our budget?

The congressman explained that he wanted to know what portion of COP funding I planned to allocate to the Republicans and what portion I planned to keep for the Democrats.

I reminded him that we were all working on the same investigations and the same reports. Congress hadn't specified the exact budget, but they were willing to give us the funds we needed to get the work done—and that's what we'd do. I told him that I felt strongly about one thing: There's no money for one side versus the other. This shouldn't be a my-party-your-party exercise. We should work together with one nonpartisan staff.

The congressman took a few more passes at his point. Sure, he understood that we were working together, and that was all very nice. But I obviously didn't know the ways of Washington. He chuckled and smiled, but he kept coming back to the same point: What part of the budget would the Democrats get to control and what part would go to the Republicans?

After a few more rounds, his tone got hard. "Look," he said, "the game is shirts-and-skins." A vivid image immediately shot into my brain: boys with sharp elbows playing pickup basketball, everyone hogging the ball, one team in shirts and the other bare-skinned. (No girls on either team, of course.)

Hensarling's point was obvious: he wanted to make sure his team got its share.

I guess I shouldn't have been surprised. The *very first* question the congressman had asked back in our *very first* phone meeting two weeks earlier had been about dividing up the staff. I'd never thought about such an idea, and on that first call I was unprepared for the question. But now we had just spent two weeks bashing our brains out to write an oversight report to pin Treasury down. We still had no office space, no phones, and no coffeepot. We certainly had no clear plan for overseeing the biggest bailout in the history of the United States. There were a million things we needed to figure out—and the congressman thought the most important thing we needed to do was slice up the operating budget so each political party was assured its "fair share"? Welcome to Washington.

Once I had gotten over my shock after that first call with Hensarling, I'd had a chance to think about this issue. The way I saw it, we were a short-term committee trying to operate in the middle of an earthshaking crisis. The bill authorizing TARP and the oversight panel had been bipartisan. And the problems our country faced would definitely require bipartisan solutions. I thought Hensarling's plan—he wanted the Democrats and Republicans to have separate staffs and separate priorities—would mean that the panel members would spend too much of their time sniping at each other and not enough time overseeing the biggest bailout in the history of the country.

Besides, the government had already proven that a nonpartisan approach could work. The 9/11 Commission, for instance, had conducted an in-depth investigation and written a clear, powerful report—all of it done with one staff and one budget. I thought that was the right approach: COP should avoid partisan divisions all the way.

So I drew a line in the sand right there in the congressman's office: The staff would be nonpartisan and would work for all of us. The panel would have one budget, not two. Period. If Hensarling wanted to go to war over this issue, so be it. As he said, I didn't understand the ways of Washington. The part *he* didn't seem to understand yet was that I didn't really care about the ways of Washington.

Later that day, the House held a hearing on TARP, and Congressman Hensarling testified. He used the occasion to explain his vote against the report. He said that he was not yet assured "that every panel member has the resources and rights necessary to conduct effective oversight." Until that happened, Hensarling said, he could "not in good conscience approve any reports." It didn't matter what we would write in our reports, he announced he would be voting no.

I guess I wasn't the only one to draw a line in the sand that day.

There was a lot of jockeying, but in the end we stuck with the nonpartisan approach. We hired an executive director who had worked for Democrats and a deputy director who had worked for Republicans. For the rest of the staff, we did our best to hire first-rate people to do a first-rate job, without regard to party affiliation. We asked all the panelists for recommendations for who should be hired and what we should work on. And I did my best to pull everyone together—panelists and staff—as one team.

Even so, I worried about the lesson from the shirts-and-skins lecture. No matter the crisis, no matter the urgency of the moment, in Washington it was always "my team vs. your team." And in all that pushing and pulling, too many times the people we were supposed to serve got left behind.

COP on the Road

With our first report out the door, it was time to hold our first hearing. We thought Clark County, Nevada—the epicenter of the foreclosure crisis—was a good place to start. So we scheduled a hearing for December 16, about a week after COP's first report came out.

Las Vegas had been a boomtown, and now the bust had exploded with a vengeance. This was nothing like the quiet, formal hearings from my days on the National Bankruptcy Review Commission, with all the lobbyists in expensive suits and carrying elegant briefcases. This was more like a PTA meeting or a church revival.

The hearing was held in a bright new auditorium at the University of Nevada–Las Vegas. A practice space for law students, the auditorium was outfitted as a mock courtroom. Damon, Richard, and I sat in front where the judges would sit, and I had the gavel. The room was crowded with people in jeans or work uniforms, and they were fired up. A few bank lobbyists may have been sitting in the audience, but if so, they were lying low.

A number of reporters showed up, and the hallways were crowded with television cameras. We had scheduled several people to testify, including policy wonks and businesspeople. But we also heard from some of the people whose lives had been torn apart by the crisis. The witness I will never forget—the man who made it clear what this catastrophe was all about—was Mr. Estrada, the father of two little girls.

Mr. Estrada wore a jacket over his T-shirt and had on a red US Marine Corps baseball cap. He and his wife both worked, and they had stretched their budget to buy a home that would get their girls into a good school. Their home meant everything to Mr. Estrada: "This is my dream house, because I can open my garage door and see my daughters playing right directly across the street because that's where their school is at." When the payments on their mortgage jumped, they fell behind. He tried to negotiate with the bank, and he thought he and the bank had arranged a settlement. Then—*poof!*—the house was sold at auction. "So at the end," he said, the bankers "tell me that I have fourteen days to get my children out of the house."

Mr. Estrada explained what happened next:

My six-year-old came home the other day with a full sheet of paper with all of her friends' names on it. And she told—she told me that these were the people that were going to miss her because we were going to have to be moving. And I told my daughter, I says, "I don't care if I have to live in a van. You're still going to be able to go to this school." I'm trusting in God that we're going to be able to be back into this home again.

Several times Mr. Estrada paused to try to get control of himself, and his pain and desperation seemed to push all the air out of the room. I held my breath, hoping I wouldn't cry, and I noticed that Damon's hands were shaking. Even now, I think about Mr. Estrada and his little girls. This wasn't supposed to happen.

Others came forward to tell similar stories. The oversight panel didn't have any money to give out, and we didn't have the power to stop any of the foreclosures. But we promised to tell their stories and to remember them when we did our work. It wasn't anywhere near enough, but at least it was something. People thanked us for coming and filed quietly out of the auditorium.

After the hearing, Damon, Richard, and I drove through Las Vegas neighborhoods not too far from the beautiful hotels and dramatic fountains. We saw vacant homes and a pickup loaded with furniture, foreclosure postings, and abandoned construction sites. No glitzy casinos here. Instead, we saw evidence everywhere of the countless people who had believed in the American dream, worked hard to make it a reality, and then lost it all.

Treasury Ignores COP

I left Las Vegas and spent the next week worrying about Treasury's response. Our report had asked just ten questions of the Treasury Department. If they planned to cooperate, we should be getting some good answers any day now.

Bruce and I went to California for Christmas with our children and grandchildren. By this point, Octavia was seven and Lavinia was three. The girls were at delicious ages—they loved baking holiday cookies and dressing up like princesses. They thought their "Gammy" (as Octavia had dubbed me) was the best. But that Christmas holiday passed in a blur, as I paced up and down the sidewalk in front of Amelia's home, exchanging anxious cell phone calls with other panel members, while the rest of the family was inside wrapping presents.

On December 30, I got the call: Treasury had responded. I opened my laptop and downloaded their letter, eager to see what they had given us. The answer? A big nothing sandwich. I was stunned. Later, ABC News summarized the Treasury response this way:

> Cut-and-paste reports were once the domain of high school cheats cutting corners on their term papers. . . . Rather than write original answers to questions posed in December by a congressional oversight panel, U.S. Treasury officials appear to have creatively repurposed old testimony and even Web site copy into a 13-page report that left some questions entirely unanswered.

The secretary of the Treasury had just blown off the COP panel.

As I saw it, this was a make-or-break moment for us. We had asked the simplest possible questions in the bluntest possible language so that everyone could see the insiders' plan for rescuing our economy. By not taking our questions seriously, the Treasury Department had treated oversight as irrelevant. In effect, they had said, "Trust us to do the right thing. Now go away." This time we had a choice: We could either call them out on it or go hide in a corner for the rest of our tenure.

The next COP report was due in ten days. What should we do?

Easy: We decided to make it clear just how completely Treasury had ignored COP's oversight questions.

For our second report, we made a table. We put each question from the first report in one column, wrote Treasury's answer to that question in a second column, and then added our own comment in the third column. If Treasury hadn't responded to a question, we wrote "No Response" in the second column. In the end, out of ten questions, Treasury gave no response or only partial responses to all ten. As we filled in "No Response" over and over, I could hear the BS whistle loud and clear.

Once again, it was about keeping it simple. The report was like a grocery list—here's what we asked for, here's what we got. People could see for themselves exactly how Treasury had blown us off.

Congressman Hensarling dissented from this report as well. But by now we had another Republican on the panel, former New Hampshire senator John Sununu, and he joined the three Democrats to make it a bipartisan report.

After all those years of fighting for families in bankruptcy—and all those years of hardly anyone paying attention—I guess deep down I expected that our second report would be ignored. It wasn't. People knew what was at stake, and the financial crisis had put the bailout at center stage.

Media coverage for the new report started early in the morning of January 9, 2009, when I appeared on *Good Morning America*. I talked with more reporters as the day rolled on, and I did interviews on ABC, CNBC, and CNN. Several news outlets came down hard on the Treasury Department. The *Boston Globe* put it this way: "If taxpayers are spending billions to bail out banks, they deserve to know how that money is used." (Go, *Globe*!)

The watchdog barked, and the public paid attention. But still we heard nothing from Secretary Paulson. He left his job as secretary of the Treasury less than two weeks later. No meetings, no phone calls, no meaningful response to either of our reports.

Don't Tell What's Really Going On

The second report was out, and COP was already hard at work on the third. By now we'd hired Naomi Baum to serve as executive director for COP. Although I knew very little about getting things done in Washington, Naomi knew Capitol Hill inside and out. She was tiny, barely five feet tall, but no one got away with underestimating her strength. Naomi had spent nearly twenty years working in Washington, and she brought calm confidence to our chaos. She got us out of the business of all-nighters, organized our operation, and hired staff. Now COP could begin multiple investigations at once; we could walk and chew gum at the same time.

Damon had an idea, and it was a big one: Let's dig into whether the public got a fair deal on the TARP investments. The idea was to take a closer look at the price when the Treasury Department handed billions of dollars to the megabanks in return for bank stock. Secretary Paulson had told the public that all the transactions were at or near par, which meant that when taxpayers put in $100, the value of the shares they got back was also $100.

What Secretary Paulson described sure sounded like a fair deal, and we could have stopped there. But we were the COP on this beat, and Damon figured we should check out the numbers for ourselves. So COP hired a first-rate investment research firm to analyze the transactions. And then we got two separate panels of experts to check and recheck their work.

When we met to review the numbers, our experts passed out thick reports laden with pages and pages of numbers and technical explanations of their analysis and their findings. Their conclusions sent a chill through me.

Treasury had overpaid—and not by just a little. In the bailout deals with the ten biggest banks, every time Treasury spent $100, it received assets worth just $66. By January 2009, that already added up to a $78 billion shortfall.

Treasury was subsidizing these banks, pure and simple. Treasury had said one thing in public and then had done something very different in private. The BS whistle was screaming.

As it turned out, the government eventually recovered the money it put into Citibank and the other banking giants. But at the time those deals were struck, no one knew what the future held, and the risks were all on the taxpayers. All the American people had to go on was what Secretary Paulson had told them. And what he said simply wasn't true.

Democracy had just taken another brutal punch in the gut.

Insiders Don't Criticize Insiders

By the time our February report came out, America had a new president. This might have been a moment for a new direction in economic policy and a chance to rethink the bailout strategy. But the crisis was still accelerating, and the economy remained on the edge of collapse. After his election, President-elect Barack Obama had quickly signaled that the new administration would continue Paulson's strategy, especially with his choice for a new Treasury secretary: Tim Geithner. As head of the Federal Reserve Bank of New York, Geithner had worked as a regulator of the Wall Street banks for years, and in 2007 he had been approached about becoming CEO of Citibank. He was experienced with bailouts, too: in the spring of 2008, he had managed the rescue of Bear Stearns, and as the markets collapsed in the fall of 2008, he had worked alongside Secretary Paulson to engineer the bailout for insurance giant AIG.

The COP panelists met with the new secretary a few times during his early months on the job. In mid-March, the story broke that AIG had paid $168 million in bonuses—bonuses that would go to employees in the very same division that had brought the company to its knees. People were furious; one Republican senator called for the AIG executives to either "resign or go commit suicide."

COP was expanding its investigations, and we were starting to make a stir about what we saw as the shortcomings of Treasury's approach on the bailout. I started hearing that many Washington insiders were surprised (and some were aggravated) that we were going just as hard on the Democratic administration as we had on the Republicans, but I wasn't going to stop and worry about that.

In early April, I got a call from the office of Larry Summers. I didn't know Larry well, but I'd met him a few times while he was president of Harvard in the early 2000s. According to reports, Larry had been Tim Geithner's mentor when they were both in the Treasury Department in the 1990s. Now Larry was the director of the National Economic Council, which meant that, along with Secretary Geithner, he advised President Obama on economic issues. Would I be interested in meeting him for dinner?

Sure, I replied. Larry's office suggested the Bombay Club, an Indian restaurant near the White House. Quiet and softly lit, it served Washington's power elite.

When Larry arrived for our dinner, he ordered a Diet Coke as soon as he sat down. He glanced at the menu, ordered quickly, and soon the food started coming.

It was a long dinner, with plenty of intense back-and-forth about everything from the bailout, to deregulation, to the foreclosure crisis. I also talked to Larry about an idea I'd been working on for a new consumer financial agency, and he seemed interested. We didn't agree on everything, but I give Larry full credit: I'll take honest conversation and debate any day of the week over the duck-and-cover stuff I so often saw in Washington that spring.

Late in the evening, Larry leaned back in his chair and offered me some advice. By now, I'd lost count of Larry's Diet Cokes, and our table was strewn with bits of food and spilled sauces. Larry's tone was in the friendly-advice category. He teed it up this way: I had a choice. I could be an insider or I could be an outsider. Outsiders can say whatever they want. But people on the inside don't listen to them. Insiders, however, get lots of access and a chance to push their ideas. People—powerful people— listen to what they have to say. But insiders also understand one unbreakable rule: *They don't criticize other insiders.*

I had been warned.

Jon Stewart

I had been doing short interviews about the bailout and COP's work for several months, but I was still nervous about appearing on national television. On April 15, a week after my dinner with Larry Summers, I had more than a bad case of nerves.

It was early evening. I was standing in the tiny guest bathroom near the set of *The Daily Show with Jon Stewart*. I glanced nervously at the front of my jacket to see if it was clean. I examined my face closely in the mirror, specifically my mouth, nose, and chin. I had just vomited.

I blotted my face with wet paper towels, and then I was hit by another wave of nausea. As I leaned over the toilet again, I wondered if I had messed up my lipstick and powder. The show's makeup person had already fluffed and buffed me for the show, and I didn't want to have to explain why I needed repairs.

I was miserable. I had stage fright—gut-wrenching, stomach-turning, bile-filled stage fright. And I was stuck in a gloomy little bathroom, about to go on *The Daily Show*.

At home, Bruce and I always recorded the show on TiVo and delighted in watching Jon Stewart skewer people who needed skewering. But now I was having serious doubts about going through with this. I had talked to reporters and been interviewed plenty of times, but this was different. At any second, the whole interview could turn into a giant joke—and what if the joke turned on the work I was trying to do?

For the zillionth time, I asked myself why on God's green earth I had agreed to sit down with Jon Stewart. For the zillionth time, I gave myself the same answer: Because oversight will mean something only if a lot of people—millions of people—get engaged. *The Daily Show* gave me one more way to draw people in, to talk about what had gone wrong and what we should do about it.

So I washed out my mouth with cold water and went back to the little waiting room. Pretty soon a director was pulling me at breakneck speed through narrow hallways, past tiny rooms, and behind heavy dark curtains. We came to an opening onto the stage, and then I stepped out into the lights, feeling like an astronaut who had just left the space capsule— except I hadn't practiced this maneuver back on my home planet.

When I sat down opposite Jon Stewart, what struck me first was how close we were. Stewart seemed to be mere inches from my face—and he immediately began hurling baseballs straight at my forehead. The beginning was a disaster. We rambled through questions about TARP and the Congressional Oversight Panel. I fumbled while Stewart made jokes. The way I heard it, his message was clear: The whole idea that our tiny little panel would be able to watch over the Treasury's $700 billion bailout was idiotic.

The first couple of minutes were terrible, and then it got worse. Jon Stewart got an acronym for a Treasury program wrong and I automatically corrected him. "P-PIP," I interrupted. (For the record, it's pronounced "pee-pip." Three-year-old Lavinia thought this was hilarious bathroom humor.) The instant "P-PIP" popped out of my mouth, I was horrified. What was I doing correcting Jon Stewart on his own show? We locked eyes for an instant, and I must have made a face, because Stewart asked me, "Madam, are you about to curse?"

I endured the wave of laughter from the audience, and then he dropped the obvious question: "What does P-PIP stand for?"

Uh-oh. Pause. "I forget."

In the instant after I said "I forget," my heart slowed down. No need to stress now: my work in Washington was over. I thought, Well, this is it. I'll call Senator Reid tomorrow and resign. If I can't even remember the names of the TARP programs, then I should quit now. Maybe they can get someone to run this panel who *isn't* an idiot.

Stewart asked a few more questions, and then, mercifully, it was time for a commercial. As I started to bolt out of my chair, Stewart grabbed my forearm and said something like "You wanted to deliver an important message here, and you didn't get to it. If I gave you one sentence, what would you tell people?"

We looked hard at each other again, our heads inches apart, and then I told him what I really thought. He said, "Okay, hold on."

By now we were well into the commercial break, and the stage director came over to hustle me off the set. Stewart said, "No, she stays." The manager said, "No, we're out of time." Each repeated their statements with a little more intensity; then Stewart insisted with the air of The Boss: "*She stays.* I know how we can make room."

The stage director backed away, and Stewart looked around at the camera and fiddled with some papers. Then he warned me: "You don't have much time."

A couple of seconds later, the cameras were rolling again. I thought he would pitch me a question that would give me a chance to say on camera what I had just said to him. But no: he asked me some other question. I thought, What the heck, I'm going to say what I have to say. And that's what I did. It was a little longer than this (and a lot more rambling), but basically it boiled down to the following:

This crisis didn't have to happen. America had a boom-and-bust cycle from the 1790s to the 1930s, with a financial panic every ten to fifteen years. But we figured out how to fix it. Coming out of the Great Depression, the country put tough rules in place that gave us fifty years without a financial crisis. But in the 1980s, we started pulling the threads out of the regulatory fabric, and we found ourselves back in the boom-and-bust cycle. When this crisis is over, there will be a once-in-a-generation chance to rewrite the rules. What we set in place will determine whether our country continues down this path toward a boom-and-bust economy or whether we reestablish an economy with more stability that gives ordinary folks a chance at real prosperity.

Done. I took a deep breath.

And then Jon Stewart pointed at me and said, "That is the first time in six months to a year that I felt better. . . . For a second, that was like financial chicken soup for me. Thank you. That actually put things in perspective and made sense for me."

Too Big to Fail

I may have frozen up over what P-PIP stood for, but there was another acronym that was burned into my brain: TBTF.

The idea behind TBTF—Too Big to Fail—had been around for a long time. But when the government stepped in during the spring of 2008 as financial giant Bear Stearns was failing, the idea had taken on new urgency. In the fall of 2008, a few weeks before Harry Reid called, I had taught the concept to my class at Harvard.

I began the session by making a few quick notes on the blackboard— I still like good old-fashioned chalk—while we talked about the bundles of bad mortgages that were scattered throughout the economy. And then I put a question to the class: The economy is obviously headed for rough sledding, and some companies may not survive. So if you ran a very large financial company right now, what would you do to make sure that you'd still be around in ten years?

Hands shot up. I called on one student who said something along the lines of "Hoard cash. Lots of it. Sell off the bad stuff fast, hang on to the cash, and try to ride out the storm."

I said something like "Hmmm . . . Anyone else?"

All the hands went down. The student who'd answered had provided the textbook response. Why would I be looking for any other answer?

In the long silence, one student jumped, just a little. His hand went up. I waited and let the silence stretch.

Another hand popped up and then another and another. Ultimately, about a third of the students had their hands up, and nearly all of them were smiling at the genius of the alternative, while the others looked on with puzzled expressions.

Finally, I let one of the students explain. The less obvious answer was to grow your bank as big as you possibly can, as fast as you possibly can. Even if it means taking on big risks. Even if it means overpaying to acquire smaller companies. Even if it means entering shaky or unprofitable markets. Do it anyway, so you can grow, grow, grow. And then—here's the important part—borrow from everyone else to finance all that growth.

Why? Because a financial company that was truly gigantic and owed lots of money to lots of other big companies would be so important to the economy as a whole that the government would not let it fail. Throw in a few billion dollars of FDIC-insured checking accounts, and the government would always make sure that this megabank stayed in business.

Of course, reality was a lot more complex than a few words on a chalkboard. But the basic concept wasn't rocket science, and we were hardly the first to figure it out. It took my students about two minutes to see how to build a bank that would be Too Big to Fail.

By the time TARP came along, pretty much everyone had grown to hate TBTF—except for the bankers who benefited.

Yes, our economy was crashing and the government needed to step in to stop the downward spiral. But the major banks didn't need to be so big and interconnected—that part wasn't inevitable. And the government made a huge mistake in *how* they handled the bailout.

I'd taught classes about business failure for nearly thirty years, so that's my prism for looking at a company that's in trouble. Typically, when a company is on the brink of bankruptcy, any rescue effort comes with lots of strings attached. CEOs get fired, shareholders get wiped out, creditors take a big haircut, and new business plans are drawn up—or there's no new money.

A similar approach should have applied during the 2008 crash. And in the case of the insurance giant AIG, it almost did—until Treasury stepped in with no-strings TARP money.

As troubles mounted for AIG in August and September 2008, the process was under way. The company had gone to its creditors and asked them to write down the debts, and creditors were starting to fall in line for partial payment. No one would get 100 percent of what they were owed, but no one would get shut out, either.

But then the government bailed AIG out, and—*shazam!*—every creditor got 100 percent of what they were owed. In other words, the US taxpayers gave AIG's creditors a better deal than they had already agreed to take. Goldman Sachs, for example, was one of AIG's largest creditors, and they walked away with $12.9 billion. It must have seemed like Christmas in October—free money!

And it wasn't just AIG. TARP sent truckloads of cash to the banks, but the banks gave virtually nothing in return—no haircuts for the creditors, no CEO firings, no promises to abandon risky trading. And that's when Too Big to Fail went on steroids—not just a bailout, but a pain-free bailout.

TBTF allows the megabanks to operate like drunks on a wild weekend in Vegas. They can take on any kind of crazy risk—put $1 billion on black 22!—and if the bet pays off, the CEOs and the shareholders will be richer than kings. If it doesn't pay off and the bank is wiped out, the taxpayers will foot the bill.

A no-strings-attached bailout created a Too Big to Fail monster, and I was pretty sure we'd be paying for that mistake for a long time.

Where Did the Money Go?

Six days after my appearance on *The Daily Show,* we got our first public hearing with Secretary Geithner. The exchange wasn't especially revealing, but we thought it was an important step in our effort to shine more light on what was really going on.

The bailout had never been sold as just a Save the Banks plan. Instead, the American people were told that the bailout would make it possible for banks to start lending to small businesses again and to help relieve the foreclosure crisis. But once those no-strings-attached checks were distributed to the big banks, that promise evaporated like a tiny ice cube in the desert. Sure, Treasury would try out a few mortgage foreclosure programs here and there. And they would talk about small-business lending. But the actual policies were anemic. Despite the way that it was sold, TARP was about saving the banks, plain and simple.

So what did the big banks do with the money they got? Reports vary. Some put the money in their vaults and hunkered down. Others used the money to buy other banks or make other acquisitions—and grew their TBTF banks even bigger. They also did exactly the opposite of what TARP was supposed to encourage: they cut back on small-business lending and got even more aggressive in their efforts to foreclose on home mortgages.

Of course, even after Treasury started handing out TARP money, not all the banks got a big check. Many small banks were left out in the cold, trying desperately to get approval for relatively small infusions. Some died while waiting. By April 2009, nearly fifty small banks had gone completely under—and many more were drowning. Without access to credit, many of their small business customers went down, too.

The lost opportunity still makes me want to scream with frustration. Small business owners, home owners, men and women whose jobs had disappeared: these weren't numbers on the page; these were millions of people who lost everything.

Late Nights at the GPO

In the middle of the maelstrom, COP was racing to turn itself into a proper organization. The old adage about building the plane and flying it at the same time was out-of-date. We were drawing up blueprints for a jet fighter while executing a catapult launch from an aircraft carrier.

By May, we had about twenty employees. Naomi Baum's right hand was Tewana Wilkerson, another tough woman who also had extensive Capitol Hill experience. Steve Kroll, a brilliant and quirky lawyer who always wore a bow tie, and Sara Hanks, a tough-as-nails lawyer with years of experience in securities law, led our key investigations.

By the time we were done, we'd put together an eclectic crew. We hired investment bankers and government regulators, courtroom lawyers and economists, accountants and a Hollywood screenwriter (okay, he was a credit rating agency specialist before he went out to California). And we enlisted Wilson Abney, a well-respected ethics expert, to come out of retirement to help us.

The hodgepodge of backgrounds was deliberate. I figured we were facing an unprecedented crisis, and we needed as many good ideas as we could muster. Besides, some of us thought that "groupthink" had contributed at least in part to the crisis. A bunch of big-time financial titans running enormous financial companies had all approached their business in roughly the same way—and so had many of the banking regulators. In fact, there was a long tradition of executives and regulators moving back and forth between government and private sector jobs, which meant that the key players in the financial industry almost never received serious input from anyone with a different worldview. We figured COP could do better.

As we added staff, we needed an office for them to work in. Finding really good space in Washington to house a brand-new government organization on a moment's notice was like looking for an affordable one-bedroom apartment with a nice view in Manhattan. Not an easy job, but possible. We turned up an unlikely landlord: the Government Printing Office.

The GPO was near the Capitol, on a side street near Union Station. The printing office does just that—it prints up Supreme Court opinions, laws, and other official documents. Its home is a huge factory that cuts and binds tons of paper every workday. Constructed in the 1860s, the building is heavy and square, with reinforced floors and thick outer walls that make it feel like a fortress.

In an earlier time, it took thousands of people to tend the huge printing presses and to bind and box up millions of documents. But like many other factories in America, the GPO had been changed by automation and computerization, and now there were far fewer human operators.

That's how we ended up on the third and sixth floors of a working factory, set apart from the GPO employees by thin slabs of wallboard. Our conference room had an old lavatory on one wall. Damon swore we were in a converted men's room, but I never confirmed that with our landlords. (We'd already rented the space, and I didn't really want to know.) The elevators were slow and the space was quirky, but during the day the building was perfectly fine. At night, the factory floors were empty, with hulking pieces of machinery illuminated only by nearby streetlamps that cast dim light through the tall windows. When the COP staff worked late, we usually stayed huddled together in our brightly lit haven. But venturing to the restrooms on the other side of the vast, darkened factory floor—or outside to the deserted streets—triggered visions of every horror movie ever made.

The GPO's management had installed closed-circuit television sets above the elevators to get messages to everyone. ("Congratulations, Norma, on twenty years of service!") Some of these messages were accompanied by pictures. On my first visit to our new offices, I was greeted by a large television screen with a photo of a bigger-than-life rat. Confession: I have a morbid fear of mice and rats—I don't even like squirrels. I actually screamed out loud when I saw that oversize rat up on the screen. This wasn't a cute cartoon; it was a close-up of the thing. The picture was accompanied by a stern reminder to keep your lunch sealed up. Whenever I was in the office after dark, I would wonder about those rats. If everyone kept their lunches sealed up, what were the rats eating now?

The GPO staffers were gracious hosts. They were incredibly friendly and put up with our crazy hours. They helped us find furniture and erect more temporary walls. They offered tours to show off their work. Best of all, they rooted for us. Riding the elevators or walking down the hall, they cheered us on, telling us to go get the bad guys. And that's what we tried to do.

More "Trust Us"

By law, the COP panelists' work was temporary and part-time, with the understanding that all five of us would keep our regular jobs. During the spring of 2009, I continued teaching at Harvard and did a lot of flying back and forth between Boston and DC.

Whenever I flew home from Washington, Bruce would pick me up at Logan Airport, and then we'd head to the Summer Shack. The Shack is a big, boisterous place that features a giant chalkboard announcing the daily catch. When fried smelts are in season, they even serve those—not for me, but Bruce loves them.

We always sat in the same booth and started with the same order—light beer for me, Fisherman's Brew for Bruce, and an order of fried clams to get us started. Sal Chillemi had worked at the Shack since it opened, and he would see us coming and bring the beer along with the menus. I always set aside a piece of cornbread to take home to Otis, who would gobble it down in a single bite.

Some nights I was elated, eager to tell Bruce about how we'd brought attention to this issue or turned up good data on that one. Other nights I was so frustrated, I could only spit out bits of stories. A few nights I was so depressed that I just leaned back in the booth with my eyes closed and pressed the beer mug to my forehead.

COP soon hit another "just trust us" moment with Treasury. Secretary Geithner had recently announced that the big banks would be subjected to "stress tests," which were supposed to show whether the banks had enough capital to begin to stand on their own. The Federal Reserve would run the actual tests, and if the banks passed, the public could have more confidence in their stability—or at least that was the idea.

COP swung into action with a very direct question: Exactly how stressful are the stress tests? We lined up some first-rate experts to evaluate the test, and we were all ready to go when the Fed and Treasury informed us that they wouldn't let us in the clubhouse door. Our access to the data they used to assess the banks would be severely limited; in fact, we couldn't even get full access to the test they were using to score the banks. We pushed and pulled. We sent our lawyers. We asked nicely and not so nicely. But nothing worked. The stress test remained top secret.

When Treasury announced the results of the test, lo and behold, every bank was in good shape. Half were great, and half were a little bruised and needed to raise some more money, but they were all on the road to recovery. Secretary Geithner declared, "None of these 19 banks are at risk for insolvency." Really? Once the results were announced and Treasury had reported that everyone was on the right path, we asked again: Now can we have more information about the test? Answer: Nope, not a chance.

Over and over during the spring and summer of 2009, we complained loudly and publicly about the Fed and Treasury refusing to give us information, but they wouldn't yield. We still don't know what was in those stress tests.

We pounded on the door to the house of TARP, but they hunkered down and never came out.

$8.6 Billion for the Taxpayers

In June 2009, Treasury started negotiating another round of deals with the big banks. As part of the original TARP arrangement, when the banks had borrowed money, they had promised to sell a certain number of shares of the banks' stock to the government at a reduced rate. The idea was that if the bailout worked and the bank became profitable again, the taxpayers were guaranteed a bonus at some point in the future. Now the future was here, and some of the banks were ready to cut a deal with the government and give the taxpayers their bonus.

So how big would the bonus be? It depended on the deal struck between Treasury and the banks. If the government settled too cheap, the banks would be getting one more very sweet subsidy at the expense of the taxpayers.

So COP did another investigation. Once again, the first few deals were done behind closed doors. (Surprise, huh?) Once again, we had our experts dig in. And once again, COP found that Treasury had gotten a raw deal for the American people. The closed-door negotiations had yielded only sixty-six cents for every dollar of value that Treasury was entitled to.

But this time, COP was on high alert—and we got there before all the money was gone. In fact, we got there so fast that most of the deals were still in the middle of negotiations. Working with the special inspector general of TARP, Neil Barofsky, who was doing great work to help oversee other parts of the bailout, we nailed down our analysis and cranked out our report. Once we went public, the pending negotiations came out from behind closed doors and were conducted in public view. Within days, for example, the private negotiations with Goldman Sachs became public, and this significantly increased the amount Goldman was willing to pay the Treasury. By the time we were finished, COP calculated that we helped put $8.6 billion back in taxpayers' pockets.

Not bad for a COP whose only power was to write reports!

Who Is to Blame?

The one-year anniversary of the financial collapse was fast approaching, but the foreclosures just kept piling up, week after week. We wrote more reports, we met with Treasury, and we prodded the various regulators, but we kept running smack into a rock-hard reality: The Treasury Department's foreclosure relief plan was a bust. I felt as if I were watching a You-Tube video of car crashes, played over and over in a continuous loop, while the guys who could have directed the traffic showed up too late and did too little.

The mortgage crisis had prompted plenty of finger-pointing—and a lot of it was directed at the families who were losing their homes. Earlier in the year, when talk of writing down mortgages surfaced, a televised rant about "losers" went viral and was generally credited with sparking the Tea Party. Now everybody seemed to have a favorite story about a bus driver who bought an $800,000 home or somebody's brother-in-law who flipped houses, made a fortune, and then lost it all when the music stopped. The pundits were ready to blame the housing crash on your neighbor down the street—and they had plenty of politicians on their side.

It all seemed backward. It was as if people were saying: "Oh gosh, we can't blame poor Mr. CEO Banker. He gets paid millions and millions of dollars because he's really good at his job, so how was he supposed to know that his bank was about to collapse?" And then they turned around and said: "Hey, stupid homeowner! Why did you sign those confusing mortgage papers? Didn't you know that your balloon payment would come due just at the moment your job disappeared?"

The hypocrisy drove me nuts.

In fall 2009, Secretary Geithner invited people working on TARP oversight to a meeting. By now COP had met with Geithner a few times, and he had answered questions twice before the panel in public hearings.

The meeting was held in the Treasury Building in an incredibly fancy room that was loaded with historic furniture, rich draperies, and heavily framed paintings. It looked like a room for kings to negotiate over who was going to get what colony.

People talk about Secretary Geithner's boyish looks. I guess that's right, but what struck me about this meeting was that we were in *his* house. He had invited us here, and it felt as if he owned this big, powerful space and we were his guests, welcome as long as we behaved ourselves. The secretary and his aides sat on one side of a huge, heavy table. The rest of us lined up on the other side: the COP panelists, Naomi Baum, Neil Barofsky, and Gene Dodaro, who represented the GAO.

Secretary Geithner spoke quickly, often dropping his voice into a barely audible monotone, rushing ahead so fast that there was no room for inter-ruptions. He was clearly smart and in command of the facts, but he didn't offer much opportunity for questions. Maybe he was a little anxious. It probably wasn't much fun to face more than half a dozen people whose job was to look over your shoulder and second-guess your decisions.

This meeting seemed headed in the same direction as COP's earlier meetings with the secretary—he would talk and we would listen, and suddenly the session would be over, with little time for questions and answers.

I tried not to fidget. But after we had listened to the secretary go on and on about his department's cheery projections for the recovery, I finally interrupted with a question about a new topic. Why, I asked, had Treasury's response to the flood of foreclosures been so small? COP had been sharply critical of Treasury's foreclosure plan. We thought that the program was poorly designed and poorly managed and provided little permanent help, and we worried that it would reach too few people to make any real difference. After the rush-rush-rush to bail out the big banks with giant buckets of money, this plan seemed designed to deliver foreclosure relief with all the urgency of putting out a forest fire with an eyedropper. As I saw it, millions of people were running out of time—and so was the country.

The secretary seemed annoyed by the interruption, but he quickly launched into a general discussion of his approach to dealing with fore-closures, rehashing the plan that COP had already reviewed. Next he explained why Treasury's efforts were perfectly adequate—no need to worry. Then he hit his key point. The banks could manage only so many foreclosures at a time, and Treasury wanted to slow down the pace so the banks wouldn't be overwhelmed. And this was where the new foreclosure program came in: it was just big enough to "foam the runway" for them.

There it was: the Treasury foreclosure program was intended to foam the runway to protect against a crash landing *by the banks*. Millions of people were getting tossed out on the street, but the secretary of the Trea-sury believed that government's most important job was to provide a soft landing for the tender fannies of the banks.

Oh Lord.

What do you say to such a thing? I wish I'd responded with some bril-liant comeback, but I didn't. I felt as if one of us was standing on a snow-covered mountaintop and the other was crawling through Death Valley. Our views of the world—and the problems we saw—were that different.

In the following months, COP wrote more reports about the Treasury's inadequate response to the foreclosure epidemic, about what the flood of foreclosures meant for mass unemployment and long-term economic growth. And COP wasn't the only one to sound the alarm; FDIC chair Sheila Bair raised the issue repeatedly and tried to suggest alternative approaches to keep more people in their homes. Leading economists and housing counselors wrote op-eds and gave speeches. Protests sprang up. We did everything we could, but the foreclosures just kept piling up.

Choosing Sides

As the fall rolled into winter, the partisan battles that marked COP's early days faded into the background. We stayed true to our vision of running a nonpartisan commission, and I think people forgot about who came from what side of the aisle, at least for a while. Even Congressman Hensarling ultimately relented and voted in favor of a few of the COP reports. I was glad to have his vote from time to time.

One day in December 2009, the congressman called to say that he had resigned. As his replacement, the Republicans appointed Mark McWatters, a seasoned tax lawyer and CPA. Earlier that year, Senator Sununu had left as well; several months later, his replacement, Paul Atkins, did the same. This time, the Republicans named Dr. Ken Troske, a highly respected conservative labor economist. Mark and Ken had strong points of view about many of the issues our panel was grappling with, and though I didn't always see eye to eye with them, they consistently worked hard to dig at the truth. Both men were sharp-witted and deeply engaged, and they helped drive the COP investigations to greater depths.

COP taught me something important about nonpartisanship: It didn't have to be timid. Despite our different backgrounds and perspectives, the panelists didn't search for the lowest common denominator and issue statements saying, "The sky is blue" because that's all anyone could agree on. We pushed and prodded and sometimes argued. We sweated over our analysis, but the result was that our reports were strong, and our language was bold—and when we couldn't work things out, the dissents were just as strong. In the end, I think our eclectic, nonpartisan team produced better work than any one individual (or any one political party) could have produced alone. During my time at COP, 10 of our 23 reports were unanimous, and 16 out of 23 were bipartisan. Not bad.

Who Goes to Jail?

COP kept churning out reports, month after month. Secretary Geithner came back to testify three more times, and a clip from one of those hearings went viral on YouTube. Vikram Pandit, the CEO of Citibank, testified, as did the CEO of Ally Bank. We asked the CEOs of several other big banks to testify, but they turned us down, and since we didn't have subpoena power, there wasn't much we could do about it.

In June 2010, we wrote a special report focused entirely on the AIG bailout. Clearly we struck a nerve. The report got an unusual amount of media coverage and revived interest in what was happening at AIG. A few weeks later, Hank Greenberg, the former CEO of AIG, demanded to see me in my office at Harvard. He was pretty angry about our report, although he didn't dispute what we'd said about the wildly dangerous risk taking at AIG and the threat it posed to the whole economy. Instead, he wanted to talk about why he was underappreciated as a great CEO. When he realized that I wasn't going to back away from our conclusion that AIG had become a risky tangle under his leadership, he turned his wrath on an investigation years earlier by New York's then attorney general Eliot Spitzer. When that rant also yielded no sympathy, he abruptly left, unsatisfied. The encounter reminded me that CEOs of giant financial companies seem to have very different worldviews from those of most people.

Greenberg had lost his job, but that was before the crash. Once TARP arrived, the CEOs of the bailed-out banks fared a lot better. By now I was more or less resigned to the fact that the federal government wasn't going to force any of these guys to step down. But I still hoped that the government would launch investigations into whether any of the top management had violated the law.

COP had no authority to file civil or criminal cases, but the Department of Justice and plenty of other agencies had the power to do so if that seemed warranted. For months, I assumed that sooner or later some regulator would think to himself, The banking system just collapsed—I wonder if any banking executives did anything illegal? I figured it was just a matter of time until there would be a string of announcements that major players in the financial markets had been indicted.

But the silence stretched out. No perp walks. No mass indictments.

Were the banks really above the law? That certainly hadn't always been the case. Back in the 1980s, the country had suffered through another banking crisis, this one involving savings and loan institutions that took advantage of a recent round of deregulation to become giant Ponzi schemes. (Did I mention how stupid it was to deregulate the banks without putting safeguards in place?) In those days, federal officials did not take such a generous line toward errant bankers. When an institution failed, the government launched a detailed investigation, and if the executives had cooked the books, they had to answer for it. People went to jail—lots of people. More than a thousand executives were indicted. As my uncle Billy said at a family reunion during the S&L crisis, "My banker friends used to work nine to four. Now they are in prison, serving five to seven." Then he gave his big belly laugh.

I don't know for sure if anyone at the giant banks engaged in criminal activity in the months and years leading up to the financial meltdown. But that's the point: I don't think anyone knows for sure. Where were the full-scale public investigations? Where were the armies of auditors, seizing hard drives and poring over the financial statements? Where were the teams of regulators who were supposed to be checking the books all along? Where were the signs—any signs at all—that real resources were being devoted to a series of thorough investigations and that somebody with real power was taking this responsibility seriously?

Think of it this way. Big banks give their regulators certified financial statements every three months, year after year, showing that the bank is in good shape. Meanwhile, they sell billions of dollars' worth of mortgages that stink to high heaven, dress those mortgages up in phony-baloney AAA-rated wrapping paper, and peddle them to retirement funds and local governments across the country. Then the banks suddenly need *tens of billions of dollars* in government money just to stay afloat. The government gives the banks the money but never puts major resources and manpower into finding out whether the sudden, gaping hole in the banks' balance sheet was caused—at least in part—by illegal activity.

So the high-powered CEOs collect millions in bonuses, and Flora moves into her car. And the US government "foams the runway" for the giant banks, never seriously investigating whether the guys flying the planes were up to no good.

Sheriffs of Wall Street

In the spring of 2010, *Time* magazine called. They were writing a story on what they called "the new sheriffs of Wall Street," and they wanted to interview me. The "hook," as they called it, was that the three people they planned to feature were all women: Sheila Bair, chair of the FDIC; Mary Schapiro, chair of the Securities and Exchange Commission; and me. COP didn't have nearly the power of the FDIC or the SEC, but that didn't seem to matter to the editors at *Time*.

I hadn't met Mary, but I already knew Sheila. She was a highly accomplished lawyer and academic who had been named by President Bush to be the chair of the FDIC back in 2006, when most people figured running the FDIC would be a pretty boring job. She had shaken up the place, pushing through reforms that strengthened oversight of the smaller banks and beefed up the FDIC insurance fund. Sheila and I had met a few years earlier, and recently I had been working in a group she led that was trying to help lower-income people get better access to banking services.

The three of us gathered for interviews and pictures. When the time came to put us together for the cover shot, the shoot director realized that I was considerably taller than the other two women and declared that this "simply won't do." But the *Time* people had come prepared. They brought out a box for Mary to stand on and a smaller lift for Sheila. Once our sizes were adjusted for the camera, we were told to look like sheriffs.

The whole situation seemed a little surreal, and we all got a good laugh out of it. In fact, I loved spending that time with Sheila and Mary. We fell into easy conversations about a lot of topics, including why it mattered that the person responsible for the banking insurance fund (Sheila) didn't have the right lipstick color and whether it was significant that the person fighting to restore the effectiveness of a badly weakened SEC (Mary) was having trouble with her hair. Did guys have to put up with this?

But all three of us knew what this photo shoot was really about: it was an opportunity to deliver a message to a lot of people about why Wall Street needed to be held to a higher standard of accountability. And I suspect each of us felt that the cover story raised a question we'd all thought about, even if we didn't dwell on it: Given that women were so conspicuously absent from the ranks of top executives in high finance, how was it that three women had ended up in leadership positions when it came time for the badly needed cleanup?

Over the next few years, Sheila, Mary, and I had several variations of that conversation. We always kept it light, but the topic touched a nerve. After all, of the twenty commercial banks listed in the Fortune 500 at that time, only one had a woman CEO. Just one. I've been going to financial conferences for a long time, and I've never seen a line in the ladies' room.

And then there's my little corner of the TARP world. During the nearly two and a half years that COP was in operation, ten panelists would come and go. Out of those ten, all were men except me.

So what is it about finance that makes women so scarce in the corner offices? And why indeed were three women now the sheriffs of Wall Street? I can't answer for Sheila or Mary, but I do have a thought about why I had ended up in this position: I was an outsider. I had never inhabited the cozy world of high finance, never played golf with a foursome of CEOs, never smoked cigars at the club.

Some people argue that if you're never in the club, you simply can't understand it. But in this case, I think not being in the club means never drinking the club's Kool-Aid. I had studied the banking system from the outside, so none of it was sacred to me. I thought most of the finance guys were smart, but not any smarter than a lot of other people I knew. Sure, they made a lot more money, but that didn't mean they couldn't be blind to a catastrophe happening right in front of them or that they wouldn't be willing to skirt the rules if it would plump up the bottom line.

Late one evening while we were working on a COP report, Damon told me a story he'd heard from someone who had participated in a memorable event. Not long after COP had first come on the scene with our plainly worded ten questions, there was a small, private going-away party for Secretary Paulson, held at some swanky establishment. The stock market had crashed and the economy was teetering, but there were toasts and backslaps over Paulson's superb tenure as Treasury Secretary and his handling of the crisis. As the evening drew to a close, the conversation turned to COP. After some general harrumphing about our work, someone mentioned my name. Said one participant, "She just doesn't get it," and everyone nodded in agreement.

I asked Damon if he knew whether any women had been present. "Nope," he said. "From what I heard, no women."

I didn't think so.

What If She Finds Out?

I stayed with COP until September 2010, when I took another Washington job. In nearly two years of tangling with the Treasury Department and the big banks about TARP, I'd say we came away with a win-some, lose-some scorecard.

The losses were obvious. We didn't have the power to stop Treasury from flooding the big banks with no-strings-attached TARP funds, and for the biggest financial institutions, Too Big to Fail became the new reality. We didn't have the authority to launch criminal investigations, and no senior banking executives were marched out of their offices in handcuffs. We were never able to prod Treasury to provide the little banks with faster help, and by September 2010, more than three hundred small banks and credit unions had failed. We were never able to push anyone to get enough credit flowing to small businesses, and 170,000 of them folded as well.

All that was bad enough, but what really ate away at me was that we were never able to get the Treasury Department or the White House to do something meaningful about foreclosures. The president chose his team, and when there was only so much time and so much money to go around, the president's team chose Wall Street. America had the biggest bailout fund in history, and the Goliaths of banking gobbled it up. Meanwhile, millions of people lost their homes, and even now, years after the crash, millions more are scrambling to pay down underwater mortgages. I still think about Flora, and I still think about Mr. Estrada—and I know there are millions of people just like them.

In my darkest moments, what really shut me down was this: COP couldn't change a system that seemed hell-bent on protecting the big guys and leaving everyone else by the side of the road.

But we also had some wins, and some of them were big. We blew the BS whistle more than once, a lot of people heard us, and some of those hidden policy decisions moved into public view. COP helped put money in the pockets of the American people. Our July 2009 report about the bonuses owed to the taxpayers helped return billions to the US Treasury. Under Naomi's capable leadership, we built a world-class team of experts and investigators. As just one more example of their superb work, the team's analysis of the auto bailout backed up the government, making it clear that the decision to save an industry—and an estimated 1.1 million jobs—was well grounded in both law and economic policy. And although we didn't stop Too Big to Fail, we sure did make a stink about it. I also think we helped shine a spotlight on a too-cozy, too-Byzantine, underfunded regulatory system that had utterly failed when it was most needed—and that spotlight spurred on those who would later push for real financial reform in the aftermath of TARP.

Maybe there were some other, less visible wins. After I left COP, my next job required that I spend a lot of time in the Treasury Building. Every now and then I'd walk down those hollow, high-ceilinged halls and bump into a member of the staff who would stop to say hello. During some of these conversations, I heard different versions of the following comment: "You don't know me, but I was working in the XX section during the financial crisis. When we talked about what we should do, someone always seemed to ask, 'What will Elizabeth Warren say when she finds out about this?' That usually made people stop and think again."

I never thought that comment was about me. I believed it was about all of the panelists who served on COP, as well as our great staff. But I also thought the comment was about democracy. To me it was another way of saying, "What if everyone knew what we were up to?" I didn't need any better proof that speaking up—and speaking up loudly and clearly—was worthwhile.

Before Harry Reid called me on the night of the student barbecue, I had never thought much about government oversight. With COP, we had a chance to involve the American people in events as they were happening. Our job was to give regular folks a window into the decisions that would shape their economy and their lives—and ultimately to help them have the information they needed to decide whether their leaders were taking the country in the right direction.

My time as a COP changed me. I still didn't have a badge or a set of handcuffs, and I was still nervous about going on television (although

I never threw up again), but I learned a couple of important lessons. I learned that insiders don't appreciate questions from outsiders, including pesky professors who don't know the unwritten rules of Washington. I also learned an essential truth: When you have no real power, go public—really public. The public is where the real power is.

Those long days and weeks on the oversight beat weren't always fun. But Otis didn't complain: he ate a lot of cornbread and began to put on weight. I poured my troubles out to Bruce, often over fried clams and beer. Sometimes I wanted to shout curses at the gods of finance over what I couldn't accomplish. But the fury was tempered by the sadness I felt when I thought about all the injustice and all the heartbreak that so many families had suffered. Despite how awful the crash had been, I was not sorry that I had been part of the fight to improve the government's response to it. I was deeply grateful for the chance to serve our country, to do whatever I could, at such a critical time.

Our oversight of the bailout wasn't perfect, not by any stretch. But I saw what was possible. We took an obscure little panel that could have disappeared without a trace and worked hard to become the eyes and ears and voice for a lot of people who had been cut out of the system. And every now and again we landed a blow for the people who were getting pounded by the economic crash.

That felt good. It felt really good.

4 | What $1 Million a Day Can Buy

I N THE MIDST of the COP work, I took on another project, one that came at me sideways. The project had nothing to do with congressional oversight but everything to do with the financial meltdown. It grew out of an idea that had been knocking around in my head for a while, and when the opportunity arose to make the idea a reality, I couldn't hold back. I guess it was like holding a missing puzzle piece and seeing right where it fit in the jigsaw—almost impossible to resist trying to put it where it belonged.

Ideas grow in lots of ways, and my idea was born of years of wonky research and teaching technical details of the law. But it wasn't enough to have a good idea. I also needed to explain it, and one way to do that was to recall one of the times when I nearly set my kitchen on fire.

When we lived in New Jersey in the 1970s, I liked to make toast for breakfast. One morning when Amelia was little, probably three or four, she was sitting in a booster chair at the kitchen table, eating cereal. I popped a few pieces of bread in our toaster oven, got busy doing six other things, and quickly forgot about the toast. When I saw smoke pouring out of the toaster oven, I grabbed the handle and pulled out the tray, exposing four slices of bread that were on fire. Always a quick thinker, I screamed and threw the tray at the kitchen sink. Three pieces of toast hit the target, but the fourth went high—setting the cute little yellow curtains on fire.

I screamed again, then grabbed Amelia's cereal bowl and threw it at the burning curtains. The milk doused most of the fire, and I calmed down enough to realize that throwing things was probably not my best strategy. Then I noticed that the toaster itself was shooting sparks and seemed to be on fire. (How long had the darn thing been on?) I got a glass, filled it with water, and poured the water on what remained of my flaming curtains. Then I grabbed a towel and beat on the toaster until everything seemed quiet and I could unplug it.

That may have been the year I started so many kitchen fires that Daddy gave me a fire extinguisher for Christmas. Oh, happy day.

Back then, our toaster oven had an on-off switch and that was it. On was On, which meant that it was possible to leave toast under the little broiler all day and all night, until the food burned, the wiring melted, and the whole thing burst into flames. At some point—I have no idea exactly when—someone had the bright idea of adding a timer and automatic shutoff. This simple change made it a whole lot harder for distracted mothers, or anyone else, to leave the broiler running until it set the kitchen on fire.

Thirty years later, while working on an article about how the government could protect consumers from predatory financial companies, I thought about those old toaster ovens. By then, it was all but impossible to buy a toaster that had a one-in-five chance of bursting into flames and burning down your house. But by the 2000s, it *was* possible to refinance a home with a mortgage that had a one-in-five chance of costing a family their home and putting them out on the street. In fact, it wasn't just possible; those mortgages were bursting into flames all over the country.

Likewise, it wasn't possible for a manufacturer to change the price of a toaster oven after someone had purchased it. (Imagine getting the bill in the mail: "Send us another $100 immediately or else your toaster will stop toasting your English muffins!") But long after the papers had been signed, it *was* possible for a credit card company to double or triple the interest rate on a balance that someone had already taken out. ("Send us more money immediately or else your credit rating will be destroyed!") Read the fine print: it was all perfectly legal.

Why the difference? The United States government was—and is—the difference. By 2007, the year I was writing my article, a government agency actually monitored toasters for basic safety, and if anyone tried to sell a toaster that had a tendency to burst into flames, the agency would put a stop to it. In fact, government agencies ensured the basic safety of pretty much every product offered for sale. The agencies worked to keep us safe: No lead paint in children's toys. No medicines laced with rat poison. No cars without functioning brakes. And no exploding toasters. But in 2007 there was no government agency that would stop the sale of exploding mortgages.

Despite their name, financial products were *not* treated like products. They were regulated as contracts—which meant that two sides, supposedly negotiating as equals, could form pretty much whatever agreement they wished. And this meant that when it came to dealing with the giant banks, consumers were mostly on their own.

I figured the fix could be pretty simple: Treat mortgages and other financial products like, well, *products.* No one expects a consumer to evaluate the wiring diagram for a toaster. I thought no one should expect a consumer to digest thirty pages of tiny print to evaluate every trick in a credit card agreement. Common sense and basic safety—to my mind, that's what this was all about.

In the article, I compared the safety of toasters with the safety of financial products. I proposed the creation of a new government agency, one whose sole mission would be to look out for consumers, and to serve as the cop on the beat who would make sure that financial companies follow some commonsense rules. People could still use mortgages and credit cards however they wanted, but the products themselves would be clear. No tricks hidden in the fine print, no traps buried in complex legalese.

It was a pretty simple idea. Getting it done would not be so simple.

Cheated

Over the years, I had heard a lot of stories from people in bankruptcy. The stories so often started with something unexpected and sad. A job that was going great—until the pink slip arrived. A beloved wife—lost to cancer. An aging father—who broke his hip, forcing his daughter to cut back on her hours at work.

And then, more often than not, the story would take a turn that would make me furious—blood-boiling furious. Because then, just when a family was down on its luck, some giant financial company would come along and make things worse.

Sometimes the lenders lied. Sometimes they cheated. Sometimes they baited a trap. And sometimes, even when the target figured it out, the lender just brazened it out.

I remember a guy (I'll call him Jason to protect his privacy) who lived on the edge of a small southern town with his wife and stepson. As Jason told the story, he had lost his job, but after a few months of searching he had found a new one, working at a warehouse about forty miles from home. Meanwhile, he had racked up some debt. He owed on his credit card, and he had borrowed money from his brother-in-law (which he found mortifying, and he planned to pay him back as soon as possible). But now that he had a new job, Jason figured he was on his way to getting back on his feet.

His pickup was a gas-guzzler and it had broken down a few times, so he decided to trade it in for something a little smaller and more reliable for his long commute. One Saturday, he drove to one of the big car dealers that advertised heavily on the radio. He kicked a few tires, thought long and hard about which car would suit his needs, and finally settled on a two-year-old Ford Taurus. He haggled on the price, arranged for the trade-in, and drove home in his new car, feeling pretty good about his decision. He hadn't exactly wanted to make the change, but he felt responsible, like he was getting his life back on track.

Several days later, the phone rang. It was the car dealer: there was a problem. When Jason had come to the car lot, the dealer had offered him a 4 percent interest rate, but the man on the phone explained that this was just a *preliminary* offer. The actual rate was higher—more than *five times* higher, according to Jason—than the preliminary rate, so the monthly car payment would be $105 higher than the dealer originally estimated.

Jason panicked. The new job didn't pay as much as his old one, taxes were chewing up more of his paycheck than he had planned, and he needed to watch every nickel. He didn't have an extra $105 each month. He told them to call it off. He would return the Taurus and take back his pickup.

No dice. They had already sold his pickup. Jason could either take the car dealer's terms or he could return the Taurus and walk. Literally.

And it was all perfectly legal. Somewhere in the fine print, the rate on his car loan was marked "preliminary." No one was obligated to spell out what that meant, and what it meant was: "Preliminary means that after you buy the car we can increase your monthly rate by $105, just because we want to."

I knew there were millions more people like Jason. He got in trouble with his car loan, but it happened with all kinds of financial products. Big banks across the country had been sneaking in ways to charge sky-high fees for bounced checks. Payday lenders would charge upward of 400 percent effective interest—rates that would make Tony Soprano blush.

And then there were the credit card companies. Their shifting payment dates. Their sudden interest rate hikes. And their torrent of fees— late fees, over-the-limit fees, just-because-it's-Tuesday fees. The language was convoluted, and the cross-references and defined terms made it unreadable. Let me put it this way: I'd taught contract law for more than twenty years, and I couldn't understand some of those contracts. How many people who were busy trying to get dinner on the table and check the kids' homework had a chance to wind through this kind of legalistic wiring diagram? Not many.

So why not put a cop on the beat? Why not create an agency to put a stop to all these shenanigans? We could put some commonsense rules in place and force the industry to use plain English to explain what the products really do. No cheating anywhere—not credit cards, not mortgages, not payday loans or student loans.

The idea was to keep Jason and millions of people like him from getting ripped off.

Don't Shoot!

My article proposing this new agency was published in 2007, in a journal called *Democracy.* At the time, a consumer financial protection bureau seemed like a pipe dream. George W. Bush was still president, and the Republican leadership was still talking about *de*-regulation, not stronger regulation.

But by the beginning of 2009, the world looked very different. America had a new president and a newly crashed economy. Suddenly a little more financial regulation didn't sound like such a bad idea.

By early 2009, I was spending nearly all my time teaching or on COP work. But in February of that year, Damon Silvers—my co-panelist at COP and associate general counsel of the AFL-CIO—invited me to a meeting about another topic: financial reform. Everyone knew that Congress would soon start working on a law that would overhaul banking regulation. A number of us also figured that the big banks would quickly begin to marshal their forces, revving up their lobbyists and getting their publicists ready. They had won big-time with the $700 billion no-strings-attached TARP bonanza, and now they were gearing up to fight any reforms that could cut into their future profits.

This meeting would bring together many of the leaders of the non-profit and advocacy groups dedicated to fighting for working families. Damon—and a lot of other longtime activists—knew that real reform was desperately needed. And they thought that all those who wanted to protect the financial interests of American consumers should start getting ready to fight back.

The meeting was held at the AFL-CIO headquarters in Washington. It was supposed to start at nine, but I was running late, so I started jogging through the lobby. The floor was hard and shiny, but I couldn't keep my eyes off the building's magnificent two-story mural: its monumental figures of working men and women were interlaced with small gold tiles that glinted in the morning sun. As I ran, the heel on my shoe slid sideways and I lost my balance. As I started falling, I vaguely wondered whether I'd be more likely to break a leg or knock out my front teeth—I figured it would depend on how I landed. But somehow, arms and legs flailing, I found my feet again just before crashing to the floor.

The meeting took place in the big conference room on the eighth floor. I'd never been there, but Damon had told me about it. The room had a balcony that looked out on the White House. During the Bush years, the AFL-CIO had been sternly cautioned that no one should step on the balcony or the sharpshooters might fire at them. So far, no one in the Obama White House had issued the same warning.

Every seat was taken, maybe seventy-five or so in total. I didn't know most of the people in attendance, but I think there were representatives from civil rights organizations, consumer groups, labor unions, and religious groups that viewed economic security as part of their core mission. It was a hodgepodge of leaders from organizations populated by people I thought of as "the good guys"—those who spend their lives fighting for the well-being of regular folks.

When I stepped into the meeting, everyone was already seated and quiet. The room was dominated by a huge conference table, and sunlight coming from a long bank of windows running beside the table briefly blinded me. I had the sense of stepping onto a brightly lit stage before I was ready.

Damon had organized the meeting, and he sat at the head of the table. On his right was his boss, John Sweeney, the legendary seventy-four-year-old president of the AFL-CIO. On Damon's left was an empty chair, which Damon motioned me into.

I'd never met Mr. Sweeney before, and I was surprised by how old he looked. His voice was thready and hoarse, barely above a whisper, and his body was bent. But like a good host, he welcomed us all, and when he spoke, no one moved. Here was a man who had organized millions of workers. Thirteen years earlier, he had risen to the presidency in the first contested election in the union's history. His message to the group that morning was short and clear: This financial crisis is historic, and our country's response should be historic. We should make the changes we need to make to protect the American worker. Then Damon turned to me. "Tell them."

So this was it. There would be a lot of topics on the agenda today, from regulation of derivatives to international capital standards, and I had one brief chance to make my case.

I started talking about the idea of a consumer agency. It was a simple concept, but that shouldn't fool anyone; it was pretty bold just the same. I wanted our government to create an entirely new agency, one whose purpose would be to rein in the financial institutions that were taking advantage of families across the country. The agency would serve as an aggressive watchdog, with the power to oversee and regulate all consumer lending—credit cards, mortgages, student loans, payday lending, car loans. Its sole mission would be to look out for the interests of families.

Big banks had perfected the art of circumventing new laws designed to protect people. I pointed out that more than a dozen federal laws already addressed issues involving consumer credit, but the responsibility for enforcing these laws was spread out among seven different federal agencies—seven! Moreover, each of those agencies had some other first job, like making sure the banking system was stable or administering housing policy. Not a single one of those agencies had as its primary job protecting consumers from dangerous credit products. Not one.

And there was another ugly problem: Guess who picked the regulators who had oversight responsibility for the individual banks? Often it was *the banks themselves*. Two federal banking regulators competed for business, and the more banks they signed up, the bigger their budgets became. The results shouldn't have surprised anyone: regulators often tried to outdo each other to be the friendliest, which shifted their role from watchdog to lapdog.

As if that weren't bad enough, there was one more problem: The mishmash of agencies left giant holes in the regulatory fabric. In fact, a growing number of lenders were left out altogether. No federal agency was responsible for overseeing payday lenders, title lenders, or an increasing number of mortgage lenders. Those guys could do pretty much whatever they wanted. Worse, many of them were financed by the big banks.

So credit regulation was a tangled mess, and enforcement of the rules was spotty at best. We needed an agency—one agency—that would be responsible for writing new rules, for updating the rules as lenders changed their practices, and for enforcing the rules. With a new agency, every mortgage and credit card would be regulated the same—no more shopping around for lax regulators or figuring out how to avoid oversight altogether. The system would be a lot more efficient and a whole lot more effective.

I didn't say so at the time, but I also thought that this agency could help us navigate a practical political problem. If the groups in this room lined up behind a hundred different ideas about how to provide financial protection for consumers, we'd get negotiated down to a dozen or so. And then those dozen would be like fence posts on the prairie—the giant banks could see them from a mile off and run right around them. But if we all rallied around a truly comprehensive idea—a long-term structural solution that would keep momentum behind reform over time—that might give us a fighting chance to create an effective counterweight to the big banks.

For many of the people in the room that day, the idea for the Consumer Financial Protection Bureau (as the agency would eventually be known) was new, and it would require a huge leap of faith. How could all these organizations, each with its own agenda and history, get behind a relatively unknown and untested idea, one that at the time had very little active political support?

People would find plenty of other reasons to be skeptical about the consumer agency. The banks would almost certainly hate it, and they would instruct their lobbyists to fight to the death to stop it. Even though the agency would streamline government and make it more efficient, the very idea of a new government agency would probably enrage the small-government advocates on the political right. Many in the media would try to rip the idea apart, and Fox News would have a field day.

And even if we won, what if the agency got a lousy director who failed to take on tough problems or was bad at spotting emerging threats? After all, other government agencies had been started with high hopes, only to sink in a bureaucratic tangle. We might fight an epic battle, somehow manage to get the agency launched, and then see it amount to little.

Still, I believed in this dream; American families desperately needed a consumer agency like this one. I knew that if the groups represented by the people in this room didn't get behind the proposal, there was zero chance of getting it through Congress. I also knew that if our first conversation focused on all that was wrong or risky or unfamiliar, the idea would die that very morning. So this was the moment.

I finished my presentation and glanced nervously around the room. No one spoke.

I looked at Damon. He looked calm, unusually calm for Damon. Then he said: "Comments?"

I could feel my heart pounding. This was like the day I stood on the corner holding hands with five-year-old Amelia, waiting for the school bus on her first day of kindergarten. My prayer that day was intense and addressed to all forces in the universe: Please please please be kind and give her a chance. Now I felt the same way, because when they are still young, ideas—like children—can be knocked over so easily.

A hand shot up. Damon called on a man at the far end of the long table. Heads turned. I didn't know who he was. I didn't breathe.

"Great idea!" the man said.

I don't remember anything else he said, just the feeling that I could breathe out—at least a little.

Damon called on someone else and got a similar response. And then a third person offered support.

Damon smiled.

After that came plenty of questions and some real concerns about whether the agency would be strong enough to succeed or if the banks would whittle it down to nothing. People were nervous, but the first guy had saved it. He gave the idea some credibility, some enthusiasm, some wind in its sails.

We were still ridiculously outgunned by the lobbyists and giant banks. But a small army began forming that day as a handful of good guys endorsed the idea and decided to fight for it. I didn't know it then, but they would become the most important soldiers in the battle that was to come.

Consumer Safety

We had one big advantage in talking about the idea of a new government agency to a skeptical public: we could point to plenty of agencies that had already done a lot to protect consumers.

In the 1970s, the Consumer Product Safety Commission (CPSC) had been created to establish safety standards, recall unsafe products, and ban products that pose unreasonable risks. That agency works to keep us safe from arsenic in toys, car seats that collapse on impact, and, yes, toasters that catch fire. In fact, the CPSC estimates that standards for three products alone—cigarette lighters, cribs, and baby walkers—save American consumers more than $2 billion every year and prevent a lot of terrible injuries.

Congress can pass a law to make something illegal, but the usual "one and done" approach is fairly rigid. Agencies, by contrast, can be nimble. The CPSC didn't pass a regulation about the safety of, say, infant car seats back in 1982 and then sit around and do nothing for the next thirty-five years. Instead, the CPSC constantly tests new products and gathers new data as things change in the market. When the agency discovers that a new model of infant car seats has a tendency to collapse on impact, it researches the problem, figures out a solution, and issues a new regulation. In many cases, it orders recalls. The world changes, products change, and so do the agencies' rules.

That could also be the mission of an agency designed to protect consumers from financial traps. New financial products come out every day—they're often created when just a few new words are added to a long and complicated contract—and the agency could keep up with changes in the industry. It could eliminate deceptive terms and help make disclosures shorter and clearer. And it could stamp out marketing that advertises a 5 percent interest rate in large print and buries the 35 percent interest rate hike in the fine print.

Not surprisingly, a lot of people were dead set against this idea when I first started talking about it. I heard the arguments against the agency over and over, sort of like a continuous-play music list with only a few songs.

The agency would engage in price fixing. Nope, the new credit agency would have the power to make prices clearer, but it wouldn't set prices.

The agency would grow the nanny state. Nope, the agency wouldn't try to prevent people from charging too much on a credit card or buying an overpriced car. Again, this was about transparency, making the terms of the deal clear and then letting people make their own choices.

The agency would stop innovation. Nope, banks could still come up with cool new products, but they couldn't build new things just to trick people about the price or trap people by hiding the risks.

The agency would put banks out of business. Well, it depends. If a bank built its profit model around tricks and traps, then it would be in real trouble. On the other hand, if a bank wanted to compete straight up and make the terms of its deals clear, then that bank should be very happy about the new agency.

The last point was really important. Through the years, a lot of reputable banks had struggled to extricate themselves from a terrible bind. Their problem reminded me of the drug industry back when snake oil salesmen promised to cure cancer and baldness with just one bottle: the honest players found it difficult to sell an effective product at a reasonable price. Who could compete against companies that were willing to deceive and cheat their customers? After all, when so many contracts were awash in fine print, how could people tell the honest companies from the cheaters?

But in a world where everyone is required to be on the up-and-up, honest banks with an honest product should find it easier to get their message through. Over time, customer confidence should improve. Ultimately, this would be a good thing for the free market. Tell the truth about a product, and customers can take it or leave it. Better products attract more customers, and bad products gather dust on the shelf. What's not to like about that?

The President Talks Toasters

As some of the nonprofits started to champion the idea of a consumer agency, I did my best to ratchet up my help. I talked to just about everyone I knew (and plenty of people I didn't know), trying to gin up more support. I knew next to nothing about how to get a bill passed in Washington. At this point, my only experience in the legislative arena had involved an effort to get a bankruptcy bill stopped, and I'd failed at that. But I figured the best way to begin was just to start talking and see if I could convince people that the agency was a good idea.

I found some unexpected support from one of my students. He was a tall, redheaded kid who in 2006 had sat in the front row in my freshman contract law class at Harvard. In fact, he had the honor that year of being the first student called on—and the first to botch the answer. During the year, he had come by my office several times to learn more about the economic pressures on American families. When the crash hit in the fall of 2008, the redhead was in my advanced bankruptcy class. By now, he was volunteering as an unpaid, part-time intern for Massachusetts congressman Bill Delahunt, who represented a district that stretched from the southern Boston suburbs out to Cape Cod and the Islands. In one more twist of fate, Congressman Delahunt had already been working with Congressman Brad Miller from North Carolina—a real hero to struggling families—to try to boost the consumer agency. After the crash, the redhead offered to work with the congressmen to help promote the idea.

And that redheaded student? That was Joe Kennedy, Bobby Kennedy's grandson. (A few years later, Congressman Barney Frank would retire, and thirty-two-year-old Joe would win his old congressional seat.)

I also went back to our champion from the bankruptcy wars, Joe's great-uncle Senator Ted Kennedy. The senator and I had talked about the concept of a consumer agency a year or so earlier, but at the time my idea seemed improbable at best. When I talked with him again in February 2009, he was battling a brain tumor, but he was driving himself hard. I told him I thought this was the time to push for the agency.

The senator said cheerfully, "You know the bankers will hate this?"

I said I understood it wouldn't be easy.

He laughed and said, "It never is with you."

And just like that, he was in.

Senator Kennedy joined forces with Senator Durbin from Illinois and Senator Schumer from New York and quickly came up with a plan. In early March, the three senators would introduce the consumer agency as a stand-alone bill in the Senate, well ahead of the broader financial reform bill that would be coming later. Congressman Delahunt (with Joe Kennedy's help) and Congressman Miller were ready to go, eager to take on the fight for the agency in the House. The lawmakers would announce the new bill at a press conference—and I was invited.

I was goose-bump excited. Wow! A year earlier, the agency had been little more than an article in a small policy journal. Now it was picking up steam in Congress. Zing! Bang! I had visions of a huge public push, debates on the floor of the Senate and House, a great signing ceremony.

On March 10, the lawmakers held a press conference inside the Capitol, just a short distance from a flock of reporters whose full-time job was to stake out the Hill. We had some pretty fancy senators and congressmen, right there in person, ready to answer questions. I figured it would be a standing-room-only crowd and that everyone would be breathless to hear about a new idea.

In fact, the whole thing was, um, orderly and efficient. We got some solid news articles out of the announcement, but hardly the brass bands and confetti of my fevered dreams.

Senator Kennedy later gently explained to me how a press conference like this worked. Introducing the bill to the media and the public was a way to signal that the agency was important, and getting a round of news stories about it was really good. But this was just a first step, and big changes take time. Trying to reassure me, the senator said he was confident that someday we would get the agency.

I wanted to believe him, but I had really hoped this announcement would give the bill a lot more momentum than it did. The press coverage was helpful, but after a couple of days, the media moved on. I was impatient—wildly impatient—because I thought that if we couldn't get the agency airborne now, it would never fly.

Then, nine days after the press conference, the agency got another boost.

President Obama appeared on *The Jay Leno Show*. He was just fifty-nine days into his first term, and he spent a good deal of his time on the show talking about the mess on Wall Street. And then he said we needed better laws to protect consumers who buy financial products—and he talked about toasters!

> When you buy a toaster, if it explodes in your face—there's a law that says your toasters need to be safe. But when you get a credit card, or you get a mortgage, there's no law on the books that says if that explodes in your face financially, somehow you're going to be protected.

Now we were moving! Go, Mr. President, go!

Barney's In

Meanwhile, the Senate and the House were beginning the heavy-duty work of crafting a bill that would provide the basis for financial reform. The White House was working through its own ideas about reform, but on Capitol Hill, Congressman Barney Frank was in the eye of the hurricane.

I wanted to make my pitch for the consumer agency directly to Congressman Frank, but I dreaded it. I knew he was deeply focused on other parts of financial reform, and I was hesitant to ask him to add the consumer agency to his already heavy burden. Besides, the two of us had met a couple of years earlier, and we'd had a bumpy beginning.

Barney Frank was the gravelly-voiced, smart-as-a-whip congressman who was equally loved and feared in Washington. He was the first member of Congress to come out as gay, and that was back in 1987 when America was a lot less open. I admired his sharp one-liners and his ferocious willingness both to fight for what he believed in and to hammer out compromises that produced half a loaf when most people thought there would be no bread at all. Here was a man who knew how to negotiate.

The congressman represented a portion of Massachusetts that sprawled from the leafy Boston suburbs down to the fishing communities and former factory towns along Buzzards Bay. He had been in Congress for more than twenty years and was now the chairman of the powerful House

Committee on Financial Services. When Congressman Frank barked, a lot of people jumped.

The congressman and I were first brought together in 2007 by the Tobin Project, a think tank that put together meetings between academic policy wonks and Washington policy makers. (I was the wonk.) Before the crash, Congressman Frank knew the financial system was crumbling, and he was intensely focused on the need to bring the huge financial institutions—hedge funds, investment banks, giant commercial banks—into a regulatory system that made some sense. The issues were devilishly complex, but Congressman Frank could talk as knowledgeably as any seasoned Wall Street trader about credit swaps or collateralized debt. He was shrewd, he was tough, and he knew what he was talking about.

Of course, that didn't stop me from arguing with him if I thought he was wrong.

At the meeting in 2007, we duked it out (metaphorically, of course) in front of a roomful of other professors and think-tank leaders. We engaged in a wide-ranging exchange about everything from derivatives and capital reserve requirements to my baby idea for a consumer agency. Underneath all our apparent disagreements, I think we agreed on 95 percent of the substance, but we ordered the priorities for financial reform very differently—and neither of us backed down.

Now it was the spring of 2009. The crash had hit with a vengeance, and the economy was still tumbling. The House would be the first to take up financial reform, which meant that as the chairman of the House Financial Services Committee, Congressman Frank would be the key player in the negotiations involving the new financial rules. He was a champion for the good guys, but a lot was broken, and as he began to sort through the nuts and bolts of reform, he had his hands full with thousands of moving parts. Still, I figured that if the consumer agency had a chance of becoming law, it absolutely had to be part of any package that he moved forward. There wouldn't be any second chances for the agency.

And that's how I came to be driving around Newton, Massachusetts, looking for Barney Frank's apartment, on a Saturday morning in April 2009. The day was lovely, and the road threaded between trees that were just starting to bud. Almost perfect, except that I was lost. (Yes, lost again.) I could see a street sign, but it was nowhere on my printed directions. I didn't have GPS, so I pulled over and used my own personal help-me-I'm-lost device: I took out my cell phone and called Bruce. I told him the name of the road. He looked at an online map, figured out where I was, and directed me to the congressman's apartment complex. I parked in an adjacent lot, figuring I was home free.

No such luck.

I saw several modest, two-story brick buildings. They were turned this way and that, with no obvious pattern to the numbering. (Who designs these places?) I was still wandering around when Jim Segel, the congressman's longtime friend and senior advisor, called out, "Over here!" He laughed as I came up. "This place can be a little confusing." A little confusing? Yeah, and the Empire State Building was a little tall.

Jim showed me into the congressman's apartment. It was a small space; on one side of the living area there was a king-size mattress on the floor, complete with a tangle of unmade sheets and blankets. Jim sat down next to a small table in the kitchen part of the room. I said hello to the congressman's surfer-dude-handsome boyfriend, Jimmy, but before we had a chance to visit, Congressman Frank burst in.

There's no ignoring Barney Frank, and he was no more relaxed in his kitchen than he was on the floor of the United States Congress. He sat me down with my back wedged up next to the refrigerator, then jumped right in.

In his usual rapid-fire delivery, he said it was clear that families had gotten cheated in the mortgage market, and he liked the idea of the consumer agency to clean things up. (Yes!) But his first obligation was to make sure we could really get something done. Financial reform was already too complicated, and he was worried the consumer agency might have to wait. In the fight for any financial reform, we would be up against an army of lobbyists, and he thought it might make more sense to take them on one issue at a time. If we tried to push through everything at once, we could lose it all. So he would start with the bank regulations that obviously needed fixing, focusing on the rules covering derivatives, capital reserve requirements, and so forth.

The same reasons that made Congressman Frank uneasy about including the consumer agency from the start made me want to move it to the front of the line. I was sure the lobbyists would fight tooth and nail against the new agency, and I worried that if the rest of the reform package made it through first, no one would feel any great urgency about continuing to battle the lobbyists. We had to make this agency a priority. I figured this was our moment: now or never.

Wedged up against Barney Frank's refrigerator, I wanted to talk about all the problems the new agency could fix and all the families it could help. But Congressman Frank knew all that, and he cared as much about these families as anyone did. Besides, he didn't disagree about policy—he was arguing over how to get things done in Washington. This was about politics, and he knew a billion times more about that than I did.

So I took a breath and tried a totally different tack. I said I wanted to tell him a story. He was clearly impatient, but he nodded for me to go ahead.

I told him that when I was a kid, I would hear stories about my grandparents' lives in Oklahoma. In the early 1900s, my grandfather was a carpenter, doing repairs and building small homes and the occasional one-room schoolhouse in Indian Territory. My grandmother raised ten children. My mother was the baby, and she still lived at home when the Great Depression hit. I don't think my grandparents knew anyone who owned stocks or other investments. For them, the Depression had nothing to do with Wall Street and the stock market crash. It was about local bank failures and families losing their savings and their farms.

My grandmother had never been very political, and she sure didn't follow high finance. But decades later, she was still repeating her line that she knew two things about Franklin Roosevelt: He made it safe to put money in banks and—she always paused here and smiled—he did a lot of other good things.

And that was my pitch to Congressman Frank. Start with something that people understand, something that solves a problem they can see. Do that, and then they'll have confidence in the work you do to fix the parts they can't see. Yes, derivatives and credit default swaps were huge problems. He was totally right about that. But for a lot of people, those were just words that fly by in news reports. On the other hand, a mortgage broker who lies about the terms of a mortgage he sells to a homeowner—that's something everyone understands. Hidden fees on a credit card bill—that's a problem millions of people had been living with for a long time. Fine print and confusing legalese—everyone had signed loans that were loaded with it.

Start simple. Fix something people can see.

My whole pitch might have lasted two minutes, tops. Congressman Frank sat still for maybe ten seconds, then said, "I get it. Let's do it."

He would push to get the consumer agency into the reform package, right out of the gate. Wowee-zowee! It was a cartwheel moment.

Somewhere in that conversation, we stopped being Congressman Frank and Professor Warren. From that day on, it was Barney and Elizabeth.

Barney was good to his word. He fought like a tiger to keep the consumer agency in the financial reform package. With Barney on board, the agency wouldn't be left at the station like so much unclaimed baggage. We had a new champion, the best we could ever have hoped for.

The chances that we'd get a consumer agency were skyrocketing. Now, instead of no chance at all, we were up to *almost* no chance at all.

Announcement Day at the White House

April rolled into May and then June. I went on *The Daily Show with Jon Stewart* and questioned Tim Geithner in our first public COP hearing with him. Ted Kennedy called to tell me he was pushing hard to build support for the new agency. "We're working it," he said. Classes ended at Harvard, and COP kept churning out reports, month after month.

Early that summer, Bruce and I took off for a family reunion in Oklahoma. By now, all three of my brothers had retired. In a very sad twist of fate, all three were widowers. All three had lost their wives too early, to cancer. Don Reed had been blessed to find a wonderful new partner, so he had remarried, but David and John were alone.

I was eating barbecue and visiting with my nephew Mark when my cell phone buzzed. An official-sounding voice came on the line and said: "The president will be announcing his financial reform package in two days at the White House, and you are invited."

Holy cow—the White House! A presidential announcement!

I immediately told the whole clan. Even Don Reed and David, both dyed-in-the-wool Republicans, were excited. (Of course John, who was a President Obama man, was even more excited.)

I changed my plane tickets so I could fly straight back to Washington. Then I had a moment of panic. I'd come from Boston to Oklahoma carrying a suitcase with my usual family reunion attire—shorts, T-shirts, swimsuit, and sandals. I couldn't exactly wear that kind of gear to the White House. Besides, I'd gotten barbecue sauce on my best shorts. I didn't have time to get to my own closet in Boston, so I had to go on an emergency shopping trip.

My two nieces, Michelle and Melinda, went with me to the mall in northwest Oklahoma City. Time was short, and I ended up grabbing something fast in one of those desperate shopping moves that makes me wonder afterward what on earth I'd been thinking.

Two days later, on June 17, 2009, I was standing in a long line outside the White House gate. It was hot, and I was discovering that the fabric on my new jacket itched like crazy and made a funny *whooshing* sound when I walked. The new shoes made my toes throb. Great start for an afternoon at the White House.

After we were all processed through security, we were herded into a big room inside the White House. People milled around and talked with one another. I spotted a couple of familiar faces from Capitol Hill and a few people I knew from the nonprofits, but I didn't recognize most of the people in the room.

Finally, we were called into an ornate room that was jammed with tiny folding chairs. The space between the rows made airline seating seem generous. I was in the back of the crowd as we surged into the room, so by the time I made it in, only a few seats were left. I spotted a chair on the aisle, but to sit down, I had to scoot the chair back a little, right into the shins of the man in the row behind. I recognized him: it was Rich Trumka.

Rich and I met for the first time that day. At that time he was the secretary-treasurer of the AFL-CIO, although a few months later he would replace John Sweeney as the new president of the eight-million-member union. Rich had started out in the mines, and he was built like a Mack Truck, solid and radiating a barely contained energy.

As I sat down, I turned around and said with a tentative laugh, "You're not going to kick the back of my chair, are you, Mr. Trumka?"

Rich leaned forward and said, "Nah. Sit down. I've got your back, Elizabeth. I'll always have your back."

Before the president came out, copies of a white paper prepared by the Treasury Department were passed around. Various proposals for financial reform had been percolating in Congress for a few months, but everyone was waiting to see what the White House would do. This was the administration's opening shot in the battle for reform.

Sure, the president had talked about toasters on television, but it worried me that the banking industry had so much access to the White House. I knew that senior White House staffers had been holding meetings with the CEOs and lobbyists from Citibank, JPMorgan, Bank of America, and other giant banks, and I had no clue about what had been promised in those meetings.

The press was reporting that the agency was somewhere on the White House's wish list, but I needed to see for myself what that really meant. Would the White House propose a strong consumer agency with real teeth? Or would it float the notion of some empty advisory thing or maybe some minor initiative that could easily be bargained away? Would the agency be "another possible idea" in a long string of "possible ideas," or would it get a "we've got to have this" push?

The document being handed out that day was eighty-nine pages long. My hands shook as I opened it. Completely missing the table of contents, I tore through the pages. Financial Services Oversight Council. Capital and Prudential Standards. National Bank Supervisor. I was getting panicky. Was there anything in here about the agency?

Finally, on page fifty-five I found the right section: Protect Consumers and Investors from Financial Abuse. Skimming, I spotted two paragraphs about what had gone wrong—got it, got it—and then I hit the magic sentence: "We propose the creation of a single regulatory agency, a Consumer Financial Protection Agency (CFPA), with the authority and accountability to make sure that consumer protection regulations are written fairly and enforced vigorously."

Bingo—the White House was in all the way!

At the time, I was too buzzed with excitement to marvel at how truly astonishing this was. I'd heard rumors that some of the president's top financial advisors were unenthusiastic about the concept for the new agency. Besides, the administration was in the midst of the largest financial crisis in living memory, and the staff had a billion things to worry about and was overwhelmed. So where had the support come from?

Months afterward, I would find out. When push came to shove, the agency had a powerful champion on the inside. As I would later learn, he believed passionately that the White House needed to support a reform measure that would help regular people, and he saw the agency as the best way to do that.

His name was Barack Obama.

Going Door-to-Door

After the White House announced its position on financial reform, it was time for Congress to go all out. Barney Frank took the lead in the House, and later Chris Dodd, a Democrat from Connecticut, picked up the ball for the Senate in his role as chairman of the Senate Banking Committee. Together, they took on the monumental task of designing a bill and getting their colleagues behind it. It was an uphill battle: when the campaign for the reform bill began, we sure as heck didn't have the votes in the House or the Senate. And the bank lobbyists were fighting full out.

Michael Barr, assistant secretary of the Treasury, and his top deputy, Eric Stein, directed the painstaking work of drafting the administration's proposed language. Community advocates also stepped up in a big way: in June 2009, a number of nonprofits joined forces and set up Americans for Financial Reform (AFR), an organization whose main mission would be to fight for a range of financial reforms that would benefit regular people. AFR was launched with help from nonprofits like AFL-CIO, Consumer Federation of America, and PIRG, and eventually more than two hundred groups would join the cause.

AFR managed to scrape together some money, and they used it to hire a handful of employees, including Heather Booth as executive director and Lisa Donner as her deputy. Creating a small team to organize the overall campaign for reform was a brilliant move. Instead of each nonprofit putting a little time into fighting for this or that provision, AFR coordinated the efforts of dozens of groups, magnifying the work of each one by helping them speak with a single voice. Heather and Lisa and the rest of their crew put out press releases, coordinated briefings on Capitol Hill, and organized groups of volunteers. The staffers and lobbyists and lawyers for the megabanks outnumbered them by a zillion to one, but the AFR people were there—day in and day out—hammering on the need for financial reform. They worked their hearts out.

I was still pouring much of my time into teaching and COP, but I figured we were approaching the make-or-break moment for financial reform and the consumer agency. I offered to jump in to help however I could, and that summer, Dan Geldon offered to jump in with me. The Roosevelt Institute offered Dan a job to help develop ideas and advocate for financial reform, and Dan said yes. He quit his job at COP. Never mind that this would be his third job in eight months. Dan wasn't in this to build a résumé that would look good to some future employer. He wanted to make a difference—right now.

Dan and I started with no long-term plan and no obvious path to victory, a two-man platoon picking up the fight wherever we could. Dan was only a year out of Harvard Law School, but he already had a passion for politics and a natural feel for Washington that I'll never have. We met and shared research with anyone who would talk to us. We visited with nonprofits and labor leaders. I made cold calls, asking reporters if they had heard about the consumer agency, and we followed up with people who had written articles in the past. We called editorial boards and wrote op-eds, joined in conference calls and spoke at events.

We also met with a lot of banking groups—at least the ones who would meet with us. The big banks were funding a huge push to get rid of the consumer agency, but Dan and I tried to meet with the representatives for the small banks and credit unions. The pitch was straightforward: You're getting hammered by giant banks and unregulated lenders that build their businesses by tricking their customers, and the consumer agency could help level the playing field. Many of the smaller lenders opposed the agency even so, but sometimes we sparked a little interest.

We looked for meetings everywhere, and we often ended up on Capitol Hill, trying to get someone to listen to our pitch. A lot of those meetings were hard. Several members of Congress told me that customers just needed to pay closer attention to the financial agreements they signed. Others said they couldn't support a bill that they claimed would mean a bigger government. Others met with us but barely seemed to listen and hardly said anything at all.

I remember one meeting particularly well. A congresswoman who seemed really interested in what we had to say told me that she supported consumers and wanted to see them treated fairly. Then she raised a specific objection to the agency. I answered, but instead of talking about the issue, she moved on to another objection, and so on through a list of about half a dozen more problems.

Despite her many objections, I felt a little encouraged. Once Dan and I were out in the hall, I said, "Well, she didn't agree with much of anything, but at least she was talking. Maybe we have a shot at persuading her."

MAIN STREET LOOKING NORTH

My grandmother wrote "Wetumka, Okla" on the back of this picture, which dates from around the time my mother and father were born. During World War II, my parents left Wetumka and moved with my three older brothers to Muskogee, where Daddy was a flight instructor and Mother ran the house. Daddy loved to fly, and these were good years for them.

By the time I was born, my parents had taken some hard knocks. In the 1950s, we lived in the last row of houses in Norman, Oklahoma. Daddy built me this sandbox in our backyard. Aunt Bee often looked after me. Every year, she bought me a dress for the first day of school. I always wore the newest one for the school picture, including this third grade shot.

There were lots of strong women in my mother's family, and they loved nothing better than family reunions. Here I am with my Aunt Bee, my mother, my grandmother, my Aunt Bert and my Great Aunt Laura.

I was crazy about my middle brother, John, and very happy when he was home for Christmas just before he was sent to Africa.

Debate was the one thing I could do well—fight smart, fight hard. My partner and I won the Oklahoma state championship, and I got a scholarship to college.

College was a dream come true, and I loved attending George Washington University. I made nearly all my clothes, including this blue velvet number.

Jim Warren was the first boy I'd ever dated, and when he came back into my life after my sophomore year, I dropped out of college to marry him. I was nineteen.

Amelia arrived when I was twenty-two; I was amazed that this perfect little creature was now part of my life.

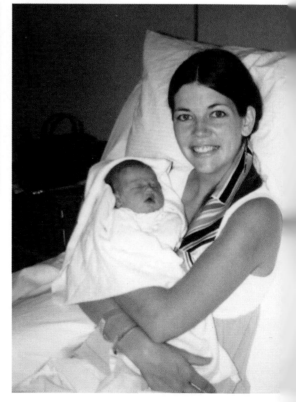

Amelia and I were buddies who ventured out together to explore the world. I went to the state law school near our home in New Jersey. When I graduated, I was very pregnant and thought I might melt in the blistering sun. Once Alex was born, I hung out a shingle and practiced law out of my living room.

Still in braces and taking care of
Amelia and baby Alex, I eventually got
a job teaching law school. That was
tough to manage, but Aunt Bee moved
to Houston to help. Even so, Jim and I
were headed for divorce.

Teaching law school was the most fun in the world; I even liked grading papers. Bruce and I got married and toasted to a new life. As two young law professors, we spent years teaching at different universities around the country.

My three handsome brothers—Don Reed, John, and David—posed with their baby sister at Thanksgiving in 1980.

Alex was a Boston Celtics fan from early on, which made Christmas shopping easy. In 1996, family dinners expanded when Amelia came home from grad school with her husband-to-be, Sushil.

It was always hard to get Daddy to stand still for a picture, but this time we caught him for a split second.

Socratic teaching means calling on everyone—even the kid hiding out in the back row.

My research on the economic pressures on middle class families began to get attention, and in 1990 I was invited to appear on the *Today* show. Bruce's dad took a whole roll of film of me on his television set—just to prove it really had happened.

I love being a grandmother—it's even better than people say. Here, my first grandchild, Octavia, is three years old, and we've got the giggles as we're dying Easter eggs.

A few years later, when my second granddaughter, Lavinia, needed someone to play a supporting role for her Halloween version of Little Bo Peep, she knew where to turn.

With my two granddaughters and all their cousins, we were ready to take on Legoland. This was the picture I took with me to the first Senate debate against Scott Brown—the one that reminded me why I was in this fight.

After months of worrying that he would come too soon, Atticus arrived fat and healthy and just in time to make Christmas 2010 one of the best ever.

It was clear in the COP hearings that Treasury Secretary Geithner and I had very different views about how TARP money should have been used. Here, the secretary is facing me while a photographer takes his picture.

I was still teaching at Harvard Law School while I was chair of COP and fighting to get a new consumer agency through Congress.

After the president signed the Dodd-Frank bill, which created the new consumer agency, he took a victory lap with the audience cheering him on. He was pumped, and everyone in the front row got a solid smack on the shoulder.

On the day the president named me to set up the new Consumer Financial Protection Bureau, I was ready to go.

As our work at the new consumer agency got under way, we met with as many people as we could. We wanted to craft regulations that would be tough and effective, and that meant lots of outreach.

The consumer agency was a start-up. Meeting space was pretty limited, so for our all-hands meetings on Tuesdays, we met by the elevators.

I was so knocked out by how many people showed up in Framingham to volunteer a year before the Senate election that I jumped up on stage and took this picture with my cell phone.

On the campaign trail in the summer at the Northhampton Pride Festival and shortly before the election near a bridge in Concord.

Organizing volunteers for one of the biggest get-out-the-vote drives Massachusetts had ever seen.

I loved the enthusiasm of the supporters I met during the Dorchester Day parade.

The firefighters union told me that once they were in, they would be in all the way—but I hadn't realized that "all the way" meant driving a big yellow bus around the state.

Art Ramalho offered up the West End Gym in Lowell for a campaign rally. He said he liked seeing me in a boxing ring—he figured it was good practice for Washington.

Otis helped me with my debate prep.

Octavia and Lavinia introduced me at the State Democratic Convention in Springfield. Lavinia was very disappointed that she was not allowed to do cartwheels during Octavia's speech.

Amelia and I had been buddies in lots of adventures, including writing books together, and now she was with me during the Senate campaign.

© TOM FITZSIMMONS

At the Democratic National Convention in September 2012, I said the game was rigged, and a lot of people in the audience seemed to agree.

Pickup trucks rumbled through West Roxbury on the night before the election.

Down to the wire, I was still out stumping, this time with lots of help.

SARAH BASTILLE PHOTOGRAPHY

When we made history, Bruce gave me one of the biggest and best hugs of my life.

PRESIDENT OBAMA RE-ELECTED

Boston **Herald**

Warren becomes first woman elected senator in Bay State

MAKING HISTORY!

MATT STONE / BOSTON HERALD

Elizabeth WARREN FOR SENATE ★ ELIZABETHWARREN.COM

For a moment, Dan looked like he was weighing whether to give me the bad news. But Dan never holds back long on bad news. He explained that the congresswoman had just run through every talking point included in a press release issued by the American Bankers Association that morning. In order.

Oh.

The most discouraging meetings were with those members of Congress who seemed to understand the problem but refused to do anything about it. Representatives on both sides of the aisle—Republicans and Democrats—said, in effect, Yeah, people are getting tricked, but the banks aren't going to let this agency go through, so why should I be a martyr for something that won't even happen? If everyone else agreed to the bill, they'd go along. But a lot of people we met with were hesitant to stick their neck out.

I wasn't giving up, but I started to understand why the banks seemed invincible. As summer wore on, the hallways got more and more crowded with lobbyists—and I mean that literally. The halls in Congress are wide and gracious, yet Dan and I would often have to step to the side with our backs against the wall while a herd of bank lobbyists thundered down the corridor. They were easy to spot: a group of a dozen or more men and maybe one or two women in the mix, all wearing custom-tailored suits. They walked with a bounce in their step as they spoke with great assurance about their "counts" and which member of Congress was next on their list. Well dressed. Well coordinated. Well connected.

Financial reform was complicated, and the bank lobbyists used a clever technique: They bombarded the members of Congress with complex arguments filled with obscure terms. Whenever a congressman pushed back on an idea, the lobbyists would explain that although the congressman *seemed* to be making a good point, he didn't *really* understand the complex financial system. And keep in mind, the lobbyists would tell the congressman, that if you get this wrong, you will bring down the global economy.

It was the ultimate insiders' play: *Trust us because we understand it and you don't.*

The pressure on elected officials to master the ins and outs of financial reform put them in a tough spot. As one congresswoman put it, "There's so much going on around here, it's like they attach your lips to a fire hydrant and turn on the water. No one can keep up." She was wrong. The lobbyists kept up.

Another meeting from that summer also stands out. Dan and I sat down with a congressman who asked some very specific questions about the current law and the proposed consumer agency. The questions were reasonable, if a little obscure. I thought he might—just might—be someone who would join our side. Offhand, I didn't know the answers to some of the questions, but I knew they were out there somewhere. It would take the better part of a day to track down the research, write up a memo, and then have a meeting with the congressman's staffer to go over our answers.

When we left, I asked Dan if he could take care of the follow-up work. Dan said he would do his best. Then he paused, evidently deciding that it was time for me to learn the facts of lobbying life. I could tell I was about to get another more-bad-news-from-Dan speech.

Dan explained that when the lobbyists showed up to talk with someone in Congress, they always brought a group. But the well-dressed men and women who strode up and down the hallways weren't the whole team. They were just the front line, the smooth talkers and beautiful smilers whose job was to make friends and persuade people. Behind them was a phalanx of support staff that worked for the lobbying groups, law firms, trade associations, PR partnerships, and financial institutions all over town—a whole second squad that we never even saw. It was their job to help make sure that before the lobbyists on the front line walked in the door, they knew everything about the congressman's background: how he had voted, who was on his staff, and where those staff people had worked before. The back office also helped provide information about the congressman's home district, including the number of people employed by banks, the names of the local bankers, and a summary of the local newspaper's editorials about the financial crisis.

Once they sat down with a congressman, the frontline lobbyists generally made a highly individualized presentation. Ideally, the presentation would be handled by someone who had either served in Congress or had worked for a member of Congress. For important meetings, stars would be rolled out. The CEO of a major bank might pay a call. Local bankers might be flown in from the home state. The younger lobbyists were instructed to take notes and build relationships with the staffers in the congressman's office.

Following the visit, the lobbying team would confer. Questions from the congressman? Have the team do a full research workup, write a memo, hand-deliver it, talk with the congressman's staff about it, and make follow-up calls. More arm-twisting needed? Write up notes to provide guidance for the next conversation, and start making plans for the next visit.

And up against all that, I had Dan.

I was certain that Dan was as smart and hardworking as anyone at any Washington lobbying firm—probably more so. But Dan was one person.

That was a humbling summer, and it didn't feel like we were making much headway. Lots of other terrific consumer advocates were out there banging on doors, too; the nonprofits were doing everything they could to stand up for consumers. But the nonprofits were just that—groups with no profits. Their resources were modest and their staffs were stretched tissue thin. And they weren't focused on only the consumer agency; they were trying to act as watchdogs on behalf of the American people for the entire financial reform bill—and a gazillion other issues to boot.

Meanwhile, the megabanks just kept pouring more money into their campaign. According to one source, the financial industry was spending more than *$1 million a day* on lobbying and campaign contributions during their drive to kill any meaningful financial reform.

I still wonder how such a thing is possible.

In addition to all the lobbying money, the industry was ponying up huge contributions for the reelection campaigns of influential members of Congress. Consider the House Financial Services Committee, the group that would determine the basic shape of the financial reform bill. That committee had *seventy-one members*. Why so many? One congressman explained it in simple terms: "It's a great place for a congressman to raise money. The banks pay."

Do they ever.

By July, health care reform was at center stage, and it looked like the financial reform legislation would be delayed until fall. The banks used the time to double down on their lobbying efforts, and they seemed to be concentrating their efforts on eliminating the provision they hated the most: the consumer protection agency. As the campaign continued to heat up, one of the lobbyists gave a blunt assessment of the banks' intentions toward the agency: "Our goal will be to kill it."

The rhetoric pitched into high gear. At one point, Congressman Hensarling, my fellow panelist on COP, wrote a furious op-ed in which he declared that the consumer agency was "a great assault on consumer rights" that was "positively Orwellian." Seriously? *Orwellian?*

We knew the banks—and a number of Republicans—were gunning for us, but we didn't slow down. AFR drove ahead, the consumer groups continued fighting, and Dan and I kept at it. Some days I felt like a door-to-door salesman. "Hi, my name is Lizzie and I'd like to show you a great new agency!"

Dan and I pushed and pitched and pushed some more. And when I'd catch the seven-thirty plane back to Boston, Bruce and Otis would be waiting for me, and Sal would always have fried clams and a light beer ready at the Summer Shack.

Credit Scores, In. Car Loans, Out.

In August, the inevitable finally happened: Senator Ted Kennedy lost his final battle. He was buried in Arlington National Cemetery near his brothers John and Bobby.

I thought about our meeting on the twenty-fourth floor of the JFK Building. I thought about his battered, overstuffed satchel. I thought about how many times he had taken up the fight for working people. No one could ever take his place.

In September, classes resumed at Harvard and I started teaching again. That fall, I kept working at COP, and we kept producing reports every thirty days. I continued to meet with pretty much anyone who wanted to talk about the consumer agency, and Dan kept fighting full-tilt.

In late 2009, I was working in my office at Harvard one day when the phone rang. "Elizabeth. It's Barney. Come down here tomorrow."

I asked what was up, but Barney, as always, was in a hurry. "It's important. Get here." And he hung up.

When I arrived in Washington the next day, I went straight to Barney's office, but he wasn't there. I was directed to a fancy meeting room near the House chamber. In the center of the room were about eight chairs arranged in a horseshoe, and behind each chair was a second chair. At the opening of this double horseshoe sat Barney.

Barney called us to order. All the men—and they were all men—took a seat. I grabbed a chair in the inner horseshoe, but no one sat behind me. I suddenly realized that all the inner chairs except mine were occupied by congressmen. The chairs behind were for their staffers. (Oops, was I supposed to sit in back? Not sure, but it was too late now.)

Barney had spent weeks negotiating dozens of provisions in the financial reform bill. Now, he told the group, we needed to work out three issues regarding the new consumer agency. He began by briefly describing a complex issue that had proved especially divisive, and then he outlined one possibility for how the law could be written. One congressman objected and offered his own proposal. Another didn't like that approach and suggested something else. I jumped in to offer my own idea, but Barney was six steps ahead of me.

It was an intense conversation. After about ten minutes, Barney cut in. "Here's what I think we can agree on." Then he quickly and clearly laid out a compromise that would resolve the problem.

Barney looked at each person in turn and asked, "Are you all right with this?" Each signaled his okay. Barney looked at me. "Can you live with this?" I said yes.

Barney said, "Done." All the people in the outer row of chairs scribbled on their notepads, and Barney turned to the second issue.

This one went faster, and Barney brought the group to an agreement in a couple of minutes.

Abruptly, I realized that these might be the final negotiations over the financial reform bill, including the consumer agency. Sure, it was always possible that we could push amendments through later on, but this would be the main engine chugging forward. We had to get all the right pieces on *this* train. My heart started pounding. It was all going so fast.

Barney was already on to the third problem. Minutes later, he declared that this issue was resolved as well.

Then Barney looked around. "Good. I think we're ready to go. Does anyone else have anything?"

My mind was racing. This wasn't a battleground; everyone in the room was on the same side, and we were all fighting to help working people. What if we missed something?

"Anything?" Barney was getting out of his chair.

And suddenly I remembered a key issue. "Wait!" I shouted it louder than I had intended; I think I startled some congressmen. "What about credit reporting?" I asked.

Barney looked sharply at me and sat back in his chair. "What *about* credit reporting?"

Credit-reporting agencies determine people's credit scores. These scores become a key factor in what people end up paying for mortgages, credit cards, and the like. In some cases, employers even use credit reports to make hiring decisions, so bad credit can block someone from getting a much-needed job. But studies had shown that credit reports were loaded with errors. Some experts believed that the credit-reporting companies weren't making the corrections required by law, and this caused a lot of trouble for a lot of families—and no federal agency was keeping a close eye on the credit-reporting companies.

Barney got right to the point: "What do you want to do about this?"

I said, "Make sure the new agency has the power to oversee the credit-reporting companies."

Barney thought for about five seconds, then said, "That makes sense. Anyone have a problem with that?"

Everyone murmured no, and Barney said, "Done."

The staffers in the outer horseshoe scribbled on their pads.

Barney looked straight at me and said, "Anything else?"

I tried to think. Had we left out anything? Did the agency need something more to do its job? If I forgot something important during those few seconds, I might end up cursing myself for years to come. I chewed on my lip for a minute, then took a deep breath.

"Nope. That's it."

"Good," Barney said. "Let's go."

Everyone hurried out of the room, off to meetings or hearings. For a minute, I sat still, absorbing what had just happened. I had always been content to coach people—to offer ideas or warnings—in the hope that they would fight the good fight behind closed doors. But my worldview had just shifted. I had seen firsthand what it meant to be in the room when the law gets negotiated.

The part I'd asked for stayed in the bill through the House version and through the Senate version and was signed into law. After that meeting, I knew that if we got the agency, there would be a watchdog keeping an eye on the credit agencies to make sure they followed the law. I loved it.

As the House version of the financial reform bill came together, Barney was everywhere and did everything. He negotiated every part of the bill, meeting with stakeholders and reluctant members of Congress from before dawn until long after dark. He worked out deals among his colleagues in the House and Senate; he hashed out compromises with the White House. He cajoled and badgered and cut deals, and ultimately he nailed down the key pieces needed to make the consumer agency work. Barney was amazing.

In the final flurry of negotiations that took place that fall, one assault on the consumer agency came on swiftly, and Barney and the consumer advocates couldn't beat it back. Car dealers wanted their auto loans to be exempt from the agency's oversight. I immediately remembered Jason and how he'd been cheated. The thought of allowing that to happen again (and again and again) to other people made me want to smash my fist through a wall. But there were car dealers in every congressional district in the country, and they were riled up about the agency. Once the car dealers started calling Washington, members of Congress started caving, one after another. Barney did everything he could to fight them off, but in the end, the car dealers got their way.

The consumer agency was a little battle-scarred, but the important provisions were all there. The agency had survived—strong and independent. And in December 2009, Barney steered the financial reform bill through the House of Representatives.

Now all that remained was to get the bill through the Senate.

Death in Committee

It was Friday morning, January 15, 2010, and the calls started coming in early. I was at home, up early to work out on the treadmill in the basement, and I was still huffing and puffing when the phone rang the first time.

Had I seen this morning's *Wall Street Journal*? The rumors were flying on Capitol Hill: The consumer agency wasn't going to make it. In an effort to move the larger financial reform bill forward, Senator Dodd would trade it off. There might be some face-saving attempt to set up a new consumer protection department somewhere else in the government, but there would be no strong, independent agency with the authority to get much done. The insiders sent the word out: Too bad. So sorry. It was a good idea, but unless the agency was dropped from the reform bill, the whole package of legislation would fail. Better to toss the consumer agency overboard and get the other reforms through.

I listened. This was it: the consumer agency was dead.

All the families who had been cheated by the big banks and the credit card companies. All the hard work by Barney, the consumer groups, Heather, Dan, the president. All that knocking on doors and all those meetings. And now it was coming to an end.

I asked if there would be a vote—even a losing vote—but the answer, apparently, was no. The death wouldn't be a public execution. Instead, the Senate Banking Committee would propose a financial reform bill with no consumer agency. No one in the Senate—not a single Democrat or a single Republican—would ever have to vote against the agency. Instead, it would just be suffocated quietly in its crib. No one would ever know exactly who had killed it, or why.

So I asked my last question: When? How long before the locked-in version of the bill would be introduced in the Senate Banking Committee, with or without the consumer agency?

Best estimate: three weeks. The deal wasn't finalized, and there were a lot of moving pieces that still needed to be worked out.

I called Dan. "We've got three weeks."

Blood and Teeth on the Floor

The way I saw it, we had nothing to lose. I didn't want a job in the Capitol, so what did I care if I ticked off a lot of people in Washington? This was our last chance to get this agency into law. If we lost now, we lost forever.

We had very little information about what had led to the latest assault on the agency, but we did know one thing: The Senate did *not* want a tough vote on this issue. Dan explained what that meant: The consumer agency was popular, and, to a lot of senators, a vote on the new agency meant having to choose between angering the public and angering the banks—and they didn't want to anger either. They preferred a quiet and slightly mysterious death.

So I figured: Too bad. Too *damn* bad. If a bunch of senators were going to pick the banks over families, then the American public had a right to know. And if we didn't win, we could at least make one hell of a stink.

Word of the agency's fate got around fast, and the consumer groups were as fired up as I was. No one talked about quitting. The nonprofits doubled down on their efforts. E-mail campaigns and rallies erupted across the country. Progressive bloggers joined the fight. Some of the state attorneys general weighed in, including the attorney general from Ohio, a guy named Rich Cordray.

Within a matter of days, the bad news got worse. On January 19, Massachusetts held a special election to fill the vacancy left by Ted Kennedy's death.

The Tea Party was in full throat, decrying all the ways they believed Washington had failed. A smiling, energetic National Guardsman named Scott Brown had waged a creative campaign, and once he proved that he might be able to seize the seat that had been held by the Liberal Lion and put it in Republican hands, Tea Party money poured in faster than he could spend it. Brown rode a wave of national anger, and on Election Day, that wave carried him to the Senate.

Brown's victory ended the Democrats' sixty-vote majority in the Senate, giving a newly energized Republican Party the leverage to block—or at least to rewrite—legislation they did not like. To those of us fighting for the consumer agency, it looked like another nail in the coffin.

Heather asked me to talk to as many people as I could. Conference calls, meetings, interviews with all kinds of media—I tried everything. I wrote an op-ed for the *Wall Street Journal*. I met with consumer groups and congressional aides. I showed up on *The Rachel Maddow Show* and *Morning Joe*. I went back on Jon Stewart's show, and this time I didn't throw up. I talked about the agency, and Jon said he'd like to make out with me. (All in good fun, of course—he knew Bruce was backstage.) Okay, it was getting a little crazy.

But to me the issue was simple: Banks versus families.

And the request was reasonable: A public vote.

Three weeks stretched into four and then to five, six, and seven. The pressure from the consumer groups seemed to be working. New rumors started flying. The agency's heartbeat was faint, but reports of its death now seemed premature.

The lobbyists bore down. Plan A: Kill the agency. Plan B: Maim it so that it won't interfere with the big banks' business plans. They attacked the whole idea of the agency, but they also went after the agency's structure, trying to ensure that it would be independent in name only. The lobbyists' message was clear: If we have to, we'll let the politicians have their show agency, but we'll cripple it so that it'll never be able to get anything done.

By now, this was a pitched battle. AFR launched a television ad in Montana targeting a recalcitrant senator. There was a protest at the Wells Fargo annual shareholder meeting, and rallies were held in Kansas City and Denver and Chicago. Petitions appeared online, and newspapers across the country published editorials and op-eds about the agency.

In early March, Hollywood weighed in. Composer Hans Zimmer and writer-director James Brooks wanted to give the agency more public attention. The result was the first ever reunion of all the stars who had played presidents on *Saturday Night Live*. Ron Howard directed, and Will Farrell, Dana Carvey, Chevy Chase, Dan Aykroyd, Darrell Hammond, and Fred Armisen were all in great form as they played presidents from Ford through Obama. The ersatz former presidents urged Obama to "grow a pair" and fight for the consumer agency. Jim Carrey delivered the knockout punch, starring as the ghost of Ronald Reagan and strutting around the set with an oversize pair of steel balls clanking in his pants. Produced for the website Funny or Die, the video got millions of hits and some great news coverage.

Meanwhile, Senator Dodd went on *Hardball with Chris Matthews* and argued in favor of a strong consumer agency. The same day, we heard puzzling reports that Dodd was trying to water down the agency. But the Senate Banking Committee doors were firmly locked, and I was on the outside. I didn't know what the Senate would do.

I continued talking to the media whenever possible, and that spring, the *Huffington Post* asked me about some of the proposals to gut the agency. Was I willing to accept a shell of an agency?

In the bluntest possible terms, I said no. "My first choice is a strong consumer agency. My second choice is no agency at all and plenty of blood and teeth left on the floor. . . . My 99th choice is some mouthful of mush that doesn't get the job done." I said that we should either stand and fight for something worthwhile or go get honest work somewhere else. I wanted nothing to do with a watchdog that could do nothing but whimper.

And then, in mid-March, Senator Dodd delivered a financial reform bill that included a strong, independent consumer agency, and he shepherded it through the Banking Committee and on to the full Senate. The giant banks had tried mightily to stop us, but they had failed. The agency would have the powers and the funding it would need to make a real difference. A coalition of consumer advocates and impassioned citizens—helped out by some very funny actors—was on the verge of beating back the best-funded lobby ever assembled. It was a good day for the American people and a good day for democracy.

When Bruce and I went to the Shack for clams and beer this time, it was to celebrate.

One Last Big Giveaway

Life doesn't stop for politics, and the spring of 2010 was no exception. Our son-in-law called to say that his younger brother was getting married. It was time for the family—all the family—to gather in India to celebrate.

Just before we took off, Amelia made a big announcement: She was pregnant again. Bruce and I would have a third grandchild.

I absorbed the news with a mix of delight and worry. I was (and am) crazy about my two granddaughters. For nearly nine years, I had flown to Los Angeles as often as I could—sometimes for a weekend and sometimes for longer—so that I could be part of their lives. Now a new grandchild was coming, and between COP, fighting for financial reform, and teaching at Harvard, I was stretched thin. I wanted to spend a lot of time with this newest member of our family, but I worried that I couldn't.

When we arrived in India, it was hot—really hot. Rolling blackouts meant that air-conditioning was hit or miss, and the power went out most afternoons. But for Bruce and me, the wedding was a complete delight. It was a three-day affair, with singing and parties and visits from the Tyagi clan, which stretched all over northern India. For a little while I left Washington behind and marveled over the bride and giggled with my granddaughters. It was glorious.

Back in Washington, there was more pain to come. After the financial reform bill passed the Senate, it was the job of a conference committee to iron out the differences between the House and Senate versions. Then the bill would go back to the House and the Senate for a final vote.

The Democrats had lost their sixty-seat majority in January, and now the bill needed the support of Massachusetts's newest senator, Republican Scott Brown. Suddenly the senator found himself sitting in the catbird seat. Wasting no time, he threatened to hold up the financial bill unless the Democrats agreed to reopen the nearly completed package to add one more provision: a financial break for the big banks.

Ever since the United States began writing rules for financial institutions, the banks have always paid the costs of regulation. The price tag for enforcing the new bank reforms was estimated to be about $19 billion, and the current version of the reform bill specifically said that the biggest financial institutions would pay for it.

Now Senator Brown threatened to hold up the bill unless that provision was changed. He insisted that the taxpayers, not the big banks, pick up the tab. Barney Frank was furious, but he didn't have much choice: this last change was the price of making financial reform a reality. The deal was cut, the final bill was passed by the both the House and the Senate, and the legislation was sent to the president for his signature.

A Pen to Remember

The White House invited me to the signing ceremony, which was set for July 21, 2010. The law was named the Dodd–Frank Act, after its sponsors in the Senate and the House.

That morning it was Washington hot—steamy, sticky, and nasty. The ceremony was to be held at the Ronald Reagan Building in an amphitheater that could seat more than six hundred people. I wanted to go, but on that same morning, I was scheduled to testify at another Senate hearing as the representative for COP. It seemed all but certain that the hearing would last long past the scheduled time for the signing ceremony, so I figured I'd just have to miss it. Serving as the chair of COP was my job.

At the last minute, I got permission to testify first and then leave the hearing. If I ran, I might make the ceremony just in time—and run is exactly what I did.

For any event involving the president, there's a point at which the doors are closed, security is locked in place, and that's it, no one else gets in. But Senator Durbin, who had also been invited to the signing, promised he would get me there. The minute I finished testifying, I dashed out of the hearing room and sprinted down the hall with one of Durbin's aides. We ran outside and jumped into a black SUV with the senator. Racing along one street and another, we wheeled into the Reagan Building, bailed out of the car and sprinted to the door just ahead of the final lockdown. What a way to start a party!

At the signing ceremony I was seated in the front row, tucked in next to the legendary former Federal Reserve chairman Paul Volcker. Huge cheers greeted President Obama when he took the stage. Everyone was on their feet, clapping and shouting. The president had supported financial reform right from the start, and this was his triumph.

Woo-hoo! The American people had won a great victory. Too bad fireworks weren't permitted inside the auditorium.

A week or so later, I got a package in the mail. Inside was a note from the president, and it was accompanied by a pen. It was one of the pens he had used to sign the consumer agency into law.

David's Slingshot

The battle had lasted for more than a year, but this time David thwacked Goliath hard.

From the beginning, the odds had been stacked so completely against us that I doubt Las Vegas would have given anyone a betting line. The big banks were organized and committed. They had PR people, lawyers, lobbyists, researchers, and consultants galore. They presented a united front—virtually no public quarrels or dramatic defections. The financial services industry assembled the best lobbying force money could buy, and it was reported that they ultimately spent more than *$500 million* on lobbying and campaign contributions during their drive to kill the reform bill.

The fight over the consumer agency was a battle between the people and rich and powerful corporations. The big banks didn't want this agency. They saw it as a direct threat, and their motivation for trying to kill it was simple: They wanted to run their businesses without a watchdog barking at them.

By the usual rules of Washington, the powerful banks should have beaten the people so easily and so thoroughly that the consumer agency would be nothing more than a tiny grease spot on the trouser cuff of a $1,000-an-hour lobbyist.

So how did the people win? There were individual heroes, like the law-makers who had championed the idea when no one thought it had a prayer of becoming law—Congressmen Brad Miller and Bill Delahunt and Sen-ators Ted Kennedy, Dick Durbin, and Chuck Schumer. When it came time to turn the concept into actual legislation, Barney Frank and Chris Dodd got down in the trenches to twist arms and cut deals and find a way to keep the agency alive. There were also behind-the-scenes heroes, like Michael Barr and Eric Stein, who spent endless hours drafting, negotiat-ing, and redrafting strong language. And there were many champions like Travis Plunkett at Consumer Federation of America and Ed Mier-zwinski at PIRG, consumer advocates who have dedicated their lives to fighting for the American people.

But in the end, I think most of the credit for this win goes to the American people. Sometimes they were organized—through nonprofit groups and unions and coalitions. Sometimes they were a little disorga-nized, as single voices burst forth in funny videos and online blogs and old-fashioned letters to the editor. But organized or not, the people made themselves heard.

I also believe that the people who worked on the consumer side got smarter. When the moment to begin the fight arrived, people moved. There was no hesitation or hanging back. Instead, longtime advocates and first-time volunteers jumped in and fought like there would be no tomorrow. They settled on One Big Idea for protecting consumers. They organized early, and they made every nickel count. They crowd-sourced and tweeted and posted on Facebook. They harnessed volunteers, from high school kids to Hollywood stars. They didn't allow their efforts to get too complicated, and they stayed clear on what they were fighting for. Most of all, even when the agency was reported dead and the big banks declared victory, nobody gave up.

And they harnessed the energy that swept the nation that year. The financial crisis had rocked this country to its core, and people were furi-ous. They were hungry for a change that didn't smack of cozy deals for insiders, a change that cleaned up at least one little corner of the world. It was a mad-as-hell moment, and that meant change was possible.

Our democracy has been beaten up pretty badly. The political influence enjoyed by big-bank CEOs and their high-priced lobbyists is shameful. When people talk to me about how broken Washington is, I really can't argue with them: it's a mess, and too often its priorities are all wrong. But I hope—I fervently hope—people won't give up.

Because this time, when the people fought an against-all-odds battle, democracy worked. It was a little dented and scratched, but it worked.

5 | An Agency for the People

THE DAY AFTER the president signed Dodd–Frank and the consumer agency into law, I was on a plane again, this time to Los Angeles.

A few weeks earlier, Amelia and Sushil had called with the results of a sonogram—it's a boy! But only days after that happy call, they rushed to the emergency room when Amelia went into early labor. The doctors barely managed to stop her contractions, and Amelia was ordered on strict bed rest for the duration of her pregnancy. The baby wasn't due until November, meaning she would have to spend *five months* on bed rest.

Each day was a victory, as the tiny baby got a little stronger before he made his appearance in the world. But each day was also touch and go, and for much of the summer Amelia was in and out of the hospital. Now Bruce and I were back in Los Angeles, and it was scary to see Amelia flat on her back in bed, strapped to monitors and barely allowed to move.

Amelia is a lot like me—she doesn't embrace the idea of "rest" very well—so this long confinement felt like punishment. The girls were rattled, struggling to understand why their mother was spending every day in bed. I wanted to be with all of them, caring for my granddaughters and holding Amelia's hand.

The minute our plane touched down, I called Amelia. Everything was the same. My next call was to Dan, who said that the press was reporting that an open letter had just gone to the White House, urging President Obama to nominate me as the director of the brand-new Consumer Financial Protection Bureau. The letter was signed by fifty-seven members of the

House and eleven senators. It was accompanied by a petition that had already been signed by 140,000 people, all supporting me for the job.

Wow: that seemed like a lot of people to even know the name of a new government agency, let alone sign a petition about who ought to be its director. I felt deeply touched that so many people were invested in this agency and that they would trust me to take on this extraordinary job.

During the months I fought for the consumer agency's creation, I spent almost no time thinking about actually running it. Occasionally, someone would ask me if I wanted the job, but I brushed it off. For a year and a half, I'd been juggling teaching, chairing COP, and doing everything possible to help get the agency passed into law. I didn't want to think about another job. Now the agency was law, and I needed to get to Los Angeles to be with family.

But my mind was already racing. Somewhere in the middle of fighting for the agency, sometime after the zillionth explanation of what the agency could do, I had gotten really fired up about *doing* it. The director of this new agency would have the chance to get it off to the right start, to set the priorities and to build a structure that would make this thing work. We had fought hard for an agency that would help keep people from getting cheated. The agency could fundamentally change the market for consumer credit. It could forever banish a profit model that was based on tricking people. In time, it could help establish a marketplace that really worked, one where it would be easy to compare products and get the best deal. It might help people like Flora, who fell prey to that nice mortgage broker, or Mr. Estrada and his family, who were shoved out of their home in a matter of weeks. The potential was huge, but the agency needed a strong start.

A strong director could build a strong agency, and now the president would choose someone for the job. The question was: Who?

A Cheerleader?

I think the president was in a bind. (Well, he was in *another* bind; this was hardly his first.) No matter whose name he put forward, he would make somebody unhappy.

On the one hand, he had a petition from a bunch of lawmakers— along with 140,000 people—asking him to pick me. Several media outlets weighed in. A *New York Times* editorial said he should nominate me precisely because the banks would oppose me. Congressman Barney Frank jumped in with both feet (does Barney jump in any other way?) and urged the president to appoint me. A rap video made the rounds starring a supercool-looking guy in cowboy duds waving a lasso and rapping, "Sheriff Warren, she's what we need, yo."

On the other hand, the banks hated the idea that I might become the agency's director, and many of the politicians who had fought against the CFPB were also adamantly opposed to the notion. Republican senator Richard Shelby from Alabama thundered: "I would hope she's not confirmable. I would not support Warren. . . . This is a power grab."

Then Senator Chris Dodd, a lifelong Democrat whose name was at the top of the Dodd–Frank Act, threw cold water on the nomination. He questioned whether I had the administrative skills to manage the agency; he also declared that the agency needed someone who could be confirmed quickly and that I would be hard to confirm. This surprised me—and it hurt, too.

Of course, Senator Dodd had put his finger on an important point. The president would nominate the director of the CFPB, but the position would require approval by the Senate. If enough of the senators didn't like his choice, they could prevent the president's nominee from ever coming up for a vote.

Reports also began to surface that Treasury secretary Tim Geithner opposed me for the role. This was not such a big surprise. Over the past year and a half, Secretary Geithner and I had disagreed—often quite publicly—about many aspects of the TARP bailout. But Geithner's opinion was critical. The law required that the new agency be operated from within the Treasury Department until the agency had a permanent director. That meant Geithner was himself in charge of the agency immediately after Dodd–Frank was enacted.

That summer, I had a string of conversations with the president's three senior advisors, Valerie Jarrett, Pete Rouse, and David Axelrod. They were always very thoughtful, and it was clear they genuinely wanted to give the agency the strongest possible start. But it was also clear that the White House was under tremendous pressure from a number of different directions. Ultimately, this would be the president's decision alone.

The push and pull in Washington reflected the debate outside. Like it or not, the nomination had become a symbol in the larger fight over financial reform, and I had become a political lightning rod. I would attract a lot of ire from the big banks, and the banks have lots of friends on Capitol Hill.

No doubt some people were also worried that I might be a little too independent or that I couldn't be trusted not to mouth off to the press. After all, I had called for "blood and teeth on the floor" during the Dodd–Frank battles—not the kind of rhetoric some people expect from a reputable agency director. There was also quite a bit of talk about whether Tim Geithner and I could get along. Nobody wanted internal discord that could somehow be embarrassing to the president.

And although no one said it directly, it was generally known that some of the president's advisors preferred to avoid confrontation with the big banks, and they weren't thrilled by the idea of an aggressive new leader for an aggressive new agency. Various alternative proposals began to float around the White House. Would I agree to be a part-time advisor to the new agency? What about becoming the agency's new public spokesperson while someone else made the real decisions?

One of the president's advisors even suggested that someone else be named director, while I could serve as "cheerleader" for the new agency. I assume that was meant as a metaphor, but I had to wonder: Cheerleader? Would the same suggestion have been made to a man in my position? I did not rush out to buy pom-poms.

The weeks went on, but nothing was resolved. According to one of his senior advisors, the president was "holding his cards close to his vest."

A Meeting in the Oval Office

In mid-August, I was invited to the Oval Office for a meeting. I had never seen the Oval Office except in pictures, so as soon as I stepped inside I wanted to take a minute to look around at one of the most famous rooms in the world. It was light, with lots of soft gold and pale colors. But all I had time for was a quick impression, because I couldn't stand and gawk. The president of the United States was talking to me.

"Is the agency really good?" the president asked. "*Really* good?"

He had swept me from the outer office into the Oval Office with a cheerful, "Elizabeth!" and a familiar hug, even though we had met only a handful of times before. He asked if I wanted something to drink or eat and then joked about the terrific White House kitchen and how he was like a movie-version president who was amazed—and tickled—to be able to order whatever food he wanted. But that took only seconds. Valerie Jarrett, the president's senior advisor and longtime friend, was the only other person in the meeting. She and I were barely inside the office when the president got serious. He wanted to know if the new consumer agency was strong enough to get the job done.

He held both my hands in his and scrutinized my face. I had the sense that he didn't really know what I would say back here behind closed doors. Would I praise the new agency or would I find fault?

"It's really good, Mr. President. It can do the job." I meant it.

The president visibly relaxed. Then he flashed his ten-thousand-kilowatt smile and maneuvered me over to the seating area—two couches facing each other, with a couple of upright chairs at the end. He took one of the chairs and motioned for me to sit on the couch nearest him. Valerie sat on the other couch.

The president started telling a story about getting a car some years earlier. I didn't catch the specifics, but he made fun of himself for not knowing all the details of the terms of the agreement he'd signed. And it seemed that even now, he was pretty irritated about how he had been treated. The story's punch line: As great as the new agency was, the president was still worried about the auto-dealer carve-out in the law and the people who might get hurt.

I was a little surprised; I figured this was the moment for a well-deserved victory lap. The president had every reason to feel good about what he'd achieved—getting the agency signed into law was a big win for him. Instead, he was lamenting the part he couldn't accomplish. I had to respect a man whose eyes were not on the political victory, but on the regular people whose lives would be touched by what he did.

Still, I knew what we'd been up against, and I knew that this agency was strong. "Mr. President, we got ninety-five percent of what we needed, and the agency will do a huge amount of good." I told him I thought this was a really, truly genuine victory.

He laughed and then turned to the business at hand. He opened with: "This isn't a job interview. You should head up the agency."

I could feel the "but" coming and so wasn't surprised when he said: But we have a real problem with the Republicans and the bankers. "You make them very nervous."

The bankers didn't want me, and since the Republicans now had forty-one seats in the Senate, they would likely filibuster my nomination so that I couldn't be confirmed as director. And that was that. Nominating me to head the agency was off the table.

But the president didn't talk about nominating anyone else, either. Instead, he suggested that I could serve in an unspecified interim position to help launch the agency, reporting to Secretary Geithner. But he didn't offer specifics on what my duties would be and what I'd be able to do.

I was uneasy with his proposal. I didn't know Secretary Geithner very well, and I figured he would do his best to set up a good agency. But he and I just didn't see banking the same way. I was worried that the secretary would pull one way and I would pull the other, and the agency would get caught in some no-man's-land in between, a sitting target for the big banks that still wanted to kill it.

The president and I went back and forth for a while but didn't come to any agreement. We stood up, and after a perfunctory hug, I was back in the hallway.

What's at Stake

Summer ended, and Bruce and I made our way home to Massachusetts for the start of classes. Amelia had another setback and returned to the hospital. In their continuing attempt to stop early labor, the doctors tried one medication after another. At one point, Amelia turned beet red from head to toe. As the days ticked by, the baby was still holding on, but just barely.

Meanwhile, the CFPB was just beginning to stir. A handful of employees inside the Department of the Treasury had begun to map out some of the agency's early infrastructure. It was good, thoughtful work, but only the beginning. The real shape and scope of the agency remained anyone's guess.

The struggle over who would launch the agency was at its core a debate about the agency's future. Would the agency be relatively passive and soon sink below the radar screen, a hopeful idea that faded away? Or would it be a vigorous example of how government *can* work? This was a rare opportunity to build a new agency from the ground up, one that wouldn't have a hidebound bureaucracy or an entrenched "serve the banks" culture. Those who launched the CFPB would have a chance to build a twenty-first-century watchdog—a watchdog that was lean and tough, knew exactly what its mission was, and used powerful new tools to make itself effective. But the agency couldn't simply promise to be and do all these things. The agency had to deliver.

Deliver. That meant cracking down on the scams that target poor neighborhoods. Stopping the little tricks—bank fees that nibble $5 here and $20 there. Stopping the big tricks—mortgages that zoom from unbelievably low monthly payments to unbelievably high monthly payments. Making sure that families going through foreclosure are treated fairly and honestly. Making credit agreements simpler, so comparison shopping would be possible. The list was long.

One thing about the agency's future was clear: It would be under attack from the get-go. The big banks had lost the fight over the CFPB, but they still had plenty of friends on Capitol Hill. If the agency was successful, it would put an end to tricks and traps that had produced some very fat profits. No one doubted that the big banks would try to cripple the agency if they could.

So the question was: What's the right way to set up an agency that will be under constant attack? The usual answer in Washington: Go slowly. Tread carefully. Don't offend anyone.

Not me. I thought the agency should go fast and fight hard right from the beginning. (Surprise, right?) The banks wouldn't hesitate to attack us aggressively in the battles to come, and I figured that nobody wins this sort of fight by worrying too much about stepping on toes. I believed that if people saw what the CFPB could do—if millions of consumers were actually helped—then people would keep fighting for it.

Trust the President

In early September, I was invited back to Washington for a second meeting with the president.

While he finished up a long call, I sat in the tiny waiting area. This time he walked me through the Oval Office and suggested we sit outside. He said there wouldn't be many more summer days, so we should enjoy the weather while it lasted.

"Enjoy" was a relative term, because it was hot—really hot—and humid. The president wore a white shirt with the sleeves rolled back, and he looked relaxed and cool. I had dressed for air-conditioning, and after two minutes outside, I probably looked as if I were going to burst into flames. I wore a blazer with a shell underneath, but the shell was skimpy enough that I didn't feel right about shedding my jacket in front of the leader of the free world. Everything I was wearing felt glued to my body.

It was just the two of us, sitting at a little outdoor table. Once again, I didn't have much chance to look around, but the space was tightly enclosed by dense hedges and felt small—and there was no breeze at all. The president described it as a hidden retreat. I thought it felt like a green version of hell.

The president dived straight in. He still wanted me to help set up the agency. I would work directly for Tim Geithner, and he wouldn't offer any guarantees about what my specific role would be or how long I'd be around to do it. And he gave no indication that he'd be willing to nominate me for permanent director in the future.

I said no.

We talked about the need for a strong agency and the inevitable opposition to it, and we talked about what the agency's first initiatives might be. But we always circled back to the same question. Would he offer me a job that was all show, or would he give me a job that would allow me to really get something done?

The president was frustrated. I was hot. We pushed back and forth for an hour. Twice his assistant came out to remind him about his next meeting.

Finally he said: "You're jamming me, Elizabeth." He urged me not to overplay my hand.

Got it.

Our conversation was going nowhere—this just wasn't going to work. Then he said: "Sometimes you have to trust the president. Let me work this out." He pronounced each word separately: "Let—me—work—this—out."

Leaning toward me across the little table, he promised that I would have all the tools I needed to get the job done and get this agency off the ground. He reminded me that he wanted the agency to be successful, that it was an important part of his legacy. Then he said, "Trust me."

And there it was. He hadn't said he would nominate me for the directorship, and he'd made no specific commitments about the responsibility I'd have.

But he was the man who had stood behind the agency throughout the Dodd–Frank negotiations when others wanted to kill it. He was the man who had signed the agency into law. He was the man who worried about what family might get cheated next.

I thought about what he said: all the tools I needed. That wasn't very specific, but "all the tools" was in the right direction. Besides, with the Republicans and the big banks on the attack, the president was the best hope the American people had.

"All right," I replied. "I'll trust you on this."

Put Your Seatbelt On

In the end, the president actually offered me two jobs. I was named special advisor to the secretary of the Treasury on the Consumer Financial Protection Bureau *and* assistant to the president. The title was a mouthful, but the "assistant to the president" designation was also held by some very senior people who sat nearest the Oval Office, and it was an important signal to the world that the president would back the new agency's work.

I understood that this was only a temporary role, although I didn't know when it would end—or how it would end. But right now, it didn't matter. I would get to help launch the agency.

After we reached a deal, I resigned from my position on the COP. I also requested a leave of absence from Harvard. Since I wanted to be at the new agency 24/7, Bruce said he would (once again) be a commuter. (Thank you, sweetie.) Washington would now be home base for Otis and me, while Bruce would fly back and forth each week.

We needed a place to live in Washington, immediately. There was no time for house hunting—heck, things were moving so fast that I felt like there was no time to brush my teeth. Someone told us about a vacant apartment that was within walking distance of the Treasury Building, and the landlord would allow us to bring Otis. Thankfully, my old friend from the bankruptcy wars, Brady Williamson, happened to be in Washington that week, so he took a look and called with a report. "Um, the living room is nice, but the stove looks weird. . . ."

Weird stove and all, we rented the apartment sight unseen.

I flew to Washington, and on Thursday, September 16, 2010, Bruce loaded up the car with our things, and he and Otis made the eight-hour drive down to D.C. (I suspect they made it in seven hours. I'm pretty sure Bruce drives a lot faster when I'm not in the car, but that's one of those "don't ask, don't tell" things in our marriage.)

On Friday, Bruce and I went to the White House for the public announcement of my new role. Amelia was still confined to bed, and Sushil couldn't leave her. Alex was in the middle of a work crisis, and he wanted to stay in Los Angeles in case Amelia needed extra help, so there were no children or grandchildren to turn it into an occasion.

Right after lunchtime, there we were in the Oval Office, just the president, Tim Geithner, and me. The president said he was sure we'd all get along fine. Secretary Geithner and I both smiled uncertainly. Gesturing to the door that opened onto the Rose Garden, where a medium-size throng of reporters and photographers waited, the president explained that the three of us would step outside together. Then he paused and said, "Well, not all at once. This isn't a Three Stooges routine." We laughed and then started into a round of Three Stooges gags. By any objective measure, I'm sure we were all pretty lame, but I was impressed. The president and the secretary knew a lot of Moe, Larry, and Curly routines. Surely the country was in good hands.

The announcement went smoothly, followed by a quick swearing in.

Saturday was another whirlwind day. No more policy discussions and welcome meetings; it was time to go shopping. Off to Target, Staples, and a couple of furniture stores for bar stools, a reading lamp, dishes—I can't remember everything we bought, but I think Bruce and I clocked fourteen straight hours of shopping. At ten that night, just after snagging a desk and chair, we celebrated over pancakes at an IHOP somewhere in Maryland.

I spent a lot of time on administrative duties during my first days on the job. I got fingerprinted—electronically and in ink, twice each way on each finger of both hands. I was also photographed, briefed on security, lectured about dozens of forms I needed to fill out, issued a badge, and given a flu shot.

During my days at COP, I'd attended a couple of meetings in the Treasury Building, but now I had my own office, and I had a chance to wander around a bit. My office was beautiful, unlike anything I'd ever worked in before. Like the other Treasury officials, I had an office with a high ceiling, a fireplace, antique furniture, and giant windows that faced a statue of Alexander Hamilton. It felt a little like a movie set. If there hadn't been so much work to do, it would have been a great place for a tea party with my granddaughters.

Like the offices in many other monumental old buildings, these offices weren't built for the modern era. My assistant, Alyssa Martin, sat in a tiny carved-out space at the front of my office. Alyssa was just twenty-two, and though she had been slated to start her first year at Harvard Law School that fall, she postponed school for a year when I asked her to come with me to Washington.

The skeletal staff that Treasury had already begun assembling for the agency was scattered in offices that had been chopped out of other spaces. Many of these people would go back to their regular Treasury jobs in the coming weeks, but not all. As we got under way, Eric Stein, who had poured zillions of hours into negotiating the line-by-line drafting of the statute creating the consumer agency, made the shift from Treasury to help launch the new agency. Wally Adeyemo, who had an amazing talent for getting things done at Treasury, now took on the role of chief of staff for the baby agency. I quickly figured out that he was indispensable.

On my first day on the job, Secretary Geithner asked me out to lunch. When I showed up in his office, he said, "I have a present for you." He held out a cop's hat. Perfect!

Heading for a restaurant that he said was one of his favorites, we bounced along in the backseat of an SUV driven—very fast—by one of his security guys. I had put on my seat belt before the car pulled out of the Treasury encampment, but as we sped along I noticed that the secretary was still unbelted. Like a bossy third-grade teacher, I looked at him and said, "Put on your seat belt, Mr. Secretary."

Like a naughty kid, he looked back and said, "I don't have to."

He explained with obvious pride that the car was bulletproof and that the driver and his partner were both highly trained and carried big guns. "We're safe here," he said in a tone meant to end the conversation.

"What? Are you kidding?" I said. "What good is that if we get hit and this thing turns over a few times and you smash your head against that great bulletproof window?" I think I may have raised my voice a little.

He didn't put on his seat belt all the way to the restaurant.

We sat at a table in the back, and while we ate, we debated a number of issues involving markets, market failures, and the role of government. More than once, he said he was surprised that I believed so strongly in markets. More than once, I emphasized that markets are great—but only if there really is a level playing field where both sellers and their customers understand the terms of the deal.

On the drive back to the office, Secretary Geithner put on his seat belt.

Late in the day, several Treasury lawyers came to call. This session started like all the other get-to-know-you meetings I'd had that day. But the lawyers were all carrying file folders, which put me on alert. No one makes a social call carrying a file folder.

After we shook hands all around and everyone was seated, one of the lawyers said he had some bad news. No one made eye contact with me. Reluctantly, a second lawyer explained that the law had a little glitch. With that, my visitors reached into their file folders and pulled out photocopies of a single page from the long Dodd–Frank Act. It seemed there was a one-word error: a provision setting up the consumer agency referred to powers under this "subtitle" rather than powers under this "title."

Huh. It was just one word, yet the difference was huge.

The statutory language was a tangle, but using the wrong word in this sentence meant that the new agency would likely get its full powers only after a director was confirmed by the Senate (or, as we eventually figured out, appointed by the president during a congressional recess). The Department of the Treasury had some ability to get the agency moving before there was a director, but its power would be limited.

One little word. I had one little thought: Oh crap.

The lawyers handed me a copy, and I read the language again and again. Could it be interpreted another way? Apparently not.

Okay, but could the mistake be corrected by getting Congress to provide a technical fix? Nope. Evidently, someone had already quietly reached out to friends in Congress to see if a fix might be possible, but everyone agreed that the politics made it impossible to correct the error.

And the final question: How had this happened? The lawyers said they didn't know. I pushed a little, but at this point it didn't really matter. The bill was hundreds of pages long, and as different staffers and committees negotiated over this sentence and that paragraph, the text of the legislation had probably gone through thousands of revisions. Mistakes happen, and what was done was done. Now we had to live with it.

Bruce was teaching classes that week, so he had already gone back to Massachusetts. I let myself into the apartment late at night. I checked in by phone with Amelia and Sushil, as I did every day. She was still flat on her back in bed. One more day had come and gone, and the baby had grown just a little bigger and a little stronger. Amelia's due date was now two months away. I imagined the tiny baby who would soon be born, and I said one more silent prayer, asking that he wait just a little longer before making his appearance.

Will You Behave Yourself?

Less than two weeks after starting my new job, I was scheduled to speak to the Financial Services Roundtable, a group of CEOs of big-deal banks, mortgage companies, and the like. They were the titans behind the lobbyists, the ones who had fought tooth and nail against the agency. My sweet husband thought I was nuts to show up at a place where a posse of CEOs would be armed with knives and forks.

But the director of the Roundtable was Steve Bartlett, a former congressman who was cheerful, charming, and committed to the idea that in politics, nothing is permanent, not even enemies. I appreciated Steve's invitation, and I welcomed the chance to talk with anyone about the new agency, including CEOs of big banks. Besides, it was a chance to make the argument that the new agency was good for competition—and good for banks that wanted to make their money from selling honest products.

Luckily, Elizabeth Vale came with me. After a successful career in banking, Elizabeth had served the president by doing extraordinary work in business outreach. She agreed to leave her very cool job in the White House to help us launch the new agency, and she was now my guide in what felt like a trip to a foreign land.

The dinner was held in a huge ballroom filled with dinner tables laden with elaborate centerpieces, heavy linens, multiple wineglasses, and little presents wrapped with fancy paper. I was seated next to Jamie Dimon, the famous CEO of JPMorgan Chase.

Dimon is a sturdy man, solidly built and supremely self-confident. I'd never met him in person, but I'd already taken him on by name in a *Wall Street Journal* op-ed. I'd quoted his remark that a financial crisis every five to seven years was inevitable and given my own blunt assessment: He was wrong. The real cause of the crash was not some inevitable cycle; this crash was the direct consequence of years of deliberate deregulation and the resulting dangerous actions of the big banks. I'd repeated this view multiple times, saying that we needed a cop on the beat to make sure that a crash didn't happen again.

I wondered if Dimon would argue with me over the salad course, but he didn't. In fact, there were no arguments of any sort. Dimon did most of the talking, complaining loudly about how painful it was for him to be a Democrat when the Democrats were trying to regulate the banks. He talked about his many, many conversations with the president and offered details about the advice he had repeatedly given him.

After a while, our host stood up, thanked everyone, noted a few of the Roundtable's accomplishments, and then turned to the next item on the agenda. He started by calling out table one, recognizing the member of Congress seated with a group of banking CEOs. A congressman stood up, and everyone applauded. He must be really close to people in the banking industry, I thought. Then it was on to table two. The host announced the name and home state of another member of Congress, the congressman stood and waved, and everyone applauded. And on it went. I was amazed by how many tables in the huge ballroom had at least one senator or representative sitting with the CEOs.

That evening was not the first time the Roundtable had found a way to make nice to members of Congress. Over the preceding decade, the financial industry had spent more than $2 billion in political contributions. And the Roundtable itself had spent more than $70 million on lobbying just to make sure their friends knew where they stood on each detail of banking regulation.

I don't remember exactly which senators and representatives were there that night, but I do recall being surprised by who was there and how long they stayed. I'd been to a few Washington dinners by this point—mostly dinners honoring consumer advocates—and sometimes a member of Congress made a quick in-and-out appearance. But I'd never seen anything like this.

All those tables and all those lawmakers. Two hours of dinner and conversation. That's a lot of access.

When it was finally time for my speech, the Roundtable's president smiled mischievously and said that since I was the scheduled speaker, the knives had been removed from the table settings.

I'm not sure if anyone laughed, but at least now Bruce would have no reason to worry about the knives.

In my speech, I went back to what Joseph Kennedy Sr. had said in the 1930s after he was sworn in to set up the brand new Securities and Exchange Commission during the darkest hours of the Great Depression:

> Everybody says that what business needs is confidence. I agree. Confidence that if business does the right thing it will be protected and given a chance to live, make profits and grow, helping itself and helping the country.

Standing before all those bankers and all those people from Congress, I said I believed Joe Kennedy had it exactly right. I underlined his point with my own: "Good regulations create an opportunity for good businesses to thrive."

Polite applause, and soon the dinner was over. On the way out, one banker from the Midwest said to me, "We just want to know if you are going to behave yourself."

I smiled and didn't say anything.

Arizona Sunset or Terra Cotta?

My first few weeks on the job were loaded with meetings, job interviews, speeches, and more meetings.

In addition to Alyssa, I had brought along three new people to help me get started. Dan Geldon shifted jobs yet again—this was now his fourth job in two years—to become my senior advisor, which meant that he helped set priorities, oversaw our media and legislative affairs work, worked on policy issues, and basically did whatever else needed doing.

Raj Date had established a successful career in banking, but then he did something that was considered pretty unusual in the banking circles: He started a think tank and wrote long, technical papers about everything he thought was wrong with the banking system. During the previous months, he had also joined forces with the AFR to help fight for a strong consumer agency, and now Raj was going to set up our research and regulatory work. And Peter Jackson, who had done a great job handling press at COP, agreed to take on the same role for the new agency.

Right from the start, we were all working flat out. We would do interviews and meetings from early morning until late at night, then head back to our respective apartments and do our homework to get ready for the next day. We were drafting the agency's basic design—the architecture that would shape its work for decades. We met with other agency heads and with the consumer groups and financial institutions that would be most affected. I scheduled regular meetings with Secretary Geithner and his staff to keep them up-to-date on our progress.

As the CFPB began to take shape, there was a fair amount of press coverage, most of it about the new agency's work. But one tiny piece appeared in late October that took me by surprise.

NEW PAINT JOB—We also hear that while Warren is out west, her Treasury office is getting a makeover (Warren will have digs both at Treasury and the CFPB's L Street headquarters). That's something of a rarity for Treasury officials, who usually leave their offices as-is. There is much internal debate as to exactly what color it is that is going up on Warren's walls. One person called it "Arizona sunset," another "terra cotta."

A headline the next day took Treasury to task for the leak: ARE TREASURY'S KNIVES COMING OUT AGAINST ELIZABETH WARREN? The reporter called the item "petty." (You think?) But he also noted that there had been a series of nasty little items leaking from Treasury since I'd arrived, all aimed at painting me "as an ego-centric fluff-monger, not a serious policymaker." Oh, yuck.

I tried to think about how the article had come about. A Treasury employee had come by and offered to schedule my office for routine repainting; he showed Alyssa and me a book with some colors and we had picked one. The conversation was short, and I could barely remember it in the flurry of those early weeks.

After the story appeared, Secretary Geithner called. We didn't have a scheduled meeting, so this was a surprise. He was direct: I'm sorry about the story about painting your office.

I brushed it off, but the secretary was insistent. No, he said, he was really sorry. It was wrong.

He obviously had nothing to do with the article, but he knew that someone in his vast department was to blame. Treasury employed a lot of people, and the secretary couldn't possibly know what they were doing every minute of every day. Nonetheless, he told me there would never be another nasty leak about me while I was trying to do my job. He said, "I give you my word on that."

I knew Tim hadn't chosen me for this role. I knew I had been pushed on him by the president. And I had begun to understand that he could probably take me down with carefully placed traps and leaks if he wanted to. But when he gave me his promise, I believed him.

I don't know what Tim did, and we never spoke of it again, but I don't remember there ever being another nasty leak.

Welcome to the World, A-Mann

In late October, I was scheduled to give a lecture at Berkeley about the new agency. The day of the speech, I got the call I'd been waiting for.

Amelia was thirty-seven weeks pregnant, and the baby would wait no longer. Wonder of wonders: after all those months of worrying that he would be born prematurely and be too small to survive, when he came into the world he was chubby! Weighing in at a solid eight pounds six ounces, he had pudgy thighs and a round little tummy. I don't think I've ever been so delighted about a roll of fat in my entire life.

Bruce and I flew to Los Angeles the next day. We wrapped the baby in a pumpkin costume—what else would a chubby Halloween baby wear?—and took the girls out trick-or-treating.

I love Halloween—dressing up, trick-or-treating, handing candy out at the door. (Confession: I have a real weakness for Mounds.) One year Lavinia talked me into becoming "the Sparkle Queen," complete with a pink glitter wig—all so that I would complement her "Sparkle Princess" costume. (Fortunately, I believe all the relevant photos from that Halloween have been deleted.) I've also been a lost sheep for her Little Bo Peep. This year we dressed up as a rose (Lavinia), Cleopatra (Octavia), a pumpkin (tiny baby brother), the Mad Hatter (Bruce), and Robin Hood (me, tongue firmly in cheek).

The baby was named Atticus Mann Tyagi, after Bruce (Mann). Bruce didn't say much—that's just his way—but I could tell he was proud as punch. He and A-Mann were now a team.

Nothing Personal

As I settled into my new job, I embarked on another round of visits to Congress. I wasn't a political pro, but it didn't take a genius to figure out that a lot of people were gunning for the agency to fail. I figured it was a good idea to talk to anyone in Congress who was willing to meet with me.

The early conversations had one element in common: Behind closed doors, both Republicans and Democrats said they understood that the country's credit markets weren't working. No one disputed that too many people had gotten cheated—they just disagreed over the right response.

One meeting in particular stands out. Spencer Bachus had represented Alabama's Sixth Congressional District for nearly twenty years. He had a smooth southern accent and a thin smile. During the height of the financial crisis, he was privately briefed by top government officials. The news was bad: The economy was on the brink of collapse. The congressman's response? According to *60 Minutes,* he shorted the market, and in a couple of days he nearly doubled his money. And now he was the ranking Republican on the House Financial Services Committee, which meant that he was next in line to be chairman of the committee if his party took back the House in the November elections.

The congressman agreed to meet with me soon after I took the CFPB post. He spoke movingly about people who had been swindled; he really seemed to feel their pain. He concluded by saying that if he had more courage, he'd go after the people who did that to families. In other words, if he stood up for the families who'd been hurt, he could find himself sidelined in Congress by the leadership of his own party. I was stunned by his use of the word *courage* and his small, tight smile.

As Congressman Bachus ushered me out of his office, he took my arm and leaned close to me. "I'll go after the consumer agency, but I hope you understand, it isn't personal." He said it in a quiet, gentle tone, with his accent twanging through each syllable.

I took him to mean that he didn't particularly disagree with the idea behind the agency. But politics was politics, and he was warning me that the agency would stay in the line of fire.

I thought that it may not be personal for you, but it *is* personal for me.

Airing the Dirty Laundry

The political knives were out, but we pushed on.

Everyone on the team understood what a special opportunity we had. We talked a lot about a twenty-first-century agency. We had a chance to build something really innovative and cutting-edge and maybe even reimagine parts of the federal government.

We started with the consumer complaint hotline.

Okay, complaint hotlines don't exactly sound "cutting-edge" (more like "really boring to talk about"). But we were required by law to create one, and we got down to business right away to make sure it would be operational by the following summer.

First we had to answer a few questions. Should we create the hotline ourselves, or should we ask another government agency to run it? Should we outsource it to a private company? How much should we budget?

Everyone had an opinion, and most people had two or three. We spun our wheels for a few weeks, trying to fit the pieces together. One day I asked a different question: "What will the complaint hotline really do?"

After a little eyeball rolling, someone finally answered, "Uh, it'll take complaints."

I figured we could be stupid for a while. "Uh-huh. And what will we do with the complaints?"

"Uh, take them."

"Take them where?"

"Oh, uh, make a record."

"And then what?"

"Uh, what what?"

The conversation got dumber, but we eventually got to the key point: A lot of government agencies collect complaints from consumers, but to those who complained, the process often seems like a dead end. Angry consumers file complaints and nothing seems to happen.

I worried about the government's consumer complaint departments. Rarely is an agency in Washington held accountable based on the quality of its response to consumer complaints. Agency budgets are perpetually tight, and the consumer complaint hotline can be an easy target for cuts. Besides, all government agencies face a basic problem with their complaint hotlines: No one has the resources to conduct an investigation every time a consumer has a problem. Even if an agency could help solve a problem for, say, one in one hundred people, the other ninety-nine consumers would always feel nothing had been done for them.

So the process for handling complaints too often evolved into little more than filling out a form and putting it on a stack of other forms. If the stack got high enough, maybe someone at the agency would investigate some particularly awful problem. But the vast majority of the other complaints would just lie there until they quietly expired.

Surely there had to be a better way.

To begin with, a twenty-first-century agency could use new technologies to take complaints online, tag them electronically, e-mail them to the appropriate bank—and then track what happened. If the bank settled quickly, we'd know it because they would have to send the information back to us; meanwhile, the customers could verify the response with a few clicks on a computer. If the bank resisted, we'd know that, too. Some banks would probably blow us off, and we'd have to work out our responses. But some might not—and that would mean that at least a few customers (hopefully a lot of them) would get their problems solved quickly and easily.

And what if we also made the complaint data *public*? And not just a little bit public, but public in a way that would expose exactly how consumers were getting cheated?

A lot of people thought the idea was nuts. After all, the big banks would *hate* this. It would be their worst nightmare come to life: we'd be taking their dirty laundry and airing it in public. As word about the idea began to leak, the bank lobbyists got more hostile. There was even talk of a lawsuit if we went ahead with the plan.

But we went ahead anyway. We figured that by telling the world how many complaints we'd received about each of the big banks and how those complaints were resolved, we might make the market for credit work better.

Shoot, who knew? Maybe consumer groups or bloggers would start writing about which banks responded the fastest and which banks had the fewest complaints. Maybe banks would start treating customers a little better, and maybe the market would fix a lot of problems all by itself.

Of course, we wouldn't publish the names and addresses of people who complained—privacy is important—but we could name the banks and tell how they treated their customers. Besides, if the hotline got a reputation for being really helpful, it would almost certainly attract a whole lot of customers who had problems, and then we'd really know what was going on out there. What was the latest scam? Which lenders and which products were generating the most complaints? The American people would tell us directly. They could be our eyes and ears, and we could focus our resources wherever their complaints led us.

The hotline also gave us an opportunity to lay down a marker: We intended to build this agency out in the open. No cozy deals behind closed doors. This would be the people's agency, and we took transparency seriously.

As for the banks, here's the way I saw it: If it turned out that they were a little scared about this new way of doing things, they could solve the problem by treating their customers better. So who would object?

I should have known the answer: Their pet senators and representatives would object. And sooner or later, that would mean trouble.

A Proud Profession

In early November 2010, most of Washington was focused on the midterm congressional elections, not least because the Tea Party had blasted onto the scene, riding a wave of antigovernment ire. But I was focused on a different election—the race for attorney general for the state of Ohio. Rich Cordray was running for reelection, and the race was tight. Rich had earned a reputation as a fierce consumer advocate, and he had led one major lawsuit against Bank of America and another against AIG.

The morning after Election Day, Dan came into my office with the news: Rich Cordray had lost. I jumped up and shouted: "Hurray!" (Sorry, Rich, that wasn't very sensitive of me.) I waited a decent interval (forty-eight hours), then called him. Before long, Rich had agreed to be the head of enforcement for the new agency. I still believe that Ohio's loss was America's gain.

Rich's work was just the beginning: the CFPB had a lot of pieces to put in place before it could get up and running. We were on the hook for setting up the consumer hotline, establishing a financial literacy department, and writing new regulations. We would be responsible for monitoring big banks, verifying that they were following consumer protection laws, and then holding them accountable when they didn't. We were also required under Dodd–Frank to set up offices for seniors and military service members. In other words, we needed people—smart, courageous people—who were up for a fight.

From the day I arrived at Treasury, I was amazed by how many résumés were pouring in. First dozens then hundreds of them, so many that we lost count. Freshly minted college grads and experienced lawyers. Consumer advocates and military veterans. Bankers and bank protesters. We even had a cowboy apply. I was overwhelmed, and I felt just a bit of awe. Who knew that so many people were so eager to work for the government?

Government service had once been a proud profession. The jobs were widely respected. True, not all government service conjured up the heroism of working as a firefighter or a teacher. But I think positions in government were seen as requiring a little more dedication and loyalty than ordinary jobs. "Public service" evoked images of people with integrity, and the "service" part meant something real.

But over the past generation or two, many Americans had come to believe that government service was synonymous with bureaucracy and complacency. Ronald Reagan's famous line—"The nine most terrifying words in the English language are: 'I'm from the government and I'm here to help'"—had inflicted an injury, all the more painful because it came from the president of the United States. Every dismissive comment ("Well, what do you expect—it's the *government*") had left a small cut.

As I got to know more people in government service, it seemed to me that those complaints were pretty unfair. I met many, many dedicated people who obviously cared about doing a good job, people who had turned down higher-paying jobs in the private sector, people who spoke with pride about helping others. Even so, the bad rap persists. Just ask a bunch of the brightest college kids: "How many of you dream of working for the federal government someday?" Not enough hands go up.

I hoped that the new agency might have a chance to prove the cynics wrong. Sure, government fails sometimes. (By the way, corporations fail sometimes, too.) But I don't believe that the response to government failure—such as the inept response to Hurricane Katrina or the slew of failures that led to the financial crisis—should be a snarky "I told you so" or a heavy sigh of resignation. No: the response should be *outrage*. The government—*our* government—should be held to a higher standard.

Let's be honest: America is facing some really, really big challenges. Climate change, educating kids for the jobs of the future, taking care of an aging population—the list is long and daunting. And let's also admit that our government isn't perfect, and it can't solve everything. But we're going to need a well-functioning government if we're to have a prayer of tackling these very complex problems.

America has faced difficult problems before—and we've solved them together. We passed laws to get children out of factories. We set up a system that allowed aging workers to retire with dignity. We built schools so that every child would have a chance for a better life, and we created a network of highway and mass transit systems so people could get to work. We built an astonishingly tough military, superb police forces, and squadrons of first-class professional firefighters.

No, the market didn't build those things: Americans built them. Working through our government, we built them together. And as a consequence, we are all better off.

We can't bury our heads in the sand and pretend that if "big government" disappears, so will society's toughest problems. That's just magical thinking—and it's also dangerous thinking. Our problems are getting bigger by the day, and we need to develop some hardheaded, realistic responses. Instead of trying to starve government or drown it in the bathtub, we need to tackle our problems head-on, and that will require *better* government.

As I started setting up the agency, America was still in the depths of the Great Recession, and a lot of people needed jobs. But as I began to interview people, I realized that many of the candidates saw the consumer agency as a small beacon of hope, a sign that Americans really can work together to make things better. For many, this was more than just a job. Coming to work for the agency would give people a chance to make a difference.

I began to see that we had a real opportunity to put together a team of passionate, tough-minded people who had a fresh vision for how to change things. Maybe, just maybe, this agency could serve as yet another counterpoint to the familiar complaint that the government can't do anything right.

Don't Believe in Government

The new cadre of Tea Party–supported lawmakers shifted the political dynamic in Washington, and by January 2011 the Republicans had control of the House. I knew that if the banks kept the Republicans trained on attacking the agency, this would be very bad news. But I needed to get the agency set up, so I just kept plowing straight ahead.

I continued calling on members of the House and Senate, both Republican and Democrat. In January, I met with Representative Michael Grimm, a newly elected Republican from Staten Island, New York. In his early forties, he was serving in his first elected office. He told me all about himself. He'd joined the US Marines when he was nineteen, and he had been decorated for his service in Desert Storm. He got a degree from Baruch College, a public university in New York, went to law school, and then joined the FBI, where, among other things, he was part of the Financial Fraud Squad. He talked in animated terms about the great work he'd done with the FBI and the terrific training he'd received. Then he launched a small business and later became CEO of another business before running for office.

It was a great story, and at first I thought: Now here's a Republican I can build some real rapport with. I didn't care about his Tea Party ties. He'd been in law enforcement and dealt with Wall Street corruption. I was sure that someone like him would really appreciate the importance of having a watchdog like the consumer agency.

When I launched into an enthusiastic description of what we were trying to get done at the agency, the congressman looked surprised. After a bit, he cut me off so he could make one thing clear: He didn't believe in government.

I thought I'd misunderstood him. What?

I asked him about the FBI, and he amended his statement to say yes, he believed in the FBI, but not other forms of "big government" and certainly not a consumer protection agency.

The meeting didn't last much longer, and afterward I kept thinking about Congressman Grimm's remark: *He didn't believe in government.*

I thought about the congressman's life. A tour of duty in the military. A degree from a public university. Eleven years working in a federal government agency. Government training. And now a seat in the House of Representatives. Heck, he had even been quoted as saying that he wanted the government-paid health insurance when he joined Congress, because "God forbid I get into an accident and I can't afford the operation. That could happen to anyone." It seemed to me that he ought to be the poster boy for someone who understood all the good things that government can do.

I wasn't calling on congressmen so I could make more enemies for the agency, so I hadn't pressed him. And sure, I understood the basic point that government plays a limited role in a lot of people's lives and that government isn't the solution to every problem. But someday I hoped to get a chance to ask him: Would you rather fly in an airplane *without* the Federal Aviation Administration checking air traffic control? Would you rather swallow a pill *without* the Food and Drug Administration testing drug safety? Would you rather defend our nation *without* a military and fight our fires *without* our firefighters?

But I wasn't a member of Congress and he was. And the Tea Party had just helped dozens of people like him make it into public office, all loudly committed to unraveling just about everything the federal government had ever built.

The new consumer agency wasn't even off the drawing board, and it was a long way from being launched. Boy, this was going to be hard.

The Lady with the Eagle

On January 18, 2011, I rode through the military checkpoint at Joint Base San Antonio. I looked this way and that, hoping I could spot something I remembered. As a little girl, I had visited each of my brothers during their basic training in San Antonio, but now everything looked so crisp and new that I couldn't get my bearings.

Beside me was Holly Petraeus, the wife of the four-star general who was the commander of our troops in Afghanistan. I had first met Holly a few months earlier, back in my office in the Treasury Building. Shortly after I'd been sworn in, I had invited her to come by so we could talk about loans that were marketed specifically to military families.

She was short, with graying hair cut in a straight bob. The first time I saw her, she wore a simple tailored suit, a sort of civilian equivalent of a soldier's dress uniform. Her only jewelry was a gold eagle, which she wore fastened on the front of her jacket. The pin was amazing—big, heavy, and ornate, right down to the bird's jeweled eyes.

The antique couch in my office was low, but her feet still didn't touch the floor. Her posture was ramrod stiff, and she didn't waste any time getting to her subject.

In short, staccato sentences, Holly told me about her work at the Better Business Bureau running a national program designed to address the financial problems of military families. The stories she recounted were heartbreaking.

She described the vulnerability of the youngest in service, kids fresh out of high school who were picking up the first regular paychecks in their lives. They were about to be sent off to fight in Iraq or Afghanistan or deployed to another military base somewhere around the world. From the moment they enlisted, Holly explained, these young soldiers became targets for a number of aggressive scams. As soon as they showed up for basic training, they would be pursued relentlessly by lenders who would sign them up for loans that took a huge chunk of their paychecks. Once the young soldiers arrived on base, they ran a gauntlet of businesses set up near the gates and at nearby malls, including stores that hired pretty young women to flirt with the young male soldiers and sell them overpriced electronic equipment on installment loans that charged 100 percent interest or more. Just sign here, sweetie.

Holly talked about how a bad debt could ruin not just a service member's credit score, but also the person's career. Not paying a debt is deemed "dishonorable conduct," a black mark that can cause soldiers to lose out on security clearances they need for promotions and special assignments.

She also talked about how frequent moves and unexpected deployments made young families especially vulnerable. To cover a security deposit on a new lease or to pay for Grandma to fly in to help with the kids, they often faced a sudden need for cash. And lenders lined up to offer that cash at ultrahigh interest rates, springing a trap that would leave some service members repaying for years and years.

Holly spoke with particular urgency as she described the hardship caused by double deployments, which happened when both spouses were military. Very quickly, many of these families got tangled up with homes they couldn't live in and mortgages they couldn't pay. Rules had been written that were supposed to help them, but in Holly's experience lenders often skirted those rules and tossed military families out of their homes.

Holly's list of concerns was long. She was clearly angry, and I thought she was right to be angry.

I already knew that these weren't isolated incidents. In 2006, the Department of Defense studied predatory lending that targeted service members and concluded that such lending "undermines military readiness, harms the morale of troops and their families, and adds to the cost of fielding an all-volunteer fighting force." The study was loaded with specific examples, including one about a woman in the air force who had originally borrowed $400 and over the years paid the lender $3,000 in interest and principal. Even then, she still couldn't escape her monthly payments and finally had to declare bankruptcy.

Sure, military families were protected by a number of laws, but not enough of the laws had real muscle behind them. For example, Congress had passed a specific prohibition on charging excessive interest rates on payday loans to service members. But Holly pointed out that anyone who Googled "military payday loans" would find dozens of links that would take them to companies that were ready to lend at truly shocking interest rates. And just to rub a little salt in the wound, many of those sites had official-sounding names that included words like "Armed Forces" or "Military Loans," suggesting that the money was coming from someone official who would do right by the service member.

As we ended that first meeting, Holly swung into her pitch. "*You* can do something about this." She sounded like a recruiting poster come to life. I leaned back a little, but she didn't slow down. She pointed out that the new agency had "real potential" and that if we made protecting members of the military a priority, we could stop these terrible practices.

I knew Holly was right, and every time I thought about her visit, I got angry all over again. The service members Holly described were people who had dedicated themselves to keeping us safe. Couldn't we find a way to make sure they didn't get cheated when they took out a loan? The scam artists and predatory lenders who targeted our men and women in uniform were a national disgrace, and I sincerely hoped there was a special circle of hell just for them. The consumer agency needed to make fixing this problem a priority, but to do that, we would need a leader with passion and commitment.

So shortly after our first meeting, I asked Holly to be that leader. She was surprised, but she quickly said yes.

And now here we were at Joint Base San Antonio for Holly's public kickoff.

We started with a roundtable discussion with the commanding officer, lawyers, counselors, and other experts on debt and military families. After that, it was time to talk directly with service members and their spouses. The stories we heard that day were intense. They reminded me of the stories Holly had told me, the stories the DOD had reported in its study, the stories I'd heard in my own conversations with military families over the years.

But now there was a difference: Holly was at the helm of an important section of this new agency. And soon the new agency would have the power to *do* something about these problems. There would be a new cop on this beat, and that cop was getting ready for action.

Cops on the Beat

By that winter, I was feeling a little more settled in our temporary apartment in Washington, although I missed Bruce a lot during the week, and I missed our home in Massachusetts.

Otis, on the other hand, didn't miss home a bit. He had always hated the stairs in our house in Massachusetts. He was now five years old and very large for a golden retriever. I thought he was fat, but Bruce insisted he was just "big-boned." Either way, climbing the steep stairs at home was a challenge. Whenever Bruce and I went upstairs, Otis would sit near the bottom step, carefully calculating whether we would be on the second floor long enough to make it worthwhile to heave himself up the stairs. And on the way down the stairs, Otis was like a fully loaded eighteen-wheeler barreling down a steep hill. We just got out of his way.

But in the new Washington apartment building, Otis had an elevator. As far as he was concerned, life was sweet.

As the agency continued to grow, Holly Petraeus and Rich Cordray weren't the only cops about to go on the beat. That winter, we began to hire what would eventually become a whole squad of banking supervisors under the leadership of Steve Antonakes and Peggy Twohig. Patrice Ficklin would later join us to head up fair lending, where she would fight on behalf of the elderly, communities of color, and other groups that had been targeted for some of the worst mortgages in the housing crash. Together, these dedicated public servants were the enforcers and supervisors who provided the frontline defense against predatory lenders.

But our cops faced a challenge. It wasn't unique to us; pretty much every agency that oversaw banking (or any other industry) faced it.

The challenge could be summarized by one question: Who are you there to protect?

The answer seemed obvious: Just like any other cop, you're supposed to protect the people. Right?

That's certainly how it works in much of the world. Regular cops hear from ordinary citizens every day. They talk to people on the streets when they make their rounds. When a crime happens, the cops meet with victims and their families and ask a lot of questions. And when there's a particularly high-profile crime, the police chief and the mayor and the press constantly ask them: Did you catch the criminal? Did you put him behind bars? In subtle and not-so-subtle ways, a whole system helps ensure that the cops stay focused on catching the bad guys.

But that isn't how it works for most people in agencies that watch over the financial industry. I have no doubt that the majority of them have the best of intentions, but let's face it: Given the way their jobs are designed, they spend most of their time talking to bankers. "Show me the books," they say. "Explain this practice." "Comment on this new mortgage form or proposed regulation." All the while, they are inundated by a constant stream of push-back and pressure from industry people. In the normal course of things, banking regulators simply don't hear from many ordinary citizens. After all, someone who gets ripped off in a $40 credit card scam might call a consumer complaint hotline, but that person doesn't have access to the agency lawyers and investigators who supervise the banks on a day-to-day basis. Nope. Bank regulators spend a lot of time with bankers and almost *no* time with bank customers.

In those early days at the agency, I spent a lot of time talking with

Rich, Peggy, and Steve about how to make certain this baby agency wouldn't someday drift away from its core mission. How could we ensure that someone working for the CFPB would spend most of her time working on behalf of the consumers who *didn't* show up at our door—rather than the representatives of banks who did?

One answer was to run straight up the middle and hit the biggest targets, and that's exactly what Rich Cordray did. Rich was fearless, and he led by example. Among other things, he investigated Capital One for misleading customers about the costs of "free" add-ons to their credit cards—"free" services that actually cost customers a total of $140 million. (He ultimately forced Capital One to send the hidden fees back to every customer—and not one customer had to file papers or ask for a refund because the checks came automatically in the mail. Rich and his team also hit up the company to pay an additional $25 million fine.)

We also tried hard to make sure that the agency's staff would never forget who they served: regular people. We made plans for people from different corners of the agency—including the director—to have a chance to listen in to the work of the complaint hotline and read consumers' feedback. The idea was to do more than gather the bare numbers, but also to hear the stories, to hear how people described their problems with financial institutions and what they believed were fair resolutions. We built an open website and talked to people around the country. We met regularly with representatives from consumer groups so we could make every effort to weigh their concerns against what we heard from the big banks and their trade associations. We wanted the voices of consumers to echo loudly through the halls of the agency, at least as loudly as those of the bankers.

I figured it this way: Every day the wind would blow over this agency from one direction. We would hear the voices of those who were organized, those who had money, and those who were powerful. If we weren't careful, their point of view would eventually seep into every crack and crevice in the place. We needed a strong wind from the other direction. We needed to create an agency that would be transparent about our mission, our goals, and the work we were doing—so that the public could call us out if we fell short.

I hoped—and I still hope—that the agency would be a place where the mission was part of the air that every employee breathed every day: We exist to serve the people.

One-Page Mortgage

In spring 2011, we had another breakthrough when Pat McCoy and a number of other staffers sat behind a one-way mirror in a test lab just outside Baltimore. Pat—who was a professor at the University of Connecticut and had written a book called *The Subprime Virus* (what a title!)—was now leading the agency's mortgage policy division.

The backstory on how Pat and her team came to be behind the mirror that day takes a little explanation. The mortgage crisis made it clear that untold numbers of people had ended up with mortgages they didn't understand, partly because a thicket of paperwork had been used to hide extra fees and confusing terms. Too many homeowners (like Flora) had trusted what they'd been told by their mortgage broker, and they didn't understand until far too late that the fine print committed them to something entirely different. When their payments skyrocketed, many homeowners couldn't afford to keep paying their mortgage and had to either refinance (and pay a gigantic fee) or give up their house.

Dodd–Frank called for rules to simplify the mortgage process, and I set an ambitious goal early on. I told Pat's group: Let's create a short, easy-to-read disclosure, and let's keep it to just one page. A simple mortgage form—one that a customer could easily read and understand—could go a long way toward making homeowners safer.

People (maybe even the whole mortgage team!) thought I was crazy. *One page?* In Washington, it's not possible to requisition a copy machine in one page. But I figured we should think big—or in this case, think short.

Our first drafts of a one-page mortgage were clunky and unreadable. Why? Federal law had long required certain disclosures that had been designed with the best of intentions—to protect consumers. But over the years, the disclosures had become a tangled mess: there were pages and pages of legal mumbo jumbo, and it was difficult for us to untangle them. The team was working hard, but they kept putting in lousy language that the law seemed to require.

It took a while, but eventually we came up with something that worked. The staff drafted and redrafted, testing versions on friends and co-workers. They consulted with design people. They modified and rejiggered.

And when they had the first draft of the form ready for public viewing, Pat's team did something that, as far as I knew, no federal banking regulator had ever done before: The team put two competing drafts of the form on our new CFPB website and asked the public to help evaluate them. I think Pat hoped to get maybe a few hundred responses—after all, mortgage forms aren't exactly prime-time TV. But no: we got more than *twenty-seven thousand* responses.

After we put out the draft forms, we got a lot of input from the bankers. Many of the credit unions and smaller community banks (and some of the big banks, too) sold honest, simple mortgages, and they loved the draft forms. They figured that a simple form that made it easier to comparison shop would help them compete against the slick operators.

And one other thing: The team did some real-life road testing. That's how Pat and several other CFPB staffers ended up behind the one-way mirror, watching this man (I'll call him Mr. Harris, to protect his privacy) who would be one of the first people to take the form for a test drive.

Pat told me Mr. Harris was an African American man in his mid-fifties, a little older than most of those who had volunteered for that early test drive. He had a soft voice, he was a little stocky, and he worked with his hands for a living. He already owned a home, knew how much he could afford, and was starting to think about refinancing his mortgage.

Mr. Harris was ushered into the testing room, where the interviewer greeted him. After some preliminaries, the interviewer got down to business. If this had been the real thing, Mr. Harris would have been staring at a stack of papers and loan officers saying, "Just sign here . . . and here . . . and here . . ."

Instead, the interviewer pushed a single page across the table and asked him to read it. According to the form, the monthly payment on the loan being offered started out at about $850, but it could eventually go up to over $1,800 a month.

Mr. Harris looked down at the paper. He paused. Wait a minute, he said—something's wrong. My payments could go up *that* much if interest rates rise? Is that right?

The interviewer said yes. This was an adjustable rate mortgage. If interest rates stayed low, his payments would be low. But if interest rates rose, that was how much he could have to pay.

Mr. Harris thought about it for a minute, then shoved the paper back across the table. "No. I don't want it. I can't afford that loan."

That's when Pat McCoy felt like bursting into song. Hallelujah! The form had done exactly what it was supposed to do. It gave Mr. Harris clear information, so he could make a choice. Plain and simple.

Okay, it wasn't exactly the Red Sox winning the World Series, and there was still a whole lot of work to do before this form and others would be final and lenders would be required to use them. And we knew that getting through the whole regulatory process with just one page would be tough. But we thought it was pretty exciting. We'd been under way for only a few months, and already the agency was taking concrete steps toward changes that would make a real difference for millions of families.

Who's the Bad Guy?

By now, the consumer agency was gaining some momentum. We had launched our website, the plan for the complaint hotline was taking shape, and Holly Petraeus was ramping up her visits to military bases. Our work to develop a shorter mortgage form was getting some traction. We were on the move—literally. We had set up shop in our new, temporary head-quarters in an office building several blocks away from the Treasury Building.

Finally, we were beginning to get our feet under us. I stopped waking up at three in the morning with my heart pounding. I almost started to believe I could relax a little.

Almost, but we still had a long way to go. And if I'd been a little more savvy in the ways of Washington, I probably could have sensed that trouble was coming.

In March, the first bomb landed. It was an all-out attack on the agency and on me personally. It began with a headline-grabbing accusation that we—and I—had stepped way out of line. What did we do wrong? The short story is that we stood accused of helping the US government defend consumers. Yup, that's pretty much what it added up to.

The longer story, of course, was more complicated. Back in October 2010, the press broke the news that several giant banks had violated the law while foreclosing against homeowners. It wasn't just a technical error here or there. The banks had flat-out lied, over and over and over. Foreclosure is a complicated process for a very good reason: The law requires safeguards to make sure that a family isn't thrown out of their home by mistake. But it took time and resources for the banks to comply, so several of the big banks had apparently decided just to ignore many of those laws. "Robo-signing" was rampant; one loan officer famously testified that he signed off on ten thousand foreclosure documents *every month*. Documents had been falsified, and tens of thousands of families had been trapped in a nightmare of lost paperwork and endless delays that had turned their lives upside down and landed many out on the street. The stories were genuinely awful.

The foreclosure scandal quickly engulfed JPMorgan Chase, Bank of America, Citibank, and a few others—the list was a *Who's Who* of the major banks (and a *Who's Who* of the banks that got the biggest TARP handouts). And as with the crash, the problem was concentrated in the big banks, not the community banks and credit unions. It seemed that the little banks—the ones with small staffs and part-time legal advice—could manage to follow the law, but the big guys couldn't be bothered. Meanwhile, the regulators who were supposed to be watching over the big banks had once again seemed not to notice or care about the abuses until the media started to stir the pot.

So many different laws had been broken and the scandal got so much press attention that a busload of government agencies began to look into suing the big banks. Before long, the media began to report that the OCC—the Office of the Comptroller of the Currency, the main agency in charge of regulating the banks—was ready with a settlement number: $5 billion. The OCC seemed to think that this was such a large figure that everyone should be a little breathless. (I couldn't help but think of Dr. Evil in the Austin Powers movie, announcing that he would destroy the world unless he was paid *$1 million*.) Collectively, these big banks earned more than $1 billion every single day, so the settlement would amount to less than five days of revenue in payment for deliberately and repeatedly breaking the law for years. Whoop-dee-doo.

When the scandal first broke in fall 2010, the consumer agency was brand-new and didn't yet have most of its authorities under the

Dodd–Frank Act. But we were slated to have jurisdiction over mortgage servicing at big banks by the summer of 2011, and Secretary Geithner asked for my advice on the issue. I asked our team to dig in, and we examined the numbers and shared our analysis with Treasury and other regulators.

Not surprisingly, many lawmakers were pretty upset about the foreclosure scandal. One of the most vocal was Richard Shelby of Alabama, the senior Republican on the Senate Banking Committee. Now approaching eighty, the senator was tall, with a deep voice and the confidence that twenty-five years in the US Senate seems to give some men. This was the same Senator Shelby who the summer before had thundered against any suggestion that I might head up the new consumer agency.

Shortly after the scandal exploded, Senator Shelby expressed outrage that government regulators appeared to have been "asleep at the switch" and demanded an "independent investigation." But as the months went by, the investigation he called for never really happened.

Now, in March 2011, he was madder than ever about the scandal. But he wasn't angry about the lack of an investigation or the ugly things done by the big banks (and make no mistake, they were ugly). Nope—he was incensed about the rumors that the banks might be asked to cough up some serious cash.

Instead of the OCC's reported $5 billion settlement, some of the other agencies favored a number closer to $30 billion. Senator Shelby called this a "shakedown." He laid the blame with "the new Bureau for Consumer Protection, the FDIC, the Fed, certain Attorneys General, and the Administration, led by Elizabeth Warren."

So there it was: Senator Shelby and his fellow Republicans were furious, not with the mortgage servicers that broke the law and stole people's homes, but with government regulators who were pushing for more accountability—and specifically with me.

In the end, Senator Shelby could do little more than fume: he still faced a Democratic majority in the Senate, which meant that he didn't have the power to call hearings or launch investigations. So it was left to the House, which was now controlled by the Republicans, to do the banks' dirty work.

Hearings Before Congress

By the time Senator Shelby launched his broadside, our little agency had attracted a lot of attention. We'd won the support of some powerful friends and made some powerful enemies. On March 16, I was called to appear before the House Financial Services Committee to testify about the agency. I knew I'd be asked about the foreclosure scandal, and I was sure I'd have to defend the CFPB and its mission.

This wouldn't be my first appearance before Congress: I had testified more than half a dozen times before various committees during my days on COP. But this one felt entirely different. While at COP, I went into each hearing feeling that since my job was to serve as the eyes and the ears for Congress, the committee members genuinely wanted to find out what I knew. But this hearing wouldn't be "Help us understand." This would be an assault on the new agency. And this time, the response to my testimony would fall along partisan lines. The Democrats were lining up to support the agency (and me), and the Republicans were out for blood.

The CFPB was a high-profile operation, so the attacks could come from anywhere. At the agency we spent days preparing for my appearance. My staff warned me that I needed to be ready to answer questions about anything and everything. What policies were we putting in place for enforcement? What was our hiring process? How were salaries set in the federal bureaucracy? (I actually did get a question on that.) The staff put together several giant briefing books, which I read late into the night. I prepared written testimony, producing a document of more than thirty pages that provided a detailed account of our work. We had spoken often of our commitment to transparency, and we were doing our best to be an open book with the public and with Congress.

When the day of my appearance finally arrived, I took a seat at a table in a hearing room for the House of Representatives. Members of Congress sat behind a raised dais, a number of them seeming to glare down at me. C-SPAN cameras blinked from the corners, but it was the guys carrying professional cameras with big telephoto lenses who made me want to throw a blanket over my head. They are not allowed to stand up and block the views of members of Congress, so a protocol has developed where they scoot on their behinds along the floor and take photos from below the dais. I figured that all the newspapers would run flattering pictures of my nostrils the next morning.

Appearing in front of a panel of mostly hostile members of Congress is like testifying in court—everyone is on edge and very formal. The agency was off to a strong start and we hadn't done anything wrong, but I sure felt as if I were on trial.

Most of the questions from Republicans concerned the foreclosure scandal. In particular, several of the representatives asked why I had offered advice about the bank settlement. They didn't ask nicely. Whatever their words said, their tone said, "How dare you!"

The Democrats did their best to defend the agency, but for the most part it was two and a half hours of the same questions over and over, with each attacker working on his or her five-minute turn in the C-SPAN spotlight.

Over the next three months, I would be called back to the House to testify two more times. The second hearing was dubbed "Who's Watching the Watchman." Each session was worse than the last. After one hearing, a reporter observed that several members of Congress "seemed to lack the basic facts about the new agency they were trying to oversee." One congressman was confused about how long other bank regulators serve in office; he accused the CFPB of being the only banking agency whose head served a five-year term (not true: several others do, too). He also didn't understand the rules for how funding is set in Washington and seemed to think the agency was the only banking regulator that was outside the political appropriations process (not even close: all of them are). Another congressman asked me to explain what was meant by a clause in the Dodd–Frank Act, as if *I* had enacted the law instead of Congress itself.

That was embarrassing enough, but then Congressman Patrick McHenry, a Republican from North Carolina, flatly accused me of lying. Not lying about anything substantive, but lying about our previously agreed-upon schedule.

I had triggered this outburst unintentionally. All the members of Congress in the room had finished asking their questions, and I asked to be excused, noting that we had arrived at the agreed-upon end time for the hearing. Congressman McHenry declared: "You're making this up."

Huh? He got pretty worked up about it. Congressman Elijah Cummings seemed genuinely appalled and tried to calm down McHenry, but it didn't work. McHenry "absolutely blew a gasket" (or at least that's how Rachel Maddow described it when she ran the video later that day).

The video of the hearing went viral, and the congressman's Facebook page was overrun with tens of thousands of angry messages. I was surprised that so many people paid attention to the incident, and I felt a little embarrassed. In retrospect, I should have just stayed for as long as he wanted to make me sit there. But the whole thing—from the first attack to the YouTube moment—made me feel like Alice in Crazyland.

As the manufactured "scandal" about trying to hold the mortgage companies accountable continued to excite the Republicans, Secretary Geithner got a lot of questions about the consumer agency's role. By now, he had a pretty good view of what the agency could do. Our work was still in the preliminary stages, but I think it was becoming clear that we were building tools that would help make the credit markets work for families.

That spring, Secretary Geithner appeared before the Senate Banking Committee to testify about the economic state of the country. Senator Shelby used the opportunity to question him repeatedly about the role that I had played in the controversy over how the banks should be penalized. The secretary never wavered. He backed me up, verifying that he had asked for my involvement. It would have been easy for him to point a finger or just stay silent, but he didn't. Secretary Geithner and I had had our differences, but when the consumer agency came under attack by the Republicans, he had our back.

I had no doubt—zero—that the banks should be held accountable for breaking the law. And I thought the repeated grilling about my role in trying to hold these banks accountable was ridiculous. It was so obviously a concerted effort to distract attention from the terrible behavior of the banks. Even so, I worried that I would make some little misstatement in a hearing and cause a problem for the agency. The attacks—the constant demands for e-mails and the endless prep sessions—sucked up time, time that should have been spent on solving real problems. And all the political nonsense distracted from what should have been the focus: Would the big banks ever be held accountable, and would they ever be forced to repair the damage they had done to so many families?

Who Will Be the Director?

As the spring rolled on, two questions came up more and more: When would the president nominate a permanent director for the CFPB? And who would he pick? The new director wouldn't report to Tim Geithner; he or she would be confirmed by the Senate and run an independent agency.

After spending many months setting up the agency, I realized that I had come to love this job. I had never thought I would love any job as much as I loved teaching, but it had happened. I loved the difference we were making; I loved the feeling that we had a chance to level the playing field for people who needed it. We were just getting started, and I felt worse and worse about the prospect of leaving the agency. So I took a deep breath and asked if the president would let me stay.

Once again, I had a round of talks with various of President Obama's senior advisors. The conversations generally ran to a pattern. First came the nice stuff: They told me I was doing a great job setting up the agency. That I was an effective consumer advocate. That the agency was getting lots of praise for its work. Lots of nice words, always followed by "but." As in: "But . . . for some reason, you are like a red-hot poker in the eye of the Republicans." According to the president's team, the Republicans in the Senate were still adamantly opposed to me. Worse, the Republicans would never even let the issue come to a vote, so there was no way I could get confirmed.

So I tried a different tack: If I can't get confirmed, would the president consider appointing me during a congressional recess? The tenure of a recess appointment is limited by law, but it could give me up to two years in the job of director while we established the agency's course. The answer was the same: No. The president wanted a director to be confirmed through the proper channels.

The rumors continued to swirl through the press, and speculation that the president would name me grew over time. In May, Senator Shelby and the other Senate Republicans decided to apply a little counterpressure.

They sent a letter to the president saying they would not agree to confirm *anyone* to be the director unless their demands were met. Their demands? They all added up to one thing: The agency must be substantially weakened.

The Republicans included a lot of items on their wish list, but one was the most telling: They insisted that Congress have control over the agency's funding. In US history, no banking regulator has *ever* been funded through Congress; instead, the regulatory agencies had covered their costs directly or indirectly through banking fees. The reason is pretty obvious: to keep the regulators safe from political pressures. But the Republicans informed the president that Congress (and, of course, the banks) wanted to determine how much food the consumer watchdog would get. They knew that a starving watchdog wouldn't be nearly as big a threat.

Some people saw that letter as a declaration of war (Washington style, that is). Never in history had a minority in the Senate "pre-rejected" a presidential nominee just because they didn't like the agency he or she was due to run. The Republican minority was using the filibuster threat to try to change the law of the land—a law that a majority of the Senate had passed, a majority of the House had passed, and the president had signed. Progressives were outraged, and a number argued that this was the right moment for the president to fight back: He should nominate me, have a showdown with the Senate Republicans, and then, if needed, make a recess appointment.

The Memorial Day recess was coming up. The Republicans upped the ante: not only were they refusing to confirm a director, they intended to prevent the president from having any opportunity to make a recess appointment. How? They would go on vacation as they always did, but they would use a parliamentary trick to keep the Senate officially in session so they could claim it wasn't a recess. The press immediately declared that this was another move to keep me from becoming the head of the consumer agency.

Once again, the agency and the question of who would become its director had become the center of a gale-force storm. Calls from the media came in every day. Reporters tried to stop me on the street. Friends telephoned from all over the country. I got encouraging e-mails and atta-girl messages left on our home phone. I couldn't get my hair cut without people stopping by to tell me to hang in there. Otis faced repeated interruptions of his late-night walks when people stopped to ask about the agency and promise their support.

In the midst of all the hubbub, I got a letter that stood out from all the others. Handwritten on congressional stationery, it looked a little like a thank-you note for a wedding gift. Ever polite—I guess that for him it still wasn't personal—Chairman Spencer Bachus wanted to let me know that he wouldn't support me or, for that matter, George Washington himself to be head of the consumer agency.

Deal . . . or No Deal

In June, the president called me in to talk about the agency and the question of who would run it. This was our first one-on-one meeting since he'd asked me to take the interim job almost a year earlier.

He left no room for ambiguity: I wasn't going to get the nomination.

I was disappointed, but not surprised. The president had never promised to nominate me. In fact, it was pretty clear from the beginning that he wasn't itching to give me the post. He hadn't nominated me a year earlier, he hadn't given me a recess appointment during the past several months while I'd been doing the job, and his advisors had consistently told me not to get my hopes up.

The president then explained that he planned to make a deal with those who opposed me: He would agree not to nominate me, and in return he would get the Republicans to stop the filibuster threats and allow a vote for the nominee.

I pressed the president: Was he sure he could lock in this deal? Along with everyone else, I had read the letter from the Republicans, and it sounded like they were in no mood for compromise.

The president told me not to worry; he was pretty confident they could work out the deal. They just needed a nominee who wasn't me.

If I couldn't do it, I thought that Rich Cordray should be the president's nominee. Rich, who had done a great job putting together the CFPB enforcement team, has both nerve and skill, exactly what would be needed to lead the new agency. The president was on board with Rich.

The White House plan was based on the premise that I was radioactive, but someone else could get through the Senate. If that was correct, then I felt like I knew an inside joke: *any* tough director would cause the bad guys a mess of trouble—and Rich is as tough as they come. The Republicans and the banks had succeeded in their effort to push me out the door, but I knew that Rich would work his tail off to make this agency a fighting force for working people.

On July 18, 2011, I stood beside the president in the Rose Garden while he announced his nomination of Rich Cordray as director of the CFPB.

But the decision to choose Rich changed nothing. Within hours of learning about the Cordray nomination, the Republicans declared that his candidacy for director of the agency was "dead on arrival."

Oh. It turned out there was no deal after all.

The Last Meeting

Bruce and I gave up the apartment, and Otis gave up the much-loved elevator. We gave away our furniture to young CFPB staffers and packed up the car with our personal stuff. There were good-bye parties that nearly tore my heart out. I'd asked so many of these people to come work for the consumer agency, and they had put every fiber of their being into giving the agency the best possible start. I wanted to stay and fight alongside them. But I needed to suck it up and move on. My time was over.

On my last day at the agency, I went to the White House to hand my letter of resignation to the president in person. Once again, he took me outside. Once again, it was hot. But this time, the conversation was different.

We talked about the foreclosure disaster and the millions of families still in trouble. We talked about the increasing stress on the middle class. And we talked about the future—about where the country was headed, about a growing band of Republican extremists.

Eventually we got around to the big Senate race that was brewing in Massachusetts. He talked about the Senate and how, if I ran and beat Scott Brown, I'd have a lot of opportunities to fight for the economic issues I cared about.

The president said he liked Rich Cordray, and he thought he would be a good leader for the consumer agency. I agreed that Rich would be terrific.

I thanked him for the chance to serve, and I left.

A Victory

After I left the agency, people in the media all asked a version of the same question: What would I do next? I told everyone the same thing: We're taking a trip to Legoland.

And that's exactly what we did. Bruce and I flew out to California, where we gathered a herd of nieces, nephews, kids, and grandkids—we were more than a dozen in all—and traipsed across Legoland, Disneyland, and the Los Angeles beaches. I proved yet again that I can get lost anywhere, including the kiddie boat ride at Legoland, where I somehow managed to get my putt-putt boat turned completely backward. My passenger, Lavinia, and I got rammed repeatedly by a dozen other boaters—and I was severely warned about bad boating from the skinny teenager running the ride. All I can say is, steering a boat at Legoland is trickier than it looks.

The break was comforting and peaceful—at least as peaceful as anything involving a mob of rowdy children can be. But I still woke up in the night thinking about the agency. I was worried: Rich's nomination was already stalled in the Senate and the Republicans were on the attack, demanding again that the CFPB be weakened. Without a confirmed director, the agency would not be granted its full powers. And no one knew if the Republicans in the Senate would ever allow a vote or if the president would ever make a recess appointment.

I was worried, but that's not the same as being afraid. I knew the agency itself was on strong footing. Just before I'd left, we had endured a top-to-bottom inspection by the inspectors general. (The very title *inspector general* made me want to check to make sure my fingernails were clean and my shoes were shined.) We had received a glowing review for all our administrative organization and execution—we'd set up the agency without a hitch. And now the agency's real work was under way. In the next two years alone, Rich would recover nearly $500 million that the banks had fraudulently charged their customers. Holly would help save lots of homes for service members deployed in Afghanistan and Iraq. By June 2013, more than 175,000 people would turn to the consumer hotline for help.

We were starting to prove our case to more and more Americans: This consumer agency was worth fighting for. And every day the agency did some good, that fight would get easier—or so I fervently hoped.

Did David or Goliath win? The fight wasn't over. Even so, I'd give this round to David.

But my role was over. It was time to hand this slingshot to someone else.

6 | The Battle for the Senate

HOME AT LAST. It was August 2011. We unpacked from Legoland and went to the Summer Shack for fried clams and beer. Bruce mowed the lawn and I attacked the overgrown holly bushes and maimed a couple of evergreens. The new school year would start soon: I got out my books and posted the reading assignment for the first class.

But life wasn't quiet. Speculation was at high pitch about whether I might run for the Senate. The very popular Scott Brown had been in office for only a year and a half, but in November 2012 the seat that had been held for decades by Ted Kennedy would be up for grabs again. The press and online media were quick to offer opinions: She should run! She shouldn't run! Plenty of people called the house, e-mailed advice, or stopped me on the street: Buy new glasses! Change your hair! Get married! (Whoa—again? I was pretty crazy about my *current* husband.)

I'd been back from California for a week or so when I got a call from a local Democratic Party official. He introduced himself, then said he was calling to urge me to get in the race. "Get your name out there," he said enthusiastically. "Stir things up!" After offering a few more thoughts about why I should run, he paused, as if suddenly remembering that he was speaking to a stranger about the strange land of politics. "Of course, I don't think you'll win. But don't take it personally—I don't think anyone can beat Scott Brown."

Run and lose. Gee, that sounded like fun. Maybe I'd do that right after I deliberately slammed my fingers in a car door.

But the guy who called had a point. If I jumped in, it would be a tough, tough fight. Unlike me, Scott Brown had grown up in Massachusetts. He was a longtime member of the National Guard, and over the years he had risen to the rank of colonel. He was well-liked and handsome, the kind of guy who might be played by Tom Cruise in the movie version of his life. He had developed a reputation as a moderate and bipartisan Republican, he had high approval ratings, and he already had nearly $10 million in the bank. He had been dubbed one of "Wall Street's Favorite Congressmen," with all the promise of future fund-raising that the title implied. To a lot of the pundits, he looked to be in a great position.

When Massachusetts held its special election shortly after Senator Kennedy's death, Brown had beaten Martha Coakley, a popular attorney general who was well known and had strong support across the state. A lot of people were downright nasty in their criticism of Martha after her loss, but even her critics acknowledged the exceptionally strong political skills of Scott Brown. After years of quiet backbenching in the state legislature, he had swept through Massachusetts politics like a gale-force wind.

My work on COP and then the consumer agency had gotten a fair amount of attention, and a number of progressives thought I might make a good senator. A petition made the rounds on the Internet, and seventy thousand people signed on, urging me to run against Brown.

Although I appreciated the support, no one could pretend that I didn't have a stack of liabilities. I had never run for *any* office, let alone a highly contested national office like this one. Even before Martha Coakley's defeat, women had not done well in statewide races in Massachusetts, and conventional wisdom held that this was a man's game. Plus, I wasn't born in Massachusetts or even New England; I was from Oklahoma of all places, and when I get a little excited, I have a twangy accent. I was not only a professor, but a *Harvard* professor. When the all-important question came up—"Which candidate would you rather have a beer with?"—I would lose, hands down.

Then there was money. I didn't have a nickel in the campaign-fund bank, and the last time I'd raised money was when I'd organized a ferocious effort to help Amelia's Brownie troop sell more cookies than any other troop in town. A lot of progressives had followed my work and might make contributions, but Scott Brown started with a huge war chest and the promise of much more to come.

And let's not forget my age: I was sixty-two years old. *Sixty-two.* Wasn't I supposed to be thinking ahead to rocking chairs and retirement plans, not crazy new ventures that require eighteen-hour days and months of grueling work? If I got into this race, I'd have to go all out, because I wouldn't just be battling nice-guy Scott Brown here at home. I'd be swept up into a much bigger fight against the giant banks and the right-wingers like Karl Rove who were determined to give Republicans control of the Senate.

Okay, so the liability stack was high, and right at the top was something buried in my heart of hearts—I really didn't *want* to run. I'd had enough of Washington. I'd never yearned for a life in politics. I missed teaching; I missed my research. I missed hiking with Bruce and time with our grandchildren. Atticus was a gorgeous nine-month-old, and I wasn't likely to have another chance to hold a baby on my shoulder until he fell asleep.

I made the family calls. Our son, Alex, was blunt. "No way," he said. "Don't do it. It'll ruin your life." He advised me to return to Harvard and enjoy my life for a while. "You've done enough fighting." My brothers took pretty much the same view: "Spend time with the grandkids."

Alex—and my brothers and my cousins and my best friend—worried about what a campaign would do to me. They all offered versions of the same message: Politics is ugly and personal and nasty. You haven't spent a lifetime developing the necessary armor. We love you and we don't want to see you hurt. Please stay out.

They were right.

And yet . . . there was so much at stake in this election. I'd spent nearly twenty years fighting to level the playing field for the middle class, and I'd seen millions of working families go over the economic cliff—and it was getting worse. What kind of country would my grandchildren grow up in? What if the conservatives and the big banks and the big-time CEOs got their way, and Washington kept helping the rich and powerful to get richer and more powerful? Could I really stand on the sidelines and stay out of this fight?

And what would I feel like on the day after the election, if Scott Brown won and Wall Street had one of its favorite congressmen back for another term? What if Republicans took control of the Senate and undid the new financial regulations and crippled the consumer agency? What if they tried to repeal it? What if all that happened and I knew I hadn't done everything I possibly could to stop it? Could I live with myself?

I had no experience in electoral politics, but I had learned enough to know that if I did get in the race, the other side would raise millions of dollars with one main goal—to make me look bad. I thought I'd lived a pretty clean life, but I wasn't perfect. Would they dig up something— anything—that could be distorted to embarrass me? Even worse, what if they made up a bunch of lies about me? And what if they spent truckloads of money spreading those lies, and people actually believed them? What if my children or my brothers or my granddaughters got hit by any of this? It was a stomach-clenching thought.

Someone suggested I meet with a campaign research pro, an expert in so-called opposition research, or "oppo." These were the guys who dug into opponents' backgrounds to find out where there might be trouble. The idea was for them to turn that around and start looking at my own background.

The research guy asked me all kinds of questions about my personal life—taxes, health, troublesome kids, alcohol, drugs. I understood that there were things everyone had a right to know, but this was so detailed and so invasive—nothing private, nothing sacred. And then he asked more about my married life. At the beginning of our conversation, I'd told the researcher about Bruce, and since we'd been married for thirty years, somehow the guy had missed the fact that I'd been married before. When I mentioned it, his head snapped up as if a dozen alarm bells had just gone off.

He wrote down some basic details, then asked, "And where is your ex-husband now?"

"He's dead. . . ."

Before I could take a breath and explain about Jim's terrible illness— about the awful cancer, about the blow to Amelia and Alex, about how he never had the chance to know his beautiful grandchildren—the research guy shouted, *"Great!"*

I felt as if I'd been punched. The guy saw my face and tried to cover his blunder: "I mean, not 'great' that he's dead . . ." But it was out there. And I couldn't help wondering: Who *are* these people? Who could say such a thing? And what comes next?

Yes, I'll Fight

I decided to dip my toe in the water, just to find out whether I could do even the simplest sort of campaigning. If I couldn't, then there really wasn't anything to decide.

In mid-August, I started meeting with small groups of people in living rooms and backyards around the state. A few days into this test run, I went to a gathering in downtown New Bedford. Ganesh Sitaraman, who had helped out in the early days of COP and was now a beginning law professor, offered to drive me to the meeting. We found a parking space, hopped out of the car, and were hit by a wall of heat. It was one of those steamy, end-of-summer mornings when your hair frizzes and your shirt sticks to your back about sixty seconds after you step outside.

The meeting was held in a building located on a cobblestone street, just down the block from the public library. Built in the 1890s, when the town had been both a thriving port and a manufacturing center, it featured an ornate front entrance and lots of marble, but the corkboard covering the entry walls and the peeling paint on the radiators spoke of years of hard use. We climbed the stairs, heading to a room that had been offered for the meeting. Inside the room, big fans whirred, but they didn't do much good.

Fifty or so people showed up and took their seats in neat rows of metal folding chairs. I spoke for about fifteen minutes, talking about the hollowing out of America's middle class and about how it would get worse if the Republicans in Congress kept cutting back on our investments in one another. I took questions for a while. When the meeting was over, we were all sweaty and the room was even hotter than before.

Not everyone rushed out. Some people stayed to ask for a picture, and others wanted to urge me to run, to offer advice, or just to wish me luck as I figured out what to do. It was noisy, a blur of voices and electric fans. Someone was starting to stack the chairs.

As the crowd thinned out a bit, a woman in her midfifties walked over. Her face was flushed and her hair was a tangle of tight curls. She looked hot and tired, maybe a little angry. She stopped a few steps away from me and said, "I walked two miles to get here."

Okay, she had my attention.

She dropped her voice a notch. "I walked because I don't have a car that runs. I don't have a car that runs because I don't have a job."

As we stood facing each other, she laid out her life in just a few sentences:

I have two master's degrees. I'm smart. I taught myself computer programming. I've been out of work for a year and a half. I've applied, I've volunteered, I've gone everywhere, but nothing.

She paused for a long time, then plunged back in. She explained that she had held one job or another since she was seventeen. She had put herself through school. She had always, always, always worked hard.

Then she stopped, took a step forward, and lowered her voice to a whisper, as if she didn't want to hear what she was about to say.

Now I don't know if I'm ever going to get a real job again.

I held out both hands and she took them. We stood there, not moving, just holding hands. I muttered something bland like "I'm so sorry," but she didn't give any sign of hearing me. She was well past the polite social conventions. She was hot, and she was exhausted—mind, body, and soul.

She focused again, looked me straight in the eye, and said:

I'm here because I'm running out of hope. I've read about you for a long time, and I'm here to see you in person, to tell you that I need you, and I want you to fight for me. I don't care how hard it gets, I want to know that you are going to fight.

I looked back at her and said, "Yes, I'll fight."

I didn't really think about the size of the commitment I was making or what it would cost me or Bruce or the rest of our family. I simply thought, I can't stand here and cry. And I can't just walk out on her. She asked for a commitment, and I made it. Stand and fight—there was nothing else to say and nothing else to do.

She didn't smile. She didn't encourage me. She just held my hands and looked at me. Then she was gone.

That night, while Bruce and I walked Otis, the enormity of that meeting in New Bedford began to sink in. No public fanfare and no announcements in the papers, but I had promised to run for the US Senate.

I took a few more weeks to do some hard thinking and come to a final, official decision, but my heart was already in. And once I was in, I knew that the only way I could do anyone any good was to win—so I intended to win.

Nobody Got Rich on His Own

A few days later, I declared war on the rich. Well, not really. But the right-wing blogs and Fox News sure made it sound as though I'd started stock-piling weapons and would soon be storming the mansions of Fifth Avenue.

After that gathering in New Bedford, I continued meeting with voters all around the state. These meetings were supposed to be quiet affairs, a chance to sit in someone's living room and visit with people about what changes we needed in Washington. On Saturday, August 20, I was invited to speak at someone's home in Andover.

Early that afternoon, we pulled up to a nice family home on a quiet street. The houses in the neighborhood had been built in the 1940s and '50s, and now there were plenty of trees and a comfortable, settled feeling. But today there were cars parked everywhere. The hosts came out to meet me. They were as nice as could be, but a little flustered. They had thought they might get a couple of dozen people, but it seemed that more than a hundred had shown up. People were crammed into the living room, the dining room, the entry hall, and the back porch. The hosts explained that the word had gotten out and people just kept appearing. They hated to turn anyone away, so they sure hoped I could speak loudly.

It was warm—not as bad as New Bedford, but with all those people packed into the house, it was hot enough to turn my face red and make me wish for a jug of ice water.

I spoke for a bit, then took questions. Really, it wasn't all that different from a lot of house parties during those weeks, except for one thing: someone had a video camera. Whoever it was recorded my little talk and later posted a clip on YouTube. The clip got a lot of attention, and the next thing I knew, Rush Limbaugh was calling me names and accusing me of being the worst sort of radical. So much for discreetly testing the waters.

At the time, I thought the argument I advanced that day in Andover was pretty uncontroversial. Someone had asked me how we were going to tackle the deficit, and in my response I got a little wound up. We hear about the deficit as if it's a monster and America's only choice is to slash and burn huge swaths of our budget immediately or face total destruction. All or nothing, live or die.

Yes, the deficit is a problem, and it deserves serious attention, but I don't buy that there's only one way out. I think we have to face a more fundamental issue first: How we spend our government's money is about values, and it's about choices. We could cut back on what we spend on seniors and kids and education, as the Republicans in Congress insisted we should. Or we could get rid of tax loopholes and ask the wealthy and big corporations to pay a little more and keep investing in our future. How we spend our money isn't some absurdly complicated math problem. It's about choices.

Here's what I said in that video:

> There is nobody in this country who got rich on his own. Nobody. You built a factory out there? Good for you. But I want to be clear: You moved your goods to market on the roads the rest of us paid for. You hired workers the rest of us paid to educate. You were safe in your factory because of police forces and fire forces that the rest of us paid for. You didn't have to worry that marauding bands would come and seize everything at your factory, and hire someone to protect against this, because of the work the rest of us did.
>
> Now look, you built a factory and it turned into something terrific, or a great idea? God bless! Keep a big hunk of it. But part of the underlying social contract is you take a hunk of that and pay forward for the next kid who comes along.

Okay, I confess—the marauding bands was a little over the top. But I hoped the basic point came through: Without police, schools, roads, firefighters, and all the rest, where would those big corporations and "self-made" billionaires be? For capitalism to work, we all need one another.

When I first saw the video a few weeks after that Andover house party, I winced. My arms were all over the place, and it sounded like I was shouting. (Well, I *was* shouting, hoping the people standing out on the porch could hear me.) Not a very polished speech, but it would have to do.

I decided that if a surprise video of one of my appearances was going to get out, this wasn't so bad. I hadn't sat down to plot it out, but it was a pretty good statement about why I was running for the Senate. I wanted this race to be about the question at the heart of the video: How do we build a future? I made the case for what I believe: We are stronger and wealthier because of the things we build together. We are more secure when we create a foundation that allows each of us to have a decent chance to build something on our own. We are better off when we invest in one another. It's economics and values, tied tightly together.

A lot of people got excited about the video and sent around the link. Pretty soon there were more than a million views on YouTube. Moveon .org posted the clip under the headline THE ELIZABETH WARREN QUOTE EVERY AMERICAN NEEDS TO SEE. The *Street* said I "was able to articulate—in a few words—what the Democratic Party has been unable to communicate for years." (Wow—that was kind of depressing.) A *Business Insider* column called it "sheer political brilliance." (Really? That made it sound as if the video were part of some grand strategy instead of totally unplanned.)

Before I could begin to imagine that I had some instinctive under-standing of how to run for office, however, the conservatives swung into action. Fox News aired the clip and brought on a commentator who declared some of my words "not true" and "patently silly." Rush Lim-baugh jumped in and called me "a parasite who hates her host . . . [and is] willing to destroy the host while she sucks the life out of it. . . . This is the thinking behind Mao Zedong's Cultural Revolution."

Whoa. Two minutes of off-the-cuff remarks about deficit reduction and how the wealthy should pay a little more in taxes, and suddenly I'm a parasite who hates her host? My campaign was off to quite a start.

The big banks kept a low profile at first, but before long they started weighing in against my campaign, too. One executive was quoted as say-ing: "It's not even about Scott Brown. . . . It's about: Do you want Eliza-beth Warren in the Senate?" The answer came quickly: Wall Street bankers sent out "urgent appeals" to raise money for Scott Brown.

Wall Street's response probably didn't have anything to do with the video clip. The big banks had made up their minds about me long ago, and for good reason—they knew where I stood on financial reform. The election was a long way off, and already these guys were in all-out assault mode. I knew that a super-motivated Wall Street was much more dangerous than a blathering Rush Limbaugh. Limbaugh could talk (and talk and talk), but the bankers had something a lot more powerful—endless buckets of money to throw into elections.

The campaign was just getting started, but already I felt like I was on the Tilt-A-Whirl ride at the carnival. Rush Limbaugh? Big-deal bankers who were squeezing their well-heeled friends to send money to Scott Brown? What was I in for?

Keep Your Clothes On

Before I could run against Scott Brown, I had to win the nomination of my own party. Five other Democrats had already thrown their hats in the ring. A debate was set up for October 4 at the University of Massachusetts–Lowell.

By that time, I had officially announced that I was a candidate for office. I had also found a terrific campaign manager, Mindy Myers, an experienced hand who had run two successful Senate campaigns. She was calm and steady and had great judgment, a perfect counterbalance to my damn-the-torpedoes-full-steam-ahead tendencies. Mindy brought organization and enormous savvy to the campaign. In addition, for her deputy she brought in Tracey Lewis, another experienced and coolly efficient pro who had done some great work on Hillary Clinton's presidential campaign.

And then there was Dan. Dan Geldon still had the same iron will as that seven-year-old kid who gave up meat, and he never wavered in any battle. This would be our fourth fight together: first COP, then Dodd–Frank, then the consumer agency, and now a Senate campaign. Only now he wasn't on his own anymore. Somehow, during this wild ride, Dan had found time to fall in love. He was engaged to be married, and he and his fiancée, Heather Geldhof, were settled in Washington. But the campaign would be in Massachusetts, so Dan—and Heather—agreed to pick up and come back to Boston.

The team came over to my house to help prepare for the debate. A couple of my former students played other candidates, and friends filled additional roles. But Dan boiled the session down to one lesson: Don't screw up. Not exactly confidence-inspiring advice, but I knew why he was offering it. Pundits were saying that I was the front-runner for the Democratic nomination. That was great news, except it also meant that I wasn't going to get a few trial runs below the radar. People would be watching to see if a first-timer could pull this off, and there might be no second chances if I messed up.

I'd been a high school debater, but with six people onstage and questions about any topic at all—and only one minute allowed for each answer—I felt like I was trying to learn how to walk backward on the moon.

The debate was held in an auditorium that could seat about a thousand people, and it was a full house. When we arrived that night, a big, noisy crowd stood outside, waving signs and cheering for their candidates. I shook hands with nearly everyone—including people holding signs for the other candidates. If felt like a big party.

The stage was big and brightly lit—so bright that the only people I could see clearly were the other candidates. A seated panel of students began asking us questions, and they covered stuff I'd expected ("Do you support Planned Parenthood?" Yes!) and stuff I didn't expect ("What superhero would you be?" Um . . . Wonder Woman! Who wouldn't want a Lasso of Truth?). There were also questions that might have made news if anyone had given the wrong answer ("Have you driven drunk?" No.).

And then another question, this time from a young man in a dark jacket. The student began by pointing out that to help pay for his law school education, Scott Brown had posed for *Cosmo*. (In fact, he'd been chosen "America's Sexiest Man" in June 1982, and a photo of him had run as the magazine's nude centerfold.) Then the student asked us: "How did you pay for your education?"

When it was my turn to answer, I joked: "Well, I kept my clothes on." I then hit what I thought was the real point:

> I borrowed money. . . . I went to a public university at a time when they were well supported and tuition was cheap and I had a part-time job, so the combination got me through.

I was glad for the chance to talk about student loans. Costs were soaring out of control, and families were being asked to shoulder an ever-growing share of that burden. A lot of people were overwhelmed by their student debt loads, and I wanted Washington to step up and do more to help people who were trying to get an education. I wished I'd had more time to talk about this—a minute wasn't nearly long enough.

Two days later, Senator Brown called in to a local radio show. The host asked him about my remark, and that's when the conversation took a surprising turn:

> HOST: Have you officially responded to Elizabeth Warren's comment about how she didn't take her clothes off?
> BROWN: (laughing) Thank God.
> HOST: (laughing) That's what I said! I said, "Look, can you blame a good-looking guy for wanting to, you know . . . ?"
> BROWN: You know what, listen, bottom line is, you know, I didn't go to Harvard.

Really? That was the bottom line? This seemed like stupid locker room stuff to me—but a lot of women were getting tired of stupid locker room stuff. As one of my friends said, "Enough! Women get hit like this all the time, and when we complain, the guys say, 'Geez, can't you take a joke?' Well, no more." The National Organization for Women called for Brown to apologize to the women of Massachusetts and step out of the race.

Some in the media declared Brown's crack the "first major gaffe" of the campaign. As it turned out, it wouldn't take me long to join him in the ranks of the big-time gaffe makers.

Gaffes, Gaffes, Gaffes . . .

On a sunny morning in early October, I headed to Quincy to start the day with breakfast at McKay's, an old-school city diner with a counter and a dozen or so tables. The state senator, John Keenan, introduced me to many of the customers, and I had the chance to feed pancakes to a toddler while I talked with his grandparents.

Kyle Sullivan, who ran communications for the campaign, also came along. I felt lucky to have him as part of the team; he was cheerful and easygoing and he knew all the reporters in Massachusetts. He had set up a meeting at the diner with Samuel Jacobs from the *Daily Beast*. The three of us sat at a small, four-seat table and had a lively and engaging conversation that lasted twenty minutes, maybe longer.

During my time on COP and then at the consumer agency, I had talked with a lot of people in the press about the need to hold big banks accountable. A typical interview would last a while—sometimes a half hour or more—and the conversation would usually include plenty of back-and-forth about ideas and sometimes even an in-depth discussion about data. So I waded into the *Daily Beast* interview the same way I always had—expecting a lively exchange about whatever issues particularly interested the reporter.

That fall, Occupy Wall Street was going full throttle and Occupy Boston was making headlines, so Jacobs and I spent much of our time talking about Wall Street—the lack of accountability, the fury people were feeling, the need for change. I talked about the consumer agency and the kind of difference it was beginning to make. He really seemed engaged, and Kyle said he thought it was a good interview. Me too.

I said good-bye to the customers, waved to the toddler, and headed on to our next event.

A week and a half later, I was surprised when a *Daily Beast* headline blared, WARREN TAKES CREDIT FOR OCCUPY WALL STREET, followed by a story that quoted my brother David declaring, "She's not a lesbian."

My first thought was, He called my seventy-year-old brother? Why? And I had to wonder: I'd been happily married to the same man for thirty-one years; why would anyone be talking about whether or not I'm a lesbian? And what difference would it make if I *were* a lesbian?

It took a minute for another thought to hit me: Surely the headline about my taking credit for Occupy Wall Street wasn't accurate. Why on earth would I have said that? When people on the campaign trail had asked about the activists involved in Occupy Wall Street, I'd said that I understood their frustration but I had no connection to the protests.

I called Kyle. There must have been a mistake—right? Kyle kept recordings of most of the interviews in case of problems like this one. But Kyle had seen the story and already checked: "The sentence is in your interview."

Huh?

Kyle was right: the sentence was there. Incredibly, I'd said: "I created much of the intellectual foundation for what they [Occupy Wall Street] do." I was trying to say that I'd worked on these issues for a long time and felt really angry about what the banks had done to families. But the quote didn't come out that way at all.

I was deeply embarrassed. My words sounded so puffy and self-important, and they made it seem as if I were trying to take credit for a protest I wasn't even part of. I wondered if some alien had invaded my body and said something stupid while the real me was visiting a desert island. I wondered if politics turned everyone into an idiot—or was it just me? I wanted to cover my head with a blanket and never come out.

I was as fired up about the crash and about Wall Street as anyone, but the Occupy protesters were putting together their own movement in their own way. I tried to take back those words every time I was asked about them. But the words were out there, and I couldn't erase them.

I learned a painful lesson from that interview. The old way of talking with the press—long conversations and lively discussions—was gone. There was a huge difference between being an "expert" and being a "candidate." The game had changed.

I wanted to spend the campaign talking about what had gone wrong in America and what we could do differently, but to make that happen, I had to learn not to step on my own tongue. I was starting this race behind, and I realized that if I let even one sentence go sideways, the story wouldn't be about the foreclosure crisis or the rising cost of college—it would be about the gaffe.

When I first started talking to people about running for office, a lot of people said to me, "Don't let the consultants change you," and I'd always assured them that I wouldn't allow it to happen. But like it or not, I had to change. Not because of a consultant, but because I started to understand the cost of a stupid mistake. I wasn't going to change who I was or what I was fighting for, but I was in a different boxing ring now. I needed to learn the new rules, and I needed to learn them fast.

And there was another reason to be careful: The Republican Party had hired someone with a video camera to follow me around. The so-called tracker was a big guy who pointed his camera at me every chance he could. I was filmed talking with people on the street, asking one of my staffers where the bathroom was, and blowing my nose while walking across a parking lot.

At the end of one event, I thanked the supporters and my staff and said good-bye. After Bruce and I got in the car, he put his arms around me and gave me a kiss. I'd just started to unwind a little when Bruce yelled, "The tracker!" and we jumped apart, like two high school kids who had been caught making out.

Bruce and I made jokes about it—"Wanna go outside and get a big smooch?"—but every time I left the house, I could feel my shoulders tighten up.

Now I needed to change: I needed to measure every sentence. The really awful part was that I wasn't sure I could.

A Rally in Framingham

On October 25, the day after the *Daily Beast* article came out, we had our first organizing meeting for volunteers. I'm not sure what I expected. For one thing, our brand-new campaign team was pretty distracted by the tornado of questions from reporters about my stupid Occupy quote.

Instead of starting out in Boston or Springfield for our first volunteer gathering, we picked Framingham, a town about twenty miles west of Boston. The election was still so far off that we didn't know what sort of turnout to expect and tried to keep our expectations low.

My senior advisor, Doug Rubin, put the event together. He had helped run Governor Deval Patrick's campaign and served as the governor's chief of staff. He gave the kind of solid guidance that was enormously valuable. Doug was sure that a public event for volunteers was a great idea, and I trusted his savvy and judgment when he set this up.

But now, half an hour before the start of the event, I was loading up on calories at the nearby McDonald's and having serious second thoughts. What if nobody came? I was pretty sure that my idiotic gaffe had ruined any chance of the event being a success. Since it was too late to do anything about it, I didn't say it to Doug at the time. Better just to keep smiling.

The meeting was held in an auditorium at Framingham State University. As people started drifting in, I stood near the main entrance and greeted them. There were lots of young people—no surprise: we were on a college campus. But there were also lots of seniors. And families with kids. And vets wearing their service caps, a couple of people with walkers, and a middle-aged guy with his arm in a sling. Mothers and daughters. Sisters.

A number of people said something about their earlier political experiences: "I was with Teddy Kennedy in '94." "I helped Martha Coakley two years ago in her fight against Scott Brown." "My husband and I had a coffee for Governor Patrick when he first got started."

Others said they weren't sure if they were going to volunteer, but they came because they wanted to hear what I had to say. Some said they were independents, and a few said they were registered Republicans.

But a lot of people said something very different:

"I've never been involved in politics in my life."

"I've never campaigned for anyone."

"This is my first time."

Mine too.

When the line at the door was down to a trickle, I turned around to walk to the stage and realized that we'd filled the entire auditorium. There were several hundred people, a number of them standing around the edges of the room. I gasped—I mean really, not metaphorically.

I was so excited that I jumped up onstage and took a photo of all those volunteers on my cell phone, and we sent it out later that night on Twitter. The picture shot around the Internet. A few days later, one blogger wrote, "This looks more like the kind of crowd you'd see at a presidential volunteer meeting late in the campaign than a rally for a Senate candidate 13 months before the general election." Wow.

The interest and enthusiasm I encountered that night knocked me over. I had barely started running for office, yet hundreds of people showed up. All these men and women and kids, out on a dark, chilly night, filling out forms so they could volunteer to spend time holding signs or making phone calls or knocking on doors. These people weren't getting paid to help the campaign. Most of them had jobs and kids and mortgages and a long list of obligations. But they were here because this race mattered to them.

I was excited about all those volunteers, but I was also anxious. What if I let them down? My job was to win this race, and I had just screwed up pretty badly with the *Daily Beast*. What if they stood in the rain holding signs, gave up their weekends to knock on doors, and put their hopes in me? What if they made real sacrifices and I lost?

Later in the campaign, I ran into a college student at a T-station. Bruce and I had decided to sneak out to the movies. We took the T to a big movie theater in downtown Boston, then had dinner at a little Italian place. By the time we headed home, it was about eleven o'clock. We stood on the subway platform with a few other late-night travelers, waiting for the train.

A thin young man—really just a kid—in a loose-fitting suit, with a backpack slung over his shoulder, looked at me and smiled. A minute later, he came over. "Are you Elizabeth Warren?"

He was from central Massachusetts, the first in his family to go to college. He was attending school in Boston and he loved it, but he said he worried about money all the time. He worked a full-time job during the school year and took two jobs during the summer to try to cover as much as he could. As we waited for the subway, we talked about student loans, declining government investment in universities, and rising tuition. Finally, he asked if he could take a picture. Bruce snapped the shot on the young man's phone. The kid smiled and started to walk away, then turned around.

"I give you money every month, and I'm taking on hours so I can give more."

I felt as if he'd hit me with a spear right between the ribs. Good Lord— this kid was working until nearly eleven o'clock on a Saturday night and he was sending *me* money? I smiled weakly and said something along the lines of, "Uh, I'm doing okay in the campaign. Maybe you should keep your money. I'll be fine. Really."

He looked back at me. "No, I'm part of this campaign. This is my fight, too."

And that really was the answer. It wasn't just my campaign. My name was on the ticket, but these folks weren't volunteering and donating for me. They were supporting something a lot bigger. When I said that we were better off if we invested in the future together, they already knew it was true—and they lived it. They thought America could do better, and they wanted it every bit as much as I did. And they would do everything possible to try to make that better future a reality.

This is my fight, too. It still gives me goose bumps.

Worth the Investment

As the fall raced by, I continued dividing my time between politics and teaching. At the end of the term, I planned to stop teaching and start campaigning full-time. Late that fall, it began to sink in that it was at least possible that I would soon teach my last class ever.

It was a bittersweet thought. Sure, I was revved up about the coming election, and I wanted very much to win. But if I joined the Senate, I would miss the classroom terribly. I loved holding a piece of chalk and watching the lightbulbs go on for my students—love love loved it. It's what I had wanted to do since I was a little girl. Leaving it behind would be hard.

But I was starting to discover that although running for office was sometimes awful, the experience could also be deeply personal. Not when I was smiling for cameras or giving a speech to a big group—it would happen unexpectedly, during the intimate moments of campaigning. One day I sat in an ice-cream shop with the mother of two boys, both of whom had been diagnosed on the autism spectrum. They were handsome little guys, active and ready to bolt from their chairs at any moment. As the boys ate, their mother instinctively kept a hand on one and a close eye on his brother, but that didn't distract her from making a passionate plea. Please, please work for more funding for research, she said. "We're so close."

The boys' mother was right. Autism, Alzheimer's, diabetes, cancer—science is advancing at a pace people only dreamed of a generation ago, and now we are right on the edge of discoveries that will change the world for millions of people. Besides, money invested in research creates opportunities for businesses to develop. Nanotechnology, MRIs, fiber optics, GPS, tumor detection—federally supported research has propelled our businesses forward, giving us a competitive edge around the world. Even medical research is a solid financial investment. Every $100 spent supporting basic medical research generates an estimated $221 in new business activity. We get healthier *and* we double our money—that's how to build a stronger future.

For more than half a century, that was part of America's strategy: Invest in science. But as a share of our gross domestic product (GDP), today our federal investment in research is half what it was when I was growing up. *Half!* I thought that now more than ever—with so many discoveries right on the cusp—we should be pushing harder on the accelerator and investing more money in research, not putting on the brakes.

Later, after a rally on the South Shore, an attractive woman in her fifties stayed around to introduce me to her tall, good-looking husband. She was losing him to the mists of Alzheimer's, and she pleaded with me for more investment in Alzheimer's research. She also worried that his day care center would fall victim to budget cuts. She just wanted to hold on to her job and keep her beloved husband at home a while longer.

She was right, too. Keeping her husband at home, and keeping her working, made sense economically and was worth fighting for on those grounds alone. But her story raised a much deeper point. Fighting for the man with Alzheimer's or fighting for the two little boys was also about our basic humanity. What kind of people are we? What are our shared values? Many congressional Republicans think it's fine to give billions of dollars in tax breaks to giant oil companies and corporations that park their money overseas, even as medical research budgets are hit by another round of cuts and care centers have long waiting lists. But those spending choices don't reflect the values of the American people.

A mother and a wife were fighting for their loved ones, and I wanted the chance to fight alongside them. I wanted it passionately. I wanted to remind people that every one of these policy fights is also deeply personal. When we make choices about investments in scientific research, millions of people are touched, one person at a time.

Jobs are personal, too. At one construction site, I asked the workers how long they were going between projects. A big guy in his fifties, a heavy-equipment operator, talked about what it was like to go eleven months with no work. "I'd show up every day, follow every rumor and every lead, but nothing—I mean, nothing." He talked about his kids, an older boy who wanted to go to college, and about his wife trying to get an extra shift at the diner. Others added their own stories—seventeen months without work, six months, nine months. They talked about how hard it was between jobs. The big guy said, "I sat home and wondered how far the life insurance would go. Would they be better off if I just died?"

He had worked so hard and played by all the rules, and it hadn't been his decisions that brought down the economy. He hadn't asked for any special deals. He just wanted a fighting chance.

For a long time, I would wake up in the night and think about the big guy, about the two little boys, about the man with Alzheimer's. I'd feel a weight on my chest. More than ever, I wanted to win this race. I wanted the chance to fight for them.

I Am Woman

In those early months in the race, reporters would sometimes ask me a variation of the question "What's it like to run as a woman?"

I always smiled mildly, but I hated the question. I was pretty sure no one asked Scott Brown how it felt to run as a man.

Still, I knew the subtext. No woman had ever been elected senator or governor in Massachusetts—and a lot of people thought no woman *could* be elected senator or governor. The Woman Question delivered a not-so-subtle message: Don't kid yourself, girlie. Big-time politics is a boys' game.

Early on, I spoke to several women who helped me think about whether I should run for office. One of them was Stephanie Schriock, the dynamic head of EMILY's List. Stephanie spends a lot of her time recruiting women to run for office, and she promised that if I decided to run, she would help me through the campaign. She wanted me to jump into the race, but she never sugarcoated how tough it would be. One of her remarks stuck with me: We need to try. When a woman runs, she makes it easier for the next woman to run, and that's how we'll win.

Back in the summer, I had also spoken with Patty Murray, a senior member of the US Senate, about whether I should run. I started listing the reasons I might not be good enough for this job.

After a few minutes, Patty cut me off: "Oh, please." Then she told me that women always think of reasons they aren't good enough. Men never ask if they're good enough to hold public office, Patty said; they just ask if they can raise enough money to win.

Huh.

I also talked with Mandy Grunwald, who had worked with a lot of women who'd run for office and who signed on as my media consultant. She knew more about electing women to office—and men, too—than pretty much anyone on earth. Early on, she explained one of the facts of public life: "It happens with every woman. People have to talk about how she looks before they can talk about what she says."

I tried to get over it, but I always winced when I saw a news report that started with a description of my appearance. The day after I announced my candidacy, some clever reporter said I was "a strand of pearls short of looking like the head of the PTA."

Oh goodie. Anyone want to offer a witty comment about my glasses or my hair?

Whose Kids?

When I had a spare minute, I spent it studying. I tried to digest the new job numbers or the latest developments in Iran. Ganesh took a leave of absence from his job as a law professor so he could be policy director for the campaign. In short spaces between campaign events and fund-raising, he gave me policy briefings and arranged for experts to give me mini tutorials on energy policy or health care or advanced manufacturing. Madeleine Albright came to help, and she spent a day talking to me about issues from all around the globe. It was like being back in the classroom, except this time I got to be the student. It felt as if my brain was being stretched in a thousand directions at once.

I slept less, ate less, worked more.

Part of campaigning was telling my own story. At first it felt a little funny. I had spent years talking about the stress on middle-class families. But it's one thing to discuss stagnant wages and dangerous mortgages and economic issues that affected millions of people; it's another thing to talk about me and my family. Over time I found that describing my background and saying a few things about how I got here seemed to strike a chord with people—the story of the daughter of a maintenance man who graduated from a commuter college and ended up as a professor at Harvard.

When I mentioned paying $50 a semester for college some people gasped, but a lot of people nodded. Pretty much everyone I talked to agreed that young people needed a shot at a college education, but support for education was shrinking. A kid going to a state college today would pay (adjusted for inflation) about three times more than his or her dad had paid a generation earlier. America had once invested in young people like me, but we weren't providing those kinds of opportunities to kids anymore—at least not at a price middle-class families could afford.

Late one afternoon, I spoke in the dining room of a house in a small town near the south coast. The chairs had been pulled out of the room, and about twenty people had crowded in, standing around the table or leaning against the walls. It was clear from their uniforms and work shirts that several of those in attendance had stopped off after their shift at work was over. A couple of people had parked their children in the living room, where the television had been turned down low.

I talked about building opportunities, about building a future for all our kids. As we moved to questions, the conversation took on more energy. We talked about children in overcrowded classrooms and what it takes to build an economy that will produce good jobs for all our kids, not just a few. We talked about why kids need safe neighborhoods and access to health care.

As the group broke up, a man in his sixties came over to me. He was thin, with the leathery skin of someone who had worked outside for many years. He wore a Vietnam vets cap that was frayed on the right side of the bill; he'd probably grabbed it there a million times.

He didn't smile, and his voice was flat. I looked for clues—maybe a little hostile? I wasn't sure.

"Yeah, you talk about building a future," he said. "But what about transgender? What about them?" Now he looked full-on angry.

Wow. That seemed to fall out of the sky. I felt the instinctive need to crouch, as if we were about to get into a fight.

I said just as flatly: "We build a future for all our children. And that means transgender children. *All* our children—no exceptions."

He held my gaze for a moment and then said: "Damn right."

He went on to explain that he had a grown son who was transgender. "In a million years you'll never know the special kind of hell he has gone through. I want somebody who fights and doesn't back off."

I relaxed. A future for all our kids, every one. *This* was a fight I was ready for.

Running a Campaign Without Karl Rove

In November, Karl Rove got in the race. He and his Super PAC, American Crossroads, and its sister organization, Crossroads GPS, were targeting Democrats they thought were vulnerable, and apparently I was high on that list. Control of the Senate would hang in the balance in 2012, and the Republican Party had every intention of keeping Scott Brown in office. They were taking no chances.

Rove was one of the wiliest political operators in the country. He had been the mastermind behind George W. Bush's two terms in the White

House, and since then he had built a reputation for launching ads that were (according to a blogger for the *Washington Post*) "full of falsehoods and distortions that were widely debunked by independent fact checkers." Since Rove's donor list was secret, Crossroads GPS didn't even pretend to be embarrassed if they were caught in a lie. These guys were playing for keeps, and they seemed to be perfectly willing to lie and cheat if that's what it took to win.

A full year before the election, Rove's group took out two attack ads against me. The day the first ad came out, I was taping an early-morning interview for a local news program. When I arrived at the station, no one showed any particular interest in talking with me about the issues at the center of my campaign. The question everyone wanted to talk about was: Had I seen the Karl Rove ad?

Um . . . What ad? I'd heard that Rove had bought advertising time, but I'd been up late the night before, and that morning I'd barely had time to get dressed and gulp down a mug of tea before heading for the studio. I hadn't seen anything.

The station's staff took me into the darkened control room and ran the ad on a bunch of screens. Everyone watched me while I watched the ad. I wondered if they thought I was about to burst into tears.

Up came this truly awful picture of me, my face puffy and weird-looking, and in the background was this creepy zombie-movie music that seemed to suggest I intended to eat voters' brains. Then came a series of images that linked me to Occupy Wall Street, riots, attacks on the police, and heavy drugs.

My first impulse was to say, Good grief, where did they get that awful picture? My second impulse was to laugh—the ad was beyond bizarre. It didn't feel real. It was so screwy that it didn't even seem personal, as if they were talking about some other person, maybe someone who starred in horror movies.

Several weeks later, the second Rove-backed ad came out. This ad was just plain cuckoo. It blamed *me* for the bank bailout and ended with: "Tell Professor Warren we need jobs, not more bailouts." What? My official response was to call the ad "ridiculous," but that doesn't capture what I was feeling. Charging that I was too cozy with banks was like attacking Newt Gingrich for being too shy or George W. Bush for being a pacifist. We were entering a new kind of crazyland.

What frustrated me, though, was the fact that it's very hard to hit back against this kind of thing. Karl Rove was making outlandish claims, but for all practical purposes, they were anonymous. His name didn't appear in the ad. The names of his buddies, the rich guys who financed the ad, didn't appear—and no one could find out who they were. I was fighting a shadow opponent, and I could flail all day and never land a blow.

But I wasn't the only one under attack: an environmental group had already gone after Scott Brown for his votes supporting Big Oil. The race was barely under way, and it wasn't hard to see where one of the hottest Senate races in the country was headed. Brown and I would both do our best to make our case to the voters, but we could easily wind up drowning in ads by outside groups.

Scott Brown spoke a lot on the campaign trail about stopping outside ads. At first it seemed to me like empty talk, but I began to wonder if there was a way to make it actually happen. Could we ask the TV stations not to air the ads? (No chance—too much profit, and people would worry about censorship.) We could gripe all day long about how terrible outside ads were, but was it really possible to keep the Super PACs on the sidelines?

In January, Brown and I started talking about doing something big and even a little radical. There was no legal way to stop the outside groups from running ads, but eventually the two campaigns signed on to a deal with real teeth: Both candidates pledged that if any outsiders came in to help us, we would penalize ourselves. The penalties would carry real weight—whoever was helped by a Super PAC ad would dip into our own campaign contributions and give money to charity. We worked it out so that if Karl Rove ran $1 million in ads against me, Brown's campaign would have to give $500,000 to the charity of my choice. And the same was true in reverse. In effect, we each pointed a gun at our own feet and then said to the outside groups: "Don't come any closer or I'll shoot!"

At first, my campaign team was uneasy with the prospect of a deal. Would Scott Brown follow through? I'm sure he wondered the same thing about me. No one could force either side to go along. For this agreement to work, Brown and I had to trust each other.

I had another reason to be worried. Every time I went out on the trail, I met people who looked me in the eye, shook my hand, and then whispered that they had given me money. People told me about cutting out doughnut runs and digging a little deeper so they could pitch some money into the kitty for my campaign. People said a hundred variations of "We contributed it to your campaign because we believe in what you are doing." If some outside group ran an ad against Scott Brown and this deal forced me to divert contributions away from my campaign, would I be betraying the people who had donated their hard-earned money? Did I have any right to gamble with their contributions?

We were in uncharted territory, but Scott Brown and I were both willing to give it a try. The deal had at least a chance of working, and the alternative of allowing the race to be swamped by outside ads seemed truly awful—for Brown, for me, for every voter in the Commonwealth. Besides, maybe this new approach could make campaigns more accountable and help pull the electoral process back in the right direction—even just a little.

On January 23, 2012, Scott Brown and I signed the People's Pledge.

The reaction from the press was positive but skeptical. Politico called it a "first-of-its-kind pact." The *Washington Post* hailed it as a "groundbreaking attempt," then quickly added, "It's unclear how effective the agreement will be." The *American Prospect* predicted that the agreement wouldn't have any impact on the Super PACs, but "bless their hearts for trying."

Who could blame the skeptics? I wasn't confident this would work, either. The proof would be in the results.

As for the Super PACs and other outside groups, the reaction was also mixed. The League of Conservation Voters—the group that had gone after Brown—announced: "We are inclined to respect the People's Pledge." The response from Karl Rove's Super PAC, however, was more ominous:

> [The agreement has] loopholes the Teamsters could drive a truck through, the longshoremen could steer a ship through, the machinists could fit a plane through, and government unions could drive forklifts of paperwork through.

And then it all went quiet.

THE BATTLE FOR THE SENATE | 233

Dodging Poison Darts

By January, life had taken on a new rhythm. I had taught my last class at Harvard—maybe my last class ever—and now my long days were scheduled to the gills, with every ten-minute block accounted for. Meeting-meeting-meeting, call-call-call. It was exhausting, but exhilarating, too.

What really threw me, though, were the constant attacks from the other side. I would almost persuade myself that I was starting to get the hang of full-throttle campaigning and then—*bam!* Out of left field, the state Republican Party, or the Brown campaign, or some blogger, would launch a rocket at me.

Some of the stingers were silly, some were nasty, and some were downright nuts. They accused me of plagiarizing my own book. They said I hated people who drank beer. Whatever the particulars, I'd get home from a long day of meeting with people and giving speeches, then end up in the basement late at night, digging out old calendars or pulling up old book manuscripts so I could rebut some ridiculous claim. I half expected someone to declare that I had given birth to space aliens, but at least that one passed me by.

The attacks were a big distraction and at times nerve-racking. And they were unrelenting. It seemed as though a new missile would sail in every day—except for the days when it was two or three missiles.

One morning, I stepped out of the shower just as the radio blared some accusation from a Republican Party official. I was dripping wet, and before I could think, I yelled, "Could you please wait until I get some clothes on?"

Bruce started picking up the papers off the front porch each morning and going through them, page by page, before he put them out on the kitchen table. On good days, he'd shout, "Clear!" and ask if I wanted oatmeal for breakfast.

But a lot of mornings there was no "Clear!" and no breakfast. It felt as if I were running through a forest at full speed while a band of hooligans threw poisoned darts at me. I needed to watch where I was headed and go as fast as possible, but I also needed to duck.

Bad News

One Monday afternoon in late January, Otis started vomiting. We mopped up and took him out for a walk, but every few hours he got sick again. We felt sorry for him, but not too alarmed. For a big, hunky dog, he had a delicate constitution. We'd seen this before, and we figured he'd picked up something yucky off the sidewalk and eaten it while we weren't looking.

In the morning I hit the campaign trail, and Bruce took Otis to the vet. The vet said it was some kind of gastric thing, but he wanted to keep Otis overnight for some tests.

That was the first little ping of warning. Otis had never stayed overnight for a tummy problem.

The next afternoon I was riding in the car, headed to Worcester for some meetings, when Bruce called.

"Babe, I just left the vet." He paused, and I could hear him breathing. His voice was tight. "It's bad. Otis has lymphoma." I felt the whole car start to sway. Otis? Lymphoma?

For a moment I sat very still. Suddenly I was acutely aware that I never spent even a minute of the campaign alone. I didn't have an office where I could shut the door or even a ladies' room where I could get away for a few minutes. Instead, my young staffer Adam Travis picked me up almost every morning in what we called the Blue Bomber (a bright blue Ford Escape) and drove me around to the day's events. I would ride along next to him, making calls or reading briefings, until we jumped out and met with people. We refueled at Burger King or Chipotle, but our job was to get out and spend time with people. Some days it was just Adam and me, and other days we'd have two or three people riding with us in the backseat.

Today we had a full backseat. When Bruce hung up, I wanted to weep. I wanted to go home and hold Otis. I wanted Bruce to hold both of us. I wanted to cry out loud and blow my nose and cry some more. Instead, I leaned my head against the cold window and cried as inconspicuously as I could. I didn't want to scare the young staffers in the car. I was pretty sure that Senate candidates weren't supposed to cry.

The next two days were a blur. I had a full schedule, and Bruce was teaching, but he got Otis to MSPCA-Angell animal hospital. Otis was in such terrible shape that the vets started emergency treatments to stabilize him. From healthy on Monday morning to nearly dead on Thursday night. The world felt very uncertain.

Otis's new doctor, Carrie Wood, called us to explain that the lymphoma would eventually be fatal. But she also told us that the disease could be treated and that about 50 percent of all dogs given treatments were alive a year later. Of those dogs, about 50 percent were still alive a year after that, and so on. Otis had a good chance of being with us for another couple of years—and maybe longer.

I was worried about what the treatments would do to Otis. Would he be sick all the time? Would he be in pain?

But Carrie said none of that would happen. The treatments would generally make him feel better, and he wouldn't have any of the awful side effects that people experience with chemo treatments. We said to go ahead.

When we picked Otis up from the hospital on Friday afternoon, he was shaky but clearly happy to head home. I didn't think he could climb into the backseat, but once I opened the car door, he was halfway in before I could bend down to help him. He was taking no chances of being left behind.

The treatments worked like magic. Otis seemed to bounce back as quickly as he had fallen ill. He was cheerful and frisky—or at least as frisky as Otis ever got. He was ready for his walks, and he began to gain back some of the weight he'd lost during the Week from Hell.

But the diagnosis changed me. Time with Otis seemed more precious, something not to be taken for granted. Before I left early in the morning or when the three of us settled in late at night, I often tried to snap a picture of Otis, as if I could somehow save these minutes. I spent hours on the phone, and I started sitting on the floor and gently combing Otis and rubbing his belly while I talked to people miles away. Otis seemed changed, too. Instead of snoring softly in another room while I worked on my computer, he moved closer to me. He would more often rouse himself and come over to get his ears rubbed or ask me to lean over and put my forehead against his. We were in this together.

But the campaign never slowed down. Every day the schedulers tried to squeeze in just a few more phone calls, a few more meetings. I went faster and faster.

As the weeks flew by, all time seemed more precious. Out in California, Atticus was learning to walk. Lavinia was moving up to the next level in her gymnastics class. Octavia was in fifth grade, and suddenly she was almost as tall as Amelia. I worried that real life was passing me by.

Alex had an announcement of his own: He was getting married to his girlfriend, Elise. He was a lucky guy. She was kind and gentle, with the sweetest smile I had ever seen. Alex and Elise were planning to buy a home in Los Angeles not too far from Amelia. He assured me that he and Elise would get married *after* the election. The campaign seemed to have ripple effects everywhere.

Back in Oklahoma, my brothers were getting older. Don Reed had climbed up on his workbench to change a lightbulb, and on the way down he took a bad fall. David had a cold he couldn't shake, and John's knees were bothering him. There was a snowstorm, then a windstorm, and later there was a hailstorm. I tried to call my brothers when I could, but I was constantly on the road, traveling around the state to meet with mayors and stop by union halls and senior citizen centers.

Was I doing the right thing? I'd wake up before the alarm went off in the morning and lie there thinking, I just want to be with family today. Then I'd get up and head out to a meeting or a breakfast or a rally. I'd talk about an America that once built the greatest middle class on earth. And I'd talk about banks that preyed on those families and a Republican leadership that thought Washington's job was to serve the banks, not hardworking families. I talked about the huge number of Americans who were getting older and how we urgently needed to put money into medical research for Alzheimer's and diabetes. This is the moment we should be investing in the next generation of young scientists, not cutting their funding. And as we sped along in the Blue Bomber from one stop to the next, I'd think about how this was the moment to speak out and how much I wanted to be in this fight.

Most nights I'd go home and start making phone calls while Bruce prepared for classes. Then Bruce and Otis and I would plonk down on the couch, watch a few minutes of TV, and collapse into bed. And I would often wake up in the night, straining to hear Otis's breathing, needing to make sure he was still with us.

Mothers for Justice and Equality

By now, Roger Lau had signed on as the campaign's political director, which meant he took me everywhere in the state—absolutely everywhere—to meet with everyone. Roger is the kind of person who always tells the truth, and people trust him. He is also the only guy I know who has tried out every hot dog stand, pizza place, 99, and McDonald's from Pittsfield to Provincetown, and he was quick to provide a review of each one. This was critical information as we crisscrossed the state.

Roger had brought on Jess Torres to be his deputy, and on a dreary Saturday morning in March, Jess accompanied me to meet with Mothers for Justice and Equality. Jess is smart as a whip, but his real strength is that he's fundamentally kind, and this was a morning in which everyone could use a little extra kindness. Gathering at Faith Christian Church in Dorchester, we numbered about fifty people, nearly all women, seated at round tables with about eight to ten chairs at each one. Most were mothers who had lost children to violence. Some had lost other family members, and some were friends or supporters. Also attending were a few religious leaders and community activists and an elected official or two, but this meeting belonged to the mothers.

By this point, I had gotten pretty comfortable standing in front of a crowd of people and making an energetic pitch about what we could do to create a better future for our children. But in this room, I was wholly inadequate. I didn't have words to address a woman who had lost her child. The grief of these mothers was so overwhelming and their mission was so enormous and I had so little to offer.

Kim Odom, co-pastor of True Vine Church in Dorchester, led the group. Pastor Kim stood at her table and talked about the death of her son Stephen. She named him, and she named the moment she had lost him four years earlier. For an instant, she wasn't with us; she was with her beloved son as he died. He had been thirteen, a good kid on his way home from a basketball game. After he was killed, she dedicated her life to preventing violence in her community.

When Pastor Kim had begun talking, I left the podium and stood with her. And when another mother rose, I moved to stand with her, and then with another mother. It was all I could do.

I knew the numbers. We lose eight children and teenagers to gun violence every day. If a mysterious virus suddenly started killing eight of our children every day, America would mobilize teams of doctors and public health officials. We would move heaven and earth until we found a way to protect our children. But not with gun violence.

The politics surrounding this issue make me want to tear my hair out. I know that Americans care fiercely about keeping our kids safe. So why do we toss common sense out the window when it comes to protecting our kids from gun violence?

Of course, not every kid has the same risk of becoming a victim. A large number of those gun deaths occur in poor neighborhoods. Gang violence and street crime pose a far smaller threat in well-off suburbs than in gritty inner cities. I'd spent decades trying to ring the alarm bell about the economic stress on middle-class families, but lately I'd been talking more about poor families, too. Low-income families have it so much harder: they start further behind, so that even the smallest blows can knock a family to its knees. Car trouble or a sick baby can mean losing a day or two at work, and any emergency can mean a trip to a payday lender and stepping into a trap that can cost thousands of dollars. Piled on the economic stress is the reality that the ugly claw of violence tears more often at poor families than rich ones.

The challenges faced by poor families attempting to build economic security are far more extreme, but the same erosion of investment in the future that is hollowing out America's middle class is also destroying the more limited opportunities that poorer families have to pull themselves forward. Much of what I was fighting for in an effort to rebuild the middle class—education, a thriving economy with good jobs, a level playing field where everyone pays their share—would provide an enormous boost to those in poverty as well. Building opportunity is about building it for everyone.

It comes back to the same question: Do we take care of some of our children, or do we build opportunity for *all* our children? For the mothers at Faith Christian that morning, that question came much, much too late. For them, the answer was: No, we do not take care of all our children. There would be no future for their beloved sons and daughters.

I spoke to the group for just a few minutes that morning. My words felt too small for such big wounds, but Pastor Kim was kind, and so were the other mothers in the room. In the end, we held hands and prayed together.

We prayed for all our children.

Native American

The long months of campaigning seemed to be having some positive effect. And if a victory over Scott Brown still looked like an uphill battle, I was at least gaining some ground.

Then the race turned really nasty.

It started in April with a question. Sixteen years earlier, in an interview in Harvard's newspaper, a university spokesman had defended the faculty's lack of diversity by noting my Native American background, and now a reporter wanted to know the details. I didn't recall the long-ago article, and when the reporter asked about it, I fumbled the question. Within a few days, we found ourselves in a full-blown campaign frenzy, with Republicans demanding that I prove who my ancestors were and accusing me of getting my job at Harvard under false pretenses.

As a kid, I had learned about my Native American background the same way every kid learns about who they are: from family. I never questioned my family's stories or asked my parents for proof or documentation. What kid would?

My mother's family lived in Indian Territory but my mother was the baby in the family, and by the time she was born, Indian Territory had become part of the new state of Oklahoma. My mother and her family talked about our Native American ancestry on both sides: her mother's and her father's families both had Native American roots.

By the time my mother was in High school, she and her family lived in Wetumka, a small town (about 1,400 people by 1920) that was the kind of place where everyone knew everyone. When my daddy began seeing my mother, his family made it clear that they did not approve. They looked down on my mother and her family, and when my father announced that he wanted to marry my mother, his parents were adamantly opposed. But my daddy and mother were very much in love, so they eloped—no fancy dress and no big group of friends and family. For someone as close to her family as my mother, this was a cut that ran deep.

For years after the marriage, the two families continued to live in the same small town, but they were almost never in the same room. As kids, we got it: There was Daddy's family and there was Mother's family. We saw Mother's family all the time. But visits with Daddy's family were infrequent, planned long in advance, and always very stiff.

Despite the trouble with Daddy's family, my mother never hid anything from us. Everyone on our mother's side—aunts, uncles, and grandparents—talked openly about their Native American ancestry. My brothers and I grew up on stories about our grandfather building one-room schoolhouses and about our grandparents' courtship and their early lives together in Indian Territory. We loved them and we loved their stories. As my mother got older, as she lost first her father and then her mother, her brothers, and two of her sisters, she spoke more forcefully than ever about the importance of not forgetting our Native American roots.

Now, in the middle of a heated Senate campaign, Republicans insisted that all of that was a lie. They claimed I wasn't who I said I was; they said I had cheated to get where I'd gotten.

I was stunned by the attacks. How do you prove who you are? My brothers and I knew who we were. We knew our family stories. But the Republicans demanded documentation and, back at the turn of the century, nobody in my family had registered any tribal affiliation. In Oklahoma, that was pretty common. But knowing who you are is one thing, and proving who you are is another.

Republicans also accused me of using my background to get ahead, but that simply wasn't true. It wasn't a question of whether I *could* have sought advantage—I just didn't. I never asked for special treatment when I applied to college, to law school, or for jobs. As the story broke and people dug through my background, every place that hired me backed that up 100 percent—including the Harvard hiring committee. Harvard told the media that they didn't know about my background when they hired me; they offered me a job because they thought I was a good law professor. Period.

But the facts didn't slow the Republicans down, and their attacks continued. Right-wing blogs took to calling me "Fauxcahontas." Someone took out a billboard with a picture of me in a Native American headdress, declaring, "Elizabeth Warren is a joke." One sunny afternoon, as I marched in a parade and shook hands and waved at people, a group of guys standing together on a corner started making Indian war whoops—

patting their mouths as if they were some kind of cartoon braves. It was appalling.

As the storm continued, I talked with one or the other of my brothers nearly every day. They were getting calls from reporters and Republican operatives. People came to their homes, and someone put our mother's death certificate on the Internet. Don Reed was shocked that so many people seemed to fancy themselves experts, without knowing our family. John was hurt, wounded by vicious name-calling. David was so furious he was ready to punch somebody. I felt terrible for my brothers; they never asked for any of this.

About the same time, the story broke that JPMorgan Chase had lost billions of dollars in high-risk trading in a scandal involving a trader known as "the London Whale." It seemed pretty clear that three years after the crash and the TARP bailout, the giant bank and its CEO, Jamie Dimon, hadn't given up their high-risk trading.

This should have been the moment to draw the sharpest difference between Scott Brown and me. Brown was "one of Wall Street's favorites," and he had worked to save the bankers $19 billion through his last-minute negotiations on Dodd–Frank. And I had been fighting for bank account-ability for years. But my encounters with the press during this period were dominated by questions about my mother's background—almost nobody asked about Jamie Dimon's recklessness.

And then, just as the controversy seemed to be winding down, Scott Brown called out my parents, suggesting that they hadn't told my broth-ers and me the truth about our family.

He attacked my dead parents.

I was hurt, and I was angry. But, as I saw it, there was nothing to do except keep on pushing ahead, fighting every day for what I believed in.

The controversy never went away completely, but it got better. Over time, reporters asked more about financial regulations and student loans and less about bloodlines. And people on the campaign trail wanted to talk about what was going on with their families, not mine.

A few months after the controversy had finally quieted down, an investigative reporter with the *Boston Globe* dived deep into my ancestry, tracking down every possible far-off relative she could locate, many of them people I'd never even met. In September, a long piece on the front page that quoted two distant cousins who said their families had never talked about any Native American ancestry, while other cousins and my three brothers were quoted saying they had grown up knowing this was part of their families' lives. Ina Mapes, a second cousin from Arizona whom I'd never met, gave a long account about our family's background, concluding that she had no doubts. "I think you are what you are," she told the reporter. "And part of us is Indian."

That sounded about right: You are what you are.

Volunteers

Through it all, the volunteers kept coming out. They believed in our campaign, even when a lot of the pundits and bloggers threw cold water on our chances. We opened loads of offices around the state, all dedicated to helping people get organized, make phone calls, and knock on doors.

Vicki Kennedy called with thoughtful advice borne of years of campaigning across the state. Former governor Mike Dukakis, who was now in his late seventies, took Bruce out to show him the finer points of knocking on doors, setting a blistering pace that kept them half-running from house to house. At one home, no one answered the front door, but the governor thought perhaps someone was in the backyard. While Bruce was thinking about the laws of trespass—he's a professor of property law and takes this sort of thing pretty seriously—the governor bounded to the side of the house and began fiddling with the gate to the backyard. Just as he got it open, a big dog came racing around the corner, barking wildly, slobber flying everywhere. The governor never missed a step. After jumping onto a small side porch, he called back over his shoulder to Bruce with the first lesson of political door knocking: "Ignore the dog. You won't change his mind anyway."

The people managing the volunteer effort were incredible. Mike Firestone is a high-energy guy who led a high-energy grassroots organization, and Lynda Tocci, Tracey Lewis, and Amanda Coulombe developed new strategies for turning out voters. Lauren Miller organized a creative and successful online effort as our new media director. The team leaders throughout the state were talented and innovative, and they busted their tails. Over time, tens of thousands of volunteers showed up and said, "I'm ready to work!" I think they went through a zillion boxes of Dunkin' Donuts before they were done.

Some of our volunteers had worked for lots of campaigns, but many were first-timers. Some volunteered because they were excited about a particular issue—education, research, global warming. Some volunteered because they wanted to do their part for democracy.

And one man volunteered to honor the dead.

I was in a Springfield union hall, talking to people who had come to find out about helping out. It was cool outside, and each time someone opened the door, it let in a *whoosh* of cold air. I always gave a short speech and took lots of questions, but this was my favorite part of campaigning, standing around and talking with people about their lives and what changes we needed to make to build a stronger future.

The hall was crowded, and people were offering cheerful greetings. Several had asked for pictures, and we'd had fun shouting, "Win!" or "Hi, Mom!" as someone snapped the shot.

I noticed a man off to the side, maybe in his fifties. He was alone, his head down and his shoulders hunched. I reached out to him. He told me his name, and we shook hands. And then we stood quietly for a minute, still clasping hands. I moved in closer, and we shifted away from the crowd.

His face was tired. His voice was quiet, a little raspy. He said his son had graduated from college a couple of years ago with a lot of debt. The boy hadn't been able to find a good job, and the debts just kept piling up.

The man paused and was quiet for a long time. He explained that people don't know how that can get you down, what it does to your heart, how depressed you get. He let out a deep breath. "My son killed himself last month."

We stood there in the cool air. I didn't say anything. I just held his hand. Finally he said, "We are failing our children."

I said, "I promise I'll do my best."

He said, "I know you will."

And that was it. He paused, and then he walked away. I held out my hand to the next person, but I knew I would never forget him. Not ever. And I would never forget what this race was really all about.

Finding Peace

I think my campaign speeches were more somber during those months. The race was grueling, and I was still behind in the polls. Well-wishers offered advice everywhere I went. "Focus on different issues!" "Change your bumper stickers!" "Fire somebody!"

I knew the advice came from a good place, from supporters who just wanted to help me win. But the underlying anxiety was palpable. People were pouring their hearts into this campaign, and I could hear the dire prediction whispering in the winds at every pit stop and every rally: *She's going to lose. She's going to lose.*

So I worked harder. What else was there to do?

Moments of peace were treasures, offering calm in an otherwise crazy life. Bruce and I went to Easter services and Passover seders and joined in prayers in several languages. Reverend Miniard Culpepper at Pleasant Hill Baptist Church made a special effort to encourage me, and I joined him in prayer on several occasions. It felt healing to be able, even for a short while, to focus on values and to be in touch with the spirit that moved me into this race.

Reverend Culpepper offered me wise counsel: Be still and listen. Have faith. Let people know your heart. As the campaign progressed, I found myself thinking about Reverend Culpepper's words time and again.

I carried my King James Bible to services, the same one I'd carried since fourth grade. Sometimes the pastor called on me to speak. I had taught Sunday school years earlier, but mostly I had told Bible stories to little children. I'd never spoken to a whole congregation. But I stood up, and I talked about my favorite Bible verse, Matthew 25:40. I told people what it meant to me. Its message was very simple: The Lord calls us to action. It's what we *do* that matters most.

State Convention

June arrived, and at last it was time for the party's state convention. Democrats from around the state would come together in Springfield, endorse a candidate, and get ready for the general election in November. It was a bit like a giant pep rally crossed with a student council election.

Tom Keady jumped in and gave our campaign yet another boost.

Tom had been active in Boston politics for decades. He'd been a key operative for John Kerry in 2004, and he'd worked on several other presidential races. He arranged an old-fashioned train trip from Boston to Springfield, with red, white, and blue bunting, and rally stops in Framingham and Worcester along the way. As we pulled out of the station in Boston, I got to stand in the back of the train and wave—just like some picture in a fifth-grade history book. The train was full of supporters, and we picked up more people along the way. Amelia and the girls joined us. (Seventeen-month-old Atticus stayed home with his daddy; Amelia had decided that the little guy might not be ready for quite this much democracy.)

When we got to Springfield, we saw that some Teamsters had parked a shiny eighteen-wheeler next to the green where we rallied our supporters; it sported a huge ELIZABETH WARREN sign on the side. That night, everyone hit the bars. They were packed, and I jumped up on benches or tables to deliver impromptu speeches. People hugged me, kissed me, and spilled a lot of beer on me.

On Saturday, June 2, the Springfield arena was packed. The Senate race had started with a gaggle of Democratic contenders, but now we were down to two—Marisa DeFranco, a high-spirited immigration lawyer, and me. Both of us would vie for the nomination until the primary in September, duking it out through the summer. Or at least, that's what we would do unless the convention delegates voted by more than 85 percent for one candidate, in which case only that candidate would go forward. That seemed unlikely, since no one could recall a contested Democratic primary that had resulted in the necessary 85 percent vote.

I had exactly fifteen minutes to make my pitch to the delegates about why I should be the Democratic nominee for the Senate—with the emphasis on *exactly*. Tradition required that I pick one or more people to introduce me, and several seasoned professionals had warned me that it was important to keep these introductions short. I put my own spin on that ball: instead of short introductions, I picked short *introducers*. My little granddaughters.

They stood at the podium, eleven-year-old Octavia on a box and seven-year-old Lavinia on a larger box, facing a crowd of more than three thousand people holding signs, shouting, and clapping. The girls smiled, and then Octavia said:

My brother, Atticus, is too little to be up here with us, so I'm talking for him, too. We are here to introduce our Gammy, Elizabeth Warren. She is running for the United States Senate because of us and because of all kids. We're really proud of her.

The cheers for the girls were like those at a big family party—loud and enthusiastic. Lavinia had wanted to do cartwheels on the stage, but the space by the podium was narrow and I figured it would be way too dangerous, so she just waved. I came out on stage, gave both girls hugs, then launched into a speech about how families were getting pounded and it was time to take on Wall Street, time to take on Big Oil, time to fight back.

After the speech, I went backstage to wait. And wait, and wait, and wait some more. I think I was on my tenth game of Go Fish with Octavia and Lavinia by the time they called me back and announced the result: I had received more than 85 percent of the vote, meaning the primary process was over!

Now I was officially the Democrats' choice and officially Scott Brown's opponent. I knew the race was going to get even more intense over the next few months, but I understood that the endorsement I'd been given meant the people in this arena were ready to fight. I was ready, too.

During my speech, I had talked about Ted Kennedy, our party's long-time champion in Massachusetts and in America. Later, riding home with Bruce and the kids, I thought about him again. I remembered the first time we'd met. I remembered his battered satchel, his enormous pride in Massachusetts as he looked out that twenty-fourth-floor window, his willingness to take on the long-odds fight for all the working families who were going broke. I leaned against the car's window and thought about the election ahead and how I might have the chance to help working families, too. I couldn't be Ted Kennedy, but at least I had a strong model for how to fight for what was right.

I pulled out my cell phone. I had saved a voice message from back when we were fighting for the consumer agency, and I'd listened to it off and on for years. It begins, "Oh, Elizabeth, uh, this is Ted Kennedy, just calling to thank you for your help. . . ." The message goes on, but I just wanted to hear the first part. I just wanted to hear his voice.

Getting Down to Business

As the summer went on, we still gathered in living rooms, but now we spilled into backyards and parks, cafés and bars.

Lots of bars, as a matter of fact.

Okay, that sounds like the start of a joke, but it's not. Many times, in fact, I visited bars and insurance offices and all kinds of small businesses. Elizabeth Vale, who had helped us launch the CFPB, was now our champion for building business liaisons for the campaign. Over time, she hooked me up with tons of people who ran small businesses—restaurants and Internet start-ups, plumbers and home health care providers, florists and building contractors, landlords and dry cleaners. I met with fishermen in Gloucester, Scituate, and New Bedford to talk through the economics of their business. And yes, I met people who owned bars.

Some of these business owners were ready to support me. But others would say something like "I usually vote Republican because Republicans are pro-business."

And I'd always get straight to the point: "Do you worry about how much you pay in taxes?"

"Sure."

"So how much money do you have stashed in bank accounts in the Cayman Islands? How much intellectual property have you transferred to a foreign tax haven? How much of your income is shielded with depletion allowances?"

You can guess the response: None. None. None.

Then I would talk with these business owners about the ongoing battle over tax policy in America. A lot of it is couched in "big government vs. little government" or "pro-business vs. anti-business." But I think most of that is a deliberate distraction so people don't see the real battle. The critical question is: Who pays? Does everyone pay, or just the little guys?

For businesses, the real battle isn't whether we need the government to invest in education and infrastructure and scientific research— businesses need all those investments. There's nothing pro-business about crumbling roads and bridges or a power grid that can't keep up. There's nothing pro-business about cutting back on scientific research at a time when our businesses need innovation more than ever. There's nothing pro-business about chopping education opportunities when workers need better training. To most people, it's pretty obvious that businesses need government investments.

No, the real battle isn't "pro-business vs. pro-government"; the real battle is whether everyone pays or just the little guys. Giant companies hire armies of lobbyists to craft custom-made tax loopholes. And it's working: big corporations are paying an average tax of 12.6 percent of their profits, less than half of the advertised 35 percent corporate rate. Meanwhile, middle-class families and middle-size (and small) businesses are left to pick up the tab.

Over the course of that summer, I also talked with a lot of people who were self-employed. For so many of them, achieving any sort of financial security seemed to hover just out of reach. After completing a job, they often had to wait to collect what they were owed, but in the meantime, they had to meet their own expenses. They paid their own insurance, and they paid their income taxes straight up—no special tax loopholes for them. They weren't asking for special breaks. They just wanted a level playing field.

That sure seemed right to me.

Money Talks

Guy Cecil, a gifted strategist who helps Democrats organize Senate campaigns, is a true believer. When he talks about how his grandmother fled an abusive husband with five little children in tow and then waited tables for forty years, he turns the story into a deeply optimistic parable about what's possible in America—if people are given a fighting chance. Guy was once a Baptist minister; when he came out as gay he knew his congregation wouldn't accept him, so he left and eventually started living his values through elections.

Back when I was first thinking about running for the Senate, Guy came to see me. He told me that I'd probably need to raise $20 million to $30 million.

I was stunned. I'd never run for office, and I was ready to stop right there. I looked at Guy and said, "Thirty million dollars—are you kidding me?"

Guy has a very gentle smile, exactly the kind you'd expect from a kindly pastor. He turned that smile on me and said in a calm voice that he knew it was a lot of money, but I needed to understand the hard reality of campaigning for a competitive Senate seat. It's really, really expensive.

In fact, Guy was wrong about what it would take—or maybe he was just trying to ease me into the shallow end of the pool. By July 2012, our campaign had already raised $24 million, and we weren't even in the homestretch yet. We were headed for a number that was a lot bigger than $30 million.

Raising money was exhausting. It was endless. I spent hours on the phone, and then spent more hours, and then more. There were days I felt like a hamster on a wheel. No matter how many calls I made, no matter how many people said yes, I needed to raise more money.

Every time I sat down to make calls, I thought about the polls: I was still behind. Scott Brown still had a big money advantage. People told me that if I didn't raise enough money, in the final stretch Brown would blitz all the television and radio stations and drown out any message I tried to deliver. And then the race would be over. I would lose.

So I picked up the phone and made another call.

I was incredibly lucky—and deeply grateful—to get so much generous help. I met a couple in Newton who celebrated their anniversary by eating sandwiches at home and writing me a check for the amount they would have spent on dinner at a nice restaurant. A boy still in grade school raided his piggy bank and brought me a bucket of change. A man wrote me a check for the exact amount of his tax refund, with the comment that it was "unexpected money, so I figure it can do some unexpected good. Go win!"

Paul Egerman and Shanti Fry organized people to host house parties and breakfasts and bring their friends into the campaign. Smart and driven, they donated hundreds—maybe thousands—of hours to the campaign. In turn, they persuaded countless numbers of others to give money to our cause. And they had terrific partners in two members of my staff, Michael Pratt and Colleen Coffey.

We also raised money online, along with lots of support. EMILY's List and the League of Conservation Voters encouraged their members to help, and they really came through, adding great momentum to the campaign. The Progressive Change Campaign Committee signed on early with the petition encouraging me to run, and they stayed with me every day right through the election. MoveOn.org also put their shoulder to the wheel. And Daily Kos, Democracy for America, and Progressives United rallied their huge e-mail lists time and again behind our campaign. To say I felt humbled by these extraordinary efforts doesn't begin to cut it. So many people made real sacrifices, and I was profoundly grateful for all their help.

Eventually, we closed the money gap with Scott Brown, and we were able to open campaign offices all over the state and get television ads on the air early and stay on straight through Election Day. Meanwhile, the People's Pledge was holding, so I didn't have to fight both Karl Rove and Scott Brown simultaneously.

Still, I felt like I had my hand out all the time, and I hated having to ask, over and over. The first contest we had run during the campaign was to ask our supporters what slogan should go on the back of our Elizabeth-for-Senate T-shirts. The winner was: *The best senator money can't buy.* I thought about that slogan every day—and every time I sent yet another e-mail asking people to donate. I asked for help because I needed to compete with Wall Street money; it was my only chance.

The same wretched system that had given giant banks such extraordinary influence over Congress also forced every candidate to constantly ask for money. And I had to wonder: If politicians didn't have to raise so much money, would the bankruptcy wars have ended differently? Would Washington have responded differently in the wake of the crash of 2008? Would the government have focused more on saving homeowners and less on saving giant banks?

Money, money, money—it whispers everywhere in politics. It twists a little here, bends a little there. And far too often, it tilts in the same direction: in favor of those with buckets of cash to spend.

I believed in what I was fighting for, and I worked hard to raise money for the campaign. And I would do it all over again. But to make lasting change, to level the playing field so that everyone gets a chance, the money part of elections has got to change. I knew it during the campaign and I know it now. Our democracy deserves better. We deserve better.

Shrink the Vote

In August, the Republicans picked a new target: my daughter, Amelia.
 Ooh boy.

I didn't know it at the time, but I later learned that Massachusetts (along with many other states) had taken some heat for not following a federal law designed to make it easier for people to register to vote. The National Voter Registration Act, passed in 1993, requires states to offer people the chance to register to vote when they get a driver's license, which is why the law is usually called "Motor Voter." Seems sensible, and that part of the law was working pretty well. But since not everyone gets a driver's license—especially the disabled, elderly, and urban poor—the same law required states to invite people to register to vote when they applied for social services, such as veterans' benefits, food stamps, or Medicaid. That's where Massachusetts had dropped the ball.

And that's where Amelia figured in. Not long after we finished writing *The Two-Income Trap* together, Amelia started volunteering for a non-profit group called Demos, which tries to help strengthen the middle class and promote democracy through research and advocacy. By the time of my Senate campaign, she had been working with Demos for several years, and they had elected her chairman of the board. It was a part-time volunteer position involving things like choosing an audit committee and setting the agenda for board meetings.

Demos had been pushing a lot of states, including mine, to comply with the federal voting law. Now Massachusetts was finally mailing out half a million voter registration cards. In early August, Scott Brown issued a furious statement calling the state's mailing "outrageous," and he accused Amelia of aiding this effort in an attempt to benefit my campaign.

In fact, Amelia had nothing to do with the Massachusetts mailing. Demos had started pushing for state compliance with federal voting laws two years before Amelia began volunteering for the organization, which was many years before I had even thought of running for the Senate.

But to me, that wasn't really the point. Scott Brown was a sitting US senator, and he was outraged that his home state was making an effort to *follow federal law.* Huh? The real issue for me had nothing to do with Amelia or even Demos: the real issue was about doing everything possible to help people register to vote. I thought voter registration was supposed to be like organizing a blood drive or holding a Thanksgiving charity raffle— the kinds of values that we all support, from both political parties.

Okay, people can laugh and say I'm hopelessly naive, but this issue is a direct shot at democracy. In many states, the Republicans have made voter suppression a regular part of their arsenal, chipping away at early voting, African American voting, Latino voting, immigrant voting, student voting, you-name-it voting. As the Tea Party–affiliated True the Vote campaign famously said, they wanted voting to become like "driving and seeing the police following you." I guess attacking my daughter for her involvement in an organization that was pushing states to help more people register to vote was just one more page out of their standard playbook.

But the assault shifted the Senate contest in another way. Amelia was suddenly in the limelight. And once Scott Brown and the Republican Party started attacking her, it quickly became clear that she was deemed "fair game" for anyone who wanted to take a whack at her.

Amelia's phone rang off the hook, and several articles about her appeared in the papers. Reporters combed through her background and called up her old friends and co-workers, trying to find people who would talk about her for a newspaper story. Amelia kept assuring me that she was fine—after all, she's a successful businesswoman in her own right, and she could handle what came at her. But I felt terrible.

I knew politics was a rough business, but I had really hoped I'd be the only target. So far, the Republicans had denounced my dead parents, harassed my brothers, and attacked my daughter. And this was all on me. My family hadn't asked for any of this, and if I had kept my head down, none of this would have happened to them.

Home Front

One night a week or two later, something was worrying me in my sleep. I finally came half-awake and heard a cough. Not exactly a cough, maybe more of a hack. I drifted back to sleep, then heard it again. My brain cleared enough to locate the sound.

I nudged Bruce and said, "What's wrong with Otis?"

We both waited in the dark, but Otis didn't make any sound, so I got out of bed. I rubbed his head for a few minutes. He seemed fine, so I went back to bed. But the next morning, Bruce said he wanted to take Otis in for a checkup, just to be sure.

When I got home that night, Bruce took me out to the porch swing and sat beside me. He held both my hands. This wouldn't be good.

"The treatments aren't working," he said quietly. "The lymphoma is back."

I felt like I'd been kicked in the chest—and I hadn't seen it coming. I remembered the stats from Otis's doctor: half of all the dogs treated for lymphoma are alive a year later. Half. One year. We'd had less than eight months.

I felt cheated. If half the dogs were alive a year later, how could he possibly be sick again? Couldn't the treatments be changed? As I tried to talk this through, my voice kept rising. Finally, I was shouting at Bruce—no, I was shouting at the fact that Otis was sick again, as if I could somehow hold off reality by force of will.

Bruce let me rail on. When I finally fell silent, I was breathing hard. He gently pointed out to me the other side of what the vet had said: half the dogs die within a year, even with treatment.

I started to cry. I wanted someone to bargain with. Please, please don't take Otis.

Bruce said Otis had started a new round of treatments that day, and we'd see what they could do. When we picked him up at Angell Memorial the next day, he was obviously sick but clearly glad to be back with his people. He dropped his head and wagged his whole back end as he slowly made his way toward us.

Later that night, we huddled together on the couch. We took up our usual positions: Bruce on one end and Otis sprawled across the other, with me wedged in between them. As I rubbed Otis's ears, I whispered, "Please be okay. Please be okay."

Corporations Don't Dance

In early September, Bruce and I headed to Charlotte, North Carolina, for the Democratic National Convention. A few weeks earlier, the word had come from the White House: President Obama wanted me to speak on Wednesday night, right before Bill Clinton.

I had never been to a national convention, and on Tuesday morning, September 4, I went to a rehearsal. While I waited for my turn, I tried to think of when I had first seen this political spectacle. I must have been about seven, sprawled on the floor with my dolls, on a tweedy rug in front of a black-and-white television. All three channels carried whichever national convention was taking place just then. I thought it was boring and hoped *I Love Lucy* and *Gunsmoke* would come back on soon. While my parents dutifully half watched, my father smoked and read the newspaper and my mother kept a book propped in her lap. My parents weren't especially political, but I had some general idea that my father thought President Eisenhower was a decent man.

Now I looked around the giant arena in Charlotte and thought about how the woman standing here would have seemed as far away as the moon to that little girl in front of the television set.

"Don't shout," someone said. "This microphone is so sensitive it can pick up your heartbeat." I got jolted back to the present.

I was standing on the stage of the awkwardly named Time Warner Cable Arena, and while one technician was warning me about the sound system, another was checking the podium height. (The thing actually moved up and down so it would look just right in front of shorter and taller speakers.) The hall was largely empty, although a number of people were setting up seats or adjusting camera equipment or just wandering around.

I tried to stay calm and focused. Tomorrow night, I would speak right before former president Bill Clinton. In front of a live audience of about twenty thousand people and a television audience of twenty-five million. During the homestretch of a race in which I was still behind. Nope: no pressure at all.

The arena had been built in 2005 as a home for the Charlotte Bobcats of the NBA. The stage was big, and even though the basketball court had been filled in with rows of seats, the place still looked like a giant gym—a nice, new gym, but a gym all the same. Maybe the Democratic Party should have spiced things up by putting us all in jerseys and baggy shorts.

After we finished the run-through, I walked back to the hotel with Ganesh and Tom Keady. As we headed down the street, some women on the other side shouted, "Hey, there's Elizabeth Warren. Woo-hoo! Elizabeth! Elizabeth!" I looked over to wave and walked straight into a pole. I wasn't hurt, but I felt really stupid.

After that, Ganesh and Tom walked closer to me, watching me carefully to make sure I knew there were obstacles ahead. "Pole!" one would yell. "Curb!" the other would caution. My life now had a sound track. Worse, I had proven I needed it.

The next day, we showed up hours ahead of my scheduled speaking time, exactly as instructed. Everyone had been given heavy plastic identification badges and told to hang them around their necks. The tags were checked and rechecked as we approached the arena, entered it, and then got closer and closer to the backstage waiting room. Going to the bathroom involved a complicated handoff from one station to another, as well as a series of confusing turns. After I navigated it once, I quit drinking water.

As I waited for my turn at the podium, I thought about this chance. An audience of twenty-five million—the number sounded beyond improbable. I figured I would never in my life get another chance to speak to this many people, so I'd better use this chance to say what I really wanted to say. And now I was about to step out on the stage.

I tried to breathe. I had exactly fifteen minutes—one shot—and I needed to get it right.

The system is rigged.

That's what I wanted to talk about. For me, that captured what was wrong with the country, how our government had been hijacked by the rich and the powerful. How it didn't have to be this way. How we could do better.

My heart was hammering. The stage manager gave me a little push, and I stepped into the blinding lights. People started applauding. It looked like a zillion people, on their feet and starting to yell. That made me even more nervous. My mouth went dry. My teeth felt sticky. In a flash of deep insight, while twenty-five million people looked on, I realized why it had been a bad idea to stop drinking water hours earlier.

But after a few seconds, something shifted. I stopped thinking of the delegates and all the others in the arena as just an anonymous crowd. I could see faces. I could see people wave. They were ready. No, they were eager.

It was like the night at the T-stop in Boston when that young guy told me this was his fight, too. This wasn't just my race. This was our race.

For a brief, absurd moment, I wanted to stop. I felt a sudden urge to line up everyone in the audience so I could spend a minute with each person, shake hands or hug or touch an arm, and say, "I know how important this fight is. We'll fight together and we'll win."

And then I took a deep breath and started.

I explained that I was here to talk about how hardworking people were getting the short end of the stick. I talked about Mitt Romney's famous statement that "corporations are people":

> No, Governor Romney, corporations are not people. People have hearts, they have kids, they get jobs, they get sick, they cry, they dance. They live, they love, and they die. And that matters. That matters because we don't run this country for corporations, we run it for people.

I asked the question asked by so many of the men and women I'd met: Is America's government working for the people, or is it working only for the rich and powerful?

> People feel like the system is rigged against them. And here's the painful part: They're right. The system is rigged. Look around. Oil companies guzzle down billions in subsidies. Billionaires pay lower tax rates than their secretaries. Wall Street CEOs—the same ones who wrecked our economy and destroyed millions of jobs—still strut around Congress, no shame, demanding favors, and acting like we should thank them.

I talked about middle-class families, people who get up early, stay up late, people who run small businesses and struggle to meet payroll, people who worry about having enough money to make it to the end of the month.

> These folks don't resent that someone else makes more money. We're Americans. We celebrate success. We just don't want the game to be rigged.

Afterward, the crowd gave me a big round of applause.

President Clinton came next. I wasn't nearly as memorable as the former president, but who is? Still, I'd said what I wanted to say, and it felt great to have the chance to say it.

Union Proud

After the convention, I shifted from high gear to superhigh gear. With the election only two months away, the days were starting earlier and running later. I felt like I was putting off everything until after the election, including sleep.

I was also eating less. I was nearly always scheduled for a "luncheon" or a "dinner," but since I was always giving speeches and shaking hands, I almost never got more than a few bites at one of those events. I lived on hot, milky tea from Dunkin' Donuts and fast food from everywhere. I lost more weight, and soon I constantly felt as though my pants were falling down. I started hitching them in back with a big safety pin. Every day brought lots of picture taking, and many times, as we'd line up to smile for the camera with our arms looped behind each other's backs, I'd feel someone's hand hit the thick bulge. I wondered if anyone speculated whether I was wearing a holster or carrying a wad of money back there.

The tracker seemed to appear at every event. I'd come to understand that this was standard political fare, and I know a similar tracker followed Scott Brown, but I never got used to it. When people whispered to me about losing their homes or having a dad at home who was dying of cancer, I learned to look around for the tracker, worrying that a video of their private moment could end up in some political ad.

With the days ticking by, it was now all hands on deck. Legendary civil rights leader and longtime congressman John Lewis gave moving speeches about the power of the vote. Singer James Taylor and his wife, Kim, put on an amazing concert. John Kerry rallied the troops. Max Cleland brought together vets from across the state to underscore the importance of honoring our promises. Governor Deval Patrick had generously endorsed me back before the state convention, and he gave powerful speeches at some great rallies, accelerating the momentum of the campaign.

And then there was Boston mayor Thomas Menino. By this point he had been the city's mayor for nineteen years, making him the longest-serving mayor in any major US city. He knew every inch of Boston, and he loved his city passionately—and his city loved him just as much. He was a Democrat, but he was also fiercely independent, and there was regular speculation in the press that he might endorse Brown or, almost as telling, stay neutral in the race. For over a year, I'd telephoned the mayor regularly, and he had asked me questions and given me advice—but no endorsement. In mid-September, he called to say: "I'm ready." He told me he was convinced that I would fight for working people, and for him, that's what public service should be all about.

Once he was in, Mayor Menino jumped into the deep end of the pool—a huge rally, speeches, signs, and even his own TV commercial. His signature line—"She's good people"—was all over Boston. He brought along his ally from many battles, Michael Kineavy, who worked his magic and pulled in hundreds more helping hands. The mayor was a powerhouse, and the boost he gave the campaign was strong enough to taste.

After months of hard work, we finally seemed to be gaining ground against Senator Brown. The polls started to show real movement. I didn't think it was possible for the campaign staff to get even more excited, but they did.

Contrary to all the predictions back in January, the People's Pledge was still holding and Karl Rove was off the airways. I give Senator Brown a lot of credit: he held to the People's Pledge. As I started catching up to him in the polls, he may have been tempted to back out and hope that outside money could swing things in his favor. But he stayed true to his promise.

One afternoon in mid-September, Roger Lau called. Get to Dorchester, he said. Right now.

So Adam turned the Blue Bomber around, and we headed off to Florian Hall in Dorchester. It's a plain redbrick building with a flag waving out front, the kind of solid place that has been home to a million potluck dinners and retirement parties for firefighters and their families in eastern Massachusetts.

Firefighters had been a particular flash point in the Brown–Coakley race two years earlier. Although the union leadership officially endorsed Coakley, the rank and file were reported to have voted for Brown in big numbers. I'd been visiting fire stations for nearly a year, and it wasn't lost on me that a lot of the cars and pickups parked near the firehouses still bore Scott Brown stickers.

Roger met me in the parking lot at Florian Hall. We went inside and shook hands with Ed Kelly and Mike Mullane. Eddie, one of the youngest presidents in the history of the state firefighters' union, grew up tagging along behind his father, Jack, who served as a Boston firefighter for thirty-five years. He inherited his dad's black hair and intense blue eyes. Now in his thirties, he has a pretty wife and two active children ("future firefighters," as he likes to say). He also has the kind of solid build that leaves no doubt that he could throw someone over his shoulder and run full tilt out of a burning building.

Mike Mullane, a veteran firefighter with white hair and a little-boy smile, is a generation older. His wheezing breath and rattling cough are painful reminders of a life spent running into chemical fogs and toxic smoke.

Eddie and Mike brought Roger and me into a little office. As we took our seats, I noticed a photograph on the wall that showed one of the union leaders posing with Scott Brown.

With no preliminaries, Eddie started in. "Look, if this election is about who you want to have a beer with, Brown wins." He paused. "Hell, no offense, but *I'd* rather have a beer with him."

He looked pained. I looked at the photo on the wall and thought, Here it comes. He's going to tell me he's sorry, but the firefighters feel more comfortable with Brown and they're going to support him. At least he's got the guts to tell me face-to-face.

I looked back at Eddie, and he held my gaze with his piercing blue eyes. "But—f**k it—we gotta raise our families. And you are the best shot we've got."

I blinked.

"Yeah, we're endorsing you."

Eddie said the firefighters had talked and talked and talked about it, and from his description, I gathered that some of the conversations had been heated. He explained that one of the leaders in the union had worked on Scott Brown's campaign and another was a longtime friend. But in the end, the council had voted—unanimously—to recommend that the membership endorse me.

Finally, Eddie leaned back and smiled. Since we're in, he said, we're going to be in all the way. "You'll be family."

Eddie was good to his word and then some. The firefighters got a huge neon-yellow bus and put a giant picture of me on the side. They drove the bus all around the state, blasting its very noisy horn and often parking it near Scott Brown rallies.

During that long year of campaigning, I met lots of firefighters, but I also met hundreds of members of other unions. I met truck drivers, electricians, and sheet metal workers. Teachers and nurses, carpenters and musicians, janitors and bricklayers. Postal workers, home health care aides, steelworkers. I talked with them at construction sites and training centers, at job registries and volunteer events. They did many different kinds of work, and they had a wide range of worries, but those unions stood tall for *all* workers.

Most of the union members I met with were painfully aware that unions across the country were losing ground, as fewer workplaces were unionized. But unions were also losing ground politically. More than one president of a local union told me that other politicians would come to them for money and endorsements. But when they left the union hall, those same politicians spoke only in code, never saying the word *union* in their speeches. I think it mattered that in speeches and rallies and round-table discussions, I said the word, long and loud: *"Union!"*

The way I saw it, unions had helped build America's middle class. They fought for better wages and reasonable hours. They fought for safer factories. They fought for pensions and retirement security. They fought for health care coverage. And every one of those benefits spread to other workers—union and non-union—which made the whole middle class stronger and more secure. And when the squeeze was on, unions showed up to fight for Social Security, for Medicare, for a higher minimum wage, for equal pay for women, and, to my great delight, for the Consumer Financial Protection Bureau. They fought for the values that keep us strong.

Often enough during the campaign, I would hear the phrase *corporate and labor influence in politics,* as if "corporate" and "labor" were somehow two sides of the same coin. Really? Does anyone believe that an army of lobbyists fighting for tax loopholes and special breaks for one corporation is the same as the unions fighting for Social Security and equal pay? Does anyone believe that when corporations give money to take down unions and support so-called right-to-work laws, there are unions giving equal money to try to put companies out of business (and themselves out of a job)? Does anyone think that for every billionaire executive who can afford to write a check for $10 million to get his candidate elected to office, there is a union guy who can do the same? Give me a break.

In the battle over who Washington was really working for, the unions knew which side they were fighting on, and they fought as hard as they could. I was honored to have the chance to fight alongside them.

Debates

Scott Brown and I would debate each other three times during the campaign, and the first debate was scheduled for September 20. Polls showed that the race was now pretty close, and a lot of people found ways to tell me how important it was that I do a good job. I started getting nervous—really, really nervous.

Dan was full of Dan-style encouragement. He kept saying, "You could lose the whole race in a single bad minute during the debate."

The prep sessions were a nightmare. Nearly a dozen staffers gathered around to help me prepare. One of them would ask a question: "What is the path to peace in the Middle East?" Or, "How should we create more jobs in the economy?" I would start into my answer, and somewhere in the middle of point one in my four-point plan, someone would yell, "*Time!*"

I was supposed to answer every question in a minute and a half. Ninety seconds. One of the staff would ask another question, and again, before I could get to the main idea, someone would shout, "*Time!*"

We played this miserable loop over and over. In desperation, the team scheduled some practice sessions during which I was allowed to answer "the long way" before we focused on the clock. I think they could see I was getting frazzled, so they tried to sound encouraging: "That was pretty good in minute four! Maybe you could just say that part first." No problem!

In the end, Otis was my best coach. On the day of the first debate, I turned off my phone and shut down my computer. Otis climbed up next to me and put his head in my lap. I studied, and he snored. After a few hours, I was as ready as I'd ever be.

The first debate was held in a television studio. It was cramped and cold, a small set surrounded by giant cameras that looked like something out of a *Transformers* movie. Only the moderator, the two candidates, and some technical people were permitted in the room—not even our spouses could come in. When Senator Brown arrived, I walked over to shake hands. The moment was somehow surreal. Here was the man I was spending every waking hour trying to defeat. Our names were linked in thousands of press accounts, yet we'd met only a few times, and I don't think we had ever spoken a dozen words to each other. In some other context, we might have made pleasant small talk. After a brief hello, we moved back to our places, he at his podium and I at mine, locked in silence before the program began.

We were allowed to bring note cards to the debate, and before we got started, I saw Senator Brown shuffling through his stack. I had a stack of cards, too. Most carried statistics that I thought were important (family incomes, unemployment rates, and so forth—I didn't want to fumble a key number). But my last card was a photograph. It was a picture taken in front of Legoland with a gaggle of grandchildren, nieces, and nephews gathered around me. We all wore matching bright yellow tops, and we were all having a great time. The picture always made me smile. I looked at those children staring into the camera and thought: I'm in this race for your future.

I held the photo, and I remembered Reverend Culpepper's advice: Have faith.

Someone in the studio called out a thirty-second warning. Everyone— Brown, me, the moderator—took sips of water, our actions synchronized as if we were runners at a starting gate who'd been told to "get set."

A countdown, then the light on the closest camera came on. The moderator made the necessary introductions and asked the first question—it was about character—which he directed to Senator Brown.

Brown wasted no time. He said his thank-yous to the moderator and viewers, then lunged straight for my throat. "Professor Warren claimed she was a Native American, a person of color, and as you can see, she is not." He expanded the accusation, asserting that on applications to Penn and Harvard, "she checked the box claiming she was a Native American, and clearly she's not."

We were thirty-three seconds into the debate, and Brown had already called me a liar and then called the people who hired me liars. He had falsely accused me of using my background to get a job. And he had invited everyone watching on television to take a close look at my appearance so they could judge for themselves just who my parents and grandparents had been.

I wanted to talk about Wall Street bankers and taxes and education, but Brown wanted to go in a different direction. So I stood my ground. I talked about my family. I made clear I never sought any advantages, and I pointed out that the people who'd hired me had all verified my account—100 percent. When I got the chance, I moved to the issues that I believed were at the heart of the election. I talked about how giant companies and billionaires were exploiting a bonanza of tax loopholes and how Scott Brown and the Republicans were determined to keep those loopholes open. I talked about how we should be investing in educating our kids instead of subsidizing Big Oil. And how billionaires should pay at least as high a tax rate as their secretaries.

The reviews the next day called the debate a draw, and not many outlets featured what I had to say about tax loopholes or investing in education. But nearly every media report included Brown's attack over my background.

Two days after the debate, Brown and former Boston mayor Ray Flynn attended a campaign event inside a pub. A rally outside the pub included some of Brown's Senate staffers, and they were caught on video joining the crowd in cartoon-Indian war whoops and tomahawk chops. The video got widespread attention—and a lot of criticism. But that didn't stop Brown: he started running commercials accusing me of covering up the truth about my background and lying about my family.

It seemed this race was going to stay nasty right to the end.

Paid Actors?

Even as he doubled down with his commercials about my Native American background, Brown opened a new front in the ad wars: he claimed I'd hurt asbestos victims. Many people who worked around asbestos developed mesothelioma, a horribly painful lung cancer that is nearly always fatal. A few years earlier, I had served as a consultant on a case to protect trusts that had set aside money for asbestos victims. Most asbestos victims supported the trusts—and were on the same side of the litigation over this issue as I was—because they knew this was the best way to get some payment for their injuries.

A lot of asbestos victims were upset about Brown's attack ad, and some of them protested outside his office. Hoping to counteract the misinformation in the Brown commercials, we filmed two short ads featuring people who had lost a husband or a father to mesothelioma. Brown then claimed that these were "paid actors" rather than real victims. If many asbestos victims were upset before, now they were furious. They had gone through unspeakable suffering, and now they were being insulted. Said one victim: "Let Scott Brown tell me to my face that I am nothing but a paid actor, and I'll set him straight on what it was like to watch my father suffocate to death." Brown issued an apology.

As the race tightened, the ads were relentless. A lot of people volunteered to make ads for me, including Art Ramalho, the owner of the West End Gym in Lowell. Art has trained generations of working-class kids to box, and he is a local legend in Lowell. The first time I visited his gym, I saw the worn, wooden boxes next to the speed bags, and it took me a few minutes to connect the dots—some of the kids who came here were small enough to need a boost to reach the bag. Art has opened his gym—and his heart—to try to help the countless kids who have come his way.

Art went on camera to call me a "fighter" for working people. I wasn't as fast with my fists as the fighters in Art's gym, but I was grateful for Art's help.

Many of our other ads talked about what I wanted to do in Washington, and some criticized Brown for how he voted. Some of our ads were pretty tough, but I didn't make personal attacks—I wasn't going to be drawn into that. Even so, I suspect the good people of Massachusetts were sick to death of political ads. I know I was.

Because That's What Girls Do

As we headed into the final stretch of the campaign, women—and women's issues—shot into the foreground in an unexpected way.

It had started several months earlier, when Republicans in the Senate led another effort to cut back on the Affordable Care Act, aka Obamacare. Back in February 2012, they had introduced the Blunt Amendment, which would let a business or insurance company deny coverage for any medical service if it cited any vague "moral objection" to such coverage. No one was fooled: this amendment was intended to give any employer the right to deny insurance coverage for birth control. As it happened, my opponent in the Senate race didn't just vote in favor of the amendment;

he co-sponsored it. I had criticized Senator Brown for his vote at the time, but he had doubled down and gone on the offense, attacking me.

Then, in August, Missouri congressman Todd Akin caused a firestorm when he asserted that women don't get pregnant from "legitimate rape." That was bad enough, but in October, Republican Richard Mourdock from Indiana said he believed that pregnancy due to rape was "something that God intended to happen." Suddenly, people were talking about women's issues with a new kind of intensity. The gains that so many of us (including me) had come to take for granted no longer seemed so secure.

The speed with which this hit the campaign was stunning. Yes, I was a woman candidate. (Well, duh.) And yes, I am all-the-way committed to reproductive freedom, equal pay for equal work, and equal opportunities. But I had focused my campaign on middle-class economic security and crumbling infrastructure. Those are issues that profoundly (and sometimes disproportionately) affect women, but no one calls them "women's issues."

I was genuinely horrified that a United States congressman would call any kind of rape "legitimate." It made my skin crawl. Heck, I was horrified that a bunch of senators wanted to roll back coverage for birth control. I wanted to get right in their faces and yell: Are you kidding me? Are you guys from the Stone Age? After decades of fighting these battles, surely America's women deserved better. A *lot* better.

The Woman Question that had come up earlier in the campaign now returned with a vengeance, only this time it was framed a little differently. Now it was one version or another of "What is *up* with you women this year?"

What was up? Simple: Women were *fired up*. It's hard to describe the energy I felt among women on the campaign trail that fall. Old and young, married and single, straight and gay. Women poured into our campaign offices, and huge numbers showed up at our events. Senator Barbara Mikulski, the longest-serving woman in the history of the US Senate and a longtime force on women's issues, came to Massachusetts to rally the troops. Ethel Kennedy—well into her eighties but still full of spirit—showed up with her daughter Rory and wowed the volunteers. High school students volunteered alongside women who had been retired for twenty years or more. Parents brought baby girls, plopped them in my arms, and whipped out their cameras.

For months now, whenever I met a little girl on the campaign trail, I would bend down, take her hand, and tell her quietly, "I'm Elizabeth and I'm running for Senate, because that's what girls do." Now that statement took on special significance. More parents than ever asked for pictures, and I got to hold tiny newborns and kneel down to do pinky promises with shy little girls.

At some point in October, I met a marvelous old lady when her grand-daughter pushed her wheelchair over to me. She was tiny and frail, but she took my hand and smiled impishly. "I'm dying," she said, "but not too fast. I plan to see you win."

Early on, our campaign team had taken a close look at Scott Brown's record on women's issues. It wasn't terrible. He had broken with his party to support the Violence Against Women Act. He said he was pro-choice, although he didn't turn down the support from the pro-life groups that endorsed him. But he had voted against a bill for equal pay for equal work, and he was a co-sponsor of the Blunt Amendment. More important, he supported a national Republican leadership that seemed hell-bent on rolling right over women's rights. When it came to women's issues, a fair assessment of Brown's voting record would be "pretty good some of the time"—but why should that be good enough?

When Senator Brown and I met for our second debate, women's issues came up in a surprising way. Somewhere toward the middle of the debate, the moderator asked us to name our favorite Supreme Court justice. Brown's response: Justice Antonin Scalia. The ripple through the audience was instantaneous: Scalia? The most outspoken, conservative, anti-choice, anti-woman justice on the Court—*that's* the justice Scott Brown liked best? A few people started to boo, and Senator Brown backtracked, naming in quick succession Justices Kennedy, Roberts, and Sotomayor. As he tried to recover, the cameras caught the expression on my face. I looked like I was about to cough up a hairball. (I felt like it, too.) When my turn came, I named the pro-choice woman on the Court whom Brown had voted against: Elena Kagan.

On October 10, when Brown and I met in Springfield for the third debate, women's issues surged to the front once again. In response to a question, Brown repeated a line he had used often about how he lived in a houseful of women and that he had long fought for women's rights. I said I had no doubt that Senator Brown was a good husband and a good father to his two daughters. But I pointed out that in Washington, he voted on laws that affect all our daughters:

- He's had exactly one chance to vote for equal pay for equal work, and he voted no.
- He had exactly one chance to vote for insurance coverage for birth control and other preventive services for women. He voted no.
- He had exactly one chance to vote for a pro-choice woman—from Massachusetts—to the United States Supreme Court, and he voted no.

Those were bad votes for women, and it felt right to say so. The way I saw it, women deserved to be represented by someone they could count on, not *some* of the time, but *all* of the time.

I could feel the momentum of our campaign building, almost like a physical force. Our team was so excited that sometimes it felt as if there were lightning in the air. We knew that a lot of people were starting to focus intently on this race; they had come to understand how much their vote would matter.

Meanwhile, the polls stayed close. Some showed me ahead, some showed Brown still in the lead, and others had us within a point or two of each other. We were going to fight this all the way to the end.

Sweet Otis

Now it was time for a final surge of stump speeches and rallies and get-out-the-vote drives. Adam and I crisscrossed the state in the Blue Bomber. Mindy and Tracey ran the headquarters like seasoned generals, while Roger and Jess lived out of their cars as they rallied troops everywhere. Bruce met with volunteers and spoke at events, turning in surprisingly passionate stump speeches for his sweetie. We made plans to fly the kids and grandkids and nieces and nephews to Boston for the big day.

Six days before the election, Halloween arrived. That evening, I stood out on the front porch and admired all the kids coming by to trick-or-treat. Photographers did their best to capture the candy traditions at our house and compare them with those at the Browns' home. It seemed that nothing could escape politics, not even our choice of treats on Halloween.

As the night went on, a raucous party across the street spilled outside and turned into a parade over to our house to meet the candidate and take lots of silly pictures.

Throughout these festivities, Otis should have been right there beside me. He liked visitors. Besides, this was a night when little kids came to the door to pet him and drop yummy treats on the floor. What could be better?

When the doorbell rang the first few times, Otis pulled himself to his feet and stood in the hall while kids came in to pet him. At one point he lumbered out into the front yard to survey the sidewalks and reflect on all the activity. But after he came back into the house, he lay down and didn't get back up. He rested his head between his big front feet, his jowls spread out on the floor. As I went back and forth from the door to the candy bowl, he followed me with his huge brown eyes.

When Bruce and I turned out the porch light for the evening, Otis had trouble making it upstairs. Later, in the dark, I listened to his labored breathing.

Early the next morning, we took Otis back to Angell Memorial. His vet was kind, but she made it very clear that Otis was in a lot of pain. "He could hang on for a few more days, Elizabeth, but he's doing it just for you. He's ready to go."

I was long past the unfairness of it all, but I didn't want to lose him, at least not yet. Couldn't he stay just a little longer?

Bruce said it was time to let him go. Finally, I agreed.

We sat on the floor with him and said our good-byes. I rubbed his big head and scratched behind his ears. I remembered the puppy who had flopped down on the air-conditioning vent and the big doggie who had let the grandchildren crawl all over him. I thought about how when life was tough, he would nuzzle me and somehow remind me of more important things in the world.

After Otis died, Bruce and I held him for a long time.

With the election only five days away, Bruce and I decided not to say much about Otis. It wasn't a political calculation. I knew that if word got out, people would open their hearts. There would be hugs and "I'm sorry" everywhere I went. And once I started to cry, I wouldn't be able to stop.

So we kept the news close, just Bruce and me and a few other people. I told myself: In five days, I can cry. But right now, I've got to close it off. I have to keep going just a little longer.

We Will Win

November 6, 2012: Election Day. It was exactly fifty years to the day that Massachusetts had voted to send a young Ted Kennedy to the US Senate for the first time.

Now, after fifteen months of nearly nonstop campaigning, it all came down to this day. The meetings and the rallies, the fund-raising and the ads, the debates and the trackers—all that was over, and now it was up to the voters. Would Scott Brown hang on to the seat Kennedy had held for nearly half a century, or would I pry it loose? Today was the day the people of Massachusetts would decide.

Early in the morning, Bruce and I walked over to the nearby elementary school where we had voted for nearly twenty years. We formed a kind of makeshift parade, with a small herd of family, neighbors, and well-wishers tumbling down the sidewalk together. My niece Melinda had made matching blue satin headbands with "WARREN" spelled out in silver glitter across the top for the little girls, and they walked to the school in full glory.

Bruce and I have a running joke: I never tell him how I voted. But the joke has a point, because I take democracy seriously, and that includes the sanctity of the polling booth. And on that morning, standing in the little portable voting booth with its red, white, and blue canvas curtain, I saw my name on the ballot for the United States Senate.

Sure, I knew it would be there, but seeing it in black-and-white was a drop-dead serious moment for me. I knew that all across Massachusetts millions of voters would see what I was seeing—a choice between two very different people, a choice between two very different visions for our country. If the voters chose me and my vision, they would be asking me to carry their hopes for a better America. Voting always gives me goose bumps, but today I stood for a few seconds longer, thinking about what it would mean to have a chance to go to the US Senate to fight for working families.

After we voted, we piled all the kids and grandkids into the Blue Bomber and a couple of rented vans and zipped around eastern Massachusetts, visiting polling places and union halls, phone banks and campaign offices, urging on the teams that were still knocking on doors and holding signs. By early afternoon, we were starved, and we stopped at the Five Guys in

Medford for hamburgers. When we walked in, a woman in her fifties was sitting near the door; she looked up and yelled, "Holy s**t! It's Elizabeth Warren!"

She recovered slightly, and after glancing at the three seven-year-old girls who were with me, she apologized. Then she said, "I guess I didn't think you were real." I knew what she meant: to most people, politics seems like something that happens in a faraway place, not in the local Five Guys.

In the early evening, we all headed to the Fairmont Copley Plaza Hotel in downtown Boston to wait for results. Children and grandchildren and volunteers and state officials crowded into noisy rooms. People bubbled with cheer and early signs of victory. ("Voting is heavy in Lynn!" "They need more rides in Brockton!") But we still had a long way to go.

I slipped away to an empty room and practiced my speech. No, I practiced both my speeches—a concession speech and a victory speech. This wasn't the moment to take anything for granted.

Shortly after the polls closed, I went into the bathroom to change clothes. It was the first quiet moment I'd had since bounding out of bed before daylight. As I dressed, I thought about my mother. Would she be happy with the way I'd turned out? I'd gotten married and had children—and grandchildren—and Bruce and I owned a home and had saved money for our retirement. And somewhere along the line, I had decided to go to Washington and try to make a difference.

Mother had been afraid for me, not wanting me to venture out. But *she* had ventured out. When we needed her, she pulled on that black dress and blew her nose and did something she had never done before. She showed me what it meant to grow up, to be responsible, to do what needed to be done. And now the daughter of a telephone operator and a maintenance man might be going to the United States Senate.

The next few hours were a blur, but then one station flashed the headline and soon another: WARREN BEATS BROWN. Suddenly the race was over. Later we learned that the margin was big: 54–46.

The weekend before the election, our volunteers had knocked on more than three hundred thousand doors and made more than seven hundred thousand phone calls in what I'm told may have been the largest get-out-the-vote drive the state had ever seen. The effort paid off: people turned out in droves. It was the highest turnout for any election ever held in

Massachusetts—an astonishing 73 percent. That was thrilling to me: no one is going to strangle democracy in our state!

It was also the most expensive Senate election in the entire nation that year. Wall Street contributed truckloads of money to try to keep me out of the Senate, but in the end it didn't work. Senator Brown's campaign raised $35 million, but to my amazement, we raised $42 million, and more than 80 percent of our contributions were for $50 or less. I still have trouble grasping how much money that was. I'm stunned by how many people sacrificed and by how much effort it took to raise so much money. But I saw at least a small silver lining: The People's Pledge held. Maybe—just maybe—we created a new model for reducing the stranglehold of the Super PAC.

Finally, it was time for me to walk to the hotel's ballroom and appear onstage. As I stepped out, I was hit by a wave—a cheer that rose as a single sound. I looked out at all these people, packed in tight, standing and roaring their excitement. I saw a sea of faces, but I knew these faces. I saw hundreds of people I had come to know during this campaign, one at a time. People who held signs and made calls. People who urged me on when victory seemed so far off. People who believed that even a first-time candidate could win a tough race if we worked hard enough for what we believed.

And we did it.

Tens of thousands of volunteers did it.

Women did it. Women broke with their husbands and boyfriends and brothers and voted for me by a knock-your-socks-off twenty-point margin.

Unions did it. Vets did it. The LGBT community and black ministers and small-business owners did it. Latino activists and Asian leaders did it. Students and scientists did it. Mothers and dads and grandmothers and granddads did it. Even kids did it.

The people did it.

What was the lesson of that day? When we fight, we can win. And when we get really fired up and fight shoulder to shoulder, we can do some pretty amazing things.

Some say the rich and powerful now control Washington and always will. I say this battle isn't over yet. True, the playing field isn't level and the system is rigged. But we're putting up a heck of a fight, and we intend to keep on fighting.

This victory wasn't mine. That's not some kind of fake modesty talk—no, that statement is deep-down truth. This victory belonged to all the families who have been chipped away at, squeezed, and hammered. This time, they fought together and won. And now they were sending me to Washington to fight for them and for every hardworking family who just wants a fighting chance to live the American dream.

Epilogue | Fighting Again . . . and Again

I T WAS MAY 8, 2013, and I was working on a speech in my office in Washington.

I sat at my desk and took a last look at my notes. My temporary office surprised visitors a bit: it was in a trailer. To get there, you walked along elaborate, marble-clad hallways, took a sharp turn onto a plywood ramp, and then suddenly encountered an office featuring prefab walls, cast-off furniture, and a fake window that concealed a tangle of electrical wires and cables. But hey, fancy office or not, I was now a senator, and I could take my shot at introducing a bill on the floor of the Senate—which was what I was about to do, for the very first time.

When it came time to head over to the Capitol, I decided against taking the underground train that usually ferries people back and forth. I wanted some space to think, so I decided to walk through the tunnel on the sidewalk that runs alongside the train. Besides, I move pretty fast—sometimes I beat the train.

As I walked through the big, hollow space, the sound of my heels echoing off the walls, I remembered an encounter the previous summer, back when we were in the thick of a hotly contested campaign. The local teamsters had offered us their hall in Worcester for a Sunday afternoon rally. I gave a short speech and took a lot of questions. Afterward, a long line formed. People gave some advice or offered encouragement. There were pictures and babies and a fair amount of laughter.

Near the end of the line was a young man: early twenties, medium height, sandy-brown short hair. When I reached him, he stepped forward and, with no preliminaries, blurted out that he had done everything he was supposed to do. Counting on his fingers, he punched out the list. Worked hard in high school. Went to a good university. Got good grades. Graduated on time. Everything—check, check, check.

And then . . . nothing. No job. No new apartment. No bright future. He'd been looking for work for more than a year, and still nothing.

Actually, it was worse than nothing. Every day he fell a little further behind. His student loan debt got a little bigger. His stretch of unemployment got a little longer. His fear that he would never build a secure, independent life cut a little deeper.

Now he had moved back in with his parents—and he had no idea when he would move out or how he would get his own life under way.

I met him in Worcester. But I heard the same story in Falmouth and Dorchester. In Marlborough, Marshfield, and Methuen. In Weymouth and Westport and Ware.

I heard the story over and over and over, until I wanted to shout to the rooftops on behalf of these young men and women. They were trying *so* hard, but they felt like their futures had broken apart before they had even begun.

And now here I was, about to give a speech on the floor of the US Senate.

I stepped into the Senate chamber and walked straight to my desk— the same desk that for so many years had belonged to Ted Kennedy, and to John Kennedy before him. I clipped on my microphone and took a deep breath. And then I jumped in.

America's young people are struggling with more than *$1 trillion* in student loan debt. I asked: Why does the United States government lend to the biggest banks—the same banks that nearly broke our economy—at an interest rate that is less than one percent, and then turn around and charge our students an interest rate that is *nine times* higher? Why is the US government scheduled to make $185 billion in profits off the backs of our students? We're not investing in these students—no, we're asking them to pony up the money to subsidize the rest of us.

Then I introduced my bill, the Bank on Students Act, which would require that the Federal Reserve lend money to our kids at the same rate they lend to the big banks. I finished with:

> Unlike the big banks, students don't have armies of lobbyists and lawyers. They have only their voices. And they call on us to do what is right.

Months have passed since that day in May; I've been a senator for a little more than a year. I've seen our Congress up close, and parts of it are truly dysfunctional. I've already lived through one government shutdown and too many Republican filibusters to count. Every day I wrestle with the same ruthless reality that I've known for many years: Change—real change—is hard. Uphill, grind-grind-grind, sweat-it-out hard.

Yes, change is hard, but it is *possible*—and that's the part that fires me up.

I've heard a lot of talk about what can't be done. People said the new consumer agency was a pipe dream. But now it's the law of the land, and in July 2013 I presided over the US Senate as Rich Cordray finally became its first full-fledged, real-deal director. That agency is here to stay. After Rich's confirmation, one headline read: ELIZABETH WARREN SMILES BIG AFTER RICH CORDRAY CONFIRMATION. Got *that* right!

There are other ways to make change happen. Committee hearings are usually pretty dull affairs, the stuff that fills the 3:00 A.M. slot on CSPAN. But those hearings offer a chance to make some progress. At my first Banking Committee hearing, I pushed regulators to name the last time they took a big bank all the way to trial. They stumbled and fumbled, and a video of the exchange shot around the Internet and was viewed by more than a million people. Maybe, just maybe, more government officials will think twice before deciding that some bank executive is too big to jail.

And student loans? No, I didn't get the Bank on Students Act passed.

But at least the final deal on student loan interest rates was better than where it started: $15 billion better for students over the next ten years. And, in the end, I wasn't alone. More than a dozen senators from around the country stood up with me to say no to any deal in which the government makes a profit off the backs of our students. That's not a bad place to begin the next round in this battle—and, believe me, we will come back to this issue again.

Of course, student loans are just a start. There are many more fights ahead, and more work to be done—and I worry that we're running out of time. For a generation now, America's middle class has been squeezed, chipped away, and hammered so hard that the foundations of our economic security are beginning to crumble.

Every day I think about the people I've met who are part of this battle. The woman in New Bedford who walked two miles so she could talk to someone who would fight for her. The father who worried that basic fairness would be denied to his transgender child. The woman who brought her tall, good-looking husband to a rally and talked with me about his slide into the darkness of Alzheimer's. The big guy at the construction site who went nine months without work last year. I remember their faces, their fears, their determination.

Every one of them worries about our future. Every one of them has anxious days and sleepless nights. But every one of them is tough and resourceful. And every one of them—every single one of them—has a deep core of optimism that says we can do better.

I believe that it's this optimism about the future that sets us apart as a people, this optimism that makes America an exceptional nation. We built this country by striking out on new adventures and propelling ourselves forward on a path we named progress. Along the way, we learned that when we invest in one another, when we build schools and roads and research labs, we build a better future—a better future for ourselves and our children and our grandchildren.

Equality. Opportunity. The pursuit of happiness. An America that builds something better for the next kid and the kid after that and the kid after that.

No one is asking for a handout. All we want is a country where everyone pays a fair share, a country where we build opportunities for all of us;

a country where everyone plays by the same rules and everyone is held accountable. And we have begun to fight for it.

I believe in us. I believe in what we *can* do together, in what we *will* do together. All we need is a fighting chance.

Notes

1 | Doing What Needs to Be Done

27   *a chance to start over without a pile of debts pulling them down:* US bankruptcy law offers debtors a chance to get some relief from overwhelming debts, both by restructuring some debts (reworking a car loan, for example) and discharging a debt (writing off credit card debt, for example). Nearly all personal bankruptcies are filed either in Chapter 7 (liquidation) or Chapter 13 (restructuring). When a person files for bankruptcy, a trustee is appointed to oversee the process; the trustee's duties range from examining the debtors to make sure they have listed all their assets to selling certain assets and distributing funds to creditors. A family may retain certain forms of property through bankruptcy ("exempt property"), such as home equity and the tools necessary for that debtor to make a living, depending on the applicable state and federal law. In Chapter 7 bankruptcy, the debtor turns over her nonexempt property to the trustee, who then liquidates the property and disburses the proceeds to unsecured creditors. In return, certain debts can be discharged. (Some debts, such as student loans and child support, cannot be discharged in bankruptcy.) In Chapter 13 bankruptcy, the debtor keeps all her property, exempt and nonexempt, but surrenders a portion of her future income to repay creditors over a three-to-five-year period, with the trustee overseeing the repayment plan. When the debtor has successfully completed the repayment plan, a portion of the remaining debt will be discharged. Filing for bankruptcy also stops debt collectors and provides temporary protection from foreclosures.

28   *great defeat and, often, personal shame:* Despite claims that bankruptcy has "lost its stigma," the evidence suggests that there is still a lot of personal shame surrounding bankruptcy. For example, one long-term study found that 50 percent of bankrupt families were unwilling to admit, even anonymously, that they had filed for bankruptcy. Scott Fay, Erik Hurst, and Michelle J. White, "The Household Bankruptcy Decision," *American Economic Review* 92 (June 2002): 706–18. Other studies have shown that a large portion of households that do not file for bankruptcy would significantly benefit from filing for bankruptcy, which suggests that stigma prevents at least some people from acting in their best financial interests. See Michelle J. White, "Why It Pays to File for Bankruptcy: A Critical Look at the Incentives Under U.S. Personal Bankruptcy Law and a Proposal for Change," *University of Chicago Law Review* 65 (Summer 1998): 685–732. People on the ground, such as those who advise clients with respect to bankruptcy, further reaffirm

the sense of anguish and personal shame people feel when filing for bankruptcy. See Elizabeth Warren and Amelia Warren Tyagi, *The Two-Income Trap* (2003), 74 & n.12; see also Daniel Bortz, "Surviving the Emotional Toll of Bankruptcy," *US News and World Report*, January 18, 2013 (illustrating the perspective of financial therapists, who see bankruptcy as taking a huge toll on a person's self-esteem and emotional well-being). In the course of researching for *The Two-Income Trap*, our research team found that more than 80 percent of families said they would be "embarrassed" or "very embarrassed" if their families, friends, or neighbors knew of their bankruptcy. See *The Two-Income Trap*, 74 & n.13.

29 *housemaids who lived at the economic margins and always would:* Many scholars once assumed that all debtors were "a poverty-stricken, chronically unemployed segment of the lower class"—people on the economic margins. Teresa A. Sullivan, Elizabeth Warren, and Jay Lawrence Westbrook, *As We Forgive Our Debtors* (1989), 63; see also Philip Shuchman, "Social Science Research on Bankruptcy," *Rutgers Law Review* 43 (1990): 185.

33 *the kind of study that legal experts almost never did:* We were not the first researchers to try to understand more about the actual individuals who file for bankruptcy. For example, David Stanley and Marjorie Girth of the Brookings Institution conducted a notable study in 1971 that provided crucial insight into the sources of financial stress for those going into bankruptcy, the demographics of debtors, and debtors' postbankruptcy experiences. See David T. Stanley and Marjorie Girth, *Bankruptcy: Problem, Process, Reform* (1971).

33 *building a giant mosaic, one tile at a time:* The 1981 study relied on bankruptcy petition data. The petition data included information regarding debts and assets, income, and the petitioner's business, but it contained very little demographic information. The study covered districts in Illinois, Pennsylvania, and Texas. We coded financial information and supplemented our data with interviews with bankruptcy judges and bankruptcy lawyers.

The 1991 study relied on one-page questionnaires in addition to financial data from court records, which were vetted by the University of Texas and the University of Pennsylvania for the protection of human subjects. These questionnaires were designed to provide demographic and employment information about debtors. We asked trustees to distribute these questionnaires to debtors in Section 341 meetings, which are mandatory for debtors, in the first half of 1991. Debtors were told that participation in the study was voluntary and anonymous. We received about 59,000 questionnaires, which we winnowed down—through random selection—to a final sample of 150 cases from each district. In addition to drawing from the districts in the 1981 study, we drew from select districts in California and Tennessee. After coding the questionnaires according to a set of common criteria, we analyzed the data with an eye toward statistical significance while accounting for the possibility of selection bias and other types of data distortions. We supplemented this data with other publicly available data, such as the 1990 Census, as well as data generated by bankruptcy judges and economists.

As in the 1991 study, the 1999 study relied on core financial data and questionnaires that were distributed during mandatory debtor meetings. The study had an expanded geographical scope, covering districts in California, Illinois, Kentucky, Ohio, Pennsylvania, Tennessee, Texas, and Wisconsin. Our final sample for the 1999 study amounted to 1,496 cases. Again, we took steps to account for the possibility of selection bias and other types of data distortions.

In all three studies, we adhered to strict confidentiality protocol to protect the identities of participants.

For more information on the methodology underlying these studies, see the Appendices to *As We Forgive Our Debtors* (1981 study) and Jay Lawrence Westbrook, Elizabeth Warren, and Teresa A. Sullivan, *The Fragile Middle Class* (2000) (1991 study) as well as the 1999 supplementary study documented in Melissa B. Jacoby, Teresa A. Sullivan, and Elizabeth Warren, "Rethinking the Debates over Health Care Financing: Evidence from the Bankruptcy Courts," *NYU Law Review* 76 (2001): 375.

34   *found good jobs, gotten married, and bought homes:* In our 1991 study, we found that
     bankruptcy filers were generally better educated than the average adult population in key
     respects. Primary bankruptcy filers were slightly more likely than the average person to
     have had formal education beyond high school and to have completed one to three years
     of college. Given that education is one of the cornerstones of middle-class identity, this
     evidence suggests that bankruptcy filers were not on the socioeconomic fringe of society.
     Similarly, the average primary bankruptcy filer was currently or previously employed in
     a job rated as prestigious as the average job in society. Finally, we found that debtors'
     median age was roughly similar to the population generally. These indicators, as well as
     the racial/ethnic and gender indicators we looked at, suggest that far from residing on the
     economic margins of society, bankruptcy filers were generally part of the middle class.
     See *The Fragile Middle Class*, 27–74. Also see Elizabeth Warren, "Financial Collapse and
     Class Status: Who Goes Bankrupt?" (Lewtas Lecture), *Osgoode Hall Law Journal* 41
     (2003): 115, examining data on education, homeownership, and job status for debtors
     filing for bankruptcy in 1981, 1991, and 2001.

34   *or a family breakup (typically divorce, sometimes the death of a husband or wife):* The 2001
     Bankruptcy Project revealed that nearly nine in ten families cite three primary reasons
     for their bankruptcies: job loss, medical problems, and family breakup, which was con-
     sistent with previous empirical studies. See *The Two-Income Trap*, 81 & n.31. In the 1991
     study, more than two-thirds of debtors cited job-related financial stress, including job
     loss and job interruption, as reason for their bankruptcies. See *The Fragile Middle Class*,
     Chapter 3. Almost 20 percent of debtors cited medical reasons for their bankruptcies. See
     The Fragile Middle Class, Chapter 5. And more than 15 percent of debtors cited marital
     disruption as an important contributor to their bankruptcies. See *The Fragile Middle
     Class*, Chapter 6. The 1981 study also concluded that "job loss, divorce, illness and injury
     [were] implicated in many bankruptcies." *As We Forgive Our Debtors*, preface.

34   *full year's income in credit card debt alone:* According to the 1991 study, the mean credit
     card debt of bankrupt debtors was $11,529, as compared to $3,635 in 1981 (both figures
     stated in 1997 dollars). To put it even more starkly, in 1991 the average bankrupt debtor
     had credit card debt that amounted to about six months' worth of income, as compared
     to six weeks' worth of income for the average bankrupt debtor in 1981. See *The Fragile
     Middle Class*, Chapter 4. When it comes to homeownership, the 1991 study revealed that
     about half of the individuals who declared bankruptcy were homeowners, with the total
     climbing to above two-thirds in some districts. Although the number of homeowners in
     the bankruptcy sample was underrepresentative of the general population, these findings
     are quite significant given the relationship among homeownership, assets, and financial
     security. See *The Fragile Middle Class*, Chapter 7.

35   *the number of bankruptcies unexpectedly doubled:* In 1980 there were approximately
     290,000 consumer bankruptcy filings in the United States. By 1987, there were more than
     500,000 filings, and by 1990 there were more than 700,000 filings. To see the number of
     consumer bankruptcies between 1980 and 2010, see "Influence of Total Consumer Debt
     on Bankruptcy Filings, Trends by Year 1980–2010," http://www.abiworld.org/statcharts/
     Consumer%20Debt-Bankruptcy2011FINAL.pdf.

36   *five part-time jobs to meet rent, utilities, phone, food, and insurance:* The data used in this
     book were gathered under strict confidentiality requirements typical of human-subjects
     research protections at American universities. All data analysis was done using anony-
     mous numerical identifiers for the study participants. When referencing individuals,
     names and specific identifiers have been changed to preserve anonymity. See *The
     Two-Income Trap*, 184; *The Fragile Middle Class*, Appendix 1; *As We Forgive Our Debtors*,
     preface, 5, 49. Note that the quotes in the text are from: *The Fragile Middle Class*, "Sick-
     ness," "Unemployed or Underemployed."

37   *so that they could restructure and keep going:* Businesses may file for Chapter 7 or Chapter

11 bankruptcy. For discussion of the Chapter 7 process, see note on p. 279, *"a chance to start over . . ."* In Chapter 11 bankruptcy, the business may continue to operate, but the debtor must work with his or her creditors to negotiate a bankruptcy plan, which must be approved by a bankruptcy court. If the plan meets certain requirements, such as fairness and priority of creditors, the creditors may vote on the plan. Once the plan is approved, the debtor will continue to operate and abide by the terms of the plan. To the extent that creditors cannot agree to a plan, the court may intervene in order to expedite the process. In a large Chapter 11 case, the shareholders are typically wiped out and the new financiers, perhaps in conjunction with the old creditors, become owners. In the case of a sole proprietorship, the residual ownership of the business may be hotly contested, as the owner struggles to hang on and a single big creditor, typically the bank, attempts to seize all the assets and shut the business down. The burden of bankruptcy generally falls disproportionately on small businesses, because costs are high and many cannot survive the reorganization process without some flexibility with respect to payment schedules. See Elizabeth Warren and Jay Lawrence Westbrook, "The Success of Chapter 11: A Challenge to the Critics," *Michigan Law Review* 107 (2009): 603, 638–40; Alan N. Resnick, "The Future of the Doctrine of Necessity and Critical Vendor Payments in Chapter 11 Cases," *Boston College Law Review* 47 (2005): 183, 198–203. In addition, recent developments with regard to unsecured creditors have prompted small businesses to pursue liquidation over reorganization. See Ian Mount, "Advisor to Businesses Laments Changes to Bankruptcy Law," *New York Times*, February 29, 2012. I have elsewhere argued that we should be, and that Congress in fact was, especially concerned about the effect of bankruptcy law on small and struggling businesses. See Elizabeth Warren and Jay Lawrence Westbrook, "Financial Characteristics of Businesses in Bankruptcy," *American Bankruptcy Law Journal*. 73 (1999): 499, 553; Elizabeth Warren, "The Untenable Case for Repeal of Chapter 11," *Yale Law Journal* 102 (1992): 437, 468.

40 *the number had more than doubled in the decade since I had started teaching:* The number of non-business filings in 1980 was 287,570 as compared to 718,107 in 1990, which corresponds to a 150 percent increase in filings. See Annual Business and Non-business Filings by Year (1980–2012), Table from http://www.abiworld.org/AM/Template.cfm?Section=Non -business_Bankruptcy_Filings1&Template=/TaggedPage/TaggedPageDisplay.cfm& TPLID=60&ContentID=36302.

41 *big banks stepped up their efforts to change the bankruptcy laws:* The credit industry, claiming that bankruptcy law protected debtors too much, successfully lobbied for changes to the Bankruptcy Code in 1984. The 1984 amendments were based in part on an empirical study funded by the credit industry. However, the study was founded on empirically unsound research designed to support the industry's goals to shrink bankruptcy protection for families in trouble. See Teresa A. Sullivan, Elizabeth Warren, and Jay Lawrence Westbrook, "Rejoinder: Limiting Access to Bankruptcy Discharge," *Wisconsin Law Review* (1984): 1087, 1087–90. In addition to supporting this expensive and dubious study, the credit industry fought for amending legislation in Congress and claimed in a number of newspaper articles that debtors were discharging "as much as $1.1 billion in bankruptcy that 'they could repay.'" See Elizabeth Warren, "Reducing Bankruptcy Protection for Consumers: A Response," *Georgia Law Journal* 72 (1984): 1333–34 & nn. 3–9. After achieving some success with the 1984 amendments, the credit industry continued to lobby Congress for additional changes it desired throughout the 1990s. See Elizabeth Warren, "The Market for Data: The Changing Role of Social Sciences in Shaping Law," *Wisconsin Law Review* (2002): 1, 8 & nn. 19–22; David G. Hicks, "The October Surprise: The Bankruptcy Reform Act of 1994—An Analysis of Title II— The Commercial Issues," *Creighton Law Review* 29 (1996): 499, 501–02 & nn. 8–12 (discussing the role of the American Bankers Association in successfully quashing any "anti-industry" changes to the law).

41   *extraordinarily high interest rates, a practice known as usury:* The regulation of usury has been around since the ancient Egyptians and has a varied and deep religious heritage. See Gardner Wilkinson, *The Manners and Customs of the Ancient Egyptians* (2013), 50 (noting that the Egyptian legislature had condemned usury on the theory that "the safety of the country might be endangered through the avarice of a few interested individuals"); see also Diane Ellis, "The Effect of Consumer Interest Rate Deregulation on Credit Card Volumes, Charge-offs, and the Personal Bankruptcy Rates," FDIC: Bank Trends, March 1998 (noting that Plato had critiqued usury on the grounds that it fostered inequality and discord among citizens of the state). The Bible, including both the Old Testament and New Testament, contains thirty-five verses on usury, many of which liken usury to "extortion" and "unjust gain." See King James Bible Online. Islamic law forbids usury, gambling, and excessive risk. Shafiel A. Karim, *The Islamic Moral Economy: A Study of Islamic Money and Financial Instruments* (2010), 4. Practitioners of Hinduism and Buddhism have issued similar injunctions against usury, believing it to be incompatible with a right livelihood. See Wayne A. M. Visser and Alistair McIntosh, "A Short Review of the Historical Critique of Usury," *Accounting, Business & Financial History* 8 (July 1998): 2. Talmudic law also prohibits both borrowing and lending on interest in certain circumstances. See Louis Jacobs, "Usury and Moneylending in Judaism," *My Jewish Learning.*

41   *entrusted to the banks by their customers:* In response to the Great Depression, Congress fundamentally changed bank regulation by passing the Glass-Steagall Act. The Glass-Steagall Act protected consumers and guarded against excessive risk by separating commercial banking, such as checking accounts and savings accounts, from investment banking, which included speculative trading on stocks. Congress also established deposit insurance, limited interest rates, and prevented traditional commercial banks from engaging too much in risky non-bank activities like the securities or insurance business. In addition, Congress passed the Securities Act of 1933 and the Securities Exchange Act of 1934, which created the Securities and Exchange Commission to increase oversight of securities markets and enforce new regulations on trading and mandatory disclosures, to protect against fraud. In the 1930s, Congress also created an agency to regulate futures markets (today known as the Commodity Futures Trading Commission) as well as an agency to regulate credit unions (today known as the National Credit Union Administration). At the state level, many states had usury laws, or interest rate ceilings, which served as a meaningful constraint on the credit industry. See Matthew Sherman, "A Short History of Financial Deregulation in the United States," Center for Economic and Policy Research, July 2009.

41   *the cap on interest rates was effectively eliminated:* Usury regulation underwent a dramatic change in 1978, following the Supreme Court's decision in *Marquette National Bank v. First of Omaha Service Corp.* In that case, the Court ruled on which state's usury law would apply when a bank in one state lent money to a customer in another state: the law of the lender's home state or that of the borrower's home state. The Court held that the lender's home state law applied, which enabled banks to impose the maximum interest rate from one state on all borrowers, regardless of the interest rate cap in the borrowers' home states. The decision prompted a "competitive wave of deregulation," as states competed for banks to relocate to their states by removing any interest rate caps. See "A Short History of Financial Deregulation." Not only did the decision effectively eviscerate usury regulation, but it also placed small banks at a huge relative disadvantage to large banks, as the large banks were much better positioned to exploit this work-around of state usury laws.

42   *to people who were a lot less likely to repay all those loans:* Starting in the 1980s, deregulation of the credit industry unleashed a wave of new credit card practices, causing credit card fees and interest rates to rise throughout the 1980s, 1990s, and 2000s. For a more

detailed discussion of this period, see *As We Forgive Our Debtors*, 178–91. We documented the fall of traditional safe banking during the 1990s, which had relatively declined in profitability, and the rise in preapproved credit cards, interest rates (up to 18 percent during this period), retail cards, solicitation of debtors, and subprime lending. See *The Fragile Middle Class*, Chapter 4; *The Two-Income Trap*, 126–32. Also over the course of this period, credit card companies increasingly targeted low-income borrowers as well as young people, African Americans, and Latinos for some of the most abusive loans. Companies realized they could make enormous profits on the backs of delinquent cardholders and those who could only afford to pay the low minimum amount due each month, even after the defaults and bankruptcies were subtracted. See *The Fragile Middle Class*, Chapter 4; *The Two-Income Trap*, 129 & n.18. One study found that more than 75 percent of credit card profits came from people who made low minimum monthly payments, as credit card companies increasingly targeted this group with late fees and adjustable interest rates. See *The Two-Income Trap*, 139.

42   *and can't afford to take on more high-interest debt:* In *The Two-Income Trap* we note that business consulting firms would give banks essentially the same advice. For example, in 1997 Fair, Isaac & Co. launched a bankruptcy prediction program that it claimed "could eliminate 54 percent of bankruptcy losses by screening potential nonpayers from the bottom 10 percent of credit card holders" (233. n.55).

43   *cute little pooch who had just been offered a credit card:* There was a significant rise in aggressive advertising of preapproved credit cards and solicitation of debtors during the 1980s, 1990s, and early 2000s. As marketing tactics targeted the poor, Americans with incomes below the poverty level doubled their credit card usage during the 1990s. Over this same period, young people were increasingly offered credit cards without having to get parental approval or having to show credit history or annual income. These offers came in droves, as credit card companies solicited people on campus, using free T-shirts and key chains with university logos, and sent mailers with preapproved credit card applications. In 1997 alone, more than three billion preapproved credit card offers were sent to people. See *The Fragile Middle Class*, Chapter 4. This number rose to five billion in 2001, which translated to more than $350,000 of credit offered to each family. *The Two-Income Trap*, 129–30 & n.19.

44   *academic circles, and snagged a national prize: As We Forgive Our Debtors* won the 1990 Silver Gavel Award. It was also a finalist for the Distinguished Scholarly Publication Award of the American Sociological Association.

47   *twenty-four hours a day, seven days a week:* In 1995, the number of families filing for bankruptcy was 874,642. In 1996, the number of filings rose to 1,125,006. To translate these numbers so they reflect the number of people rather than families, we multiplied the number of filings by 1.4 because about 40 percent of those filing for bankruptcy in the 1990s were married and both adults were filing in a single petition. Thus, on average a person entered bankruptcy every 26 seconds (using the 1995 figure) and every 20 seconds (using the 1996 figure).

2 | The Bankruptcy Wars

48   *completing its review and then deliver a report to Congress:* The National Bankruptcy Review Commission (NBRC) was established as an independent commission on October 6, 1995, under the Bankruptcy Reform Act of 1994. Members included: Chairman: Initially Congressman Mike Synar, Oklahoma, later replaced by Brady C. Williamson, Esq., Wisconsin; Vice Chair: Hon. Robert E. Ginsberg, US Bankruptcy Judge, Illinois; Jay Alix, CPA, Michigan; M. Caldwell Butler, Esq., former Member of Congress, Virginia; Babette A. Ceccotti, Esq., New York; John A. Gose, Esq., Washington; Jeffery J. Hartley, Esq., Alabama; Hon. Edith Hollan Jones, US Circuit Judge, Fifth Circuit, Texas; and James I. Shepard, Esq., California.

According to Judge Ginsberg, "The charge to the commission was to (1) investigate and study issues and problems relating to the bankruptcy code; (2) evaluate the advisability of proposals and current arguments with respect to such issues and problems; (3) prepare and submit a report; and (4) solicit divergent views of all parties concerned with the operation of the bankruptcy system." "Interview with Bankruptcy Judge Robert E. Ginsberg, Acting Chair of the National Bankruptcy Review Commission," *Third Branch News*, February 1996.

50   *pack of small children and a pile of bills:* In all our bankruptcy studies, we adhered to strict confidentiality protocol to protect the identities of participants. See note on p. 281, "*Five part-time jobs. . . .*" For more linkages between domestic violence and financial distress, see, for example, Angela Littwin, "Coerced Debt: The Role of Consumer Credit in Domestic Violence." *California Law Review* 100 (2012): 1–74. Similarly, in our research we interviewed a bankruptcy trustee who said: "I'm in the abuse-prevention business. Every time I help a family get straightened out financially, I figure I saved someone a beating." *The Two-Income Trap*, 12.

53   *a bankruptcy case he had won in the United States Supreme Court:* In *Farrey v. Sanderfoot*, Brady Williamson represented the winning plaintiff, holding that the debtor could not use the homestead exemption provision of the Bankruptcy Code to avoid a valid obligation to a former spouse as stipulated in their divorce decree. See *Farrey v. Sanderfoot*, 500 US 291 (1991).

54   *northern or southern, black or white, male or female:* While there are some demographic differences between people in bankruptcy and the general population, for the most part the differences are modest, and people in bankruptcy are generally representative in terms of race, gender, and age. For more about the race of people who file for bankruptcy, see Elizabeth Warren, "The Economics of Race: When Making It to the Middle Is Not Enough," *Washington & Lee Law Review* 61 (Symposium Issue 2004): 177. For gender and bankruptcy, see Elizabeth Warren, "What Is a Women's Issue? Bankruptcy, Commercial Law and Other Gender-Neutral Topics," *Harvard Women's Law Journal* 25 (2002): 19 (Twenty-fifth Anniversary Issue); see also Teresa Sullivan and Elizabeth Warren, "More Women in Bankruptcy," *American Bankruptcy Institute* (July 30, 1999). For age and bankruptcy, see Deborah Thorne and Elizabeth Warren, "Bankruptcy's Aging Population," *Harvard Law & Policy Review* 3 (Winter 2009); see also Teresa Sullivan, Deborah Thorne, and Elizabeth Warren, "Young, Old and In Between: Who Files for Bankruptcy?," *Norton Bankruptcy Law Advisor* 1 (September 2001). For an overall discussion of the demographics of people in bankruptcy, see also *The Fragile Middle Class*, 36–59.

54   *proves to be the darkest secret of their entire lives:* For more discussion of stigma and shame often associated with bankruptcy, see note on p. 279, "*great defeat.*"

54   *best-organized, best-funded lobbies in America:* See, for example, the Center for Responsive Politics, which documents the dramatic rise in campaign contributions from finance and credit companies, from 1990 through the 2000s. They also found that by 1998 the Finance/Insurance/Real Estate industry was the number one industry in terms of resources spent on lobbying. See Michael Bechel, "Finance and Credit Companies Lobby Lawmakers as Congress Moves to Aggressively Regulate Them," *OpenSecretsBlog* (November 19, 2009). See also "Lobbying-Analysis" at OpenSecrets.org.

55   *economic failure as akin to moral failure:* "A Problem That Can Be Solved" subsection of Chapter 6, Judge Edith H. Jones and Todd J. Zywicki, "It's Time for Means-Testing," *Brigham Young University Law Review* (1999): 177–249. For more on Judge Jones's point of view, see: "The escalation in filings has revealed many little facts, the cumulative proof that in case after case, bankruptcy's powerful debt-relief tools are often misused. . . . At one time personal shame and social stigma would have bedeviled people filing bankruptcy, and their credit rating would have been ruined." Edith H. Jones, Foreword, "The Bankruptcy Galaxy," *South Carolina Law Review* 50 (1999): 269, 271; "I would like to inject the moral

issue here because I do think that it is a very important matter of personal integrity and honor not to take on obligations beyond one's means and if one has been caught in a bind to make every effort to pay them back. . . . My moral upbringing suggests to me that what is good to me as a moral person has to be applied to everybody across the board as the standard." Also, "One thing that has become very plain to us in these hearings is that a lot of people who file bankruptcy over-indulged." Edith Jones et al., "Panel Discussion, Consumer Bankruptcy," *Fordham Law Review* 67 (1999): 1315, 1347, 1353.

55 *family breakups had laid these families low:* For discussion of the causes of bankruptcy, see note on p. 281, *"or a family breakup . . ."*

55 *tried to repay long past any reasonable chance of doing so:* Research by Ronald Mann and Katherine Porter using Consumer Bankruptcy Project data found that most households who file for bankruptcy seriously struggle for two years before filing. In one of their interviews with bankruptcy attorneys regarding how long it takes their clients to file, one Georgia attorney reported that "it's very, very common for people to say[,] 'I should have done this years ago' or 'I should have done this about two years ago.' So I don't think it's a snap decision to contact an attorney." Ronald Mann and Katherine Porter, "Saving Up for Bankruptcy," University of Iowa Legal Studies Research Paper No. 10–02 (2010). Similarly, in *The Two-Income Trap* we found that the average person who filed for bankruptcy reports spending more than a year struggling with debts before filing. See p. 78.

55 *and I fought her at every turn:* During the Commission's work, a news report broke that indicated Judge Jones had led a group of Commissioners in a secret meeting with bank industry representatives—in violation of federal open-meeting laws. Diana B. Henriques, "Bankruptcy Commission Faces an Inquiry," *New York Times*, August 9, 1997.

59 *shopped it around to some friendly members of Congress:* H.R. 2500 (105th), the "Responsible Borrower Protection Bankruptcy Act" was introduced on September 18, 1997, and had 147 cosponsors. "Sponsors of the bill acknowledge that lawyers and lobbyists for the banks and credit card companies were involved in drafting it. The bill gives those industries most of what they have wanted since they began lobbying in earnest in the late 1990s, when the number of personal bankruptcies rose to record levels." Philip Shenon, "Hard Lobbying on Debtor Bill Pays Dividend," *New York Times*, March 13, 2001. "The fact that McCollum and Boucher didn't wait until the report was in to introduce HR 2500 says a lot about the overall attitude toward the NBRC's efforts, analysts say." According to a Visa executive, "Unfortunately the commission's proposal was [dead on arrival]." Judge Jones was quoted saying to the press: "The lending industry became disaffected with the commission's work pretty early on and decided, strategically, not to show us their hand." "Proposed Bankruptcy Bill Gets Overwhelming Support," *Credit Risk Management Report*, December 1, 1997.

60 *bill would make life worse for families in trouble:* The industry-backed bankruptcy bill increased difficulty for families in financial distress in a number of ways. It created means testing, which erected legal barriers to people in financial trouble trying to discharge their debts altogether through Chapter 7. Instead, debtors in trouble were turned out of the system altogether or pushed into the much more arduous Chapter 13, in which a family was put on a very strict budget and forced to make payments on their debts for three to five years. Note that our research had shown that because people sometimes lose jobs or miss work, or are faced with unexpected expenses like medical bills or car trouble, approximately two-thirds of families who attempt Chapter 13 are unable to follow through with the strict budget and end up getting kicked out of the system and lose all bankruptcy protections. See National Bankruptcy Review Commission, "Chapter 13 Repayment Plans," (1997). The method used for means testing created particular hardship on families who were going through divorce. In addition, repaying back child sup-

port payments would no longer take precedence over other kinds of debt repayment. As a result, a single parent who is due back child support from an ex-spouse would now be required to compete with professional collection agents when trying to collect monies due. Also, homeowners who had fallen behind on their mortgages would no longer be allowed to focus their resources on catching up on past-due mortgage payments until they had also paid off other debts, which increased the chances of foreclosure. Lastly, the provisions significantly added to the costs and complexity of filing for bankruptcy. See note on p. 291, *"charged more,"* for more discussion of attorney costs to file.

60   *stayed in the fight however I could:* By 1999, there were 1,281,581 personal bankruptcy filings. By 2001 that figure had climbed to 1,452,030. It would reach 1,625,208 in 2003. See American Bankruptcy Institute, http://www.abiworld.org/AM/AMTemplate.cfm?Section=Home &TEMPLATE=/CM/ContentDisplay.cfm&CONTENTID=66471.

60   *National Partnership for Women & Families pitched in, as did the AFL-CIO:* Many organizations joined the fight against the industry-sponsored bill and on behalf of consumer protection through bankruptcy. Some of the biggest supporters were AARP, AFL-CIO, the NAACP, the Consumers' Union, the Consumer Federation of America, the National Partnership for Women and Families, the Leadership Conference on Civil Rights, the National Consumer Law Center, PIRG, the Center for Responsible Lending, and the UAW. These groups played a critical role in fighting for bankruptcy reform that would benefit struggling families.

In addition, the National Association of Consumer Bankruptcy Attorneys (NACBA) was formed in 1992 to serve as a voice for consumer bankruptcy attorneys and protect the rights of consumer debtors and also played an important role.

64   *into their second terms, and they were also ready to help:* By taking on the bankruptcy issue, these lawmakers ended up fighting with some of the biggest banks and biggest credit card companies in the country. Senator Durbin mastered the details of the very complex bill, and he was constantly on the lookout for changes that would help families in trouble rather than hurt them. Senator Schumer was an amazing strategist, as his work on the abortion-protestor amendment showed. Senator Feingold and Senator Wellstone actively worked on bankruptcy issues, advocating for the families who needed them. Senator Chris Dodd pushed hard on the point about how bankruptcy helped women (and some men) collect past-due child support and alimony. On the House side, Congressman Jerrold Nadler was an active opponent of the credit industry efforts to weaken bankruptcy, along with Congressmen John Conyers, William Delahunt, and Marty Meehan. Their battles were uphill, but they kept fighting, and my admiration for each runs deep.

65   *three different studies, each of which was touted as "independent":* The number started out as a $400 hidden tax but quickly grew to $550; neither figure had any basis in fact. For the original studies, see Tom Neubig et al., Ernst & Young, LLP, "Chapter 7 Bankruptcy Petitioners' Ability to Repay: Additional Evidence from Bankruptcy Petition Files," American Bankruptcy Institute, (February 1998). See also WEFA Group Planning Services, "The Financial Costs of Personal Bankruptcy" (February 1998). See also John M. Barron and Michael E. Staten, "Personal Bankruptcy: A Report on Petitioners' Ability-to-Pay 1," Credit Research Center, Georgetown School of Business (1997).

65   *hardworking, bill-paying American family a $550 "hidden tax":* For more discussion, see *The Two-Income Trap,* 154–55 & nn. 97–99; see also Elizabeth Warren, "The Phantom $400," *Norton Journal of Bankruptcy Law and Practice* 13 (2004): 77. According to our analysis, for the $550 statistic to have been true, then the families whom the banking industry was targeting to repay more monies in the bankruptcy courts would have had to have paid $550,000 per household. In our sample of more than two thousand bankrupt families, not one even owed at least $550,000, let alone earned enough money to repay

that amount. In other words, the claim that bankruptcy cost every American family $550 was nonsense.

65 *but the press reported it as "fact" for years:* For example, see Beth Dixon, "We All Pay Note on House of Cards," *The Commercial Appeal*, December 14, 2003. "The American Bankers Association figures that the record number of bankruptcies in 2002 causes American families to pay an additional $400 a year in increased costs for goods and services." See also Donald Barlett and James B. Steele, "Big Money and Politics: Who Gets Hurt? Soaked by Congress," *Time*, May 15, 2000: "Representative Bill McCollum, a Florida Republican who has received $225,000 from the lending industry, upped the ante: 'Bankruptcy will cost consumers more than $50 billion in 1998 alone. That translates into more than $550 per household in higher costs for goods, services and credit.'"

For more examples and discussion, see Elizabeth Warren, "The Phantom $400."

65 *working families, against "that awful bill":* In her book, Hillary Clinton writes: "Proposed bankruptcy reform moving through Congress threatened to undermine the spousal and child support many women depend on." Hillary Rodham Clinton, *Living History* (2003), 384. The *New York Times* also reported on then First Lady Clinton's involvement in the bankruptcy fight: "[Mrs. Clinton] wrote dozens of personal notes to lawmakers last year as the [bankruptcy] bills made their tortuous way through the Congressional process. And she, along with Senator Edward M. Kennedy, Democrat of Massachusetts, played what the bill's opponents say was a decisive role in helping to kill the legislation last year." Katharine Q. Seelye, "First Lady in a Messy Fight on the Eve of Her Campaign," *New York Times*, June 27, 1999.

67 *inflicted chaos on the credit industry's well-laid plans:* For more on the Schumer Amendment: "The provision would bar abortion opponents from declaring bankruptcy to avoid paying court-imposed fines or damages that result from violent protests at abortion clinics. In recent years, a number of prominent abortion foes have used the bankruptcy laws for that purpose, among them Randall Terry, the founder of Operation Rescue. In declaring bankruptcy in 1998, Mr. Terry said he wanted to avoid paying debts, which then totaled more than $1 million, 'to those who would use my money to promote the killing of the unborn.'" Philip Shenon, "Abortion Issue Holds Up Bill on Bankruptcy," *New York Times*, April 30, 2002. Senator Schumer had long been pro-choice and his vigorous defense of an amendment to prevent abortion clinic protestors from discharging their debts was a critical strategic move.

69 *bankruptcy than would be diagnosed with cancer:* See *The Two-Income Trap*, 6.

69 *best predictor that a family would go bankrupt was if they had a child:* In *The Two-Income Trap*, we found that married couples with children are more than twice as likely to file for bankruptcy compared to couples without children. A divorced woman raising a child is three times more likely to file for bankruptcy than a woman without children (6).

69 *right up until something went horribly wrong:* In *The Two-Income Trap* we found that two-income families were actually more likely to file for bankruptcy than their one-income counterparts (83).

71 *"urge to splurge" was overtaking us:* Many scholars and pundits have belittled the American consumer as reckless and on a "credit binge." In *Affluenza: The All-Consuming Epidemic*, John De Graaf, David Wann, and Thomas Naylor decry consumerism in the United States.

Juliet Schor blames "the new consumerism." She points to "mass 'over-spending' within the middle class [in which] large numbers of Americans spend more than they say they would like to, and more than they have. That they spend more than they realize they are spending, and more than is fiscally prudent." Juliet B. Schor, *The Overspent American: Upscaling, Downshifting, and the New Consumer* (1998), 20.

Robert Frank argues that America's "Luxury Fever" causes middle-class people "to finance their consumption increases largely by reduced savings and increased debt." Robert H. Frank, *Luxury Fever: Why Money Fails to Satisfy in an Era of Excess* (1999), 45.

71 *pet food to boys' pajamas:* "The Consumer Expenditure Survey (CE) program consists of two surveys, the Quarterly Interview Survey and the Diary Survey, that provide information on the buying habits of American consumers, including data on their expenditures, income, and consumer unit (families and single consumers) characteristics. The survey data are collected for the Bureau of Labor Statistics by the U.S. Census Bureau." For more information, see http://www.bls.gov/cex/.

71 *the average family spent* less *on food than they did thirty years earlier:* We found that the modern family of four spends 21 percent less on clothing than they had a generation earlier, adjusted for inflation. Similarly, the modern family of four spends 22 percent less on food (at-home and restaurant eating combined) than its counterpart of a generation ago. *The Two-Income Trap*, 17–18.

71 *solid, comfortable, growing middle class of my generation:* For example, we found that a modern family spends an extra $290 per year on telephone services compared with its counterpart of a generation earlier (all numbers are inflation adjusted). On the other hand, the average family spends nearly $200 less per year on floor coverings, $210 less on dry cleaning, and $240 less on tobacco-related purchases. Similarly, today's family spends 44 percent less on major appliances today than a generation ago. For more, see *The Two-Income Trap*, 17–19 and 196–97.

72 *remained stagnant for an entire generation:* We note that the typical, fully employed male earned $38,700 in 1973 and $39,000 in 2000 (adjusted for inflation), less than 1 percent real increase in nearly thirty years. See *The Two-Income Trap*, 50. More recent evidence indicates that median male incomes declined slightly between 2000 and 2012 when adjusted for inflation. Women have fared somewhat better, as the income gap between men and women declined over the past generation and real median incomes climbed for fully employed women. However, women's economic progress seems to be slowing, as median earners have only gained 1 percent in real income over the past decade, and fully employed women continue to earn 21 percent less than their male counterparts. Calculated from US Census, Table P-36: "Full-Time, Year-Round All Workers by Median Income and Sex: 1955 to 2012."

Similarly, the Center for Responsible Lending reports: "When controlling for inflation . . . the typical household really had less annual income at the end of the decade than it did at the beginning [2000–2010]. . . . And though workers made less as the decade progressed, their productivity increased by 20% (Jank & Owens, 2012). Workers appear to be benefitting less from productivity gains than in prior periods." M. William Sermons, "The State of Lending in America and Its Impact on US Households," Center for Responsible Lending, December 2012, 9.

72 *live without, like health care and education:* In *The Two-Income Trap* we compare health care costs for a typical insured family of four and found that the average family was paying $1,650 more for insurance in 2000 than in the early 1970s, adjusted for inflation (51).

The cost of college at a public university nearly doubled during this period, adjusted for inflation (*The Two-Income Trap*, 42). Note that college costs have continued to climb even faster over the past decade. In addition, in *The Two-Income Trap* we discuss the growing importance—and the growing costs—of preschool education (37–38).

The Center for Responsible Lending reports that over the past decade, the trends we noted in *The Two-Income Trap* continued to worsen, as costs for many basic expenses continued to climb relative to incomes for middle-class families: "The declining real incomes of the last decade would not have been so hard on families if the cost of maintaining a household had also remained unchanged. While families would not have had resources to improve their standard of living, they would have at least been able to consume at the same level year after year. Instead, families were faced with increases in basic non-discretionary expenses like food, housing, transportation, medical care, and utilities with no growth—or sometimes even decreases—in income to pay for these items." "The State of Lending in America and Its Impact on US Households," 10.

72 *loans appeared, and families grabbed hold:* See note on p. 292, *"prepayment penalties,"* for more on the emergence of dangerous and predatory mortgage products.

72 *get a good education or to live in a nice neighborhood:* In *The Two-Income Trap* we discuss the role of public schools in driving housing choices for families with children (28–36). We also note that the rise in home prices during the '80s and '90s was disproportionately born by families with children. *The Two-Income Trap,* 32.

72 *huge, new homes remained the domain of the wealthy:* In *The Two-Income Trap,* we found that the size of the average middle-class family home had increased only modestly: The median owner-occupied home grew from 5.7 rooms in 1975 to 6.1 rooms in the late 1990s—an increase of less than half a room in more than twenty years. The data show that the room was typically a second bathroom or a third bathroom. We also note that the proportion of families living in older homes increased by nearly 50 percent during the same period (21–22).

72 *I had made a generation earlier: they took a job:* In the mid-'70s a married mother was more than twice as likely to stay home with her children as to work full-time; by 2000, those figures had reversed: Today a married mother is nearly twice as likely to work full-time as to stay home. *The Two-Income Trap,* 30.

72 *one-income family of a generation earlier:* In *The Two-Income Trap,* we show two budgets for middle-class families, one median single-breadwinner family from 1970, and a second median two-earner family in 2000. We calculate the average earnings, and the cost of fixed costs such as housing, health insurance, car, taxes, and child care. We found that the modern two-income family has less money left over after paying their basic bills than the one-income family of a generation ago, when adjusted for inflation. We also note that the modern one-income family that tried to live a typical middle-class standard of living had a significant gap compared with a generation earlier (50–53 and 207–8). We note that because the modern two-income family owns a more expensive home than their one-income counterpart of a generation earlier, and because they have added a second earner, their tax rate has increased (206–8).

73 *the savings rate for the average family was approaching zero:* The Two-Income Trap, 113.

73 *sucked in people who were in a crunch:* Borrowing from payday lenders, virtually non-existent twenty years ago, has grown tremendously. One study estimates that ten million households borrow from payday lenders each year, with more storefronts in the United States than McDonald's and Starbucks combined. Paige Skiba and Jeremy Tobacman, "Do Payday Loans Cause Bankruptcy?" *Vanderbilt Law and Economics Research Paper* No. 11–13 (2009). Payday lenders typically charge "10–20 percent interest for a one-to-two-week loan, implying an annualized percentage rate (APR) between 260 and 1040 percent." Neil Bhutta, Paige Skiba, and Jeremy Tobacman, "Payday Loan Choices and Consequences," *Vanderbilt Law and Economics Research Paper* No. 12–30 (2012). Similarly, credit card debt increased by 570 percent in a single generation. *The Two-Income Trap,* 20.

73 *hanging on to the cliff by their fingernails:* For example, Michelle J. White estimates that 17 percent of households in the United States are in so much financial distress that they would have significant improvements in their balance sheets if they filed for bankruptcy. "Why It Pays to File for Bankruptcy."

73 *starting to climb, even back in the 1990s and early 2000s:* The rate of mortgage foreclosure more than tripled between 1979 and 2002. *The Two-Income Trap,* 78.

74 *covered by CBS News, the* Boston Globe, *NPR, and CNN:* For examples of media coverage of *The Two-Income Trap,* see Daniel McGuinn, "Housebound: Young Families Always Stretch to Buy Their First Home but the Growing Ranks of the 'House Poor' Suggest Many

People Are Stretching Budgets Too Far," *Newsweek*, September 15, 2003. See also Christopher Shea, "Two Incomes, One Bankruptcy," *Boston Globe*, September 14, 2003. See also Rome Neal, "Broke on Two Incomes," *CBS News*, September 9, 2003. See also Jeanne Shahidi, "Are You Worse Off than Mom and Dad?" *CNNMoney*, September 11, 2003, and Michele Norris, "Two-Income Families at Risk of Financial Crisis," NPR, *All Things Considered*, September 8, 2003.

75 *in 2004 they stepped up to the plate again:* See, for example, Robert Zausner and Josh Goldstein, "Bush's Largest Funding Source: Employees of Credit-Card Firm," *Philadelphia Inquirer*, July 28, 2000. "By orchestrating mass contributions from its employees, the Wilmington-based company has become Bush's single largest source of campaign money. MBNA employees and their families have given more than $250,000 to the Republican's presidential bid, an *Inquirer* analysis found." Christopher H. Schmitt, "Tougher Bankruptcy Laws—Compliments of MBNA?," *Business Week*, February 2001, 43. Schmitt confirmed that MBNA was "the candidate's single biggest source of cash" and added: "On the soft-money side, MBNA chipped in nearly $600,000. . . . On top of that, MBNA Chairman and CEO Alfred Lerner and his wife, Norma, each kicked in $250,000 to the Republicans. Charles M. Cawley, CEO of MBNA's bank unit and a friend of Bush Sr., organized fund-raisers and gave $18,660 to Bush and the GOP."

Similarly, in 2004 the Center for Public Integrity reports: "MBNA surpasses Enron as the president's top lifetime contributor." Alex Knott, "Bush Has a New Top Career Patron," *The Center for Public Integrity*, March 11, 2004. The Center for Responsive Politics reports that MBNA slipped to ninth place in 2004, when it was outspent by employees of other banking giants like Citigroup, Lehman Brothers, Morgan Stanley, and Merrill Lynch. See analysis of Top Contributors by Center for Responsive Politics, at OpenSecrets.org.

80 *law kicked in, bankruptcy filings dropped sharply:* In 2004, there were 1,563,145 bankruptcy filings. In 2005, that number shot up to 2,039,214. Then in 2006, in the wake of the new law, the number of filings fell to 597,965. See American Bankruptcy Institute.

80 *charged more—sometimes a lot more—to navigate the more complex law:* One study found that attorney fees for the simplest type of bankruptcy filing—Chapter 7 with no assets—increased 51 percent after the new law. For more complex Chapter 13 filings, costs increased 24 to 27 percent. Lois R. Lupica, "The Consumer Bankruptcy Fee Study," American Bankruptcy Institute, December 2011.

See also Robert M. Lawless, Angela K. Littwin, Katherine M. Porter, John A. E. Pottow, Deborah Thorne, and Elizabeth Warren, "Did Bankruptcy Reform Fail? An Empirical Study of Consumer Debtors," *American Bankruptcy Law Journal* 82 (2008): 349–406. Subsequent work demonstrates that the sharp increase in attorneys' fees after the change in the laws resulted in smaller payouts for creditors. Lois R. Lupica, "Final Report: The Consumer Bankruptcy Creditor Distribution Study," American Bankruptcy Institute National Conference of Bankruptcy Judges, 2013.

80 *if they tried to use bankruptcy to clear their debts:* "Nearly a quarter [of families]—23.6%—said the debt collectors had raised the subject of bankruptcy explicitly, threatening what would happen if they filed. More than half who received such warnings recount being told by the debt collector that it was 'illegal' to file for bankruptcy, or that, if they filed, they might go to jail, the I.R.S. would audit them, or they could lose their jobs. The remainder received a mix of misinformation, including the oft-repeated 'you won't qualify.'" Robert Lawless et al., "Did Bankruptcy Reform Fail?"

80 *or stopped taking their kids to the doctor:* In *The Two-Income Trap* we describe that "60% of bankruptcy filers went without needed medical care in order to save money" (77). Similarly, a study using nationally representative data from the Community Tracking Study found, "People in families with medical bill problems also reported much greater trouble getting care because of cost concerns—one in three did not get a prescription drug, one in four delayed care and one in eight went without needed care." Jessica May

and Peter Cunningham, "Tough Trade-offs: Medical Bills, Family Finances and Access to Care," *Center for Studying Health System Change*, No. 85 (2004).

82   *get more money for asbestos victims:* For more discussion of my work relating to asbestos victims, see note on p. 334, *"payment for their injuries."*

82   *families gain access to more affordable banking services:* Sheila Bair was a highly effective chairman of the FDIC. She reorganized much of the agency to make it more efficient and to put it on sounder financial footing. She also established the Committee on Economic Inclusion to explore ways to create alternatives for underserved families who used payday loans and money orders by bringing them into the banking system.

3 | Bailing Out the Wrong People

85   *one entry: "Submit reports":* The Congressional Oversight Panel (COP) was charged with putting out "regular reports" on the actions taken by the Treasury secretary, the impact of those actions on the financial sector, the extent to which those actions contributed to market transparency, and the effectiveness of those actions on foreclosure mitigation and costs and benefits to the taxpayer. In carrying out its oversight duties, COP could engage "experts and consultants," "hold hearings," "take testimony," "receive evidence," "obtain official data," and receive and consider "reports required to be submitted [to it]." See Section 125, Emergency Economic Stabilization Act of 2008, Government Printing Office, Public Law 110–343—October 3, 2008.

86   *more bankruptcy research:* The number of people filing for bankruptcy dropped sharply in the wake of the 2005 amendments to the Bankruptcy Code, so the goal of the 2007 Consumer Bankruptcy Project was to understand who was filing now and to compare our findings to the findings that had emerged from similar studies in 1981, 1991, and 2001. The 2007 study examined a nationwide random sample of households in bankruptcy across the United States. We drew on questionnaires, interviews, and court records—in total amounting to almost a thousand pieces of information for each debtor—to sketch a detailed picture of the debtors in bankruptcy. The data were gathered under strict confidentiality requirements typical of human-subjects research protections at American universities. All data analysis was done using anonymous numerical identifiers for the study participants. When referencing individuals, names and specific identifiers have been changed to preserve anonymity.

    We found that those who filed in 2007 were very much like those who had filed in 2001. This suggested that the 2005 amendments, which led to a huge reduction in the number of bankruptcies, had not cut out the more prosperous debtors or the ones who could somehow better manage their debts, or that the new law had otherwise curbed "abuse." Instead, the data suggested that the impact of the amendments was to squeeze struggling families across the board.

87   *"prepayment penalties":* For example, "[There is] a new breed of dangerous mortgages—such as loans with introductory 'teaser' rates that reset after a few years to much higher rates; loans that did not require income verification; and loans with prepayment penalties that locked borrowers into high rates or risky terms. These loans were often made with scant underwriting and marketed without regard for whether they were suitable for the borrowers." M. William Sermons, "The State of Lending in America."

    "The option adjustable rate mortgage (ARM) might be the riskiest and most complicated home loan product ever created." Mara Der Hovanesian, "Nightmare Mortgages," *Bloomberg Businessweek*, September 10, 2006. See also, ". . . lenders are seeing a rapid rise in defaults on a type of mortgage that gives consumers with good credit several different monthly-payment options. These mortgages, which are sometimes known as 'pick-a-pay' or payment-option mortgages but are generically called option adjustable-rate mortgages, are turning out, in some cases, to be even more caustic than subprime loans, in part because the loan balance and the monthly payments on some loans is growing even as home prices are falling." Ruth Simon, "Defaults Rising Rapidly for 'Pick-a-Pay' Option Mortgages," *Wall Street Journal*, April 30, 2008. See also Kat Aaron, "Predatory Lending: A Decade of Warnings," Center for Public Integrity, May 6, 2009.

For more on how wide ranging the sales and purchase of these new mortgage products became, and what gave rise to the growth, see "The Financial Crisis Inquiry Report," The Financial Crisis Inquiry Commission, US Government Printing Office, January 2011, 34, 68, 85, 425.

87   *most deceptive products:* "Approximately one quarter of all Latino and African American borrowers have lost their home to foreclosure or are seriously delinquent, compared to just under 12 percent for white borrowers." See Debbie Grunstein Bocian, Wei Li, Carolina Reid, and Roberto G. Quercia, "Lost Ground, 2011: Disparities in Mortgage Lending and Foreclosures," Center for Responsible Lending, November 2011.

According to another study, African American and Latino borrowers were 30 percent more likely to be steered into higher-cost subprime loans than similarly situated white borrowers. Debbie Grunstein Bocian, Keith S. Ernst, and Wei Li, "Race, Ethnicity and Subprime Home Loan Pricing," *Journal of Economics and Business* 60 (2008): 110–24.

See also Sara Miller Llana, "Loans to Minorities Rise, but at a Price: The 30-Day Past-Due Rate for Subprime Mortgages Rose from 5.4 Percent to 7.1 Percent During 2005," *Christian Science Monitor*, March 24, 2006.

Many giant banks settled mortgage bias lawsuits. See, for example, "Financial Fraud Enforcement Task Force Announces Settlement with AIG Subsidiaries to Resolve Allegations of Lending Discrimination," The United States Department of Justice, March 4, 2010, http://www.justice.gov/opa/pr/2010/March/10-crt-226.html.

"Justice Department Reaches $21 Million Settlement to Resolve Allegations of Lending Discrimination by Suntrust Mortgage: Borrowers Were Charged Higher Fees Based on Their Race or National Origin in 2005–2009 Before the Company Implemented New Policies," The United States Department of Justice, May 31, 2012, http://www.justice.gov/opa/pr/2012/May/12-crt-695.html.

Charlie Savage, "Wells Fargo Will Settle Mortgage Bias Charges," *New York Times*, July 13, 2012.

Charlie Savage, "Countrywide Will Settle a Bias Suit," *New York Times*, December 21, 2011.

87   *pursued seniors like Flora:* For example, "Equity-rich, cash poor, elderly homeowners are an attractive target for unscrupulous mortgage lenders. Many elderly homeowners are on fixed or limited incomes, yet need access to credit to pay for home repairs, medical care, property or municipal taxes, and other expenses. The equity they have amassed in their home may be their primary or only financial asset. Predatory lenders seek to capitalize on elders' need for cash by offering "easy" credit and loans packed with high interest rates, excessive fees and costs, credit insurance, balloon payments and other outrageous terms." "Helping Elderly Homeowners Victimized by Predatory Mortgage Loans," National Consumer Law Center, 2008, http://www.nclc.org/images/pdf/older_consumers/consumer _concerns/cc_elderly_victimized_predatory_mortgage.pdf.

87   *urged Americans to "tap" their home equity:* See Ruth Simon, "Home-Equity Loans Hit Record Levels," *Wall Street Journal*, January 20, 2005.

Although these loans often erode the family's primary foundation for developing financial stability, and they increase the risk of foreclosure, pundits and industry leaders nonetheless have widely encouraged people to take out these loans. For example, former chairman of the Federal Reserve Alan Greenspan discussed the many benefits of homeowners tapping their home equity and the subsequent boost to the economy. See, for example, "Remarks by Chairman Alan Greenspan," March 4, 2003, http://www.federalreserve.gov/boarddocs /speeches/2003/20030304/; also Alan Greenspan and James Kennedy, "Sources and Uses of Equity Extracted from Homes," The Federal Reserve Board, March 2007.

One advertising agency concocted the slogan "Live Richly" for Citi, which was designed to encourage people to take out home equity loans. See Louise Story, "Home Equity Frenzy Was a Bank Ad Come True," *New York Times*, August 14, 2008. In my own work, I tried to discourage borrowers from putting their most important asset at risk by engaging in these types of loans. In *The Two-Income Trap* we argued, "Refinancing their homes to pay down other bills is the single biggest mistake made by homeowners in trouble" (168). In *All Your Worth* we noted that according to the data at the time, one in eleven families bet their house and lost, as they ended up in foreclosure. Elizabeth Warren and Amelia Warren Tyagi, *All Your Worth: The Ultimate Lifetime Money Plan* (2005), 150. Sadly, the odds only worsened in the years that followed.

87   *home prices caught fire:* "Seventy-one metro areas, accounting for 39 percent of all single family housing value, were deemed to be extremely over-valued. . . ." "House Prices in America," Global Insight/National City, June 2006. See also Martin Wolk, "Housing 'Bubblettes' May Be Rising," *NBC News*, February 14, 2005.

87   *speculators jumped into the game:* "Real Estate Speculation Raises Prices, Concerns," Associated Press, June 20, 2005. Also Paul Krugman, "Running Out of Bubbles," *New York Times*, May 27, 2005.

88   *more than their homes were worth:* Jonathan Stempel, "One in Five Homeowners with Mortgages Under Water," Reuters, October 31, 2008.

88   *most valuable asset:* "Owning a home has long been the most accessible way to build wealth in the United States. . . . The wealth acquired through homeownership has been a key source of economic mobility and financial security in this country for decades." The loss of middle-class wealth due to the housing crash has been dramatic." M. William Sermons, "The State of Lending in America." "Many families have experienced a precipitous loss of wealth because of the housing crash, which was sparked by high-risk subprime mortgages . . . [there has been] a loss of wealth by households of all races and unprecedented wealth disparities between white households and African-American or Hispanic households. . . . The impact of these economic circumstances has been devastating for the typical American household." ". . . the Pew Research Center used different data sources and found much larger declines from 2005 to 2009 in net worth for African-American (53% decline) and Hispanic (66% decline) households relative to white households (16% decline)." M. William Sermons, "The State of Lending in America." See also Ylan Q. Mui, "Americans Saw Wealth Plummet 40 Percent from 2007 to 2010, Federal Reserve Says," *Washington Post*, June 11, 2012. See also Jesse Bricker, Arthur B. Kennickell, Kevin B. Moore, and John Sabelhaus, "Changes in U.S. Family Finances from 2007 to 2010: Evidence from the Survey of Consumer Finances," *Federal Reserve Bulletin* 98, no 2 (June 2012). Binyamin Appelbaum, "Family Net Worth Drops to Level of Early '90s, Fed Says," *New York Times*, June 11, 2012.

88   *committed a whopping $172 billion:* TARP was passed on October 3, 2008. Within a month of TARP's passage, Treasury had pledged $172 billion to a total of fifty-four banks. See David Goldman, "Where the Bailouts Stand," *CNNMoney*, November 12, 2008.

In the month of October, Treasury had disbursed $115 billion to eight top Wall Street institutions, including, among others, Bank of America, Goldman Sachs, JPMorgan, and Citigroup. See "Bailout Events for October 2008," *ProPublica*, October 2008, http://projects .propublica.org/bailout/events/list/2008/10. By November 21, Treasury had given an additional $36.5 billion to large and medium-sized banks, including, among others, U.S. Bancorp and Capital One, and had committed at least $20.5 billion more to helping out the banks. See "Bailout Events for November 2008," *ProPublica,* November 2008, http:// projects.propublica.org/bailout/events/list/2008/11.

90   *halls of Treasury as "Citi-weekend":* On November 24, 2008, Treasury struck a deal with Citi whereby it would invest $20 billion in Citi preferred stock and guarantee $306 billion

of its assets. See Dan Wilchins and Jonathan Stempel, "Citigroup Gets Massive Government Bailout," Reuters, November 24, 2008.

In her excellent book, *Bull by the Horns*, Sheila Bair, the chair of FDIC, notes that she wasn't notified by Treasury and the Fed of the impending Citi bailout until Friday, November 21, the same day that we met with Kashkari. For more discussion, see Sheila Bair, *Bull by the Horns* (2012), 121–29.

According to a SIGTARP document entitled "Extraordinary Financial Assistance Provided to Citigroup," Federal officials referred to November 21–23, 2008, as "Citi Weekend." See Special Inspector General for the Troubled Asset Relief Program, "Extraordinary Financial Assistance Provided to Citigroup, Inc.," January 13, 2011, http://www .sigtarp.gov/Audit%20Reports/Extraordinary%20Financial%20Assistance%20Provided %20to%20Citigroup,%20Inc.pdf. The *New York Times* reported that Citigroup executives and board members "held several calls with Henry M. Paulson" on Friday, November 21. Andrew Ross Sorkin and Louise Story, "Shares Falling, Citigroup Talks to Government," *New York Times*, November 22, 2008.

90   *scientific research for the next twenty years:* I recognize that TARP was a loan that was designed to be repaid, but a loan from the government—particularly on terms that no private lender would take on—is fundamentally about investment. Thus the examples in the text include other investments that the United States could have made, such as education, infrastructure, and scientific research, that also would have paid out over time, albeit over a longer time horizon, with a more productive and inventive workforce, more efficiency in power, transportation, and other production necessities, and a boost to business innovations that come through support of scientific and medical research.

91   *previously been closed off to them:* The regulatory changes in the 1980s (see note on p. 283, *"the cap on interest rates . . . "*) enabled banks to engage in increasingly risky, nontraditional practices. In the 1980s and 1990s, regulators reinterpreted—and Congress ultimately repealed—the Glass-Steagall Act, which had separated commercial and investment banking activities. These changes, in combination with other changes that encouraged greater consolidation of financial institutions, enabled banks to enter new and dangerous terrains. As basic banking—checking, savings, mortgages, loans—were folded into increasingly complex financial institutions, regulators were called on to oversee a wider variety of intricate investment and hedging activities. Everything became more complicated, from the balance sheets to the credit ratings. A few banks ballooned in size, posing more risks for the economy and more challenges for the regulators.

See Matthew Sherman, "A Short History of Financial Deregulation in the United States," Center for Economic and Policy Research, July 2009.

During this time, the financial industry developed a number of new products, including a variety of derivatives (instruments used to hedge against risk without involving an actual transfer of underlying assets) and securitized assets (instruments used to pool assets and repackage them into securities). As discussed in the text, the risky proliferation of securitized mortgage loans contributed significantly to the 2008 financial crisis.

By selling the mortgages to investors, the banks had more money to lend. That turned out to have good and bad elements: more people now had access to mortgages and could buy homes, but with more mortgage money available, the housing bubble also began to inflate and prices began to rise. See "The Financial Crisis Inquiry Report." The 2008 crisis had many contributing factors and no one solution can address all of them, but I partnered with Senators John McCain, Maria Cantwell, and Angus King several months after arriving to the Senate in proposing a twenty-first-century Glass-Steagall Act to dial back the risk and shrink the largest institutions. The big banks remain adamantly opposed, but we've had some strong support from Americans for Financial Reform, the Progressive Change Campaign Committee, and many other groups who are fighting for a safer banking system.

91   *out to make a quick buck:* Banks became heavily involved in developing and peddling mortgage-backed securities in the 1990s and 2000s. As Fannie Mae and Freddie Mac focused on securitizing prime mortgage loans, banks, thrifts, and investment banks focused on securitizing riskier mortgage loans, such as subprime loans, "Alt-A" loans, and non-conforming loans. Since interest rates were low, many investors were looking for safe investments that would pay higher premiums. Home mortgages seemed like the perfect answer, with low default rates and higher returns. Over time, originators began to peddle more and more high-risk mortgages to satisfy the greater and greater demand for the securities. And the mortgage bundlers developed more and more refined techniques for disguising the risk, even fueling further demand for the securities. Thus originators peddled more and more high-risk mortgages to satisfy greater and greater investor demand for the securities. This was all done with the imprimatur of the credit rating agencies that repeatedly signed off on the safety of the underlying packages of mortgages. Between 2003 and 2007, financial institutions created more than $4 trillion in mortgage-backed securities. See "The Financial Crisis Inquiry Report." As the Financial Crisis Inquiry Commission noted, this "originate-to-distribute model undermined responsibility and accountability for the long-term viability of mortgages and mortgage-related securities and contributed to the poor quality of mortgage loans" (125).

91   *got more and more complicated:* "In the first decade of the 21st century, a previously obscure financial product called the collateralized debt obligation, or CDO, transformed the mortgage market by creating a new source of demand for the lower-rated tranches of mortgage-backed securities. Despite their relatively high returns, tranches rated other than triple-A could be hard to sell. . . . Wall Street came up with a solution: in the words of one banker, they 'created the investor.' That is, they built new securities that would buy the tranches that had become harder to sell. Bankers would take those low investment-grade tranches, largely rated BBB or A, from many mortgage-backed securities and repackage them into the new securities—CDOs. Approximately 80% of these CDO tranches would be rated triple-A despite the fact that they generally comprised the lower-rated tranches of mortgage-backed securities." "Between 2003 and 2007, as house prices rose 27% nationally and $4 trillion in mortgage-backed securities were created, Wall Street issued nearly $700 billion in CDOs that included mortgage-backed securities as collateral." See "The Financial Crisis Inquiry Commission Report," 127–50.

92   *mortgage bundles AAA ratings:* See "The Financial Crisis Inquiry Commission Report" on AAA ratings of bundled mortgages.

For one example, see: "In May 2007, Standard & Poor's confirmed its initial AAA ratings on $772 million of a collateralized debt obligation known as Octonion I. Within 10 months, the Citigroup Inc. (C) deal defaulted, costing investors and the bank almost all their money. . . . Octonion I underscores how inflated grades during the credit boom contributed to more than $2.1 trillion in losses at the world's financial institutions after home-loan defaults soared and residential prices plummeted." Jody Shenn, "Default in 10 Months After AAA Spurred Justice on Credit Ratings," *Bloomberg*, February 5, 2013. For more examples, see Kevin G. Hall, "How Moody's Sold Its Ratings—and Sold Out Investors," *McClatchy*, October 18, 2009. See also David Evans, "Banks Sell 'Toxic Waste' CDOs to Calpers, Texas Teachers Fund," *Bloomberg News*, June 1, 2007.

Chair of the Commodity Futures Trading Commission Brooksley Born pushed for greater regulation of derivatives and other products, "warning that unregulated financial contracts such as credit default swaps could pose grave dangers to the economy. Her efforts brought fierce opposition from Wall Street and from Administration officials who believed deregulation was essential to the extraordinary economic growth that was then in full bloom." See Henry Liu, "Financial Reform Warrior Brooksley Born Warns of More Crises to Come," Roosevelt Institute, November 2009. See also Manuel Roig-Franzia, "Credit Crisis Cassandra," *Washington Post*, May 26, 2009.

92   *a catastrophic meltdown:* A new type of insurance product played a large role in exacerbating the financial crisis—the credit default swap. Credit default swaps were designed to protect investors from defaults or declines in the value of mortgage-backed securities. In exchange for periodic payments from the buyer, the insurer would pay the buyer the face value of the debt in the event of default or other specified "credit event." "The Financial Crisis Inquiry Commission Report," 50. Unlike other insurance products, credit default swaps were not subject to federal regulation because they were treated as over-the-counter derivatives. As the Financial Crisis Inquiry Commission Report noted, credit default swaps contributed significantly to the financial crisis by "fuel[ing] the mortgage securitization pipeline," as they helped to create an illusion of safety. "The Financial Crisis Inquiry Commission Report," xxiv. AIG sold more than $79 billion worth of credit default swaps in the run-up to the crisis. The combination of credit defaults swaps and CDOs—discussed above—created a dangerous environment in which there were multiple opposing bets on the same securities spread across different sectors of the financial system.

92   *financial system might crumble to nothing:* Bear Stearns, an investment bank and securities trading and brokerage firm, collapsed in early 2008 as a result of excessive exposure to subprime mortgages. The Federal Reserve Bank of New York negotiated a sale of Bear Stearns to JPMorgan on March 16, 2008, which was supported by a $30 billion loan from the government to JPMorgan to salvage the company. Federal Reserve chairman Ben Bernanke defended the bailout as necessary to protect asset values and to prevent a "chaotic unwinding" of investments across the United States. See Yalman Onaran, "Fed Aided Bear Stearns as Firm Faced Chapter 11, Bernanke Says," *Bloomberg*, April 2, 2008.

Lehman Brothers, a leading investment bank and global financial services firm, filed for bankruptcy protection on September 15, 2008, after suffering major stock losses and devaluation of its assets by credit-rating agencies. The failure of Lehman was the largest failure of an investment bank in decades, and it sent a shock wave through the markets. Sheila Bair notes: "First, the bankruptcy defied market expectations. Bear Stearns had been bailed out, and most market players assumed that the government would step in with Lehman as well. . . . Markets hate uncertainty, and the Lehman failure confused them." She continues, "Because of that flexible accounting treatment for complex securities, Lehman looked as if it was much stronger than it really was. The lack of transparency about Lehman's true financial condition immediately created suspicion about other financial institutions that also held opaque, complex mortgage investments on their books. As a consequence, the institutions with the biggest exposures, such as Merrill and Citigroup, started having problems accessing credit even from other financial institutions. . . ." Sheila Bair, *Bull by the Horns*, 107. Merrill Lynch, a large brokerage firm, was on the verge of collapse due in large part to its involvement in the mortgage-based collateralized debt obligations market. On September 14, 2008, Bank of America acquired Merrill Lynch, with Bank of America citing pressure from the US government to follow through with the transaction.

92   *struggled to get car loans:* "In the aftermath of the panic, when credit was severely tightened, if not frozen, for financial institutions, companies found that cheap and easy credit was gone for them, too. It was tougher to borrow to meet payrolls and to expand inventories; businesses that had neither credit nor customers trimmed costs and laid off employees. Still today, credit availability is tighter than it was before the crisis." See "The Financial Crisis Inquiry Commission Report," 389. Also, from p. 214: "Securitization of auto loans, credit cards, small business loans, and equipment leases all nearly ceased in the third and fourth quarters of 2008."

See also Nick Carey, "Credit Seen Drying Up for U.S. Small Business," *USA Today,*

July 25, 2008. Bill Vlasic and Nick Bunkley, "With Credit Drying Up, Car Buyers Bring Cash," *New York Times*, October 7, 2008.

For COP's critique of Treasury reaction to inadequate credit for small businesses, see note on p. 301, *"actual policies were anemic."*

92 *financial system had stalled:* On Thursday, September 19, 2008, Treasury Secretary Henry Paulson and Federal Reserve Chairman Ben S. Bernanke began their push for broad bailout authority by meeting with members of Congress. See David Herszenhorn, "Congressional Leaders Stunned by Warnings," *New York Times*, September 20, 2008. See Edmund L. Andrews, "Bush Officials Urge Swift Action on Rescue Powers," *New York Times*, September 19, 2008. They sent a three-page written request to Congress. See "Treasury's Bailout Proposal: The Legislative Proposal Was Sent by the White House Overnight to Lawmakers," *CNNMoney*, September 20, 2008. Henry M. Paulson and Ben S. Bernanke appeared before the Senate Banking Committee on Tuesday, September 23, and the House Financial Services Committee on September 24. See "Prepared Text of Paulson's Statement," *New York Times*, September 23, 2008. Henry Paulson would later write in his book: "Going into the hearing, I knew I had to choose my words carefully. We faced a real dilemma: To get Congress to act we needed to make dire predictions about what would happen to the economy if they didn't give us the authorities we wanted. But doing so could backfire. Frightened consumers might stop spending and start saving, which was the last thing we needed right then. Investors could lose the final shred of the confidence that was keeping the markets from crashing." Henry M. Paulson, *On the Brink: Inside the Race to Stop the Collapse of the Global Financial System* (2010), 281–83.

96 *auto companies reported that they were on the verge of bankruptcy:* See December 2008 COP report, "Questions About the $700 Billion Emergency Economic Stabilization Fund," http://cybercemetery.unt.edu/archive/cop/20110402034700/http://cop.senate.gov /documents/cop-121008-report.pdf. For more on the auto companies, see Chris Isidore, "Big Three Face Bankruptcy Fears," *CNNMoney*, August 6, 2008.

96 *receiving a fair deal?:* See December 2008 COP report, 8–9. The first COP report asked the following primary questions, with explanatory text and various secondary questions as well. The ten questions, paraphrased, were:

(1) What Is Treasury's Strategy?

(2) Is the Strategy Working to Stabilize Markets?

(3) Is the Strategy Helping to Reduce Foreclosures?

(4) What Have Financial Institutions Done with the Taxpayers' Money Received So Far?

(5) Is the Public Receiving a Fair Deal?

(6) What Is Treasury Doing to Help the American Family?

(7) Is Treasury Imposing Reforms on Financial Institutions that Are Taking Taxpayer Money?

(8) How Is Treasury Deciding Which Institutions Receive the Money?

(9) What is the Scope of Treasury's Statutory Authority?

(10) Is Treasury Looking Ahead?

100 *Hensarling testified:* For Congressman Hensarling's testimony before the House Financial Services Committee on December 10, 2008, see http://votesmart.org/public -statement/401754/hensarling-testifies-before-house-financial-services-committee.

103 *here's what we got:* See COP report, January 9, 2009. Treasury "did not provide complete. answers to several of the questions and failed to address a number of the questions at all" (1).

103 *"that money is used":* "Tidy Up the Bailout," editorial *Boston Globe*, January 15, 2009. Also Justin Rood, "Bailout Czar's Secret? Copy. Paste. Repeat," ABC News, January 9, 2009.

104 *value of the shares they got back was also $100:* Treasury noted in "Responses to Questions of the First Report of the Congressional Oversight Panel for Economic Stabiliza-

tion" on December 30, 2008: "When measured on an accrual basis, the value of the preferred stock is at or near par" (8) (http://www.treasury.gov/press-center/press-releases /Documents/123108%20cop%20response.pdf).

104 *a $78 billion shortfall:* The financial valuation study of TARP assets was conducted by the COP's Advisory Committee on Finance and Valuation and by the international valuation firm Duff & Phelps Corporation (D&P). The Advisory Committee was composed of Adam M. Blumenthal, former First Deputy Comptroller of the City of New York, Professor William N. Goetzmann of Yale University, and Professor Deborah J. Lucas of Northwestern University. Together, the Advisory Committee and D&P devised a methodology for evaluating the fair market value of TARP assets. Rather than rely on any single valuation approach, the team used multiple methods to calculate, company by company, the fair market value of preferred stock and warrants received by Treasury, applying a "reduced marketability discount" under each approach to reflect the diminution in value of these relatively illiquid securities. (The team concluded that, given the liquidity and market volume in the trading of securities, it was reasonable to rely on market pricing for ascertaining economic value.) This analysis yielded a range of values per company, and the team selected the midpoint as representative for purposes of the final report. The final report ultimately revealed that for the ten largest TARP investments made during 2008, Treasury received about $66 for every $100 spent, amounting to about a $78 billion shortfall. See "Valuing Treasury's Acquisitions," Congressional Oversight Panel, February 6, 2009, http://cybercemetery.unt.edu/archive/cop/20110402010539/http://cop.senate.gov /documents/cop-020609-report.pdf.

105 *brought the company to its knees:* The story first broke on March 14–15, with the number "$165 million" quoted (others would later cite the $168 million figure). See Edmund L. Andrews and Peter Baker, "A.I.G. Planning Huge Bonuses After $170 Billion Bailout," *New York Times*, March 14, 2009. The reaction was swift and intense. There were rumors of death threats against AIG executives, and the House quickly passed a bill that called for a 90 percent tax on bonuses for certain TARP recipients. Neil Barofsky, *Bailout*, (2012), 140. There is considerable debate about the role of Treasury oversight in this debacle. Secretary Geithner told AIG that these bonuses were "unacceptable" and "demanded they be renegotiated." He also convinced AIG to reduce its bonuses for the financial products units by 30 percent. See Edmund L. Andrews and Peter Baker, "Bonus Money at Troubled A.I.G. Draws Heavy Criticism," *New York Times*, March 15, 2009.

However, Neil Barofsky, then Special Inspector General of TARP, is quite critical of Treasury's handling of the bonuses: "Had Treasury officials been more effectively monitoring the government's investment in AIG and more concerned with accountability and basic fairness, they might have helped prevent the blowup. For example, they could have forced AIG to renegotiate the terms of the contracts as a condition of the additional $30 billion in TARP funds that they had announced several days *after* learning about the imminent bonus payouts." Barofsky also notes: ". . . the rationale Neel Kashkari had given me for making the payments—that the bonus recipients were essential personnel necessary to wind down AIG's complex transactions—didn't quite wash." Barofsky, *Bailout*, 182. For more on executive compensation during the bailout and what he calls "the abject fetishization of the lords of high finance," see Barofsky, *Bailout*, 139–40. He argues that TARP recipients "showed no shame in pushing for ever-high salary awards. More noteworthy, however, was the pressure exerted by several Treasury officials, who also pushed to increase the value of the pay packages." Barofsky, *Bailout,* 140.

105 *"resign or go commit suicide":* Senator Chuck Grassley (Republican, Iowa) said on a March 16 radio interview: "I suggest, you know, obviously maybe they ought to be removed, but I would suggest that the first thing that would make me feel a little bit better towards them [is] if they would follow the Japanese example and come before the American people and take that deep bow and say I'm sorry and then either do one of two things: resign

or go commit suicide. . . . In the case of the Japanese, they usually commit suicide before they make any apology." Tahman Bradley, "GOP Senator: AIG Execs Should Follow Japanese Model—Suicide or Apology," ABC News, March 16, 2009.

110 *A similar approach should have applied during the 2008 crash:* Under current law, banks are not permitted to file for bankruptcy, but the crisis—including the hundreds of billions of dollars in bailout money—was all in unchartered territory with no legal precedent. It would have been possible for the Treasury to lay out the terms of a bailout with the primary features of a negotiated Chapter 11 reorganization, including replacing the CEOs, imposing significant losses for the shareholders, requiring the creditors to bear some of the losses, and drawing up a new business plan. In fact, most negotiated reorganizations are done in the shadow of the bankruptcy laws, with the parties agreeing that there will be no formal filing, so long as the agreed-upon conditions are met. In addition, because of the unprecedented investment of public funds, the banks could have been required to help meet certain public aims, such as reduced foreclosures and increased lending to small businesses.

Sheila Bair believes such an approach should have been considered for Citibank, and she points out that a bankruptcy-like receivership could have been used through the existing authority of the FDIC: "I took the position that we should at least consider the feasibility of putting Citibank, Citigroup's insured national bank subsidiary, through our bankruptcy-like receivership process. That would have enabled us to create a good-bank/bad-bank structure, leaving the bad assets in the bad bank, with losses absorbed by its shareholders and unsecured creditors. My request that we at least look at using our receivership powers was met with derision by the other regulators. Hank Paulson and Tim Geithner mockingly accused me of saying that Citi was 'not systemic.' " Sheila Bair, *Bull by the Horns*, 123.

Under this scenario, banks that did not want to subject themselves to a negotiated reorganization could continue operations, but they would not receive TARP bailout money. While Sheila Bair makes it clear that Secretary Paulson and Secretary Geithner were unwilling to consider such an alternative because Citi and the other huge banks were systemically important, it is worth considering that the markets (and the economy) might have responded more positively to the news that TARP money was available if the largest banks needed it, but the terms would require some serious accountability and a change in banking practices going forward.

111 *fall in line for partial payment:* When AIG was running out of cash in late 2008, it began negotiating with creditors for write-downs of their debts. Elias Habayeb, the CFO who oversaw the Financial Products unit of AIG, reportedly tried to get creditors to accept discounts of as much as 40 cents on the dollar. See Richard Teitelbaum and Hugh Son, "New York Fed's Secret Choice to Pay for Swaps Hits Taxpayers," *Bloomberg*, October 27, 2009. Although it is typical to have creditors take some haircut, Tim Geithner, then head of the Federal Reserve Bank of New York, guaranteed creditors would be paid 100 cents on the dollar, placing the burden on taxpayers without having the creditors—including the counterparties to AIG's credit default swaps—shoulder any of the losses. See Brady Dennis, "Fed Criticized for Not Negotiating Harder with AIG Creditors," *Washington Post*, November 17, 2009.

111 *walked away with $12.9 billion:* One of the biggest beneficiaries of the government bailout of AIG was Goldman Sachs, which received a $12.9 billion payment from AIG. Once Goldman learned that the government was likely going to bail out AIG in 2008, it refused to take a haircut. According to one report, Goldman would later feature AIG as a "client success story," even though its role in the bailout of AIG came at significant cost to the taxpayer. See Lauren Tara LaCapra, "Goldman, AIG and the Government Renew Their Friendship," *Unstructured Finance* (blog), Reuters, April 15, 2013.

111 *but a pain-free bailout:* Note that the "no-strings-attached" approach for the major bank bailout is in sharp contrast to how the auto companies were treated. After an initial infu-

sion of cash in the fall of 2008, Ford was in relatively secure shape but Chrysler and GM asked for huge loans, arguing that they had no other access to cash, and without help they would be forced to shut down. Ultimately Treasury lent the money, but their bailout was accompanied by a Chapter 11 bankruptcy and most of the attendant features, including the requirement that shareholders be wiped out and creditors share some of the pain. See Martin Kady, "Dems Attach Strings to Auto Bailout," *Politico Live* (blog), *Politico*, November 15, 2008. Both companies adopted new business plans, and their relatively new CEOs agreed to work for $1 a year. To help the companies survive, the unions agreed to modify their contracts and adjust their pension obligations. See also Sheryl Gay Stolberg and Bill Vlasic, "US Lays Down Terms for Auto Bailout," *New York Times*, March 30, 2009.

111   *for a long time:* In fact, the price of Too Big to Fail is still weighing on our economy. Concentration in the banking industry was one of the principle problems cited at the time TARP was passed, and yet, the largest financial institutions are now 30 percent *larger* than they were before the financial crisis and the five biggest banks now hold more than half of all banking assets in the United States. This is based on our calculation of assets for the top four banks, which grew from a combined $6 trillion to $7.8 trillion between 2007 and 2013. Similarly, one report in 2012 showed that the top five banks are about twice as large as they had been a decade earlier relative to the economy. David Lynch, "Big Banks: Now Even Too Bigger to Fail," *Bloomberg Businessweek*, April 19, 2012.

The continued faith in Too Big to Fail also gives large financial institutions access to cheaper capital, since investors believe the government would never let them fail. One estimate pointed to "a taxpayer subsidy of $83 billion a year. To put the figure in perspective, it's tantamount to the government giving the banks about 3 cents of every tax dollar collected. . . . The top five banks—JPMorgan, Bank of America Corp., Citigroup Inc., Wells Fargo & Co., and Goldman Sachs Group Inc. . . . would just about break even in the absence of corporate welfare. In large part, the profits they report are essentially transfers from taxpayers to their shareholders." "Why Should Taxpayers Give Big Banks $83 Billion a Year?" editorial, *Bloomberg*, February 20, 2013. See also COP report, January 2011.

112   *actual policies were anemic:* COP criticized Treasury's foreclosure prevention policies as insufficient and ineffectual. COP noted that HAMP, Treasury's signature foreclosure program, "ha[d] failed to make a significant dent in the number of foreclosures and [did] not appear likely to do so in the future." COP report, December 2010, 133. COP viewed these failings as particularly significant in light of the relationship between housing, unemployment, and long-term economic growth. COP also found that HAMP "was not designed to address the root causes of the housing crisis" and that HAMP borrowers were "still paying 63 percent of pre-tax income towards debt" even after receiving a modification (236–38, 385). COP also noted that "to the extent that HAMP simply kicks the foreclosure can down the road, it ends up hurting all of the people who are desperate for the economy to start growing again so that their lives can return to normal." COP report, December 2010, (450).

See also COP report, "Examining the Consequences of Mortgage Irregularities for Financial Stability and Foreclosure Mitigation," November 16, 2010. See also COP report "Foreclosure Crisis: Working Toward a Solution," March 6, 2009. See also COP report "Evaluating Progress on TARP Foreclosure Mitigation Programs," April 14, 2010.

COP found that banks cut their lending to small businesses by more than 9 percent between 2008 and 2009, prompting many businesses to close their doors entirely. "Unable to find credit, many small businesses have had to shut their doors, and some of the survivors are still struggling to find adequate financing . . . it is not clear that [Treasury's] programs [to boost small business lending] have had a noticeable effect on small business credit availability." COP also criticized Treasury for failing "to target the smaller financial institutions that often serve small businesses." COP report, May 2010, 2.

112   *Reports vary:* Neil Barofsky, Special Inspector General of TARP, noted: "TARP has become

a program in which taxpayers are not being told what most of the TARP recipients are doing with the money, have still not been told how much their substantial investments are worth, and will not be told the full details of how their money is being invested." Brady Dennis, "Lawmakers Rebuke Treasury Department Over TARP Spending," *Washington Post*, July 21, 2009. One regional bank executive said to the press: "Make more loans? We're not going to change our business model or our credit policies to accommodate the needs of the public sector as they see it to have us make more loans. . . . We see TARP as an insurance policy. That when all this stuff is finally over, no matter how bad it gets, we're going to be one of the remaining banks." Another regional bank executive said the Treasury money "really doesn't change our perspective about doing things. . . . Adding $400 million in capital gives us a chance to really have a totally fortressed balance sheet in case things get a lot worse than we think. And if they don't, we may end up just paying it back a little bit earlier." Mike McIntire, "Bailout Is a Windfall to Banks, if Not to Borrowers," *New York Times*, January 17, 2009.

112 *or make other acquisitions:* In the initial days of the bailout, Secretary Paulson urged TARP recipients to lend the new money out. But at the same time, he noted that "some banks may use the capital they receive through the Treasury program to buy weaker banks and that this could benefit the financial system." Luke Mullins, "Bailout Merger No. 1: PNC and National City," *US News and World Report,* October 24, 2008. By January 2009, at least seven banks that had received TARP money had since bought other companies. Mike McIntire, "Bailout Is a Windfall to Banks."

112 *got even more aggressive in their efforts to foreclose on home mortgages:* "One reason foreclosures are so rampant is that banks and their advocates in Washington have delayed, diluted, and obstructed attempts to address the problem. Industry lobbyists are still at it today, working overtime to whittle down legislation backed by President Obama that would give bankruptcy courts the authority to shrink mortgage debt." Brian Grow, Keith Epstein, and Robert Berner, "How Banks Are Worsening the Foreclosure Crisis," *Bloomberg Businessweek*, February 11, 2009. See also Don Lee, "Home Foreclosures Expected to Surge in Coming Months: Moratoriums from Banks, Government to Expire, Setting Off New Wave of Default Actions," *Chicago Tribune*, July 6, 2009.

112 *many more were drowning:* By April 2009, forty-seven small and medium-sized banks had already failed. "Tracking the Nation's Bank Failures," *Wall Street Journal* (last update June 17, 2011) at http://graphicsweb.wsj.com/documents/Failed-US-Banks.html. The number would grow substantially.

112 *small business customers went down, too:* According to the Business Journals of US Census Bureau data, more than 170,000 small businesses closed in the United States between 2008 and 2010. See Bonnie Kavoussi, "Recession Killed 170,000 Small Businesses Between 2008 and 2010: Report," *Huffington Post,* July 25, 2012.

115 *stress test remained top secret:* The COP report, "Stress Testing and Shoring Up Bank Capital," June 9, 2009, notes that COP had engaged two internationally renowned experts in risk analysis, Professor Eric Talley and Professor Johan Walden, to review the stress test methodology.

These experts "noted that there remain unanswered questions about the details of the stress tests. Without this information, it is not possible for anyone to replicate the tests to determine how robust they are or to vary the assumptions to see whether different projections might yield very different results. There are key questions surrounding how the calculations were tailored for each institution and questions about the quality of the self-reported data." Also, "The Panel recommends that the Federal Reserve Board release more information on the results of the tests, including results under the baseline scenario" (2–3).

115 *risk for insolvency:* On *Charlie Rose,* Secretary Geithner said, "I think the results will be, on balance, reassuring. None of these 19 banks are at risk for insolvency." See Jim Puzzanghera and E. Scott Reckard, "Big Banks' 'Stress Test' Results to Be Reassuring,

Geithner Says," *Los Angeles Times*, May 7, 2009. Note that the results of the stress tests revealed that ten out of nineteen banks tested needed to raise a total of $74.6 billion in new capital. David Ellis, "Stress Tests: Banks Need $75 Billion," *CNNMoney*, May 8, 2009. Many have excoriated the "stress tests." As one commentator put it, the tests were "about as intimidating as a 1040-EZ tax form." Frank Partnoy, "Geithner's Stress Test Sham," *Daily Beast*, May 7, 2009.

116 *give the taxpayers their bonus:* Senator Jack Reed was a vocal advocate for the view that the taxpayers would be taking a huge risk that one or more of the banks might fail and leave the government stuck with the bill. He argued that if TARP worked, it wasn't enough for the banks to pay back the TARP money; taxpayers should be compensated for the risk they had assumed. The warrants were an important component of that and he insisted that TARP include a provision for warrants. See Senator Reed's statement, "Floor Statement on TARP Warrants," May 5, 2009, http://www.reed.senate.gov/news/speech /floor-statement-on-tarp-warrants

116 *value that Treasury was entitled to:* With the support of three renowned finance experts, Professor Robert Merton, Professor Daniel Bergstresser, and Professor Victoria Ivashina, COP—along with the Special Inspector General of TARP, Neil Barofsky—set out to determine how much the warrants were actually worth. In terms of methodology, COP adopted a modified version of the Black-Scholes method for valuing warrants to account for dilution and dividend yield. COP did not apply a liquidity discount to this valuation. Using different stock price volatility scenarios, COP generated high, low, and best estimates for the value of the warrants Treasury held on July 6, 2009. COP also estimated the value of the warrants Treasury had already sold using the same Black-Scholes method, except that the relevant date was changed to the date of the sale to enable comparison. The experts independently ratified the technical valuation model and its underlying assumptions. For more information on the methodology used for this analysis, see Annex A of the July 10, 2009, COP report.

COP ultimately found that eleven small banks had repurchased their warrants from Treasury for about 66 percent of their best-estimated value. COP report, 2. In other words, Treasury failed to maximize return to the taxpayers by selling warrants to banks at below-market value. See "TARP Repayments, Including the Repurchase of Stock Warrants," COP report, July 10, 2009.

116 *$8.6 billion back in taxpayers' pockets:* In the final COP report, March 16, 2011, COP reported: "Due in part to pressure generated by the Panel's work, Treasury changed its approach, and subsequent sales recovered 103 cents on the dollar, contributing to $8.6 billion in returns."

Several articles reported that Goldman Sachs initially offered the government around $400 million to $600 million to repurchase its stock warrants. See "Chump Change from Goldman?" DealBook (blog), *New York Times*, July 23, 2009. Shortly after the COP report, Goldman doubled its offer for TARP warrants to $1.1 billion, representing an improvement of $500 million to $700 million for the taxpayer. This offer was considered "the best deal taxpayers ha[d] got to date." Kristin Wong, "Goldman Buys Back TARP Warrants for $1.1 Billion," ABC News, July 22, 2009.

COP was not the only force trying to get a better return for the taxpayer: members of Congress also clamored for greater transparency in Treasury negotiations and greater attention to the interests of the taxpayer. For example, US Representative Mary Jo Kilroy introduced a bill on July 16, 2009, that "would force TARP warrants to be sold in the open market rather than settled through private negotiations." Colin Barr, "Goldman 'Warrants' Raves from Congress," *CNNMoney*, July 22, 2009.

117 *lost it all when the music stopped:* In the wake of the financial crisis, many people blamed American consumers and government homeownership policies for the financial crisis. For example, on its top 25 list of "people to blame" for the financial crisis, *Time* magazine

listed "American consumers" as one of the key figures because Americans have "enjoyed living beyond [their] means" for decades without regard for when it would end. "25 People to Blame for the Financial Crisis," Time Lists, at http://content.time.com/time/specials/packages/completelist/0,29569,1877351,00.html. Along similar lines, some people have claimed that the financial crisis resulted from the Community Reinvestment Act and other government policies aimed at expanding homeownership. For example, Charles Krauthammer said these policies were "at the root of [the financial crisis]," as he relegated the role of lenders and banks in the financial crisis: "Were there some predatory lenders? Of course. But only a fool or a demagogue . . . would suggest that this is a major part of the problem." Charles Krauthammer, "Catharsis, then Common Sense," op-ed *Washington Post*, September 26, 2008. Similarly, "We hear a lot of blaming of the creditor, but it's almost like we're afraid to blame the consumer. . . . I would challenge really somebody find me somebody that a gun was held to their head to sign the documentation. It's like we're afraid to really admit that these folks went beyond their means." Leslie Linfield quoted in Sara Murray, "Q&A: What the 'Middle-Class' Recession Means for Bankruptcies," Real Time Economics (blog), *Wall Street Journal*, October 23, 2009. I have disputed this line of thinking more directly in the text, but it is worth noting that a great deal of evidence debunks the claim that affordable housing policies caused the crisis. For example: "While it is unquestionable that Fannie Mae and Freddie Mac held substantial amounts of subprime mortgages, and that their holdings of these securities played a significant role in their demise, the evidence in this paper refutes the claim that the affordable housing mandates were responsible for the subprime crisis." Rubén Hernández-Murillo, Andra C. Ghent, and Michael T. Owyang, "Did Affordable Housing Legislation Contribute to the Subprime Securities Boom?," Federal Reserve Bank of St. Louis, August 2012, 36. ". . . We find little evidence to support the view that either the CRA or the GSE goals caused excessive or less prudent lending than otherwise would have taken place. . . . In fact, the evidence suggests that loan outcomes may have been marginally better in tracts that were served by more CRA-covered lenders than in similar tracts where CRA-covered institutions had less of a footprint. Loan purchases by CRA-covered lenders also do not appear to have been associated with riskier lending." Robert B. Avery and Kenneth P. Brevoort, "The Subprime Crisis: Is Government Housing Policy to Blame?," Division of Research and Statistics Board of Governors of the Federal Reserve System, August 3, 2011.

118   *too few people to make any real difference:* "When viewed in light of the millions of foreclosure completions since 2007 and the large number waiting in the pipeline due to continued hardships from high unemployment rates and lower home values, HAMP has failed to make a significant dent in the number of foreclosures and does not appear likely to do so in the future." COP report, December 2010, 133. In addition to criticizing Treasury for failing to reach the vast majority of homeowners with its foreclosure mitigation efforts, COP also expressed concern that the relief offered was only temporary. COP condemned "the timeliness of Treasury's response to the foreclosure crisis, the sustainability of mortgage modifications, and the accountability of Treasury's foreclosure programs." COP report, April 2010. COP believed more of Treasury's efforts should have been channeled toward "dealing with the crisis directly by addressing home mortgage foreclosures," particularly in view of the relationship among housing, unemployment, and long-term economic growth. COP report, March 2009, 5; see also note on p. 301, *"actual policies were anemic."*

118   *"foam the runway" for them:* For more discussion of this meeting, including a discussion of Secretary Geithner's "foam the runway" comment, see Neil Barofsky, *Bailout*, 150–58.

119   *long-term economic growth:* For example, COP noted: "The Panel remains concerned regarding the long-term sustainability of HAMP modifications. High, persistent unemployment continues to present problems for many borrowers. HAMP modifications leave borrowers with continuing high levels of negative equity, and even after receiving a mod-

ification, half of HAMP borrowers are still paying 63 percent of pre-tax income towards debt." COP report, December 2010, 385. "The Panel first expressed concerns that HAMP was not designed to address the root causes of the housing crisis in March 2009. In subsequent reports the Panel has raised serious concerns about Treasury's efforts to address these problems, noting that HAMP has failed to address foreclosures caused by factors such as unemployment and negative equity." COP report, December 2010, 236–37; "The finding that [Home Owners' Loan Corporation] loans were more likely to end in foreclosure if the borrower had little or no equity has important implications for HAMP. It suggests that borrowers with less equity or negative equity will be more likely to redefault on their modified loans, and thereby underscores the importance of principal reductions to the program's long-term success." COP report, December 2010, 348. "Homeowners with unaffordable mortgages were not the only group hurt by the financial crisis. Millions of homeowners who didn't have mortgages or who had affordable mortgages saw the value of their home plummet, and this was devastating for those who were going to use the equity in their home to finance their retirement. . . . For all of these people, relief will only come once the economy starts growing again. That growth will only occur once the housing market has stabilized, and that stability will not develop until people move out of homes with mortgages they cannot afford and into housing they can afford. So to the extent that HAMP simply kicks the foreclosure can down the road, it ends up hurting all of the people who are desperate for the economy to start growing again so that their lives can return to normal." COP report, December 2010, 450; "Since any intermediate to long-term resolution of the housing crisis must reside substantially with the private sector lenders and investors who hold the mortgage notes and liens, instead of spending an additional $30 billion on a government-sponsored foreclosure mitigation effort, we believe Treasury would be best served by strongly encouraging these participants to engage in good faith, market-based negotiations with their distressed borrowers. In our opinion, this is the best way to bring stability to the housing market so that the economy can start growing again." COP report, December 2010, 451.

119 *FDIC chair Sheila Bair raised the issue repeatedly:* For example, Sheila Blair proposed making FDIC bailout funds for Citibank conditional on forcing Citi to participate in a foreclosure prevention program. Charles Duhigg, "Fighting Foreclosures, F.D.I.C. Chief Draws Fire," *New York Times*, December 10, 2008.

119 *wrote op-eds and gave speeches:* For example, Les Christie, "FDIC Chief: Intervene on Foreclosures," *CNNMoney*, December 2, 2008. See also Gretchen Morgenson, "Why Treasury Needs a Plan B for Mortgages," *New York Times*, December 5, 2009.
See also Art Levine, "As Treasury Department Stumbles, Liberals Push Tougher Measures to Stem Foreclosures," *Truthout*, November 30, 2009.

119 *to greater depths:* Over time, the Republicans named six different men to the Congressional Oversight Panel: Congressman Jeb Hensarling and Senator Judd Gregg, followed by former senator John Sununu, former SEC commissioner Paul Atkins, Mark McWatters, and Dr. Ken Troske. Later, when I resigned to take over the job of setting up the new consumer agency in September 2010, Senator Ted Kaufman took over and added his energy to the subsequent COP investigations and reports. Senator Kaufman was a longtime advisor to Joe Biden, and he had been appointed to take over Biden's Senate seat when Biden was elected vice president. He testified on behalf of the panel, and he oversaw the final report, wrapping up COP's work.

120 *16 out of 23 were bipartisan:* The Congressional Oversight Panel built up support from many Democrats as well as a number of Republicans in Congress for its efforts to hold Treasury accountable. For example, Republican senator Olympia Snowe introduced a bill to provide COP with subpoena authority in April 2009, and she criticized Treasury for withholding key information from its overseers. http://www.gpo.gov/fdsyspkg/CREC-2009-04-20/html/CREC-2009-04-20-pt1-PgS4448.htm. Republican senator Chuck Grassley was also a strong

supporter of COP's work. See, for example, his statement from July 21, 2010: http://www
.finance.senate.gov/imo/media/doc/072110CG.pdf.

120 *as did the CEO of Ally Bank:* Testimony of Citibank CEO Vikram Pandit from March 4,
2010, is available at http://cybercemetery.unt.edu/archive/cop/20110401231848/http://
cop.senate.gov/hearings/library/hearing-030410-citi.cfm. Testimony of Michael Carpenter, CEO of GMAC/Ally, from February 25, 2010, is available at http://cybercemetery.unt
.edu/archive/cop/20110401231727/http://cop.senate.gov/hearings/library/hearing-022510
-gmac.cfm. COP also heard testimony from SVP from Chrysler and Treasurer from General Motors (http://cybercemetery.unt.edu/archive/cop/20110401231815/http://cop.senate
.gov/hearings/library/hearing-072709-detroithearing.cfm), as well as the heads of a number of small banks.

120 *focused entirely on the AIG bailout:* "The AIG Rescue, Its Impact on Markets, and the
Government's Exit Strategy," COP report, June 10, 2010.

   COP also heard testimony from Robert Willumstad, former chairman and CEO
of AIG, on May 26, 2010, available at http://cybercemetery.unt.edu/archive/cop
/20110401232000/http://cop.senate.gov/hearings/library/hearing-052610-aig.cfm. The AIG
officials were quick to point out that nearly all of the business practices of the insurance
giant were conservative and well regulated and that only one tiny portion of the company
nearly brought it down. But I always heard that differently: Risk-taking at huge financial
institutions could be hidden away from the regulators and the shareholders, but, at the same
time, be so dangerous that it could blow up both the company and the entire economy.

120 *New York's then attorney general Eliot Spitzer:* During his tenure as attorney general, Eliot
Spitzer was at the forefront of prosecuting white-collar crime, securities fraud, and Internet
fraud, and he was willing to tangle with Wall Street institutions. He had sniffed out trouble
at AIG years before the company collapsed. In March 2005, AIG's board forced Greenberg
to resign from his post as CEO and chairman, in part under the shadow of an investigation
by Spitzer. In May 2005, Spitzer filed a civil complaint against AIG, Greenberg, and former
CFO Howard Smith, alleging fraud. In 2013, Hank Greenberg filed a civil lawsuit against
Eliot Spitzer for defamation. Greenberg claimed that Spitzer had engaged in a "long-
standing malicious campaign," involving allegedly false accusations against Greenberg on
multiple occasions in various media, "to discredit . . . Greenberg and damage [his] reputation and career." Chris Dolmetsch, "Ex-AIG Chief Greenberg Sues Eliot Spitzer for Defamation," *Bloomberg News*, July 15, 2013. Spitzer called the suit "ridiculous, frivolous and
stupid," Yoav Gonen, "Exclusive: No, You're 'Stupid!' Spitzer Blasts 'Ridiculous' Suit from
Former Wall Street Foe Hank Greenberg," *New York Post*, August 9, 2013.

121 *thousand executives were indicted:* Savings and loans were financial institutions that
accepted deposits and financed home mortgages and car loans. In the early '80s, the
S&Ls were given broader ability to do more kinds of lending activities—but without as
much regulatory oversight. The S&Ls loaded up on real estate loans, and when interest
rates climbed, they got caught short with money already committed on home mortgages
and not enough deposits, and many faced insolvency. Because they were lightly regulated, some of them turned to various forms of creative bookkeeping or thinly disguised
Ponzi schemes. Nearly 750 of the 3,200 S&Ls failed. The scandal was huge, entangling
political figures and Wall Street titans.

   In the wake of the S&L crisis, regulators referred more than 1,100 cases to prosecu-
tors for indictment, resulting in 839 convictions of bank officials for financial fraud. This
is in sharp contrast to the 2008 financial crisis, which has produced hardly any major
criminal convictions of individual executives.

   Kitty Calavita and Henry N. Pontell, "The State and White-Collar Crime," *Law and
Society Review* 28 (1994): 297, 302 (citing DOJ statistics). See this excellent graphic summary: "Two Financial Crises Compared: The Savings and Loan Debacle and the Mortgage Mess," *New York Times*, April 13, 2011, http://www.nytimes.com/interactive/2011

/04/14/business/20110414-prosecute.html?ref=business. In its related article, the *New York Times* notes: "Leading up to the financial crisis, many officials said in interviews, regulators failed in their crucial duty to compile the information that traditionally has helped build criminal cases. In effect, the same dynamic that helped enable the crisis— weak regulation—also made it harder to pursue fraud in its aftermath." Gretchen Morgenson and Louise Story, "In Financial Crisis, No Prosecutions of Top Figures," *New York Times*, April 14, 2011. See also Jed Rakoff, "The Financial Crisis: Why Have No High-Level Executives Been Prosecuted?" *The New York Review of Books*, January 9, 2014. Rakoff argues that the legal foundation was not difficult but that changes in government attitudes have made corporate accountability a lower priority.

122 *pretty boring job:* Before going to the FDIC, Bair was Dean's Professor of Financial Regulatory Policy at the Isenberg School of Management at the University of Massachusetts— Amherst, and she had a background in the Treasury Department, the Commodity Future Trading Commission, and the New York Stock Exchange. She had worked for Senator Robert Dole as research director when he was Senate majority leader in the 1980s. She was an outspoken advocate for sensible rules and safer markets.

123 *only one had a woman CEO:* In 2011 and 2012, of the twenty commercial banks listed in the Fortune 500, only one had a female CEO (KeyCorp's Beth Mooney). By 2010, there were no female CEOs of top commercial banks. See: http://money.cnn.com/magazines /fortune/fortune500/2010/industries/30/index.html; http://money.cnn.com/galleries/2010 /fortune/1004/gallery.fortune500_women_ceos.fortune/15.html; Laura Petrecca, "Number of Female 'Fortune' 500 CEOs at Record High," *USA Today*, October 26, 2011. Colleen Leahey, "Update: Fortune 500 Women CEOs Hits a Record 20," Postcards (blog) *CNNMoney*, July 18, 2012.

124 *more than three hundred small banks and credit unions had failed:* By September 2010, about 276 small and medium-sized banks had failed, along with sixty-six credit unions. See http://graphicsweb.wsj.com/documents/Failed-US-Banks.html; http://online.wsj .com/article/SB10001424052748703499604575512254063682236.html.

124 *pay down underwater mortgages:* "Since the financial crisis began in September 2008, there have been approximately 4.5 million completed foreclosures across the country." CoreLogic, "Core Logic Reports U.S. Foreclosure Inventory Down 33 percent Nationally from a Year Ago," Yahoo! Finance, October 8, 2013. "In late 2009, during the worst of the housing market's meltdown, 26% of all borrowers were underwater." "By the end of June [2013], 7.1 million, or 14.5%, of mortgage borrowers remained underwater on their loans." Les Christie, "2.5 Million Mortgage Borrowers No Longer Underwater," *CNNMoney*, September 10, 2013.

125 *well grounded in both law and economic policy:* See "An Update on TARP Support for the Domestic Automotive Industry," COP report, January 13, 2011. For example of news coverage, see Andy Kroll, "Auto Bailouts: A Success Story?," *Mother Jones*, January 13, 2011. COP wrote that "unless they could raise billions of dollars in new financing, they faced collapse—a potentially crippling blow to the American economy that Treasury [at that time] estimated would eliminate nearly 1.1 million jobs."

4 | What $1 Million a Day Can Buy

128 *to burst into flames, the agency would put a stop to it:* The CPSC recall system works to ensure speedy recalls of faulty products. The manufacturer has a responsibility to report any potential danger within twenty-four hours of discovering it. At that point, the CPSC begins an investigation into the danger posed. In the meantime, the manufacturer has the option to "fast track" the recall process by initiating a voluntary recall. If the manufacturer chooses to fast track, it gains voluntary recall status and avoids the stigma of facing a forced recall from the CPSC. Jennifer P. Toney, *Brief Overview of the US Consumer-Product Recall System—Old and New*, WeMakeItSafer.com, September 2, 2008, http://

wemakeitsafer.com/blog/2008/09/brief-overview-of-the-us-consumer-product-recall
-system-old-and-new/.

For example, there have been many toaster recalls, for a variety of reasons ranging from short-circuiting to failure to shut off. Most recently, in 2011 the CPSC announced the recall of a model where the toasters did not always pop up as intended, igniting the contents. Liz F. Kay, "CPSC Recalls Flaming Toasters," *Baltimore Sun*, June 30, 2011.

130 *who lived on the edge of a small southern town with his wife and stepson*: As noted previously, the data used in the bankruptcy studies were gathered under strict confidentiality requirements typical of human-subjects research protections at US universities. All data analysis was done using anonymous numerical identifiers for the study participants. When referencing individuals, names and specific identifiers have been changed to preserve anonymity. See *The Two-Income Trap*, 184; *The Fragile Middle Class*, Appendix 1.

130 *car payment would be $105 higher than the dealer originally estimated*: There are many examples of predatory car lending. Jason got caught by a "yo-yo scam," where a car lender will not finalize the terms of the financing until after the car has been taken home from the dealership. See "Auto Lending Abuses in Dealer-Financed Loans," Center for Responsible Lending, Issue Brief April 2011, at www.responsiblelending.org. Another common practice is for auto dealers to reach out to several lenders to whom the dealer could sell the loan. The lender will dictate the interest rate of the loan but will allow the dealer to increase the rate further and take a kickback from the increased rate. In a 2011 study, the Center for Responsible Lending estimated that consumers were paying more than $25 billion in increased interest rates to finance these dealer kickbacks. Delvin Davis and Joshua Frank, "Under the Hood: Auto Loan Interest Rate Hikes Inflate Consumer Costs and Loan Losses," Center for Responsible Lending, April 19, 2011. Buy Here, Pay Here dealers act as lenders themselves, selling and financing used cars at extremely high interest rates and luring buyers into paying substantially more than market price for the vehicle, http://www.responsiblelending.org/other-consumer-loans/auto
-financing/research-analysis/auto-dealers-lending-abuses-cost-billions.html.

131 *rates that would make Tony Soprano blush*: According to a 2009 study by the Federal Reserve Bank of Kansas City, the average annual percentage rate (APR) on payday loans was 451 percent. See Robert DeYoung and Ronnie J. Phillips, "Payday Loan Pricing," The Federal Reserve Bank of Kansas City Economic Research Department, Table 1 (February 2009), available at http://www.kansascityfed.org/PUBLICAT/RESWKPAP/PDF/rwp09-07.pdf. See also Carolyn Carter et al., "Stopping the Payday Loan Trap," National Consumer Law Center, 4, Appendix A-3 (June 2010). (APR for typical payday loans varies from 391 percent to 782 percent.)

131 *in a journal called* Democracy: See Elizabeth Warren, "Unsafe at Any Rate," *Democracy* 5 (Summer 2007): 8–19.

131 *would overhaul banking regulation*: As part of the TARP bill, Congress had instructed the COP to produce a report on financial regulatory reform to help guide future changes to the law. We put out the report in January 2009 and highlighted shortcomings in systemic risk management of "too big to fail" banks and the lack of transparency in credit ratings. We also called out the failures in consumer protection: "Fairness should have been addressed through better regulation of consumer financial products. If the excesses in mortgage lending had been curbed by even the most minimal consumer protection laws, the loans that were fed into the mortgage backed securities would have been choked off at the source, and there would have been no 'toxic assets' to threaten the global economy." Many of these ideas were also embraced by consumer advocates in the weeks and months that followed. See "Special Report on Regulatory Reform," COP report, January 2009.

132 *AFL-CIO headquarters in Washington*: From the early days of the bankruptcy wars, through the fight for the consumer agency, and in the years since then, I've had the privilege to work shoulder to shoulder with amazing union leaders, and I'm deeply grateful

for all the work of AFL-CIO; the Amalgamated Transit Union; the American Federation of Government Employees; the American Federation of Musicians; the American Federation of State County & Municipal Employees; the American Federation of Teachers; the American Postal Workers Union; the Bakery, Confectionery, Tobacco Workers & Grain Millers International Union; the Brotherhood of Locomotive Engineers & Trainmen; the Brotherhood of Railroad Signalmen; the Communications Workers of America; the Glass Molders Pottery Plastics & Allied Workers International Union; the International Alliance of Theatrical Stage Employees; the International Association of Bridge, Structural, Ornamental & Reinforcing Iron Workers; the International Association of Fire Fighters; the International Association of Heat & Frost Insulators and Asbestos Workers; the International Association of Machinists & Aerospace Workers; the International Brotherhood of Boilermakers; the International Brotherhood of Electrical Workers; the International Brotherhood of Teamsters; the International Longshore and Warehouse Union; the International Longshoremen's Association; the International Union of Bricklayers & Allied Craftworkers; the International Union of Elevator Constructors; the International Union of Painters & Allied Trades; the International Union of Operating Engineers; the Laborers' International Union of North America; the Marine Engineers Beneficial Association; the National Association of Government Employees; the National Association of Letter Carriers; the National Education Association; National Nurses United; the National Postal Mail Handlers Union; the National Treasury Employees Union; the Office & Professional Employees International Union; the Operative Plasterer's & Cement Mason's International Association; the Professional Aviation Safety Specialists; the Retail, the Wholesale and Department Store Union; the Seafarers International Union; the Service Employees International Union; the Sheet Metal Workers International Association; the Transport Workers Union; UNITE-HERE; the United Association of Plumbers, Fitters, Welders and HVAC Service Techs; the United Automobile, Aerospace and Agriculture Implement Workers of America; the United Brotherhood of Carpenters; the United Food and Commercial Workers International Union; the United Mine Workers of America; the United Steelworkers; the United Transportation Union; the United Union of Roofers, Waterproofers, and Allied Workers; the Utility Workers Union of America, and so many other unions who fight for the working men and women of America.

132 *might fire at them:* "When AFL-CIO officials wander onto the eighth-floor balcony of their Washington headquarters, armed guards appear a block away at the White House and the Secret Service is on the phone, telling the union leaders to get back inside, PDQ." Thomas B. Edsall, "For AFL-CIO and White House, The Great Divide Is Deepening," *Washington Post,* September 2, 2002.

133 *Not one:* The agencies are as follows: (1) The Office of the Comptroller of the Currency (OCC), whose primary mission is to charter, regulate, and supervise all national banks and savings associations, to ensure the safety and soundness of chartered institutions, and to ensure their compliance with laws requiring fair treatment of customers and fair access to credit and financial products; (2) the Office of Thrift Supervision (OTS), whose primary mission, before it was absorbed by the OCC in 2011, was to supervise savings associations and their holding companies, to ensure their safety and soundness, to ensure their compliance with consumer laws, and to encourage a competitive industry; (3) the National Credit Union Administration (NCUA), whose primary mission is to provide safety and soundness in the credit union system through regulation and supervision; (4) the Federal Reserve Board (the Fed), whose primary mission is, in its words, "to foster the stability, integrity, and efficiency of the nation's monetary, financial, and payment systems so as to promote optimal macroeconomic performance"; (5) the Federal Deposit Insurance Corporation (FDIC), whose primary mission is to maintain confidence in the financial system, by insuring deposits, supervising banks for safety, soundness,

and consumer protection, and managing receiverships of failed banks; (6) the Department of Housing and Urban Development (HUD), whose primary mission is, in its words, "to create strong, sustainable, inclusive communities and quality affordable homes for all"; and (7) the Federal Trade Commission (FTC), whose primary mission is to prevent anticompetitive, unfair, and deceptive business practices and to enhance consumer choice and public understanding of the competitive process.

134 *other to be the friendliest, which shifted their role from watchdog to lapdog*: Before 2010, the responsibility for consumer financial protection was shared among seven principal agencies, and the scattered responsibility created an opportunity for regulatory arbitrage. The banking regulators received their funding from chartering fees paid by those they regulated. This had a particularly corrupting influence on the two main banking regulators, OCC and OTC, who were in head-to-head competition for banking business. When one banking regulator adopted more permissive regulations, the banks either moved their charters to this agency or threatened to move. That dynamic put pressure on all the competing regulators to "race to the bottom" by adopting the most permissive regulations to keep their chartering fees and remain relevant. There was one regulator, the Federal Trade Commission, that had consumer protection as a primary responsibility, but its consumer protection jurisdiction didn't extend to banking entities, leaving a whole host of consumer financial products out of its purview. See Adam J. Levitin, "Hydraulic Regulation: Regulating Credit Markets Upstream," *Yale Journal on Regulation* 26 (2009): 143, 156–57.

As one example, Countrywide Financial, one of the worst abusers in the lead-up to the crisis, responded to increased regulatory pressure from the Fed and the OCC by rechartering with OTS, after OTS promised more "flexible" oversight of its mortgage lending practices. Binyamin Appelbaum and Ellen Nakashima, "Banking Regulator Played Advocate over Enforcer," *Washington Post*, November 23, 2008.

134 *many of them were financed by the big banks*: For example, giants Wells Fargo, U.S. Bank, Fifth Third Bank, and Regions Bank offer payday loans. Liz Weston, "How Big Banks Offer Payday Loans," *MSN Money*, April 19, 2013.

136 *and, yes, toasters that catch fire*: The Consumer Product Safety Commission regulates the sale and manufacture of thousands of consumer products, ranging from kids' toys to all-terrain vehicles and everything in between. According to the agency's estimates, by promulgating new regulations, initiating recalls of faulty products, and partnering with industry in prevention efforts, more than $1 trillion is saved every year by avoiding costs that result from accidents. See "About CPSC," CPSC.gov, http://www.cpsc.gov/About-CPSC/. See also "U.S. Consumer Safety Commission Strategic Plan," http://www.cpsc.gov//PageFiles/123374/2011strategic.pdf.

136 *a lot of terrible injuries*: See http://www.cpsc.gov/PageFiles/122643/05perfrpt.pdf. "For example, our work in reducing product-related injuries and deaths from cigarette lighters, cribs and baby walkers alone saves $2.6 billion annually in total societal costs."

139 *eager to take on the fight for the agency in the House*: Congressman Delahunt and Senator Durbin had introduced a similar bill on October 3, 2008, called the Consumer Credit Safety Commission Act of 2008, H.R. 7258 and S. 3629. The bill created a commission that would have the responsibility to promulgate new consumer safety rules banning abusive, fraudulent, and unfair practices; requiring adequate information and warnings on consumer credit products; and enforcing those provisions.

139 *and I was invited*: See Senator Schumer's statement: http://www.schumer.senate.gov/Newsroom/record.cfm?id=309349&&year=2009&. See also "U.S. Lawmakers Propose Financial Products Watchdog," Reuters, March 10, 2009. Also Ryan Grim, "Financial Product Safety Commission: Dems Want Mortgages Regulated Like Toys, Drugs," *Huffington Post*, April 10, 2009.

140 *somehow you're going to be protected*: For the transcript of the president's Jay Leno inter-

view, see "President Barack Obama on 'The Tonight Show with Jay Leno,'" *New York Times,* March 19, 2009.

141 *in 2007 by the Tobin Project:* The Tobin Project is an independent, nonprofit research group that was founded by Harvard Business School professor David Moss. It supports scholarly research and helps link people in government with a community of scholars across various fields who are working on significant policy issues. http://www .tobinproject.org/about.

146 *that day was eighty-nine pages long:* See "Financial Regulatory Reform; A New Foundation: Rebuilding Financial Supervision and Regulation," http://www.treasury.gov /initiatives/Documents/FinalReport_web.pdf.

146 *written fairly and enforced vigorously:* The original name proposed by the White House for the agency was the "Consumer Financial Protection Agency," and its mission would be "protecting consumers in the financial products and services markets." The administration intended for the new CFPA to be a stand-alone agency with "an independent seat at the table in our financial regulatory system" and for the CFPA to end the practice of a bank's being "able to choose its supervisor based on any consideration of real or perceived differences in agencies' approaches to consumer protection." "Financial Regulatory Reform; A New Foundation," 55–57.

147 *two hundred groups would join the cause:* AFR is a nonprofit coalition that today includes more than 250 civil rights, consumer, labor, business, investor, faith-based, and civic and community groups dedicated to laying the foundation for a strong, stable, and ethical financial system. I am deeply grateful to AFR and its member organizations for the absolutely critical role they played in the fight for the consumer agency. Heather Booth put the group together, with Lisa Donner as her deputy, and, after Dodd–Frank was adopted, Lisa became the full-time director. Two of the deans of the consumer movement who helped AFR and put their own considerable muscle behind adoption of the consumer agency were Travis Plunkett at Consumer Federation of America and Ed Mierzwinski of PIRG. They not only brought considerable skill and experience to the fight, they also inspired others to venture into the area of consumer finance. For more information, see http://ourfinancialsecurity.org.

While it is impossible to list all of the groups that played a role, I want to particularly acknowledge the contributions in this fight of AARP, AFL-CIO, American Family Voices, AFSCME, American Sustainable Business Council, Americans United for Change, Business for Shared Prosperity, Campaign for America's Future, Center for Media and Democracy, Center for Responsible Lending, Consumer Action, Consumer Federation of America, Consumers Union, Corporation for Enterprise Development, Demos, Greenlining Institute, Hastings Group, Lawyer's Committee for Civil Rights Under Law, The Leadership Conference on Civil and Human Rights, MoveOn.org, NAACP and the NAACP Legal Defense Fund, National Association of Consumer Advocates, National Community Reinvestment Coalition, National Consumer Law Center, National Consumers League, National Council of La Raza, National Fair Housing Alliance, National People's Action, National Urban League, PICO National Network, Public Citizen, Public Interest Research Group (PIRG), Roosevelt Institute, SEIU, Progressive Change Campaign Committee, USAction, and the other members of AFR that worked so hard.

147 *They worked their hearts out:* For example, the National Consumer Law Center, which was one of the premier consumer advocacy groups, supporting litigation and policy research on a range of issues, including student loans, foreclosures and debt collection, took up the fight. They provided terrific papers and analysis of the need for a consumer agency.

147 *and Dan said yes:* The Roosevelt Institute jumped into the financial reform debates with amazing speed and with some really smart people. The Institute quickly became a hub of activity, a place to find first-rate research or to meet with other experts. Under the

leadership of Andrew Rich, the Institute was one of the key partners in sensible financial reform.

150 *had worked for a member of Congress:* It is common practice for former Members of Congress, congressional staffers, and other government officials to leave government service for lobbying firms. As of 2010, the six biggest banks had hired 243 lobbyists who once worked in the federal government, including 33 who had worked as chiefs of staff for members of Congress and 54 who had worked as staffers for the Senate or House banking committees. See Kevin Connor, "Big Bank Takeover: How Too-Big-to-Fail's Army of Lobbyists Has Captured Washington," Institute for America's Future (2010), http://ourfuture.org/files/documents/big-bank-takeover-final.pdf.

Another analysis by the *Huffington Post* showed that the House Financial Services Committee has an active revolving door: Of the 243 staff members who worked on the Committee between 2000 and 2010, about half of those who left had registered as lobbyists. Most of those registered as lobbyists for the financial industry. Ryan Grim and Arthur Delaney, "The Cash Committee: How Wall Street Wins on the Hill," *Huffington Post*, March 18, 2010.

151 *they could to stand up for consumers:* Many consumer groups turned to the Center for Responsible Lending for research. Under the leadership of Martin Eakes, CRL had developed some of the best research anywhere on the impact of various financial scams on American families. CRL also provided critical data early on about the mortgage foreclosure crisis. Without its careful and detailed studies, much of the work to get the consumer agency passed into law would have been harder.

151 *gazillion other issues to boot:* For example, Jim Guest, the longtime president and CEO of Consumers Union, got into the battle. CU had a huge number of issues on its plate, from assessing the reliability of cars to evaluating the effectiveness of stain removers. But Jim jumped in, inviting me to discuss the consumer agency with thousands of e-activists by telephone conference call. Those e-activists then wrote e-mails and letters, called members of Congress, and otherwise advocated for reforms. They were smart and tough as they pressed for adoption of the CFPB, and they gave new energy to our efforts.

Similarly, Public Citizen was working on trade policy, minimum wage issues, and money in politics, and still helped to get the consumer agency passed. All their work was critically important, and they covered such a wide range of topics only by working long hours on a tight budget.

151 *drive to kill any meaningful financial reform:* According to the Center for Responsive Politics, the banking and finance industry spent, in the aggregate, more than $523 million on campaign contributions and lobbying, or $1.4 million a day, during the fight against financial reform. "As Senate Begins Financial Reform Debate, Industry Spends Tens of Millions to Influence Debate," Center for Responsive Politics Press Release, March 22, 2010. The number was found by aggregating the campaign contributions and lobbying expenditures made by accounting firms, commercial banks, credit unions, finance and credit companies, insurance companies, real estate firms, savings and loans, and securities and investment firms. One member of the House Financial Services Committee, Maxine Waters, lamented how powerful the lobbying had been: "I understand they have almost hired a lobbyist for each one of us. . . . I'm more concerned that there are members of Congress who are beginning to take on the arguments of the financial services industry about why a consumer financial protection agency is not necessary." Ryan Grim and Arthur Delaney, "The Cash Committee."

151 *reelection campaigns of influential members of Congress:* In 2009, of the ten Representatives most well funded by the finance and banking industry, five were members of the House Financial Services Committee. http://www.opensecrets.org/news/2009/11/finance-and-credit-companies-l.html. Because of the high campaign contributions to its members, the Financial Services Committee is known as a valuable committee assignment for

vulnerable members of either party who need to raise lots of money for reelection. It's a quality that has helped earn the bottom two rows of the committee hearing room—where all the most junior members sit—the reputation of being "the place where reform goes to die." Between 2009 and 2010, the eleven freshmen on the committee raised an average $1.09 million for their 2010 reelection campaigns. The House-wide average was less than half of that number. Ryan Grim and Arthur Delaney, "The Cash Committee."

151 *"Our goal will be to kill it"*: Scott Talbott, then a top lobbyist for the Financial Services Roundtable, was quoted as saying: "Our goal will be to kill [the Consumer Financial Protection Agency], or make it the least-worst way to do the wrong thing." Cheyenne Hopkins, "Banking Industry Is Underdog in Fight over New Agency," *American Banker,* July 1, 2009.

152 *was "positively Orwellian"*: Hensarling's op-ed first appeared in the *Washington Times* in July 2009. He argued that the agency would "have the power to strip from consumers their freedom of choice and restrict their credit opportunities." He also argued that it would harm consumers by "stifling innovation" and would create "less competitive markets." He concludes that "the CFPA says to the American people, 'You are simply too ignorant or too dumb to be trusted with financial products.'" He advocates an alternative Republican plan to focus on more disclosures. Jeb Hensarling, "Punishing Consumers to Protect Them," *Washington Times,* July 22, 2009.

154 *eye on the credit-reporting companies:* For example, the National Consumer Law Center (NCLC) issued a 2009 overview of studies and surveys on the extent and impact of errors on credit reports. Studies from PIRG and Consumers Union estimated that 25 percent of credit reports had errors serious enough to cause a denial of credit. Over half of the participants in a Federal Trade Commission study found an error in their credit reports, and a quarter of those participants had a materially harmful error. The types of errors found across studies included mixed files (where one consumer was mistaken for another, and vice versa), identity theft, incorrect payment history, ownership dispute, and "re-aging" of debt (where debt that gets charged off after a certain amount of time is added back on by misrepresenting the date the debt was incurred). Consumers' lengthy written complaints were reduced to one of a handful of two or three letter codes and rarely investigated. See Chi Chi Wu, "Automated Injustice: How a Mechanized Dispute System Frustrates Consumers Seeking to Fix Errors in Their Credit Reports," National Consumer Law Center, January 2009, http://www.nclc.org /images/pdf/pr-reports/report-automated_injustice.pdf. See also "Credit Score Accuracy and Implications for Consumers," Consumer Federation of America, December 17, 2002, http:// www.consumerfed.org/pdfs/121702CFA_NCRA_Credit_Score_Report_Final.pdf.

157 *Progressive bloggers joined the fight:* Many bloggers criticized Senator Dodd for his signals to exclude the agency, and they started a campaign to push him to keep the agency in the bill. One blog referenced a lobbyist who said that Dodd was paying back the bankers for keeping him in office for so long. It also depicted a cartoon of Dodd's "Dance Card," listing individuals who would benefit from the agency—"Overworked Olivia" and "Bankrupt Betty." At the end of the list was "Wall Street Fat Cats," crossed out. Mary Bottari, "Senator Dodd's Dilemma: Who to Take the Ball?," Center for Media and Democracy's PR Watch, January 19, 2010. The dance card was sent around as a petition, with the language "Senator Dodd, Tell Wall Street You Have a New Dance Partner!," banksterusa.org, http:// salsa.democracyinaction.org/o/632/p/dia/action/public/?action_KEY=2040.

Mike Lux played a critical role in introducing me to bloggers and activists and advising me on how to organize people through new media. More generally, he rallied support for the consumer agency from a broad cross-section of people and made a real difference. He understood the importance of this fight early on, and he has also stood strong for the consumer agency and financial reform ever since.

157 *a guy named Rich Cordray:* Attorneys General Tom Miller (IA), Lisa Madigan (IL), Richard Blumenthal (CT), and Richard Cordray (OH) spoke out in favor of the agency.

Cordray emphasized that "until we establish a Consumer Financial Protection Agency, we will continue to have a regulatory black hole when it comes to many of the deceptive practices and products." Austin Kilgore, "Democrat Attorneys General Push for Consumer Financial Protection Agency," Housingwire.com, February 9, 2010. Martha Coakley, attorney general for Massachusetts, and I wrote an op-ed in the *New Republic*, strongly advocating for a new agency. She was always ready to speak up on behalf of the agency. Martha Coakley and Elizabeth Warren, "The Right Way to Regulate," *New Republic*, November 18, 2009.

158 *published editorials and op-eds about the agency:* For examples of columns supporting the agency leading up to the Senate Banking Committee's markup of financial reform, see Barbara Kiviat, "Don't Kill the Consumer Financial Protection Agency, Part 2," *Time*, February 19, 2010. See also Michael Grunwald, "The Case for a Consumer Financial Protection Agency," *Time*, February 17, 2010. See also Ezra Klein, "Don't Kill the Public Option of Financial Reform," *Washington Post*, January 15, 2010. See also Paul Krugman, "Financial Reform Endgame," *New York Times*, February 28, 2010.

158 *water down the agency:* Interview by Chris Matthews with Chris Dodd (March 2, 2010), available at nbcnews.com. See also Jim Puzzanghera, "Dodd Moves to Scale Back Consumer Financial Protection Agency Plan," *Los Angeles Times*, March 2, 2010.

158 *"mouthful of mush that doesn't get the job done":* Shahien Nasiripour, "Fight for the CFPA Is 'a Dispute Between Families and Banks,' Says Elizabeth Warren," *Huffington Post*, March 3, 2010.

160 *not the big banks, pick up the tab:* During negotiations between the House and Senate, the Congressional Budget Office came out with a report showing that the reform bill would cost $19 billion over time. (This estimate was for the cost of stepped-up bank regulation and did not include the cost of running the Consumer Financial Protection Bureau, which was separately funded as part of the Federal Reserve System, which is not taxpayer funded.) The financial reform bill that first passed the Senate ensured that the new costs of regulation would fall on the hedge funds and other large financial institutions that would pay a fee to fund the work. George Zornick, "Scott Brown's Hypocrisy on Wall Street Reform," *The Nation,* October 11, 2012. But in the final weeks of June, long after the funding provision had been agreed on by lawmakers and the Dodd-Frank bill was moving toward passage, Scott Brown demanded that the tax be eliminated. Donovan Slack, "Donations Poured In as Brown's Role Grew," *Boston Globe,* December 12, 2010. Instead of charging the biggest hedge funds and banks for the cost of the regulation, the vast majority of the funds would come from unused TARP funds, which were due to go back to the taxpayers. Daniel Indiviglio, "Financial Regulation Bill Passes Through Conference . . . Again," *The Atlantic,* June 29, 2010. As Barney Frank and many others put it, Brown moved "twenty billion dollars off the backs of the banks and onto the taxpayers." Zornick, "Scott Brown's Hypocrisy on Wall Street Reform"; see also Max Fisher, "$19 Billion Bank Fee Nixed: Will It Save Financial Reform?," *The Wire,* June 30, 2010.

5 | An Agency for the People

165 *asking him to pick me:* The Progressive Change Campaign Committee (PCCC), under the leadership of Adam Green and Stephanie Taylor, organized a petition with the headline "Let Elizabeth Warren Police Wall Street" in 2010. At least thirteen senators signed on to the petition, and as of August 6, 2010, the petition had collected more than two hundred thousand signatures. Stephanie London, "Al Franken Leads Campaign to Whip Support for Elizabeth Warren," CBS News, August 6, 2010.

166 *because the banks would oppose me:* "Elizabeth Warren," editorial, *New York Times*, July 24, 2010. The editorial characterized the banks' objection to my appointment: "The banks don't oppose Ms. Warren because she doesn't get it. They oppose her because she does."

166 *"she's what we need, yo":* Los Angeles comedian Ryan Anthony Lumas was an employee

at Best Buy when he wrote and performed in a Western-style rap video urging the president to appoint me to head up the new consumer agency. The video was sponsored by the Main Street Brigade, a group supported by Hans Zimmer and Bonnie Abaunza that was dedicated to fighting for American families and consumer protection reforms in Washington. In the video, Lumas raps about how the country has a strong consumer advocate and "sheriff of Wall Street" in Elizabeth Warren. Video available at: http://mainstreetbrigade .org. See also Joe Nocera, "Consumers Clamoring for a Leader," *New York Times*, August 20, 2010.

166 *"This is a power grab"*: See Ronald D. Orol and Greg Robb, "Warren Seen Gaining Key Consumer Protection Post," *Market Watch*, July 28, 2010.

166 *and that I would be hard to confirm:* Senator Dodd said in an interview with the *Courant:* "It isn't just a question of being a consumer advocate. I want to see that she can manage something, too." Kenneth R. Gosselin, "Dodd: Is Warren 'Confirmable?,'" *Courant*, August 17, 2010. See also Shahien Nasiripour, "Chris Dodd, Top Democrat, Fights Against Elizabeth Warren," *Huffington Post*, August 12, 2010.

170 *to unbelievably high monthly payments:* For background on the rise of complicated mortgage products, including the rise of interest-only, adjustable-rate, or "teaser-rate" mortgages, see note on p. 292, *"prepayment penalties."* According to a CoreLogic study, one-third of the adjustable-rate mortgages taken out between 2004 and 2006 had initial "teaser" rates below 4 percent. On average, payments for these loans doubled after the initial teaser period lapsed. Veena Trehen, "The Mortgage Market: What Happened?," NPR, April 26, 2007.

175 *rather than powers under this "title":* Section 1066 of the Dodd-Frank Wall Street Reform and Consumer Protection Act of 2010: "The Secretary is authorized to perform the functions of the Bureau under this subtitle until the director of the Bureau is confirmed by the Senate in accordance with section 1011." Choice of the word "subtitle" over "title" had powerful implications. According to Treasury's lawyers, the statute as enacted meant that a wide range of regulatory and supervisory activities could not be initiated before a director was in place. See, e.g., letter dated January 10, 2011, jointly from the Inspectors General of the Department of the Treasury and the Federal Reserve Bank to Chairman Spencer Bachus and Chairman Judy Biggert at pages 6–7. http://www.treasury.gov/about /organizational-structure/ig/Documents/OIG-CA%2011004%20Committee %20of%20Financial%20Serivces%20Response%20CFPB.pdf.

177 *this crash was the direct consequence of years of deliberate deregulation:* In testimony before the Financial Crisis Inquiry Commission on January 13, 2010, Jamie Dimon commented on the strength of JPMorgan and the actions it took in the run-up to and aftermath of the financial crisis. See http://fcic-static.law.stanford.edu/cdn_media/fcic -testimony/2010-0113-Dimon.pdf. Dimon recounted: "My daughter called me from school one day and said, 'Dad, what's a financial crisis?' And, without trying to be funny, I said, 'This type of thing happens every five to seven years.' And she said, 'Why is everyone so surprised?'" Second, Dimon conceded that the banks did not adequately account for scenarios in which housing prices went down. I took issue with Dimon's first comment, which—in contrast to his second comment—painted the financial crisis as inevitable and removed responsibility from those who engaged in reckless and shortsighted activity on Wall Street and the regulators who should put an end to it. I noted that effective financial regulation following the Great Depression had ended "150 years of boom-and-bust cycles and gave us 50 years with virtually no financial meltdowns." The boom-and-bust cycle began when these Depression-era laws were dismantled. I encouraged bank CEOs to "acknowledge how Americans' trust has been lost and take the first steps to earn it back" by working with financial regulators and embracing meaningful consumer protection. For coverage of Dimon's comment, see Sewall Chan, "Voices That Dominate Wall Street Take a Meeker Tone on Capitol Hill," *New York Times*, January 13,

2010. For my op-ed, see Elizabeth Warren, "Wall Street's Race to the Bottom," *Wall Street Journal*, February 8, 2010.

177 *spent more than $2 billion in political contributions:* According to calculations from data provided by the Center for Responsive Politics, the Finance/Insurance/Real Estate sector contributed more than $2 billion to federal campaigns from 2000 to 2010. This figure includes contributions from individuals and PACs and "soft money" contributions reported to the Federal Elections Commission. The total reached a new all-time high of $665 million during the 2012 election cycle. http://www.opensecrets.org/industries/totals.php?ind=F.

177 *knew where they stood on each detail of banking regulation:* According to the Center for Responsive Politics, the Financial Services Roundtable has spent more than $70 million on lobbying since 1998. http://www.opensecrets.org/orgs/summary.php?id=D000021984 &cycle=A.

178 *"create an opportunity for good businesses to thrive":* In addition to discussing how effective financial regulation can benefit banks that want to offer transparent products, I emphasized the following points in my speech to the Financial Services Roundtable on September 29, 2010: (1) my commitment to helping build a consumer credit structure that "works for families, works for the financial services industry, and works for the American economy"; (2) my belief in *genuine* free markets, in which "the best products at the best prices win" because consumers and lenders have access to a level and transparent playing field; and (3) my support for a new regulatory approach that cuts through the thicket of fine print contracts and "thou shall not" rules by using simple principles to measure success, such as the principle of "fair treatment" embodied in the following question: "Can customers understand the product, figure out the costs and risks, and compare products in the marketplace?" This principles-based approach, I argued, would empower consumers while easing the regulatory burden on lenders. My speech is available at http://www.scribd.com/doc /38439729/Elizabeth-Warren-s-Speech-to-the-Financial-Services-Roundtable.

179 KNIVES COMING OUT AGAINST ELIZABETH WARREN?: Zach Carter, "Are Treasury's Knives Coming Out Against Elizabeth Warren?," AlterNet, October 29, 2010.

181 *in a couple of days he nearly doubled his money:* In his book *Throw Them All Out*, Peter Schweizer found that from July to November 2008, "[Congressman] Bachus engineered no less than forty options trades, betting that the market, a sector of the market, or an individual company would go up or down at critical times" and reported $50,000 in capital gains during this period. Peter Schweizer, *Throw Them All Out* (2011), 25. He accused Bachus of exploiting his role as a policymaker by relying on insider information about the state of the financial market when trading (25–32). As just one example, Schweizer pointed to a September 2008 incident in which Bachus traded short options—effectively betting against the market—the day after a closed-door meeting with then Treasury secretary Paulson and then Federal Reserve Bank chairman Bernanke, with the result that he almost doubled his money (Bachus bought the options for $7,846 and sold them for over $13,000) (28–29). Schweizer notes: "Congressman Bachus was not the only one actively trading stocks while setting policy during the financial crisis. But he was particularly aggressive with options; others merely cashed out of positions that were just about to worsen," and he implicated ten other lawmakers (33–34). CBS broke the story in a *60 Minutes* special, and several other media outlets reported it thereafter. See "Congress Trading on Stock Information?" *60 Minutes*, June 11, 2012. The reaction to the reports in the public and in Congress was quick and negative. For his part, Bachus denied allegations of insider trading, noting "you would have to be living under a rock not to know by September 18, 2008 that the economy was in bad shape." See Tim Mak, "Spencer Bachus Letter to 'Insider Trading' Publisher," *Politico*, November 16, 2011. Of course, his comment ignored the fact that for every trade in which the congressman profited, there was someone who didn't get confidential briefings and lost money. The Office of Congressional Ethics ultimately cleared Bachus of insider trading on April 30, 2012. See

Scott Higham, "Congress Ethics Office Clears Bachus of Insider Trading," *Washington Post*, April 30, 2012. While Members of Congress were exempt from most insider trading laws at that time, Congress subsequently made the rules more stringent.

184　*which banks had the fewest complaints:* Since the CFPB began amassing and posting information about consumer complaints in 2011, some groups have in fact started analyzing the data, shedding important light on how financial institutions treat their customers. For example, the US PIRG Education Fund found ". . . thousands of consumers with errors on their credit reports are getting relief through the Consumer Financial Protection Bureau (CFPB). The report also found that credit reporting agencies vary widely in how they respond to consumer complaints . . ." "Big Credit Bureaus, Big Mistakes," US PIRG Education Fund, November 19, 2013.

In another study, PIRG analyzed CFPB complaint data about banks: "The CFPB's searchable complaint database is the newest of a set of federal government consumer complaint databases that help consumers make better economic and safety choices by reviewing others' experiences and searching for problems or product recalls. The transparency also helps firms improve their products and services. In short, transparency improves the way markets work." "Big Banks, Big Complaints," Florida PIRG Education Fund, September 17, 2013.

In a separate study, the National Community Reinvestment Coalition (NCRC) found racial disparities in terms of both the source of complaints and banks' response to complaints, raising questions about the inequality of financial services and fair lending practices. Danielle Douglas, "Consumer Group Finds Racial Disparity in Bank Complaints," *Washington Post*, October 8, 2013.

The work of PIRG, NCRC, and other consumer groups in analyzing the CFPB data and expanding the audience for the data is critically important to the success of the agency, and the organizations' willingness to make constructive criticism about the ways the data could be enhanced are even more important. These organizations are a critical counterbalance to the big banks, helping keep the agency focused on its mission.

188　*"That could happen to anyone":* When asked to turn down government-funded health care for the sake of ideological consistency, Grimm said: "What am I, not supposed to have health care? It's practicality. I'm not going to become a burden for the state because I don't have health care, and God forbid I get into an accident and I can't afford the operation. That can happen to anyone." Two weeks later, he voted against the ACA. See, for example, Rachel Maddow, "Michael Grimm's Health Care Problem," msnbc.com, February 15, 2012.

189　*security clearances they need for promotions and special assignments:* According to Article 134 of the Punitive Articles of the UCMJ, willful nonpayment of debt is considered dishonorable conduct (http://www.au.af.mil/au/awc/awcgate/law/mcm.pdf). What's more, active servicemembers can lose their security clearances if they have significant credit issues, which could result in those members being discharged, taken off assignment, or otherwise ineligible for promotion. According to Lt. Col. James Gregory, debt and late payment has become one of the leading factors in security-clearance terminations because "a person with big debts is more likely to accept money in exchange for revealing secrets." According to one report, thirty-six thousand active-military members who hold security clearances have sought urgent financial assistance or advice to avoid this scenario. Bill Briggs, "How Big Debt Is Threatening Security Clearances for Thousands of Troops," NBC News, August 13, 2012. Defense Secretary Leon Panetta said that financial troubles are the number one reason why servicemembers lose their security clearances. Reuters, "Student Loans: Even Military Worries About Rising Debt," *Christian Science Monitor*, October 21, 2012.

190　*payments and finally had to declare bankruptcy:* In a 2006 study the Department of Defense found that predatory lenders—harnessing a variety of marketing techniques—specifically targeted military personnel who lacked the ability to repay with high-rate, high-fee loans designed to evade state consumer protection laws. The department recommended the following changes be made with respect to servicemembers: (1) lenders should make "unambiguous and uniform price disclosures" to servicemembers and their families; (2) Congress should impose a federal cap on interest rates to prevent lenders from circumventing state restrictions; (3) lenders should be prohibited from making loans to servicemembers and their families "without due regard for the Service member's ability to repay"; (4) lenders should not require servicemembers to waive important legal protections via contract; and (5) states should enforce their consumer protection laws fairly and consistently, including with respect to non-resident servicemembers stationed within their borders. See "Report on Predatory Lending Practices Directed at Members of the Armed Forces and Their Dependents," Department of Defense, August 9, 2006, 4–10. The report details the effects of predatory lending on servicemembers and their families, incorporating specific case studies such as the one involving an air force member whose $400 loan turned into a $3,000 obligation. For this impact assessment, see "Report on Predatory Lending," 37–44.

190 *someone official who would do right by the service member:* On September 30, 2006, Congress passed H.R. 5122, the Military Lending Act, which was designed to protect military families from predatory lending. The act prohibits lenders from charging servicemembers and their families an annual interest rate greater than 36 percent. In addition, it requires lenders to make certain disclosures to clarify key loan terms, prohibits abusive penalties and practices, and bans onerous contractual provisions. While these protections have made noticeable differences, lenders have found many ways to circumvent the law. For example, "Lenders have exploited loopholes in the definitions of covered credit, such as styling a payday or car title loan as open-end credit or setting a loan term slightly longer than the definitions cover, to make high-cost loans to servicemembers." Furthermore, "Some credit products described as problems for servicemembers in the DoD Report to Congress were not included in DoD's initial consumer credit definitions, including military installment loans and rent-to-own or other retail installment sales financing. As a result, servicemembers are still exposed to extremely high rates and risky forms of security, inconsistent supervision at the state level, and can still have pay drained by military allotments when borrowing or financing purchases with these creditors." Jean Ann Fox, "The Military Lending Act Five Years Later," Consumer Federation of America, May 29, 2012, 10.

192 *targeted for some of the worst mortgages in the housing crash:* The Equal Credit Opportunity Act prohibits discrimination in lending on the basis of race, color, religion, national origin, sex, marital status, age, or receipt of public assistance. Creditors may, however, discriminate on the basis of such factors as income, debts, and other indicators of creditworthiness. For more information on this act, consult the Federal Trade Commission's summary: http://www.consumer.ftc.gov/articles/0347-your-equal-credit-opportunity-rights. The Fair Housing Act prohibits discrimination in housing practices, such as setting different terms on a loan or refusing to provide information about loans, on the basis of race, color, national origin, religion, sex, familial status, or handicap. For more information on this act, see the Department of Housing of Urban Development's summary: http://portal.hud.gov /hudportal/HUD?src=/program_offices/fair_housing_equal_opp/FHLaws/yourrights. Several agencies, including the Consumer Financial Protection Bureau and Department of Justice, have a hand in enforcing these and other important antidiscrimination laws. These laws were created within a context of well-documented lending discrimination against women, minorities, and other groups. John R. Walter, "The Fair Lending Laws and Their Enforcement," *Federal Reserve Bank of Richmond Economic Quarterly* (Fall 1995): 62–67. For more on CFPB Fair Lending, see http://www.consumerfinance.gov/fair-lending/.

Investigation of lending discrimination or the violation of other lending rules typically involves painstaking collection of information from lenders, from debtors, and from other sources. Steve Antonakes, Peggy Twohig, and Patrice Ficklin put together teams of extraordinary people at CFPB to investigate lending activities and act as the frontline cops on the beat. Most of their work will be out of the public view, but their impact will be felt throughout the economy.

193 *pay an additional $25 million fine:* See http://www.consumerfinance.gov/newsroom /cfpb-capital-one-probe/.

195 *big banks, too) sold honest, simple mortgages:* During my time at CFPB, I had a chance to visit with community bankers from all fifty states to learn about their business models and get their input on mortgage rules and other policies—thanks in large part to the help of Camden Fine of the Independent Community Bankers of America (ICBA), who generously helped introduce me to his members nationwide and teach me about issues important to smaller institutions. I came to understand that community bankers were particularly interested in the Know Before You Owe project because the previous system of disclosures placed a disproportionate regulatory burden on them. In addition, most community bankers believed they were already following the basic principles of Know Before You Owe, and many viewed transparency and simplicity as core components of their trusted, long-term relationships with the families they serve. See my "Remarks to the Independent Community Bankers of America," March 22, 2011, at http://www .consumerfinance.gov/newsroom/remarks-to-the-independent-community-bankers-of -america/. From early on in the process, community bankers had many positive comments on the CFPB's mortgage disclosure effort. Ron Haynie of the ICBA made the following remark with respect to the agency's process: "I think what was probably the most refreshing was just the fact that you had a room of bankers there . . . folks who use [these disclosures] every single day and have to explain it to customers every single day. And the folks at the CFPB were asking questions—does this work? They want the feedback, and bankers are not a shy bunch." See Kate Davidson, "New CFPB Mortgage Disclosures Win Praise for Content and Process," *American Banker,* May 18, 2011. Dillon Shea of the National Association of Federal Credit Unions said the credit unions "appreciate[d] the CFPB's collaborative approach" and hailed the CFPB's first prototype forms as "a positive first step in simplifying an increasingly complex mortgage disclosure regime." See http:// www.nafcu.org/Tertiary.aspx?id=22644. The ICBA noted the prototypes were "a vast improvement." See http://www.icba.org/files/ICBASites/PDFs/cl071311.pdf. As one community banker put it, "Clearly [Elizabeth Warren] understands our model" of doing business. Andy Kroll, "Has Elizabeth Warren Won Over the Banks?," *Mother Jones,* May 6, 2011.

195 *people to take the form for a test drive:* Each participant in the initial "Know Before You Owe" study signed a privacy notice and consent form. Kleimann Communication Group, Inc., "Know Before You Owe: Evolution of the Integrated TILA-RESPA," presented to CFPB, July 9, 2012 34. www.consumerfinance.gov/knowbeforeyouowe/. The CFPB has never publicly identified individual participants in the study, instead using nonidentifiable information to characterize participant responses in its report. As such, I treat the identity in this example as confidential.

196 *clear information, so he could make a clear choice:* The study protocols and the results and stories are validated beginning on p. 53 in "Know Before You Owe." Disclosures, by Kleiman Communications Group, July 9, 2012, available at http://files.consumerfinance .gov/f/201207_cfpb_report_tila-respa-testing.pdf.

The CFPB employed a user-centered design process to test prototype mortgage disclosure forms, in which the users influenced how the design took shape. The process had several phases, including context setting (information gathering), formative development (rapid prototyping), and iterative usability testing (interviewing and testing prototypes all over the country). During the iterative usability testing phase, the CFPB tested two different thirty-year, fixed-rate loans and two different 2/1 adjustable-rate mortgages using two different designs, both of which contained a summary of key loan and affordability information, closing cost details, and information about insurance, servicing, escrow, and appraisal. Participants in the study were asked to compare the loans and answer a number of questions related to the process, which were coded using grounded theory to identify response trends and participant performance. "Know Before You Owe," xxiii.

On November 20, 2013, the CFPB finalized the "Know Before You Owe" mortgage disclosure forms, which turned out to be longer than one page. Extensive testing revealed that consumers were better able to understand the revised forms, as they proved more capable of answering questions about a sample loan. In particular, consumers demonstrated understanding of risky loan features, short-term and long-term costs, and monthly payments. In addition, consumers were better able to compare different products and evaluate the difference between an original and final loan offer. The forms will become effective August 1, 2015, following consultation with industry representatives and consumers. See "CFPB Finalizes 'Know Before You Owe' Mortgage Forms," CFPB Newsroom, November 20, 2013.

197 *The stories were genuinely awful:* News of the mortgage foreclosure scandal first emerged in fall 2010. It became clear that many banks were engaged in the practice of "robo-signing," which occurred when employees signed or forged mortgage foreclosure documents without verifying the information contained in those documents *as they were required to do by law.* In one such case, Jeffrey Stephan of GMAC (now Ally), who was responsible for reviewing foreclosure cases to ensure they were legally justified, testified in July 2010 that he signed off on ten thousand mortgage foreclosure documents per month for five years, which provides some sense of the massive scale of the fraud. Ariana Eunjung Cha, "Ally Financial Legal Issue with Foreclosures May Affect Other Mortgage Companies," *Washington Post,* September 22, 2010.

Another aspect of this fraud dealt with ownership of mortgages and chain of title. Before a bank can foreclose on a home, it must prove that it owns the property. In their haste to package and repackage and sell and resell loans, banks had often cut corners in their paperwork and ownership could no longer be documented. Some banks offered forged affidavits to "clear" the titles. Since the scandal came to light, courts have intervened to stop foreclosure proceedings in several cases where the banks were unable to prove they owned the underlying mortgages. John Carney, "A Primer on the Foreclosure Crisis," CNBC, October 11, 2010. One study found that banks failed to prove ownership of the underlying mortgage in 40 percent of foreclosure bankruptcy cases. Katherine M. Porter, "Misbehavior and Mistake in Bankruptcy Mortgage Claims," *Texas Law Review* 87 (2008): 121–82. As people began to examine the mortgage foreclosure process in greater detail and in particular the role of servicers, it became clear that improper foreclosure was not only rampant, but it was also multilayered. For example, "dual tracking" is when a mortgage servicer tells a homeowner she is being considered for a loan modification, while at the same time the servicer is moving forward on foreclosure proceedings. Rick Rothacker, "Senators Criticize 'Dual-Track' Foreclosure, Loan Modification Processes," *Charlotte Observer,* November 17, 2010.

Many bank executives claimed that no houses were taken in error and that the scandal really just amounted to a technical paperwork problem. Ruth Simon, Robin Sidel, and Jessica Silver-Greenberg, "Signs of Mistakes Aside, Banks Defend Foreclosures," *Wall Street Journal,* October 20, 2010. Jamie Dimon of JPMorgan said, "We don't think there are cases where people have been evicted . . . where they shouldn't have been," and an ex–Goldman Sachs employee dismissed the scandal as "just a clerical error" as opposed to something more "nefarious." Jill Treanor and Julia Kollewe, "Robo-Signing Eviction Scandal Rattles Wall Street," *Guardian,* October 14, 2010; Max Abelson, "The Foreclosure Fiasco and Wall Street's Shrug," *New York Observer,* October 12, 2010. One commentator published an editorial by John Carney entitled "Let's Not Start Lionizing the Anti-Foreclosure Deadbeats," in CNBC, October 13, 2010.

Despite the force with which these arguments were articulated, no one offered any proof to back them up. The eventual mortgage foreclosure settlements included payments to settle claims by people who had in fact been wrongfully moved out of their homes. See, e.g., http://www.nationalmortgagesettlement.com/.

197 *got the biggest TARP handouts:* The following banks and mortgage servicers were involved in the mortgage foreclosure scandal: Bank of America, Citigroup, Wells Fargo, JPMorgan Chase, Ally/GMAC. In later settlements, Aurora, MetLife Bank, PNC, Sovereign, and SunTrust also paid substantial penalties. James O'Toole, "Banks to Pay $8.5 Billion in Foreclosure Settlement," *CNNMoney*, January 7, 2013. All of these institutions received TARP funding, with the exception of MetLife Bank.

197 *but the big guys couldn't be bothered:* The culprits in the mortgage foreclosure scandal were by and large the big banks. As one community banker noted, the community banks could not afford to become "mortgage factories" like the big banks because their business model hinges on developing good relationships between the customers and the bank/banker. Matt Gutman and Bradley Blackburn, "Foreclosure Crisis: 23 States Halt Foreclosures as Officials Review Bank Practices," ABC News, October 4, 2010; see also testimony of Jack Hopkins, president and CEO of CorTrust Bank, on behalf of Independent Community Bankers of America, August 2, 2011. https://www.icba.org/files/ICBASites/PDFs/test080211.pdf.

197 *until the media started to stir the pot:* Several media outlets reported that federal regulators not only delayed responding to the mortgage foreclosure scandal, but some were pushing for "relatively modest fines." Paul Kiel, "Despite Finding Big Problems in Mortgage Industry, Regulator's Punishment Unclear," *ProPublica*, February 17, 2013.

197 *settlement number: $5 billion:* Shahien Nasiripour, "Bank Regulator Pushing for Modest Settlement with Industry over Improper Mortgage Practices," *Huffington Post*, February 16, 2011. For more on the scandal and the regulatory response, see Sheila Bair, *Bull by the Horns*, 243–56. "Unlike the FDIC, the OCC did not want to put pressure on its big banks to come to the table and agree to something reasonable."

197 *$1 billion every single day:* The five banks involved in the initial scandal—Bank of America, JPMorgan, Citigroup, Ally Financial, and Wells Fargo—earned a combined total of $471 billion in revenue for 2010. This translates to about $1.3 billion per day.

197 *Whoop-dee-doo:* What was the right number? The standard measure of damages would have been to measure how much the mortgage servicers had hurt people. When the mortgage servicers broke the law, some people lost homes that they might have been able to keep, if only they had more time to catch up on past-due payments, or if the banks had found their lost paperwork, or if they had received the loan modifications they had been promised. How many families were in this situation? What had it cost them to lose their home? What was that worth?

Others might have lost their homes eventually, but they lost the chance to have more time—guaranteed by their local laws—to look for a new place and to settle in their families. For some homeowners, all their possessions were unceremoniously—and illegally—dumped on the sidewalk. What's the right compensation for that? The big banks had systematically and deliberately broken the law, and so many families across the country had paid the price. To know how much injury mortgage companies had caused, the agencies would have to do a very significant investigation.

There was another way to calculate the damages too. It would have been possible to determine how much money the banks had saved with every corner they had cut and every paper they had failed to file. In other words, how much did the mortgage servicers profit from breaking the law? Once that was known, the banks could have been forced to pay a multiple on that amount. By way of comparison, in a fraud prosecution, the fraudster is often required to pay three times the amount that was taken by deception, in order to deter future fraud.

It made no sense for regulators to push for a quick settlement, but that's what several of them did.

198 *demanded an "independent investigation"*: For Senator Shelby's statement, see http://www.shelby.senate.gov/public/index.cfm/newsreleases?ID=0447c3e6-5864-452e-ab43-2b9ec7afa684.

198 *favored a number closer to $30 billion*: Abigail Field, "Sizing Up a Sweeping Mortgage Settlement," *CNNMoney,* May 20, 2011.

198 *"led by Elizabeth Warren"*: Senator Shelby accused regulators of using "strong-arm tactics" to "politicize" the mortgage foreclosure settlement process, with "serious due process" implications. Shelby called on the Senate Banking Committee to inquire into the substance and process surrounding the proposed settlement, and he urged the Obama administration to refrain from entering into any agreement before Congress had a chance to weigh in on the details. See http://www.shelby.senate.gov/public/index.cfm?p=NewsReleases&ContentRecord_id=ac820c24-1e3c-4114-a601-c8a33e2a30bc&ContentType_id=ae7a6475-a01f-4da5-aa94-0a98973de620&Group_id=876a24c9-639d-499e-8f4d-ad2b6c7cf218.

199 *provided a detailed account of our work*: See http://financialservices.house.gov/media/pdf/031611warren.pdf.

200 *served a five-year term (not true: several others do, too)*: For example, the chairman of the Federal Deposit Insurance Corporation serves a five-year term. The Comptroller of the Currency (OCC) also serves a five-year term. Federal Reserve Bank presidents serve a five-year term. The Director of the recently defunct Office of Thrift Supervision had also served a five-year term.

200 *as if I had enacted the law instead of Congress itself*: Michael McAuliff, "Elizabeth Warren Called Liar at CFPB Hearing by Republicans Who Botched Facts on Agency," *Huffington Post,* May 24, 2011.

201 *described it when she ran the video later that day*: See http://www.today.com/id/43170318/ns/msnbc-rachel_maddow_show/#.UnixCxbkhFI.

201 *overrun with tens of thousands of angry messages*: David Waldman, "Blowback for Patrick McHenry's Nastiness to Elizabeth Warren," *Daily Kos,* May 25, 2011.

201 *The secretary never wavered*: Secretary Geithner testified before Congress on March 15, 2011: ". . . the Consumer Financial Protection Bureau, does not currently have authority to administer penalties and will, therefore, not be a party to any formal settlement with mortgage servicers. Under that same law, though, the CFPB will obtain significant authority to set standards for the mortgage servicing industry on July 21, 2011, the date when the consumer finance protections of other agencies transfer to the Bureau. For this reason—and this is very important—for this reason, the CFPB has been invited to, and I personally invited Elizabeth Warren to advise the other agencies that are part of this process on how to design appropriate servicing standards for the mortgage servicing industry." See http://www.gpo.gov/fdsys/pkg/CHRG-112shrg67144/html/CHRG-112shrg67144.htm.

203 *The agency must be substantially weakened*: On May 5, 2011, forty-four Republican senators sent a letter to President Obama asserting that they would not confirm anyone to head the Consumer Financial Protection Bureau absent structural changes to the agency. In particular, the senators wanted to change the management, funding, and rule-making apparatus of the CFPB, citing "accountability" and "democratic values" concerns. See http://www.shelby.senate.gov/public/index.cfm/newsreleases?ContentRecord_id=893bc8b0-2e73-4555-8441-d51e0ccd1d17. These proposed reforms would have severely weakened the CFPB. For example, see Jim Puzzanghera, "Senate Republicans Vow to Block Any Appointee to Head Consumer Protection Bureau," *Los Angeles Times,* May 6, 2011. All of the Republicans then in the Senate signed the letter except Senators Lisa Murkowski, Scott Brown, and John Ensign. Brian Beutler, "Republicans Make Power Play to Gut Consumer Financial Protection Bureau," *TPM,* May 6, 2011.

203 *covered their costs directly or indirectly through banking fees:* For example, the Federal
Reserve, the OCC, the FDIC, and the NCUA are not funded through the appropriations
process in Congress. See http://www.federalreserve.gov/faqs/about_14986.htm; http://
www.ots.treas.gov/about/what-we-do/mission/index-about.html; http://www.fdic.gov
/about/learn/symbol/; http://www.ncua.gov/News/PressKits/Docs/PressKits.pdf.

203 *because they didn't like the agency he or she was due to run:* Senator Sherrod Brown said
publicly: "... some time ago I asked the Senate historian has this ever happened, that a
political party has blocked a nomination of someone because they didn't like the construction of the agency? And he said, no, it's never happened." Senator Harry Reid echoed
this: "This is the first time in Senate history a party has blocked a qualified candidate
solely because they disagree with the existence of the agency that's being created by law."
This was later confirmed as true by PolitiFact. Senate historian Donald A. Ritchie confirmed the unprecedented nature of Republicans' attempts to block the nomination of an
agency director unless there were drastic changes to the structure of that agency. The
closest historical analogs the historian could provide were nineteenth-century cases of
nominees being rejected because of significant policy disagreements with the president,
but even those cases "did not involve a blanket blocking of nominees to a particular
agency." "Sen. Sherrod Brown Says Republicans' Refusal to Confirm Richard Cordray to
Head Consumer Protection Bureau Was Unprecedented," Politifact.com, December 7,
2011.

203 *and then, if needed, make a recess appointment:* Representatives Carolyn Maloney (D-NY),
Keith Ellison (D-MN), and Brad Miller (D-NC) sent a letter to the president: "Since
Republican Senators have said that no one is acceptable unless the law is weakened, we
would urge you to nominate Professor Warren as the CFPB's first Director anyway. If
Republicans in the Senate indeed refuse to consider her, we request that you use your
constitutional authority to make her a recess appointment." The letter was signed by
eighty-nine members of the House: http://maloney.house.gov/press-release/89-house
-members-send-letter-president-urging-elizabeth-warren-be-appointed-head. Senator Al
Franken also wrote a letter to the president urging him to make a recess appointment of
me, http://www.franken.senate.gov/?p=news&id=1547.

203 *keep me from becoming the head of the consumer agency:* "Republicans are preventing
the Senate from completely adjourning for the Memorial Day recess. Instead, the
chamber will come in for three pro-forma sessions over the next 10 days. The cursory
sessions are a formality that will ensure President Obama does not make recess
appointments, a prospect that was considered unlikely anyway because the recess is
scheduled for only a week. Some Republicans feared that Obama would use the recess
to appoint Elizabeth Warren to head the controversial Consumer Financial Protection
Bureau, which will have broad powers over Wall Street." Alexander Bolton and Josiah
Ryan, "GOP Forces Senate Pro-Forma Session," *The Hill*, May 27, 2011. See also Brian
Montopoli, "Senate GOP Blocks Possible Elizabeth Warren Recess Appointment," CBS
News, May 27, 2011.

204 *George Washington himself to be head of the consumer agency:* In a speech to the US
Chamber of Commerce, Representative Spencer Bachus made the following remark
about the Consumer Financial Protection Bureau and the discretion vested in the head of
the agency: "If George Washington came back today, or Abraham Lincoln or Warren
Buffett signed up [to head the agency], I wouldn't give that person total discretion."
Edward Wyatt, "Warren Defends Agency at Chamber of Commerce," *New York Times*,
March 30, 2011.

205 *director of the agency was "dead on arrival":* The day of Cordray's nomination, Senate
Republican Leader Mitch McConnell said: "We'll insist on serious reforms to bring
accountability and transparency to the agency before we consider any nominee to run it."
The day after Cordray's nomination, Senator Moran said: "It is unclear why the centerpiece

of the president's financial reform package has taken so long to materialize, but what is clear is that this nomination is dead on arrival because it does nothing to increase accountability or shed light on the operations of the CFPB." Phil Mattingly, "Republicans Target CFPB, Call Nomination 'Dead on Arrival,'" *Bloomberg*, July 19, 2011. A few days later, Senator Shelby wrote a scathing anti-CFPB op-ed in the *Wall Street Journal*. Richard Shelby, "The Danger of an Unaccountable 'Consumer' Protection Czar," *Wall Street Journal*, July 21, 2011.

206 *we'd set up the agency without a hitch:* The Inspectors General of the Treasury and Federal Reserve are required to conduct audits, investigations, and other reviews of department programs and operations. The Dodd–Frank Act charged both these offices with oversight of CFPB implementation. On July 15, 2011, the joint Inspectors General released a report, in which they found that the CFPB had successfully identified mission-critical activities, developed and begun executing appropriate implementation plans, and communicated these plans to key stakeholders. "Review of CFPB Implementation Planning Activities," Offices of Inspector General, July 15, 2011.

206 *had fraudulently charged their customers:* On July 18, 2012, the CFPB ordered Capital One to pay $140 million to two million consumers as well as a $25 million penalty for engaging in deceptive marketing practices with respect to "add-on products" like payment protection and credit monitoring. See "CFPB Probe into Capital One Credit Card Marketing Results in $140 million Consumer Refund," CFPB blog, July 18, 2012. On September 24, 2012, the CFPB, in conjunction with the FDIC, ordered Discover Bank to pay $200 million to 3.5 million consumers and an additional $14 million penalty for engaging in deceptive marketing practices with respect to extra services like identity theft and wallet protection. Blake Ellis, "Discover to Refund $200 Million to Customers for Deceptive Telemarketing," *CNNMoney*, September 24, 2012. On October 1, 2012, the CFPB ordered American Express to pay $85 million to 250,000 consumers as well as a $14.1 million penalty for violating various consumer protection laws, including laws that prohibit discrimination and deceptive advertising practices. See "CFPB Orders American Express to Pay $85 Million Refund to Consumers Harmed by Illegal Credit Card Practices," CFPB Newsroom, October 1, 2012.

And then on December 23, 2013, CFPB ordered American Express to pay another $59.5 million for unfair billing and deceptive practices. "CFPB Orders American Express to Pay $59.5 Million for Illegal Credit Card Practices," CFPB Newsroom, December 23, 2012. Enforcement actions have also been used in other areas, including, for example, requiring National City Bank (successor to PNC) to pay $35 million for racial discrimination on mortgage pricing, when they added extra fees for African American and Hispanic borrowers. "CFPB and DOJ Take Action Against National City Bank for Discriminatory Mortgage Pricing," CFPB Newsroom, December 23, 2013. On November 20, 2013, Cash America was required to refund $14 million and pay an additional $5 million fine, for robo-signing and illegally overcharging servicemembers. "Consumer Financial Protection Bureau Takes Action Against Payday Lender for Robo-Signing," CFPB Newsroom, November 20, 2013. On December 20, 2013, CFPB required Ally Bank to refund $80 million for racial discrimination in how they marked up car loans and other loans. Patrice Ficklin, "Ally to Repay $80 Million to Consumers It Discriminated Against," CFPB Newsroom, December 20, 2013. The agency regularly updates its enforcement actions at http://www.consumerfinance.gov/blog/category/enforcement/.

206 *for service members deployed in Afghanistan and Iraq:* In her first year and a half at the agency, Holly Petraeus worked actively to help protect servicemembers whose homeownership was threatened by a military move or combat deployment. In addition, her team worked to help servicemembers and veterans who wanted to enroll in college, to ensure they understood the true costs of their degree and what financial aid was available to them. She was also working to help develop a new financial-education curriculum for

new recruits that could be delivered by smartphone or computer. And she continues to fight predatory lending that targets servicemembers and veterans. For more, see http://www.consumerfinance.gov/newsroom/written-testimony-of-holly-petraeus-before-the-senate-committee-on-banking-housing-and-urban-affairs/.

206 *turn to the consumer hotline for help:* Between July 21, 2011, and June 30, 2013, the CFPB received about 176,700 complaints—36,300 credit card complaints, 85,200 mortgage complaints, 25,700 bank accounts and services complaints, 6,000 private student loan complaints, 5,700 consumer loan complaints, 14,200 credit reporting complaints, and 300 money transfer complaints. "Consumer Response: A Snapshot of Complaints Received," CFPB, July 2013, 6. Consumers most often contacted CFPB about billing disputes, credit card rates, inability to make mortgage payments, mortgage servicing, bank account management, bank transaction holds and unauthorized transactions, and limited ability or inability to make student loan payments (6–15). During the same time period, companies had responded to 95 percent of the complaints sent to them for response (7).

207 *slingshot to someone else:* Rich Cordray was the new nominee for director when I left the consumer agency, but he wouldn't step into that role until the president made a recess appointment of him several months later. During the time in between, Raj Date took over as special advisor to the secretary of the Treasury for the CFPB. Raj had done a tremendous job building our research and regulatory work and taking on other critical projects, and he was now stepping into an important leadership role.

6 | The Battle for the Senate

209 *dubbed one of "Wall Street's Favorite Congressmen":* See Brian Wingfield, "Wall Street's Favorite Congressmen," *Forbes,* June 1, 2010. According to the *Boston Globe,* Brown "used the leverage of his swing vote to win key concessions" for the financial industry. See Donovan Slack, "Donations Poured In as Brown's Role Grew: With Vote Near, Financial Sector Delivered $140K," *Boston Globe,* December 12, 2010. See also Robin Bravender, "Wall Street Filling Scott Brown's Coffers," *Politico,* October 1, 2012. For more about political contributions, see also Center for Responsive Politics—the nonpartisan group that tracks money in politics. http://www.opensecrets.org/.

212 *In mid-August, I started meeting with small groups:* On the very first day I started meeting with people, Joyce Linehan invited me to her house in Dorchester. Joyce had a crowd, with people jammed in the living room, sitting on the floor, and spilling into the dining room and entry hall. The questions showed a deep level of engagement, and they made me think that running for the Senate in Massachusetts could be fun. But more important, they taught me early on that it was possible to campaign by talking about serious issues and that strong allies—people like Joyce and many of those in the room that night—would build the kind of grassroots campaign that we would need if we were going to unseat a popular incumbent. Joyce was amazing, and she was there every step of the way throughout the campaign. See, e.g., Paul McMorrow, "The New Campaign," *CommonWealth,* July 16, 2013.

That first week, we also headed out to Pittsfield, hosted by Sherwood Guernsey and Lee Harrison, with a number of the Berkshire Brigades in attendance. The plan had been to speak in the early evening from the front porch of a great old home that was now a law office, but just as I stepped out of the car, the sky started getting very dark. We were just around the corner from the house, which we hadn't seen yet, so I asked Nick Black, "Is this the right place?" And just as I finished, a bolt of lightning hit somewhere nearby with a thunderous crack, lighting up the sky and nearly giving me a heart attack. I figured it was a sign—but I wasn't sure exactly how to interpret it. But the Brigades gave it their own interpretation: as I rounded the corner, I saw the front of the house was plastered with a huge "Run Elizabeth Run" sign, and several people had made their own political buttons.

They cheered when they saw me, and when it started pouring rain so that we couldn't stay outside any longer, they crowded into the house and yelled, "Keep going!" And when the lights went out, they yelled it again: "Keep going!" And when the fire alarms were triggered, they yelled it again: "Keep going! We're with you all the way!" The Brigades don't give up. Andy McKeever, "Berkshire Democrats Want Warren to Run, Run, Run," iBerkshires.com, August 19, 2011.

214 *a hundred had shown up:* Hank and M J Powell were the generous hosts who permitted their home (and porch and lawn) to be overrun by Massachusetts voters who wanted a look at this first-time candidate. When I called later to thank them, M J said it had been "fun," which, under the circumstances, I took to be a sign of how committed she and Hank were to the whole grassroots we-build-it-together effort.

216 *"sheer political brilliance":* For the MoveOn.org quote, see http://front.moveon.org/the-elizabeth-warren-quote-every-american-needs-to-see/#.UdyC62AYR4E. *The Street* said, "She was able to articulate—in a few words—what the Democratic Party has been unable to communicate for years" and concluded, "Whether or not you agree with Warren, she is worth listening to." John DeFeo, "Why You Should Listen to Warren, not Buffet," *The Street*, September 22, 2011. Chris Weigant reports: "This is sheer political brilliance. Democrats are notorious for not being able to do what Warren just proved she's fully capable of: Explaining an issue in plain language that resonates with the average citizen. Telling a story. Crafting a narrative. I especially like the bit about 'marauding bands,' since it just proves how silly the entire concept of 'class warfare' truly is, in this day and age." Chris Weigant, "Elizabeth Warren's Campaign Takes Off," *Business Insider*, September 21, 2011.

216 *"Mao Zedong's Cultural Revolution":* The speech went viral on the Internet with liberal blogs and websites linking to the clip. Right-wing and conservative blogs, magazines, and TV used it to boost their arguments about class warfare. See Jonah Goldberg, *America Live*, Fox News, September 22, 2011, http://video.foxnews.com/v/1176435451001/: "It seems to me, what Warren says, some of it is true and where it's not true, it's just patently silly . . ."

Similarly, Rush Limbaugh declared: ". . . She's a parasite. She's a parasite who hates her host. She's willing to destroy the host while she sucks the life out of it. Roads, bridges, firefighters and policemen. . . . There's a guy at the *New Republic*—Jonathan Cohn—celebrating her rant, especially the philosophical pillar that the rich are just basically lucky. He says, 'I've met many people at the bottom of the income ladder who work just as hard, for far less reward. Between 1980 and 2005, the richest 1 percent of Americans got more than four-fifths of the country's income gains. Does anybody seriously believe that the other 99 percent didn't deserve to take home a much larger share?' This is the kind of thinking [that] undergirds it all. Again, I cannot emphasize it enough: This is exactly the way Obama views this country in the rest of the world. This is the thinking behind Mao Zedong's cultural revolution. This is the thinking behind Fidel Castro's revolution, the kind of thinking that's going on in Venezuela—and, as you can see, at our citadels and even in our government. . . ." Rush Limbaugh, "Elizabeth Warren Video: One of the Great Teaching Tools on Liberalism," Rushlimbaugh.com, September 22, 2011.

216 *to raise money for Scott Brown:* Nicholas Confessore, "Vilifying Rival, Wall St. Rallies for Senate Ally," *New York Times*, November 18, 2011.

219 *step out of the race:* Terry O'Neill, president of the National Organization for Women, said in an interview with Politico: "This is the kind of sexist misogynistic attack that we have very sadly come to expect from politicians whenever there is a strong woman who is capable and really dedicated to the betterment of all the people. And I really think that the biggest apology he owes is not to Elizabeth Warren—she is strong, trust me, she can take it—he owes an apology to the women of Massachusetts. [Brown's comment is reason enough for him to] reconsider whether he should be a United States senator. He

should seriously consider dropping out of the race." In addition, Kim Gandy, vice president at Feminist Majority, also weighed in: "By every measure, Elizabeth Warren is an attractive candidate. Scott Brown's sexist wisecrack offers women some insight into his, um, underlying attitudes. Not so attractive." Jess McIntosh at EMILY's List commented: "Scott Brown's comments are insensitive at best, offensive at worst, and just show the only thing he really cares about is Scott Brown." See M.J. Lee, "Women's Groups Dress Down Scott Brown," *Politico*, October 6, 2011.

House Minority Leader Nancy Pelosi, always an outspoken leader on issues concerning women, also jumped into the debate on ABC's *This Week*: "I thought it spoke volumes about how clueless Senator Brown is.... It really spoke volumes about, really, disrespect for women that he may not even realize. I bet you he would like to take that comment back." Sam Stein, "Nancy Pelosi: Scott Brown Is Clueless," *Huffington Post*, October 9, 2011.

219 *"first major gaffe" of the campaign:* Garrett Quinn, "Brown's First Major Gaffe of the 2012 Race," *Less Is More* (blog), Boston.com, October 6, 2011. See also Hillary Chabot, "Case Clothed: Scott Brown Quip Hits Below the Belt," BostonHerald.com, October 7, 2011.

219 *all the reporters in Massachusetts:* More often when I was out and about, Alethea Harney was along to help with press. Alethea was not only calm and well informed, she was a pleasure to be with, day in and day out. No matter what, she kept smiling. And back in the office, Julie Edwards kept all the pieces moving, efficiently and effectively managing our communications.

220 *"She's not a lesbian":* For the interview with the *Daily Beast*, see Samuel P. Jacobs, "Warren Takes Credit for Occupy Wall Street," *Daily Beast*, October 24, 2011.

The Occupy Protesters rightly took issue with my statement; see Diana Perez, "Protesters Say They Deserve Credit for Occupy Boston, Not Warren," *CBS Local*, October 25, 2011.

223 *"13 months before the general election":* Nick Baumann, "Check Out This Crazy Photo of an Elizabeth Warren Volunteer Meeting," *Mother Jones*, October 27, 2011.

225 *competitive edge around the world:* See the "Nifty50" from the National Science Foundation, which are NSF-funded inventions, innovations, and discoveries. http://www.nsf.gov/about/history/nifty50/.

225 *$221 in new business activity:* See NIH report: "It has been estimated that every $1 of NIH funding generates about $2.21 in local economic growth. Also, discoveries arising from NIH-funded research serve as a foundation for the entire U.S. biomedical industry. Long considered the world's leader in innovation, that vital sector exports an estimated $90 billion in goods and services annually and employs 1 million U.S. citizens with wages totaling an estimated $84 billion," http://www.nih.gov/about/impact/economy.htm.

225 *half what it was when I was growing up:* According to the NSF, federally funded R&D as a percent of GDP ranged from 1.74 to 1.92 percent from 1961 to 1968. By 2011, this figure was .89 percent, or less than half at the peak during my childhood. See "Table 1. Gross domestic product and research and development (total, federally funded, nonfederal): 1953–2011." Available at http://www.nsf.gov/statistics/nsf13318/pdf/tab01.pdf.

227 *is a boys' game:* Marla Romash, who has done incredible work helping women candidates get elected, just laughed when she read the nonsense. Stay steady, she would advise, and win. People like tough women—they just may not know it yet.

227 *"looking like the head of the PTA":* David Boeri, "Warren Takes Her Campaign on the Road," WBUR.org, September 15, 2011.

Britney Schultz, "Elizabeth Warren Announces Senate Run," *Truthout*, September 14, 2011.

228 *paid a generation earlier:* For more data on the increase in the cost of a college education, see Sandy Baum and Jennifer Ma, "Trends in College Pricing 2013," College Board, October 23, 2013. Over the thirty years from 1983–84 to 2013–14, average published tuition and fees

at private nonprofit four-year institutions rose by 153 percent, from $11,909 (in 2013 dollars) to $30,094. The average published price at public two-year colleges rose by 164 percent, from $1,235 (in 2013 dollars) to $3,264, while the increase for in-state students at public four-year institutions was 231 percent, from $2,684 to $8,893.

This has helped fuel the enormous rise in student loan debt. See "Total Student Loan Debt, Q1 1999 to Q1 2011," Demos, http://www.demos.org/data-byte/total-student-loan-debt-q1-1999-q1-2011.

229 *"what about transgender?"*: Over the years, the Human Rights Campaign and many other organizations have fought to raise awareness around issues that affect transgender people. I am proud to work alongside them.

230 *"widely debunked by independent fact checkers"*: "During the 2010 elections, Crossroads GPS, the group cofounded by Karl Rove, spent millions and millions of dollars blanketing airwaves across the country with ads full of falsehoods and distortions that were widely debunked by independent fact checkers. Now that's happening again—only if anything, this time the distortions are even more brazen, and the sleaze factor is even higher." Greg Sargent, "Rove-Founded Group Again Blanketing Airwaves with Falsehoods, Distortions, and Sleaze," *Plum Line* (blog), *Washington Post*, November 10, 2011. See also FactCheck.org: "A group with ties to Karl Rove sends viewers ashtray in a $2 million ad campaign attacking Democratic Senate candidates in Pennsylvania, California and Kentucky. The ads make badly misleading claims about the health care legislation that those Democrats supported." "Misdirection from Crossroads GPS," August 30, 2010, http://www.factcheck.org/2010/08/misdirection-from-crossroads-gps/.

230 *Since Rove's donor list was secret:* See Matea Gold, "Secret Donors Pour Millions of Dollars into Crossroads GPS," *Los Angeles Times*, April 17, 2012. Factcheck.org also reports: "Crossroads GPS is organized as a 501(c)(4) under the federal tax code and thus, unlike its parent group, isn't required to disclose its donors—though it says on its website there are "no limits" to the amount of money it will accept from U.S. corporations (or unions, for that matter). Officially, the full name of the group is Crossroads Grassroots Policy Strategies." See http://www.factcheck.org/2010/08/mis direction-from-crossroads-gps/.

230 *attacks on the police, and heavy drugs:* To see the ad, see Crossroads GPS: "Foundation," MA, November 9, 2011, http://www.youtube.com/watch?v=tNxez4ddpa0. The attention was strong and immediate. See Zeke Miller, "Karl Rove–Backed Group Unveils Vicious Ad Against Elizabeth Warren and the 'Occupy' Protesters," *Business Insider*, November 11, 2011. See also Brendan Fischer, "Rove's Crossroads GPS Attacks Occupy Movement, Elizabeth Warren," *PR Watch*, November 11, 2011. See also Steve LeBlanc, "National PAC Launches Anti-Elizabeth Warren Ad," *Boston Globe*, November 10, 2011. For my first television ad, see Lucy Madison, "In First TV Ad, Elizabeth Warren Blasts Wall St., Pledges to Even Playing Field," *CBS News*, November 14, 2011.

230 *"we need jobs, not more bailouts"*: Amy Bingham, "Ad Twists Elizabeth Warren's Role as TARP Watchdog," *The Note* (blog,) *ABC News*, December 8, 2011.

For my campaign's response, Kyle Sullivan noted that I had been "an outspoken critic of the bank bailout and its blank check to Wall Street. . . . The Wall Street bankers financing these attacks are desperate to stop Elizabeth Warren because she's worked so hard to stop Wall Street from ripping off middle class families." Lucy Madison, "Crossroads: Elizabeth Warren Responsible for Bank Bailouts," *CBS News*, December 8, 2011.

231 *an environmental group had already gone after:* The League of Conservation Voters made a $1.9 million ad buy in the Boston media market in late October 2011, criticizing Brown for his votes to support Big Oil. See Joshua Miller, "Environmental Group Buys Ads Against Scott Brown (VIDEO)," *Roll Call*, October 25, 2011. See also David Catanese, "League Targets Brown on Big Oil," *Politico*, October 25, 2011. Scott Brown hit back with a Web ad and an op-ed refuting some of the claims, arguing: "In reality, I have worked

across the aisle on bipartisan legislation to protect our communities from harmful pollutants, to make our homes and businesses more energy-efficient and to begin to wean us off foreign oil." See Luke Johnson, "Scott Brown Hits Back Against League of Conservation Voters 'Gone Washington' Ad," *Huffington Post*, November 1, 2011.

232 *"bless their hearts for trying"*: Clare Malone, "What's So 'Super' About Super PACs?," *American Prospect*, February 8, 2012. Dan Eggen, "Scott Brown, Elizabeth Warren Pledge to Curb Outside Campaign Spending," *Washington Post*, January 23, 2012. Manu Raju, "Elizabeth Warren, Scott Brown Settle on Super PAC Pledge," *Politico*, January 23, 2012.

232 *"respect the People's Pledge"*: "LCV Responds to People's Pledge Agreed to by Elizabeth Warren and Scott Brown," League of Conservation Voters, January 23, 2012, http://www.lcv.org/media/press-releases/LCV-Responds-to-People-s-Pledge-Agreed-to-by-Elizabeth-Warren-and-Scott-Brown.html.

232 *"forklifts of paperwork through"*: Abby Goodnough and Jess Bidgood, "Massachusetts Senate Candidates Look to Limit Outside Advertising," *The Caucus* (blog) *New York Times*, January 23, 2012.

233 *plagiarizing my own book:* Hunter Walker, "*National Review* Apologizes for Accusing Elizabeth Warren of Plagiarism," Politicker.com, May 18, 2012; "National Review's Elizabeth Warren Plagiarism Claim Quickly Debunked," *Huffington Post*, May 19, 2012.

233 *hated people who drank beer:* Devra First, "The Food-Culture Wars," *Dishing* (blog), Boston.com, April 13, 2012.

237 *gun violence every day:* For more on gun-related deaths, see Brady Campaign to Prevent Gun Violence, http://www.bradycampaign.org/?q=about-gun-violence.

Statistics were compiled using the most recent data available from CDC's National Center for Injury Prevention and Control's Web-Based Injury Statistics Query and Reporting for years 2008–2010.

See also "We Can Do Better: Protect Children Not Guns 2013," The Children's Defense Fund, July 24, 2013, http://www.childrensdefense.org/child-research-data-publications/data/protect-children-not-guns-2013.pdf, 60.

240 *including the Harvard hiring committee:* "... Officials involved in [Warren's] hiring at Harvard, the University of Pennsylvania, the University of Texas and the University of Houston Law Center all said that she was hired because she was an outstanding teacher, and that her lineage was either not discussed or not a factor." Katharine Q. Seelye and Abby Goodnough, "Candidate for Senate Defends Past Hiring," *New York Times*, April 30, 2012.

Professor Charles Fried from Harvard Law School, who had served as solicitor general under Ronald Reagan and was a registered Republican and an avowed Scott Brown supporter in 2010, came forward to identify himself as the head of the committee that hired me at Harvard, saying that the suggestion that Warren "attained her position and maintains her reputation on anything other than her evident merit is complete nonsense." Catalina Camia, "Harvard Professor: Elizabeth Warren Got Job on Merits," *USA Today*, May 7, 2012.

In other interviews, Fried gave equally strong statements: "'It simply played no role in the appointments process. It was not mentioned and I didn't mention it to the faculty,' he said. 'In spite of conclusive evidence to the contrary, the story continues to circulate that Elizabeth Warren enjoyed some kind of affirmative action leg-up in her hiring as a full professor by the Harvard Law School. The innuendo is false. I can state categorically that the subject of her Native American ancestry never once was mentioned,' he added. That view was echoed by Law School Professor Laurence H. Tribe, who voted to tenure Warren and was also involved in recruiting her. 'Elizabeth Warren's heritage had absolutely no role in the decision to recruit her to Harvard Law School,' he told the *Crimson*. 'Our decision was entirely based on her extraordinary expertise and legendary teaching ability. This whole dispute is fabricated out of whole cloth and has no connection to reality.'"

Garance Franke-Ruta, "Is Elizabeth Warren Native American or What?," *Atlantic*, May 5, 2012.

241 *"the London Whale":* On April 13, 2012, reports surfaced of a trader making huge bets, nicknamed the "London Whale," and JPMorgan CEO Jamie Dimon dismissed any concerns as "a complete tempest in a teapot." Then on May 10, 2012, JPMorgan disclosed there were $2 billion in losses. By July 13, 2012, losses had climbed to more than $7 billion. See Eric Owles, "Timeline: The London Whale's Wake," *New York Times*, March 27, 2013.

For Jamie Dimon's take on the scandal, see Dan Fitzpatrick, "JP Morgan's Dimon on Whale: There Was No Hiding, No Lying," *MoneyBeat* (blog), *Wall Street Journal*, June 11, 2013. See also Jessica Silver-Greenberg, "New Fraud Inquiry as JPMorgan's Loss Mounts," *DealBook* (blog), *New York Times*, July 13, 2012.

And for a sense of Wall Street's hubris, see Pat Garofalo, "We're Getting the Feeling That Wall Street Isn't Sorry," Opinion, *US News and World Report*, March 22, 2013.

241 *last-minute negotiations on Dodd–Frank:* Noah Bierman and Michael Levenson, "Senator Brown Sought to Loosen Bank Rules: OK'd Overhaul, Then Called for Leeway, E-Mails Show," *Boston Globe*, June 4, 2012. See also note on p. 314, *"not the big banks . . . "*

241 *truth about our family:* For more on Scott Brown's statement "My mom and dad have told me a lot of things too, but they're not always accurate," see Rick Holmes, "Holmes: The Art of Political Distraction," Opinion, *MetroWest Daily News*, June 3, 2012.

And for my response to Brown, see Noah Bierman, "Warren Sends Letter to Supporters Trying to Calm Native American Controversy," *Political Intelligence* (blog), *Boston Globe*, May 31, 2012.

242 *part of their families' lives:* Sally Jacobs, "Warren's Extended Family Split About Heritage," *Boston Globe*, September 16, 2012.

242 *half-running from house to house:* Mike and Kitty Dukakis met with me early in the campaign to give me advice that was grounded in decades of public service and hard-fought campaigns. They offered many details and strategies, but the bottom line boiled down to one word: grassroots. They believed that the only way to beat a popular incumbent in Massachusetts was to organize neighborhood by neighborhood all across the state. They explained how to do it and how much patience and hard work it would take. It was slow-going, but it was hugely powerful.

Of course, Mike and Kitty weren't the kind just to dole out advice and then turn their backs on the candidate. Both of them jumped in to help. They gave speeches and rallied the troops and were legendary in the energy they displayed knocking on doors. Bruce had never done any of this before (and neither had I), so Mike took him out on a Saturday to get him started. Mike also took Bruce to the Greek Festival in Brockton, where Bruce not only shook hands but also brought home a huge stack of pastries. Mike and Kitty worked week in and week out to help build grassroots support and they are a big part of why we had such an extraordinary turnout on election day.

244 *prayers in several languages:* Several churches in Roxbury and Dorchester invited Bruce and me for services, and as the months went by, we worshipped in more than a dozen different churches in African American neighborhoods around Boston and out in Springfield. Each church had its own personality, but it was clear that people were working hard to build communities within communities to support each other and to find ways to heal a troubled world. Interfaith services were also a source of great spiritual connection and a clear reminder that we are a people who come from many different traditions. I am grateful for the warm hearts of so many people who made Bruce and me feel so welcome.

245 *Worcester along the way:* Super-volunteer Kate Donaghue, who did so much for the campaign, put together an old-fashioned whistle-stop in Framingham, complete with signs and cheering.

246 *people in this arena were ready to fight:* With the endorsement also came the official support of the Massachusetts Democratic Party, under the leadership of John Walsh. John

had served as Deval Patrick's campaign manager in 2006 and had worked hard as party chair to build grassroots capacity and pull together elected officials. Along with Matt Patton, who moved from working directly on my campaign to working for the state Democratic party, John would be a critical ally as Election Day approached.

247 *for building business liaisons for the campaign:* Will Sealy also came along with Elizabeth Vale from the consumer agency to work on the campaign. Will worked to put together a robust network of small-business owners and had a real knack for organizing details, plotting strategy, and building alliances. He also happened to be a dynamite photographer, and many of his shots appear in this book. Will is just plain terrific.

We had a lot of endorsements, but I was particularly moved when the Massachusetts Credit Union League endorsed my campaign. This was the first time they ever endorsed a candidate for office, but I had worked with the credit unions for years on family financial issues, and they said they wanted to make their support public.

248 *advertised 35 percent corporate rate:* Nelson D. Schwartz, "Big Companies Paid a Fraction of Corporate Tax Rate," *New York Times*, July 1, 2013.

Richard Rubin, "Profitable U.S. Companies Paid 12.6% Tax Rate in 2010, GAO Says," Bloomberg News, July 1, 2013.

For additional reports on how some big corporations often pay no taxes at all and how many others get loopholes and tax benefits to avoid state and federal taxes, see Citizens for Tax Justice, www.ctj.org.

251 *veterans' benefits, food stamps, or Medicaid:* The National Voter Registration Act of 1993 was passed by Congress and signed into law by President Bill Clinton. "The NVRA set the first ever national standards for mail-in voter registration, required states to provide registration at public agencies, outlawed the purging of voters solely for non-voting, and established the nation's first federal standards for voter list maintenance and the first national voter registration application, [and] required states to provide registration at public agencies." See "Registering Millions: Celebrating the Success and Potential of the National Voter Registration Act at 20," Demos, May 20, 2013, http://www.demos.org /registering-millions-success-and-potential-national-voter-registration-act-20. See also the National Voter Registration Act of 1993 (NVRA), United States Department of Justice, http://www.justice.gov/crt/about/vot/nvra/nvra_faq.php.

For context, see "History of Federal Voting Rights Laws," United States Department of Justice, http://www.justice.gov/crt/about/vot/intro/intro_b.php.

251 *half a million voter registration cards:* Massachusetts sent out voter registration forms to nearly five hundred thousand Massachusetts residents "as part of an interim settlement with plaintiffs who argue that the state has failed to comply with a 1993 federal law designed to ensure better voting access for Americans." See Mark Trumbull, "'Welfare-Voter' Spat in Massachusetts Part of Larger Political Duel," *Christian Science Monitor*, August 14, 2012. Prior to that mailing, only 58.2 percent of Massachusetts eligible low-income voters were registered to vote, compared to 76.9 percent of higher-income citizens.

See also "Background on Delgado v. Galvin Interim Settlement," Demos, August 8, 2012, http://www.demos.org/publication/background-delgado-v-galvin-interim-settlement.

251 *attempt to benefit my campaign:* Brown released the following statement: "I want every legal vote to count, but it's outrageous to use taxpayer dollars to register welfare recipients as part of a special effort to boost one political party over another. This effort to sign up welfare recipients is being aided by Elizabeth Warren's daughter and it's clearly designed to benefit her mother's political campaign." See "Brown Statement on Elizabeth Warren's Daughter Aiding Effort to Register MA Welfare Recipients to Vote," ScottBrown .com, August 8, 2012, http://www.scottbrown.com/2012/08/brown-statement-on-elizabeth -warrens-daughter-aiding-effort-to-register-ma-welfare-recipients-to-vote/.

See also "Sen. Brown Slams Costly Push to Register Welfare Recipients as Politically Motivated," Fox News, August 9, 2012.

251 *I had even thought of running for the Senate:* See "Statement: Voting Rights Advocates to DOJ: 'Enforce NVRA,'" Demos, August 18, 2004, http://www.demos.org/press-release /statement-voting-rights-advocates-doj-enforce-nvra; see "Demos, Project Vote Criticize DOJ After Meeting About NVRA Enforcement," Demos, September 28, 2004, http:// www.demos.org/press-release/demos-project-vote-criticize-doj-after-meeting-about-nvra -enforcement.

    See also: "Demos Stands By Long Record of Non-Partisan Voting Rights Work," Demos, August 8, 2012, http://www.demos.org/press-release/demos-stands-long-record -non-partisan-voting-rights-work.

252 *student voting, you-name-it voting:* For a full discussion of voter suppression, see Liz Kennedy, Tova Wang, Anthony Kammer, Stephen Spaulding, and Jenny Flanagan, "Bullies at the Ballot Box," Demos and Common Cause, September 10, 2012. See also Scott Keyes, Ian Millhiser, Tobin Van Ostern, and Abraham White, "Voter Suppression 101: How Conservatives Are Conspiring to Disenfranchise Millions of Americans," Center for American Progress, April 4, 2012.

    See also Judith Browne Dianis, "Top 10 Voter Suppression Moments of 2012," *Huffington Post*, December 26, 2012.

    For some of the press on this, see Jess Bidgood, "Brown Questions Role of Warren's Daughter in Voter Registration Effort," *The Caucus* (blog), *New York Times*, August 8, 2012. See also "Brown Urges Warren to Pay State for Mailing Costs," Associated Press, August 10, 2012.

    And more press . . . Mark Trumbull, "'Welfare Voters' Are Latest Battleground in Brown-Warren Senate Race," *Christian Science Monitor*, August 9, 2012.

256 *"We just don't want the game to be rigged":* For my full speech at the Democratic National Convention, see ABC News at http://abcnews.go.com/Politics/OTUS/transcript-elizabeth -warrens-democratic-convention-speech/story?id=17164726.

257 *all hands on deck:* We have long had an outstanding delegation here in Massachusetts. I have a terrific partner in now senator Ed Markey, who was a great supporter during the campaign. Senator John Kerry was always a thoughtful advisor during the campaign, and we are all proud to have him represent us around the world as secretary of state. Congressman Barney Frank, a champion for the people who had been a true friend since our days fighting for the consumer agency, had been one of the first to encourage me to run for Senate. He was retiring from the House, but he campaigned with me, gave sharp advice, and took particular care to tutor me on fishing issues, determined that I get to know fishing families up and down the coast. Congresswoman Niki Tsongas was the first to endorse me, making it clear that she thought Massachusetts would be well served by a woman in the Senate. Congressman Richie Neal helped introduce me to his constituents in Western Massachusetts, and Congressman John Olver, who was retiring, showed up at event after event to introduce me to the people he had worked so hard for across so many years. Congressman Jim McGovern, a true man of conscience, offered to organize the central part of the state, which was powerfully important. Congressman John Tierney and I hit many events together on the North Shore, stressing the same issues and building on each other's energy. Congressman Bill Keating was great on the Cape and South Coast, including a rally in the final days before the election in which, at the end of my speech, I reached behind me and grabbed his hand and identified him as my sweet husband who been with me every step of the way—much to the surprise of Bruce (who was standing next to Bill) and Bill's wife (who was nearby). Congressmen Mike Capuano and Steve Lynch helped out at many events, and state officials and local officials jumped in at key points. I was grateful for everyone's help.

257 *power of the vote:* Senators Al Franken, Bernie Sanders, Sheldon Whitehouse, Bill Bradley, and Jeanne Shaheen and Congresswoman Rosa DeLauro showed up to stump for me, and they energized the volunteers and reached out to new groups.

257 *the momentum of the campaign:* From the earliest days of the campaign, Governor Patrick offered thoughtful advice. Each time we talked, he reminded me that a campaign was about values and that if I stuck to my values, I'd be all right. He endorsed me just before the state convention, giving the campaign a needed boost. Later in the campaign, he helped rally Democrats in the fight to win back the Senate seat and his powerful speeches left the crowds cheering. In short, he was terrific.

258 *more helping hands:* Caroline Kennedy offered to help, which I really appreciated. She joined Mayor Menino and me as we campaigned together in Charlestown.

258 *Karl Rove was off the airways:* Common Cause conducted an in-depth study on the People's Pledge and concluded: "The People's Pledge drastically reduced outside spending." Also, "The People's Pledge resulted in substantially greater public disclosure of political donors." Common Cause notes that other similar elections in 2012 had five times more "dark" or completely undisclosed money. "The People's Pledge increased the influence of small donor donations relative to big dollar donations" and the pledge "resulted in significantly less negative advertising." Common Cause also notes: "In response to the Pledge, outside groups did not run a single television advertisement for or against either candidate after the Pledge was signed. . . . In the few cases of print and radio advertisements financed by outside groups, candidates paid the agreed upon fine and the advertisements promptly ceased." The report concludes that limiting "the impact of outside groups in elections is a fundamental first step to an electoral process that is more transparent, fair, and accountable." Common Cause calls for future elections to have similar pledges, noting the pledge "should be replicated in elections going forward." Tyler Creighton, "A Plea for a Pledge," Massachusetts Common Cause, April 2013. At commoncause.org.

260 *stood tall for all workers:* From early in the campaign, Lou Mandarini worked to connect me to union families throughout the state. Lou, a Boston labor lawyer and son of the president of the Greater Boston Labor Council, was Labor Director for the Campaign. He was tireless, making calls, passing along names, offering advice, and showing up at events, always with one goal in mind—get to know everyone in the Commonwealth. Lou is smart as a whip, but his advice was always straight from the heart: "You're on our side—just make sure we all get a chance to see that."

As the campaign progressed, so many union members put their shoulders to the wheel, carrying signs, working the phones, opening their union halls and homes to me and to my team, and fighting with heart and soul for the campaign. I was deeply humbled by their outpouring, and I will always be grateful.

One note: Whenever I was hosted by a union family or met at a union hall, I always talked about my belief in the right of workers to organize and to bargain collectively, but the cheers were always just as loud for protecting Social Security, equal pay for equal work, and helping our kids get a college education. In other words, we fought side by side for a future, not just for some of our families, but for all of our families.

261 *In the end, Otis was my best coach:* Debate prep was frustrating and Otis was terrific, but my second-best coach was Jon Donenberg, who has since become the legislative director in my Senate office. Jon tutored me on policy issues and taught me an enormous amount about the US Senate. He played a key role, and I'm grateful.

263 *subsidizing Big Oil.* In putting a spotlight on Big Oil subsidies, I have been pleased to work alongside the League of Conservation Voters, Sierra Club, and so many other organizations dedicated to protecting our environment for our children and grandchildren. We should be investing in energy technologies of the future, not subsidizing Big Oil.

263 *war whoops and tomahawk chops:* The video can be seen at http://bluemassgroup.com/2012/09/scott-brown-staffers-do-indian-war-whoop-tomahawk-chop-youtube. Brown soon issued a statement saying he "regrets" his staff's "unacceptable behavior." Katharine Q. Seelye, "Scott Brown says He 'Regrets' His Staff's 'Unacceptable' Behavior," *The Caucus* (blog), *New York Times*, September 26, 2012.

263 *and lying about my family:* See Sabrina Siddiqui, "Scott Brown Aims at Elizabeth Warren over Native American Claim," *Huffington Post*, September 24, 2012.

See also Glen Johnson, "Scott Brown Hits Elizabeth Warren's Native American Claim in New Ad," *Boston Globe*, September 28, 2012.

263 *claimed I'd hurt asbestos victims:* For a link to Brown's ad and my response ads, see http://www.factcheck.org/2012/10/warrens-role-in-asbestos-case/.

263 *payment for their injuries:* As more and more people who had worked around asbestos, particularly in shipbuilding and construction, developed a rare form of lung cancer, lawsuits began mounting up. If each victim had sued each company individually, more money would have been spent on lawyers' fees. More important, the first people to develop cancer would likely receive payment, but at some point the companies would run out of money and the insurance coverage would be exhausted, so that later victims would get nothing. The solution was to create a trust and to fund it with all the money from the businesses and their insurance companies who would be held responsible. This way victims could get compensated while paying smaller legal fees and there would be more money available for all the victims, including those who developed cancer later. The trust system had been effective for many years, but it was challenged in the US Supreme Court. In this case, alongside an insurance company and the trusts representing thousands of victims, I argued that the trusts were the best way to compensate victims, rather than individual lawsuits. We won that case in the Supreme Court. Later, after I left the case, a lower court held that the insurance company didn't need to pay as much money as it had offered, and the case was again appealed.

For additional information, see Factcheck.org: "Warren's version of the case has been publicly backed by several attorneys representing the asbestos victims, as well as leaders of an asbestos workers' union. '[Brown is] flat out misrepresenting the facts,' Francis C. Boudrow, business manager for the International Association of Heat and Frost Insulators and Asbestos Workers Union, Local No. 6 told the *Boston Globe*. 'It's offensive to all these people who've lost lives' to asbestos-related illness, he said." See "Warren's Role in Asbestos Case," Factcheck.org, October 15, 2012, http://www.factcheck.org/2012/10/war rens-role-in-asbestos-case/.

264 *"father suffocate to death":* See Marc Larocque, "Sen. Scott Brown Suggests Warren Uses Actors in Asbestos Ads, Then Apologizes for Remarks," *Taunton Daily Gazette*, October 17, 2012.

264 *owner of the West End Gym in Lowell:* Art Ramalho lives his values every day in the work he does for kids in Lowell. He and his gym were featured in *The Fighter*, a film by David O. Russell that starred Mark Wahlberg and Christian Bale. For more about his gym, see Karen Sackowitz, "Blood, Sweat, Cheers," *Boston Globe*, June 10, 2010.

264 *"moral objection" to such coverage:* See Scott Brown, "Brown: Conscience Exemption Was a Matter of Fundamental Fairness," Opinion, *Taunton Gazette*, March 2, 2012.

For the counterargument, see Laura Bassett, "Blunt Amendment Is 'Desperate' GOP Election Strategy, Senate Dems Say," *Huffington Post*, February 24, 2012. Planned Parenthood, NARAL, and NOW organized their members on this issue, and they played a critical role in the fight against the Blunt Amendment and the ongoing fight for women's reproductive rights. As a woman, a mother with a daughter, and a grandmother of two little girls, I am deeply grateful for their ongoing leadership in this important fight.

265 *gone on the offense, attacking me:* "(Warren) and her allies on the left are dictating to Catholics and other people of faith that they must do as they are told when it comes to health care or face the consequences, regardless of their personal religious beliefs," Brown said in one fund-raising e-mail. Steve LeBlanc, "Scott Brown, Elizabeth Warren Aim to Win Over Bay State Catholics," Associated Press, October 25, 2012.

265 *to rally the troops:* Senator Mikulski was extraordinary. Her speech was energetic and

focused on why we need more women in the Senate. She is the dean of the women senators, and she proved that she was also an effective campaigner to make sure the team of women gets bigger.

265 *wowed the volunteers:* When Ethel Kennedy showed up, many of our young volunteers felt like they had a chance to touch history. Ethel was living very much in the future and she wanted to help me win this seat. She drove home for everyone the importance of who represents you in the Senate.

265 *whipped out their cameras:* Adnaan Muslim managed our mailings, helping us reach people on a personal level. When women's issues heated up, his enthusiasm, which always ran high, kicked into overdrive. Yeah, he was a guy's guy, but he was the father of two beautiful little girls, and Adnaan was in this fight for their future too.

266 *pro-life groups that endorsed him:* See Michael Levenson, "Brown Stresses Prochoice Stance as Abortion Foes Offer Backing," *Boston Globe*, August 23, 2012. "We consider him a senator who votes prolife," said Anne Fox, president of the Massachusetts Citizens for Life. "We have to take his word for it when he says he is prochoice. But what we're looking for is someone who votes prolife, and he does." Brown said he would not reject the backing of Massachusetts Citizens for Life but reiterated that he considers himself a supporter of abortion rights.

See also Shira Schoenberg, "National Pro-Life Group Sends Out Mailers Supporting Scott Brown, Who Is a Pro-Choice Republican," *MassLive*, October 25, 2012.

And for more on Scott Brown's stated pro-choice stance, see Amanda Terkel, "Scott Brown 'Pro-Choice' Message Undermined by Mailer from Group Opposing Abortion Rights," *Huffington Post*, October 25, 2012.

269 *for the first time:* On Election Day, Ted Kennedy's sons, Patrick and Ted, came to deliver rousing get-out-the-vote speeches and add to the overall enthusiasm. It was so good to see them and for them to be part of this race.

269 *up to the voters:* We had lots of help on Election Day, including from dear friends who came in to help out as poll watchers. Former students, and now law professors, Melissa Jacoby and Katie Porter came to work. Katie and Matt Hoffman brought baby Betsy Ann along. Damon Silvers also came to poll watch, ably assisted by his daughter Rosie. There were more, but in the blur of the day, I'm afraid I lost sight of many of them.

271 *an astonishing 73 percent:* Noah Bierman, "Mass. Voter Turnout Sets Record at 73 Percent," *Boston Globe*, November 27, 2012.

271 *we raised $42 million:* The Massachusetts race was the most expensive congressional race for spending by candidates only. When combined with outside spending, the most expensive congressional race was the Virginia 2012 race for Senate. See "Massachusetts, Virginia Senate Among 2012's Most Expensive Races," OpenSecrets.org, November 6, 2012, http://www.opensecrets.org/news/2012/11/massachusetts-virginia-senate-among.html. The Brown campaign spent $35 million, compared to $42 million for my campaign. http://www.opensecrets.org/politicians/elections.php?cycle=2012&cid=N00031174&type=I.

271 *$50 or less:* Mindy Myers, "One Year Ago Today, We Made History," *Huffington Post* (blog), November 6, 2013.

Epilogue |

274 *student loan debt got a little bigger:* While there are grace periods for some types of student loans, many loans have no grace period, and the grace period time for all loans is limited. For example, Direct Subsidized and Unsubsidized Loans have a six-month grace period after graduation or withdrawing from school. There is, however, no grace period for certain PLUS loans. For more discussion, see http://www.direct.ed.gov/leaving.html. Some federal loans also allow borrowers to apply for forbearance in certain situations, which can include financial hardship. However, interest continues to accrue. See http://www.direct.ed.gov/postpone.html.

274 $1 trillion *in student loan debt:* Rohit Chopra, "Student Debt Swells, Federal Loans Now Top a Trillion," CFPB, July 17, 2013, available at http://www.consumerfinance.gov/newsroom /student-debt-swells-federal-loans-now-top-a-trillion.

274 nine times *higher:* At the time of the speech, the interest rate available to the big banks through the Federal Reserve Bank Discount Window was about three-quarters of 1 percent. "Federal Reserve Bank Discount Window and Payment System Risk," Federal Reserve, available at http://www.frbdiscountwindow.org.

At that time, the rate for subsidized federal Stafford loans was slated to double to 6.8 percent, which was approximately nine times higher than the rate charged to big banks. Shelby Bremer, "It's Official: Student Loan Rates Will Double Monday," ABC News, June 29, 2013.

274 *off the backs of our students:* "The U.S. government is forecast to generate $185 billion in profit over the next decade from students and their families under an overhaul of the federal student loan program endorsed by the White House and approved by the Senate on Wednesday." Shahien Nasiripour, "Obama's Student Loan Profit Guaranteed as Senate Approves Deal," *Huffington Post,* July 24, 2013.

275 *more than a million people:* Jim Puzzanghera, "Elizabeth Warren's First Grilling of Regulators a YouTube Hit," *Los Angeles Times,* February 18, 2013.

276 *over the next ten years:* Republican senator Coburn introduced the initial student loan bill for 2013, and the final bill was modeled on the Republican variable-rate proposal, but with two key differences: the original bill had a large markup over the government's borrowing costs and no cap on interest rates, while the final bill had a smaller markup for most loans and included a cap on the amount students could be charged if interest rates rose. The Congressional Budget Office determined that the Coburn bill would have produced an additional $15.6 billion in extra profits for the government over the next the ten years. See the CBO score of the Coburn bill: http://www.cbo.gov/sites/default/files/cbofiles /attachments/s682.pdf. By contrast, the bill that ultimately passed is estimated to produce $0.7 billion in extra profits. See the score for the Bipartisan Student Loan Certainty Act: http://www.cbo.gov/sites/default/files/cbofiles/attachments/Bipartisan%20Student%20Loan%20Certainty%20Act%20of%202013.pdf.

The difference between the two bills is nearly $15 billion, which would have been additional profits to the US government but are now staying in the pockets of students. All these profits are, of course, calculated on top of the estimated $185 billion in profits that will be produced from student loans over the next ten years from all the student loan programs.

Acknowledgments

For a long time, writing books has been one way for me to fight for the people I believe in, and my daughter, Amelia Warren Tyagi, has been an extraordinary ally. After coauthoring *The Two-Income Trap* and *All Your Worth*, she was ready once again to jump into another book with me, this time helping me with the research and keeping the entire project on track. She pushed me to tell more personal stories, to let the reader know what these fights felt like. Amelia was also the one who repeatedly said, "Tell more about this story," or "This is confusing," or the much-dreaded "This is boring." She helped make this a better book, and I am deeply grateful.

Dan Geldon has been my partner as we fought our way side by side through five battles now, and much of what we've accomplished should be credited to him. From his student days, Dan has been a crucial co-conspirator—the strategist who made sure that we kept our goals firmly in mind and managed toward them every day. Where I am blunt, Dan is subtle, and he sees much that I would miss. Another former student, Ganesh Sitaraman is the great thinker of the team, the one who sees context and direction. He has a ravenous appetite for ideas, and he shares them with generous delight. Like Dan, Ganesh was a close-up partner for most of these battles. Without Dan and Ganesh, the adventures would have been fewer and the successes fewer still.

In this book, I tell what happened, what I saw, and what I fought for, but I was never alone. Thanks should be widely shared. In the Bankruptcy

Wars, no one deserves more credit than my long-time coauthors Professor Jay Lawrence Westbrook and Dr. Teresa Sullivan. We set out on our first empirical study together, venturing into uncharted territory; no one could ask for better partners in such an undertaking. Other co-researchers and coauthors joined us along the way in various groupings and regroupings in research projects that spanned more than twenty-five years—some of which are still ongoing. Professor Melissa Jacoby joined our efforts, and then Professor Katherine Porter, Dr. Deborah Thorne, and Professor John Pottow. Together they helped build some of our biggest, most comprehensive studies. Professor Bruce Markell worked on the design of a new study, until he left to become a judge. Professor Robert Lawless and Professor Angela Littwin added new depth and new directions to the studies. Dr. Steffie Woolhandler and Dr. David Himmelstein brought their health care experience to help us expand the reach of our work. Dean Michael Schill and Dr. Susan Wachter helped us explore housing issues. We went into the field multiple times through the years, with study after study, to provide hard facts about the economic realities facing America's middle class.

The battle over changes in the bankruptcy laws spanned a decade, from the National Bankruptcy Review Commission's earliest days to the final passage of the new laws. Commission members, including Representative Mike Synar, the Honorable Robert E. Ginsberg, and Brady Williamson, led the group through extraordinary challenges. Melissa Jacoby helped us through each policy twist and turn, along with Elizabeth Holland, Susan Jensen, and other staffers, as they worked to make the Commission's process and recommendations rigorous. When the credit industry came to Congress with an agenda and lobbying dollars in hand, the speeding train looked unstoppable. As this book recounts, the leadership of Senator Edward Kennedy fundamentally changed the nature of the battle. Without his work and that of his then-counsel, Melody Barnes, the fight would have been over before it ever started. Maureen Thompson helped organize volunteers' efforts, as she worked tirelessly to fight off the industry-backed bill. Other lawmakers whose leadership in this fight was essential included Senators Richard Durbin, Charles Schumer, Paul Wellstone, Russell Feingold, and Christopher Dodd, and Representatives John Conyers, Jerrold Nadler, William Delahunt, and Martin Meehan. Each of them was willing to stand up to powerful forces. And they did more than stand up; they worked hard and they committed their overworked staffs to the fight as well, expending time and effort on issues that would otherwise have been ignored.

As it has done since the bankruptcy laws were revised in the 1930s, the National Bankruptcy Conference offered in-depth analysis of each iteration of the proposed law. The leadership of J. Ronald Trost, Douglas Baird, Ken Klee, Rich Levin, Donald Bernstein, Melissa Jacoby, and many more made a big difference. Commercial law professors from around the country organized communications to Congress sharing their grave concerns about the proposed law's impact. Against the odds, that legislation was delayed until 2005, which is a testament to the dedication of more people than can be named here.

As the economy crashed in 2008 and Congress passed a $700 billion bailout bill, our little oversight panel did its best to bring some accountability to the system. I'm grateful to Majority Leader Harry Reid for the confidence he showed in a professor from Massachusetts to be part of the oversight group. Someday I hope he'll tell me how it was that he picked me. I am also grateful to my dear friend Damon Silvers, deputy chair of the Congressional Oversight Panel and long-time policy leader at the AFL-CIO, and all-around smart, strategic, and brave guy who was ready to march into battle to take on the big guys. Damon has been a life-long defender of working people, and I embrace any chance to fight alongside him. I also appreciate the efforts of Richard Neiman, who worked in careful detail on every element of every COP report, and former Senator Ted Kaufman, who took over COP when I left and saw that it landed safely. I also offer a special thanks to Mark McWatters and Ken Troske, who often started from different places than Damon, Richard, and I did, but who were strong advocates for making the reports smart and insightful, and who were willing to go wherever the data took us. My respect runs deep.

While COP panel members pressed government officials and bankers in public, a nonpartisan group of talented and dedicated professionals were working hard behind the scenes. As executive director, Naomi Baum led the group with amazing skill, always driving the process forward in an honest, evenhanded manner that made each report stronger and that helped us build public confidence in our efforts. As we added more capacity, the COP staff helped us conduct vigorous oversight in the midst of the economic crisis. They dug deep to get the information we needed, crunched numbers to follow the money, and put together hearings across the country to shed light on how Treasury's actions were helping (or not helping) the American people. In addition to the senior staff I mentioned in the book—deputy director Tewana Wilkerson, lead attorneys Steve Kroll and Sara Hanks, and ethics counsel Wilson Abney—there were almost eighty COP staffers, detailees, and interns, many of whom stepped away from careers, came out of retirement, or deferred other job opportunities to help us. Key people included senior policy advisor Alan Rhinesmith; attorneys Elizabeth MacDonald, Thaya Brook Knight, and Beth Davidson; communications directors Peter Jackson and Thomas Seay; hearing lead Patrick McGreevy; research analyst Isaac Boltansky; chief clerk Joan Evans; Nicole Callan, who kept us all organized; Michael Negron, who played a critical role in getting the panel set up; and Caleb Weaver, Ganesh Sitaraman, and Dan Geldon, who also helped get us off the ground. I deeply appreciate their hard—and careful—work.

The effort to get the Consumer Financial Protection Bureau passed into law was yet another David vs. Goliath fight. I mentioned in the book some of the key people who helped us beat the odds and win, including Michael Barr and Eric Stein at the Treasury Department, Heather Booth and Lisa Donner at Americans for Financial Reform, Dan Geldon—then working at the Roosevelt Institute—Travis Plunkett at Consumer Federation of America, Ed Mierzwinski at US PIRG, Congressman Barney Frank, and Senator Chris Dodd. But they formed just the tip of the iceberg. Andrew Rich and Mike Lux were particularly helpful in supporting this work and putting wind in our sails. And so many people in consumer groups, labor unions, netroots organizations, and civil rights groups worked tirelessly for more than a year on this fight. Nearly every week, we were on conference calls setting our strategy and making plans, and I got to see firsthand how effective nonprofits (even ones with very few resources) can be when they are standing up for working families. In addition, many bloggers took on the cause, and so many foundations, think tanks, and individual people made financial reform their fight in ways that provided enormous value. They strengthened the hand of the those in the administration and on Capitol Hill who wanted a strong agency and who spent countless hours working to get the details right. I have no doubt that the agency never would have happened without the dedication of many, many people.

I have already mentioned some of the individuals who helped build the CFPB, but I also need to say a special thank-you to all the bureau's staff. People from all walks of life heard the call of public service and came to help build the consumer agency. Building an airplane while you fly it is not an easy task, and we could not have accomplished anything without the hard work of exemplary public servants. I am particularly grateful to the CFPB executive committee for their help in making our vision of a strong consumer agency a reality: Wally Adeyemo, Sartaj Alag, Steve Antonakes, Rich Cordray, Raj Date, Patrice Ficklin, Dan Geldon, Gail Hillebrand, Len Kennedy, Peggy Twohig, Elizabeth Vale, and Catherine West. Their work was tremendous, bold, and visionary, but always executed with the care demanded in a very challenging environment. Other members of the staff made outsized contributions to our early efforts as well, including Anna Canfield, Flavio Cumpiano, Leandra English, Jen Howard, Peter Jackson, Alyssa Martin, Zixta Martinez, Pat McCoy, Holly Petraeus, Will Sealy, and David Silberman. Each of them— along with so many dozens of others on the CFPB staff—will always have my appreciation for their hard work and determination. I am also grateful to the consumer advocates and those within Congress, the White House, the Treasury Department, and elsewhere in the Obama administration who helped protect us from attempts to defund, destroy, and defang the agency. While we did our best to prove that the best defense is a good offense—for example, by taking consumer complaints before we let the paint dry—it made a huge difference to have an all-star cast of defenders.

In the early days of the bankruptcy wars, a number of labor unions that were already fighting on multiple fronts took up the cause of families in financial trouble. Later, in the fight for the consumer agency, organized labor was again at the forefront of change on behalf of working Americans. The AFL-CIO hosted that first meeting pulling together all the groups, and they, along with SEIU and so many other unions, made a huge difference. Over the years I've had the privilege to work shoulder to shoulder with amazing union leaders in Massachusetts and across the country. But as good union leaders, I know they would want the thanks to go not to them, but to the men and women who work so tirelessly in hospitals, classrooms, fire stations, constructions sites, and on factory floors every day.

Through so many of the fights for a better America, the unsung heroes have been the great nonprofits and grassroots organizations that have labored tirelessly. Despite thin budgets and stretched resources, they have aimed high. It has been my great privilege to work with many of these groups, and I am grateful for the work they do on behalf of all of us, to help create a better future. They create the infrastructure to help balance against the concentrated influence of the powerful and to give people a chance to fight for our values. I'm grateful to all of these hardworking groups, particularly the members of Americans for Financial Reform, an umbrella organization of more than two hundred groups that have put tremendous energy into making markets work for all of America's families. And I have to say: I am also grateful to all those community banks, credit unions, and other lenders who want to do right by their customers and who have, in some important cases, embraced the push for real reform.

The Senate campaign was a true grassroots effort, from start to finish, and there are thousands of people who deserve deep thanks. So many people poured their time, their money, and their passion into the race that it gives me goose bumps. We had an incredibly strong volunteer army—people who made phone calls and knocked on doors, people who agreed to serve as our team leaders, people who entered data and held up signs, people who hosted house parties and helped us raise money. Every single day I think about the people who worked so hard so that I could be in the United States Senate, and I feel renewed, absolutely certain that we can work together and build a future where everyone gets a fighting chance.

And I will also be eternally grateful to our staff. Mindy Myers was a calm and thoughtful leader. Campaigns are chaotic, but under Mindy's leadership, we were able to stay focused on our goals and keep our energy channeled toward what matters most. Roger Lau was also invaluable as political director. Roger is a person of deep integrity, a guy who always tells the truth and who never makes a promise that he doesn't keep. Mindy and Roger brought muscle to our fight for hardworking families, and I relied repeatedly on their good judgment.

Under Mindy's leadership, we assembled one of the best strategic teams in Democratic politics. Day in and day out, Mandy Grunwald, Marla Romash, and Adnaan Muslim helped me cut through the noise of the campaign and stay focused on the big picture—making the case for a progressive vision for our future. Doug Rubin and Tom Kiley offered me sharp insights and keen advice, based on years of experience about what it would take to unseat a popular incumbent and bring home a win. Kyle

Sullivan gave valuable advice every day, often laced with the latest Red Sox news. Elizabeth Vale was tireless in making new friends all across the state, proving once again her enormous talents and generous heart.

We also had dozens of field organizers and community organizers who busted their tails recruiting volunteers, and they made a huge difference. I'm very grateful to all the efforts of Jacques Abatto, Melea Atkins, Sarah Badawi, Andrew Bettinelli, Gus Bickford, Norm Birenbaum, Nick Black, Brent Blackaby, Abby Blum, Michael Blumenthal, Jason Burrell, Frank Chi, Amanda Chuzi, Abby Clark, Alana Clark, Colleen Coffey, Amanda Coulombe, Ashley Coulombe, Matt Cournoyer, Patrick Dennis, Jon Donenberg, Julie Edwards, Marc Elias, Daphne Evans, Mike Firestone, Judy Flumenbaum, Adam Freudberg, Shaan Gajria, ML Ganley, AJ Goodman, Alethea Harney, Julia Hassett, Ben Herman, James Hutchison, Larry Huynh, Chrissi Johnson, Pete Jones, Louis Katz, Nora Keefe, Charlie Keller, Alexis Keslinke, Chris Lange, Paula Levine, Tracey Lewis, Keith Lowey, Lou Mandarini, Dave Mason, Diane Masters, Greg Maynard, Heather McAuliffe, Lauren Miller, Jeremiah Montgomery-Thompson, Colleen Murphey, Dan Murphy, Eric Nguyen, Jay O'Brien, Katherine O'Koniewski, Matt Patton, Lisa Paulson, Michael Pratt, Dan Rivera, Jamie Schell, Will Sealy, Rebecca Straley, Seth Tanner, Lynda Tocci, Pat Tomaino, Steve Tompkins, Jess Torres, Adam Travis, Morgan Warners, Andrew Wright, and Michelle Wu.

I also offer thanks to the many mayors, state legislators, and other public servants of Massachusetts, who spend their days fighting for our communities. Many of them spent time helping me understand the local economy, regional growth, and other community issues that were vital to connecting federal policies to what happens at home. Many also put their own time into my campaign, and I am grateful for their help and for all they do every day to make our state a better place.

In the epilogue of the book, I discuss some of my early work in the US Senate. Once again, I have had the good fortune of having an incredible team of smart policy wonks, strategic thinkers, and can-do people who fight every day to help level the playing field for working families. They work hard for the people of Massachusetts and for Americans everywhere. Once again, Mindy Myers deserves credit for putting together a fantastic team in Washington—starting with my terrific legislative director, Jon Donenberg—and Roger Lau has my enduring gratitude for the amazing group he has built here at home in Massachusetts. They make many things possible, and I am in their debt.

When the book was in its early stages, I prevailed on my best friend, Jean Morse, to read it—as she has done for my other books. I also asked other good friends to read, and Bev Lindsey, Ed Fouhy, and Ruth Wooden stepped up to the task. They offered me an outside perspective to make sure I was telling enough detail to explain the story and not so much to put the reader to sleep. (If I got that wrong, it was my fault—not theirs.) My son-in-law, Sushil Tyagi, took on the task of sorting through endless stacks of old pictures, demonstrating once again that he sees into the heart of matters, big and small. I'm grateful for his help, and grateful that he's part of our family.

Alyssa Martin has been extraordinary. She was not only one of the key partners in the early days of setting up the consumer agency but also one of my students in my last year of teaching and the chief researcher to document all the twists and turns in this book. She worked incredibly hard and took amazing care to make sure we got all the facts and figures right. Pete Jones checked and rechecked factual details and end notes, and he added a degree of judgment and thoughtfulness to his comments that enriched every part of this book. Sarah Levin, another former student, also put in long hours to help us round out the research cited in the book. Rebecca Wharton and Anne Schwichtenberg pitched in as well, working under tight deadlines and always willing to "check one more time." It has been an honor to work with each of them to tell this story.

The book's editor, John Sterling, has been a great partner in the enterprise, offering smart editing suggestions but always being careful not to change the underlying meaning. He knew from the beginning that this was a personal book, a story from me to the reader, and John gave me plenty of space to remain true to that vision. Bob Barnett served as a thoughtful advisor, starting years ago when the idea for a book about fighting for a stronger middle class was barely a glimmer.

Brady Williamson has been a comrade-in-arms throughout most of the adventures told in this book. Brady persuaded me to stay on the Bankruptcy Commission. I didn't know it then, but that decision would shape the rest of my life. He has been the critical behind-the-scenes counselor through all my battles in Washington. Over time, I have learned that Brady had the steadiness born of a good heart and that he possesses the kind of keen judgment that is rare in any human being. He helped with the book, and he helped even more with the struggles that are chronicled here, and I will forever be in his debt.

When I thank those who helped advise, guide, or propel me through the events of this book and who helped me write it all down, I need to reserve a special place for my big brothers. My first memory of Don Reed was when he left for the service and then of his wedding. He was adventurous and dashing, and his very existence was like a distant light. John, big and kind and sweet, always offered the constancy of family and the love that would be there no matter what. And David, always faster and smarter and funnier than anyone I ever knew, taught me to live every minute right out to its edges. But most of all, with three big brothers, I learned early that I could hang back and disappear or I could fight for my place at the table.

Through the years, my son, Alex Warren, has made his own special contributions, always in his own unique ways. He is quick and insightful, always willing to challenge conventional wisdom from any direction. He has been my go-to guy on data and technology issues for years, and he has worked all the way through my books, arguing over ideas and reminding me on occasion that I'm still not that funny. Alex sharpens my thinking and makes life far more interesting.

And then there's Bruce Mann. When I married Bruce, I got me the best. I am grateful all the way down to my toes for having had the good fortune to meet him and the good sense to grab him and hold on tight. Bruce has about a million good qualities, but in the context of this book, I should note one in particular: he has never once discouraged me from taking on a fight. Besides, he's a great kisser. Without Bruce, I would never have written this book, or, far more important, never have undertaken most of the adventures that are chronicled here.

I saved one very special thank-you for the closing of this book: the people I have the enormous honor to represent in the United States Senate. I had been a senator for just three months when two bombs tore through our Boston Marathon celebration, leaving a wake of terrible deaths, life-altering injuries, and heartbroken families. In the hours and weeks afterward, the deep resilience and unbreakable spirit of the people of Massachusetts were evident to the world, as we pulled together as one people and sustained one another in a time of deepest pain. Every single day I appreciate even more the kindness, wisdom, generosity, and tenacity of the people of this great commonwealth, and I am grateful they have asked me to give them voice in Washington.

Index

AARP, 81, 287, 311n
Abaunza, Bonnie, 315n
ABC News, 102, 103
Abney, Wilson, 112, 340
abortion, 67, 266–67, 288n, 335n
Adeyemo, Wally, 174
Affordable Care Act (ACA, "Obamacare," 2010), 264–65, 317n
Afghanistan War, 189
AFL-CIO, 61, 89, 131–35, 145, 147, 287n, 308–9n, 311n
African Americans
    financial meltdown of 2008 and, 294n
    home foreclosure and, 293n
    predatory and deceptive lending and, 87, 284n, 324n
AFSCME, 311n
AIG, 105, 111, 120, 184, 297n, 300n, 306n
    bonuses, 105, 299n
Akin, Todd, 265
Albright, Madeleine, 228
Alix, Jay, 284n
Ally Financial, 120, 306n, 321n, 324n
All Your Worth (Warren and Tyagi), 77–79, 294n
Alzheimer's, 225–26, 236, 276
Amalgamated Transit Union, 308n
American Bankers Association, 149, 282n
American Crossroads, 229

American Express, 324n
American Family Voices, 311n
American Federation of Government Employees, 308n
American Federation of Musicians, 308n
American Federation of State County & Municipal Employees, 308n
American Federation of Teachers, 308n
American Postal Workers Union, 308n
American Prospect, 232
Americans for Financial Reform (AFR), 147, 152, 158, 179, 311n
Americans United for Change, 311n
American Sustainable Business Council, 311n
Andy Griffith Show (TV show), 49
Antonakes, Steve, 192, 319n
Armisen, Fred, 158
asbestos victims, 82, 263–64, 292n, 334n
As We Forgive Our Debtors (Sullivan, Warren, and Westbrook), 44, 280n, 281n, 284n
Atkins, Paul, 119, 305n
Aurora, 321n
autism, 225
auto bailout, 96, 125, 300–301n, 307n
auto companies, 298n. See also car loans
Axelrod, David, 166
Aykroyd, Dan, 158

Bachus, Spencer, 181, 204, 315n, 316n, 323n

Bair, Sheila, 82, 119, 122–23, 292n, 295n, 297n, 300n, 305n, 307n, 321n

Bakery, Confectionery, Tobacco Workers & Grain Millers International Union, 308n

Bale, Christian, 334n

bank bailouts. *See* Congressional Oversight Panel; Troubled Asset Relief Program; *and specific individuals and institutions*

bank CEOs, 146, 300n, 307n, 315n
  Congress and, 177
  lack of accountability and, 111, 120–21, 124, 306n, 307n
  Warren's speech to, 176–80

Bank of America, 146, 184, 197, 294n, 297n, 301n, 321n

Bank on Students bill (proposed), 275–76

bankruptcy, 3, 77, 89, 279–92nn, 308n.
    See also National Bankruptcy Review Commission; *and specific amendments*
  academic experts and, 37–38
  banks attempt to change law, 40–41, 43–44, 54–56, 59–61, 65
  business vs. personal, 282n
  causes of, 34–36, 44, 55, 57, 59, 62, 73, 129, 281n, 286n, 291n
  Chapter 7, 279n, 282n, 286n, 291n
  Chapter 11, 282n, 300n, 301n
  Chapter 13, 279n, 286–87n, 291n
  child support and, 60, 80–81, 279n, 287n, 288n
  Citibank seminar on, 42–43
  credit card debt and, 281n
  defined, 27, 279n
  increase in, 34–35, 40, 42, 47, 73, 281n, 282n, 284n, 287n, 291n, 292n
  Kennedy and, 61–67
  Lehman Brothers and, 297n
  means testing and, 286–87n
  military and, 190
  mortgage debt and, 302n
  National Bankruptcy Review Commission and, 48–51, 53–57

profile of people in, 28–36, 40, 50, 54–56, 69–70, 86, 280n, 281n, 285n
  shame and, 35, 46, 54–55, 59, 279–80n, 285n, 286n
  Silvers and, 89
  small vs. big businesses and, 37–38
  Warren hopes to change laws on, 46–51, 54, 57
  Warren's father and fear of, 32
  Warren's research and writings on, 32–38, 44
  Warren teaches courses on, 27–30

bankruptcy bill (industry-supported, 2000–2004), 60, 286–88n
  of 2000, vetoed by Clinton, 65
  of 2002, 66–67
  of 2005, signed by Bush, 75, 79–82, 84, 86

bankruptcy law amendments
  of 1978, 29
  of 1984, 29, 282n
  of 1994, 284n
  of 2005, 81, 292n

Bankruptcy Research Project, 86, 281n, 286n, 292n. *See also* Consumer Bankruptcy Project

banks and banking. *See also* bank CEOs; big banks; credit cards; Dodd-Frank Act; financial regulation; foreclosures; lobbyists; mortgages; predatory lending; small banks; Troubled Asset Relief Program; *and specific individuals and institutions*
  bankruptcy law and, 35, 37–38, 40–44, 55–60, 64–65, 67–68, 75, 282n, 286n
  benefits of regulation for honest, 137–38, 316n
  campaign contributions and, 75
  CFPB and, 135, 137, 148, 151–52, 156–57, 160–62, 166–67, 169, 205–6
  concentration in, and TARP, 301n
  consumer complaint hotline and, 183–84, 325n
  COP and, 89, 120
  Depression and, 143
  deregulation and, 3, 40–44, 72, 91, 283n, 284n

fees and, 43, 170, 322n
financial crisis and, 92, 121
foreclosure program to "foam runway"
    for, 118, 122, 304n
low-income access and, 82, 122, 292n
mortgage-backed securities and, 295n
National Bankruptcy Review
    Commission and, 55–60
negotiated reorganization vs. bailouts
    and, 300n
predatory practices of, 76–77, 206,
    236
profits of, 41–42
public relations and, 80
S&L crisis and, 121
stress tests and, 115, 302–3n
TARP and attempt to restart lending by,
    92–93
TARP and shareholders in, 300–301nn
TARP and shares sold to government,
    104–5, 115–16, 124–25, 303n
Too Big to Fail and, 109–11
women and, 122–23, 307n
Barnes, Melody, 61–62
Barofsky, Neil, 116–17, 299n, 301n, 303n,
    305n
Barr, Michael, 147, 162
Barron, John M., 287n
Bartlett, Steve, 176
Baum, Naomi, 104, 112, 117, 125
Bauman, Nick, 327n
Bear Stearns, 92, 105, 109, 297n
Bergstresser, Daniel, 303n
Bernanke, Ben, 297n, 298n, 316n
Better Business Bureau, 189
Betty Crocker Homemaker of Tomorrow
    Award, 14–15
Bible, 283n
Biden, Joe, 66, 305n
Bierman, Noah, 330n, 335n
big banks. See also banks and banking;
    and specific financial institutions
    accountability and, 121, 220
    bankruptcy law and, 42, 80, 287n
    CFPB, 131–35, 136, 148, 151, 157–59,
        161–63, 167, 170, 185, 198, 317n
    COP and, 124

foreclosure scandal and, 196–98, 201–2,
    320–22n
Glass-Steagall repeal and, 295n
government loans to, vs. students, 274–75
interest rates and fees, 41–43, 131, 283n
mortgage bias and, 293n
National Bankruptcy Review
    Commission and, 53, 55
power and influence of, 151, 161, 250
products of, regulated as contracts, 129
reforms of 2009 and, 131–32, 141, 146,
    151
Senate Banking Committee and, 275
size of, after TARP, 301n
targeting by, 41–44
TARP bailout and, 89–91, 93, 112,
    115–16, 132, 294n, 295n, 300–301n
TARP stock purchase and, 104–5, 116,
    124–25, 303n
Too Big to Fail and, 109–11, 301n
Warren's Senate campaign and, 210,
    216–17
unregulated lenders and, 134, 310n
big corporations, 215, 256, 260–61, 263,
    328n, 333n
    bankruptcy courts and, 37
    taxes and, 2, 215, 248, 330n
Biggert, Judy, 315n
Big Tobacco, 49
Bipartisan Student Loan Certainty Act
    (2013), 336n
birth control coverage, 264–65, 267
Black, Nick, 325n
Black-Scholes method, 303n
bloggers, 157, 162, 214, 223, 240, 313n, 326n
Bloomberg, 301n
Blumenthal, Adam M., 299n
Blumenthal, Richard, 313n
Blunt Amendment, 264, 266, 334n
Boeri, David, 327n
Boltansky, Isaac, 340
boom-and-bust cycles, 109, 315n
Booth, Heather, 147, 156, 157, 311n
Born, Brooksley, 296n
Boston Globe, 74, 103, 241–42, 298n, 325n,
    334n
Bottari, Mary, 313n

Boucher, Rick, 286n
Boudrow, Francis C., 334n
Bradley, Bill, 332n
Brady Campaign to Prevent Gun
    Violence, 329n
Brooks, James, 158
Brotherhood of Locomotive Engineers &
    Trainmen, 308n
Brotherhood of Railroad Signalmen, 308n
Brown, Scott, 314n, 322n
    asbestos issue and, 263–64
    Blunt Amendment and, 264–65
    Cosmo and, 218–19
    debates and, 261–63, 266–67
    Dodd-Frank and, 160, 241, 330n
    election of 2010 and, 157, 160
    firefighters union and, 259
    fundraising and, 250, 271, 314n
    Native American issue and, 239, 241,
        262–63
    outside ads and, 231–32
    Senate campaign of 2012 and, 205,
        208–11, 216–18, 223, 231–33, 239, 241,
        246, 249–52, 257–59, 261–67, 269,
        325n, 326n, 328–31nn, 333n, 334n
    voter registration and, 251–52
    women and, 264–67
Brown, Sherrod, 323n
Bush, George H. W., 55, 291n
Bush, George W., 55, 66, 74–75, 79, 88,
    122, 131–32, 229–30, 291n
business. *See also* big corporations; small
    businesses
    benefits of government investment for,
        225, 247–48
    credit and, 41, 92, 297n
    failures, 110–11
Business for Shared Prosperity, 311n
Business Insider, 216
Butler, M. Caldwell, 284n

campaign contributions, 64, 75, 177, 230,
    285n, 291n, 312n, 314n, 316n
    financial industry and, 151, 161
    Warren's Senate campaign and, 209–10,
        216–17, 231–32, 248–50, 271, 325n,
        335n

Campaign for America's Future, 311n
Cantwell, Maria, 295n
capitalism, 215
Capital One, 193, 294n, 324n
capital reserve requirements, 141–42
Capuano, Mike, 332n
car loans, 41, 80, 92, 130, 133, 155, 297n,
    308n, 318n, 324n
Carpenter, Michael, 306n
Carrey, Jim, 158
Carvey, Dana, 158
Cawley, Charles M., 291n
CBS News, 74, 291n, 316n
Ceccotti, Babette A., 284n
Cecil, Guy, 248–49
Center for Budget Policies and Priorities,
    287n
Center for Media and Democracy, 311n,
    313n
Center for Public Integrity, 291n
Center for Responsible Lending (CRL),
    287n, 289n, 308n, 311n, 312n
Center for Responsive Politics, 285n, 291n,
    312n, 316n
Chase, Chevy, 158
children
    bankruptcy and, 69, 288n
    government spending and, 215
    housing costs and, 290n
    investing in, 215, 228–29, 237
    protecting, 237–38, 243
Children's Defense Fund, 329n
child support, 60, 80–81, 279n, 287n, 288n
Chillemi, Sal, 114, 152
Chopra, Rohit, 335n
Chrysler, 301n, 306n
Citibank, 42–43, 120, 197, 294–95n,
    306n
    bailout vs. receivership and, 300n
    financial reform and, 146
    foreclosures and, 305n
    Geithner and, 105
    TARP and, 89–90, 98, 105
Citigroup, 291n, 294–97n, 301n, 321n
Citizens for Tax Justice, 331n
Clark, Wesley, 74
Cleland, Max, 257

Clinton, Bill, 48, 51, 53, 65, 81, 253–54, 256, 331n
Clinton, Hillary, 65, 217, 288n
CNBC, 103
CNN, 74, 103, 291n
Coakley, Martha, 209, 222–23, 258, 314n
Coburn, Tom, 335n, 336n
Coffey, Colleen, 249, 343
Cohn, Jonathan, 326n
collateralized debt obligations (CDOs), 95, 141, 296n, 297n
college costs, 2, 11–12, 41, 72, 90, 228, 289n, 327n, 333n. *See also* student loans
Committee on Economic Inclusion, 292n
Commodity Futures Trading Commission, 296n
Common Cause, 333n
Communications Workers of America, 308n
community banks, 195, 197, 319n, 342
Community Reinvestment Act, 304n
Congressional Budget Office, 314n, 336n
Congressional Oversight Panel (COP), 83–127, 131, 144, 147, 152, 159–60, 165, 172–73, 179, 199, 209, 219–20, 298n, 299n, 301–7nn
    AIG and, 120
    bank stock warrants and, 104–5, 116, 124–25, 303n
    Citibank and, 90
    Daily Show and, 106–9
    first report of, and ten questions for Treasury, 94–97, 102–3, 298–99n
    Geithner and, 105, 111–12, 115, 117–18, 120
    GOP and, 305–6n
    HAMP and, 301n, 304–5n
    hearings of, 100–102
    Hensarling and, 97–100, 103
    limited authority of, 85
    media and, 103, 106–9
    mission of, to oversee TARP, 88–94
    nonpartisan approach of, 97, 99–100, 119–20
    offices of, 113–14

Paulson and, 123–24
regulatory reform recommendations of, 309n
reports of, 93–94, 102–5, 120, 124–25, 292n
staff of, 100, 104, 112–14, 340
stress tests and, 115, 302–3n
Summers and, 105–6
Treasury foreclosure program and, 93, 116–19
Warren asked to serve on, 83–85
Warren chairs, and set-up of, 93–97
Warren resigns from, to launch CFPB, 127
Warren's congressional testimony during, 199
Warren's first meeting with Treasury on, 88–90
website of, 96
wins and losses of, 124–26
women and, 123
YouTube and, 96
consumer advocacy groups, 60–61, 132, 151–52, 157–59, 162–63, 312n
Consumer Action, 311n
Consumer Bankruptcy Project (2007), 286n, 292n. *See also* Bankruptcy Research Project
consumer complaint hotline, 182–85, 193, 316–17n, 325n
Consumer Credit Safety Commission Act (2008), 310n
Consumer Expenditure Survey, 289n
Consumer Federation of America, 60, 147, 162, 287n, 311n
Consumer Financial Protection Bureau (CFPB), 106, 127–207, 209, 219–20, 247, 260, 312–17nn
    antidiscrimination laws and, 318n
    banks try to kill or weaken, 151–52, 157–58, 322n
    benefits of, 134, 136–38
    car loans left out of, 155
    consumer complaint hotline and, 182–84, 316–17n, 325n
    consumer groups and, 131–36
    Cordray confirmed as director of, 275

Consumer Financial Protection (*Cont'd*)
Cordray hired by, 184–85
Cordray nominated as director of,
204–6
Daily Beast interview on, 220
enactment of, 161–63, 312–14n
enforcement by, 324n
fight for, in Congress, 138–55
fight for, in House-Senate conference,
159–60, 314n
fight for, in Senate, 155–59
financial literacy department, 185
foreclosure scandal and, 196–202
Frank and, 140–44, 152–55
funding of, 314n
Funny or Die video on, 158
Hensarling and, 152
Holly Petraeus and, 191
idea proposed, 106, 126–36, 310–11n
Inspector General on, 206, 324n
Kennedy and, 144
launch and design of, 169–202
military service members and, 185,
189–91, 206
mortgage forms and, 194–96, 319–20n,
322n
Obama and, 138–40, 144–46, 205
powers of, and error in Dodd-Frank,
175–76, 315n
staff hired, 174, 178–79, 185–87, 191–92,
341
toaster analogy and, 127–31, 138–40
Warren as special adviser to launch,
169–91, 194–202
Warren directorship of, opposed in
Congress, 135, 164–69, 202–5,
314–15n, 322–23n
Warren resigns from, with Cordray
nomination, 204–7
Warren's run for Senate and, 205,
211
website of, 195–96
Consumer Product Safety Commission
(CPSC), 128–29, 136–38, 307n, 308n,
310n
Consumers Union (CU), 60, 287n,
311–13nn

contracts, financial products regulated as,
129, 131
Conyers, John, 287n
Cordray, Richard, 157, 184–85, 192–93,
204–6, 275, 313–14n, 323n, 325n
Corporation for Enterprise Development,
311n
Coulombe, Amanda, 242, 343
Countrywide Financial, 310n
credit cards
bankruptcy and, 34, 42–43, 60, 64, 67,
80, 286n, 287n
CFPB and, 133, 134, 143
complaints about, 324n
debt problems and, 35, 73, 87, 281n,
290n
deregulation of, 283–84n
fees and interest rates, 41–44, 86–87,
128, 129, 131, 143, 284n
targeting by, 78, 284n
credit crisis, 92–93, 297–98n
credit default swaps, 141, 143, 296n, 297n,
300n
credit rating agencies, 92, 121, 296n, 297n
credit reports, 154, 313n, 316–17n, 324n
credit unions, 124, 148, 195, 197, 307n
Crookham, Michelle Elizabeth Herring,
145
Crossroads GPS, 229–30, 328n
CSPAN, 275
Culpepper, Miniard, 244, 262
Cummings, Elijah, 201

Daily Beast, 219–20, 222, 223, 327n
Daily Kos, 250
Daily Show with Jon Stewart, The
(TV show), 106–9, 144, 157
Date, Raj, 178–79, 325n
Davidson, Beth, 340
Dean, Howard, 74
debt and financial distress. *See also*
bankruptcy; low-income families;
middle class
All Your Worth and, 78–79
bankruptcy law and, 80–81
demographics of, 280n
interest rates and, 34

military and, 189–91, 317n
number of families in, 69, 290n
targeting of people in, 41–44, 284n
two-income trap and, 73
debt collectors, 60, 80, 291n
Defense Department (DOD), 190–91,
   317n, 318n
DeFranco, Marisa, 245
Delahunt, William, 138–39, 162, 287n,
   310n
DeLauro, Rosa, 332n
Delgado v. Galvin, 331n
democracy
   bankruptcy and, 81
   CFPB and, 162–63
   COP and, 125
   election of 2012 and, 269
   money in politics on, 250
   voter registration and, 251–52
Democracy for America, 250
Democracy (journal), 131, 308n
Democratic National Convention of 2012,
   253–56, 332n
Democratic Party, 216
   bankruptcy law and, 66
   CFPB and, 149, 199–200
   COP and, 88, 97, 100, 103
   elections of 2004 and, 75
   elections of 2012 and, 208
   TARP and, 88
Demos, 251–52, 311n, 331–32n
deregulation, 121, 177, 283–84n, 295–97n,
   315n
derivatives, 95, 141–43, 295–97nn
Desert Storm, 187
diabetes, 225, 236
Dimon, Jamie, 176–77, 241, 315n, 320n,
   330n
Dodaro, Gene, 117
Dodd, Chris, 147, 155, 158–59, 162, 166,
   287n, 313–15nn, 338, 340
Dodd-Frank Act ("financial reform bill";
   2010), 131–67, 172, 185, 194, 198, 200,
   216–17, 311n, 315n, 323n. *See also*
   Consumer Financial Protection
   Bureau
   Brown and funding of, 241, 314n, 330n

campaign for, in Congress, 125, 139–56
CFPB powers and, 175–76, 315n
CFPB proposed as part of, 131–36,
   141–44
Frank and, 141–44, 152–56
Obama announces, 144–46
Obama signs, 160–62, 164
passed, 158–60, 314n
Dole, Robert, 307n
domestic violence, 285n
Donaghue, Kate, 330n
Donenberg, Jon, 333n, 343
Donner, Lisa, 147, 311n, 340
Dr. Phil Show (TV show), 75–77
drug industry, 137
Duff & Phelps (D&P), 299n
Dukakis, Kitty, 330n
Dukakis, Mike, 242, 330n
Durbin, Dick, 51, 64, 67, 81, 139, 160–62,
   287n, 310n, 338

Eakes, Martin, 312n
education, 72, 90, 186, 215, 218, 224, 229,
   238, 247–48, 289n, 290n, 295n.
   See also college costs; student loans
Edwards, John, 74–75
Edwards, Julie, 327n, 342
Egerman, Paul, 249
Eisenhower, Dwight D., 254
elections
   of 2000, 66
   of 2004, 74–77
   of 2008, 105
   of 2010, 157, 184, 187, 327–28n
   of 2012, 208–72, 315n, 335n
Ellison, Keith, 323n
EMILY's List, 227, 249, 327n
Ensign, John, 322n
environmental groups, 231, 333n
Equal Credit Opportunity Act (1974), 318n
Ernst, Keith, 293n
Estrada, Mr., 101, 124, 165
Evans, David S., 296n, 284n
Evans, Joan, 340

Facebook, 162, 201
factcheck.org, 328n, 334n

Fair, Isaac & Co., 284n
Fair Housing Act (1968), 318n
Faith Christian Church (Dorchester),
    237–38
Fannie Mae, 296n, 304n
Farrell, Will, 158
Farrey v. Sanderfoot, 285n
Federal Aviation Administration, 188
Federal Bureau of Investigation (FBI),
    187–88
federal deficit, 214–16
Federal Deposit Insurance Corporation
    (FDIC), 41, 82, 110, 119, 122, 198,
    283n, 292n, 295n, 305n, 309n, 321n,
    323n
    Citibank and, 300n
Federal Elections Commission, 315n
Federal Reserve, 87, 115, 198, 275, 295n,
    309n, 310n, 314n, 322n
Federal Reserve Bank of Kansas City,
    308n
Federal Reserve Bank of New York, 105,
    297n, 300n
Federal Trade Commission (FTC), 310n,
    313n, 318n
Feingold, Russell, 64, 81, 287n, 338
Feminist Majority, 327n
Ficklin, Patrice, 192, 319n, 324n, 341
Fighter, The (film), 334n
Financial Crisis Inquiry Commission,
    293n, 295n, 296n, 297n, 315n
financial crisis of 2008. *See also*
    Dodd-Frank Act; Troubled Asset
    Relief Program
    causes of, 86–88, 113, 295–97nn, 304n,
        315n
    chance to rewrite rules after, 109–11, 141
    congressional insider trading and, 181,
        316–17n
    consumer financial protection idea and,
        127
    COP created after, 83–85
    COP YouTube and website on, 95–97
    Dimon on, 176–7, 315n7
    failure to prosecute bank executives for,
        307n
    impact of, 96, 302n
    Obama's effort to stem, 105
    TARP passed to stem, 92–94
    tight credit and, 297–98n
financial reform bill. *See* Dodd-Frank Act
financial regulation, 296n, 309–10n.
    See also Consumer Financial
    Protection Bureau; Dodd-Frank Act;
    and specific individuals and agencies
    benefits of, 316n
    changes in, 295n
    Depression and, 41, 283n
    financial crises and, 109, 121, 306–7n,
        315n
    foreclosure settlement and, 321–22n
    funding of, 160, 203, 314n
    need for improved, 127–31, 136–37
    relationship of, with banks, 113, 125,
        133–34, 192
Financial Services Roundtable, 176–80,
    312n, 315n, 316n
Fine, Camden, 319n
firefighters, 188, 215, 258–60
Firestone, Mike, 242, 343
Flanagan, Jenny, 331n
"Flora," 86–87, 121, 124, 165, 194, 293n
Flynn, Ray, 263
Food and Drug Administration, 188
Ford Motor Company, 301n
foreclosures, 73, 279n, 287n, 290n, 293n
    CFPB and, 170, 198–202
    COP and, 93, 96, 100–102
    FDIC and, 305n
    HAMP and, 301n, 304–5n
    military and, 190
    robo-signing scandal and, 197–202,
        320–22nn
    subprime mortgages and, 87–88
    TARP and, 93, 96, 111–12, 300–305nn
    Treasury fails to help, 93, 116–19, 124
Founding Fathers, 40, 59
Fox, Anne, 335n
Fox News, 135, 214, 216
Fragile Middle Class, The (Westbrook,
    Warren, and Sullivan), 280n, 281n,
    284n
Frank, Barney, 138, 140–44, 147, 152–56,
    160, 162, 166, 314n, 332n

Frank, Robert, 288n
Franken, Al, 314n, 323n, 332n
Freddie Mac, 296n, 304n
free market, 137–38, 175, 186
Fry, Shanti, 249
Funny or Die, 158

Gandy, Kim, 327n
GAO, 117
Geithner, Timothy, 105–6, 299n, 305n
    Bair and, 300n
    CFPB and, 166–67, 169, 171, 173–75,
        179–80, 198, 202, 322n
    COP and, 111–12, 115, 117–18, 120, 144
    foreclosure scandal and, 201
    stress tests and, 115, 303n
    Summers and, 105–6
Geldhof, Heather, 217
Geldon, Dan
    CFPB and, 147–52, 156, 164, 178, 184,
        217, 337, 340–41
    COP and, 95, 217, 340
    Warren's Senate campaign of 2012 and,
        217–18, 261
General Motors (GM), 301n, 306n
George Washington University, 12–13
Gingrich, Newt, 230
Ginsberg, Robert E., 284n, 285n, 338
Glass Molders Pottery Plastics & Allied
        Workers International Union, 308n
Glass-Steagall Act, 283n
    repeal of, 295n
GMAC, 321n
Goldman Sachs, 294n, 300n, 301n, 321n
    AIG bailout and, 111, 300n
    TARP warrants and, 116, 303n
Good Morning America (TV show), 103
Gose, John A., 284n
government
    homeownership policy and, 304n
    importance of, 185–88, 215–16, 247–48,
        225–26, 256
Government Printing Office (GPO),
        113–14
Grassley, Chuck, 299n, 305n
Great Depression, 9, 28, 41, 109, 143, 178,
        283n, 315n

Green, Adam, 314n
Greenberg, Hank, 120, 306n
Greenlining Institute, 311n
Greenspan, Alan, 87, 293–94n
Gregg, Judd, 93, 305n
Grimm, Michael, 187–88, 317n
Grunwald, Mandy, 227, 342
Guernsey, Sherwood, 325n
Guest, Jim, 312n
gun violence, 237–38, 329n

Habayeb, Elias, 300n
Hammond, Darrell, 158
Hanks, Sara, 112, 340
Hardball with Chris Matthews (TV show),
        158
Harney, Alethea, 327n, 343
"Harris, Mr.," 195
Harrison, Lee, 325n
Hartley, Jeffery J., 284n
Harvard Law School, 44–47, 50, 95,
        109–10, 138, 172, 262, 329n
    Bruce Mann moves to, 79
    Native American issue and, 239–40
    Warren's last class at, 233
Hastings Group, 311n
Haynie, Ron, 319n
health care, 72–73, 80, 151, 260, 289n,
        291n, 317n. See also Affordable Care
        Act; medical problems; scientific and
        medical research
    bankruptcy and, 34–35, 44, 55, 57, 59,
        62, 73, 129, 281n, 286n, 291n
hedge funds, 141, 314n
Hensarling, Jeb, 93, 97–100, 103, 119, 152,
        298n, 305n, 312–13n
Herring, Barbara, 52
Herring, David, 1, 10, 32, 39, 144, 210, 220,
        236, 241, 344
    death of father and, 58
    death of mother and, 51
Herring, Donald Jones, 1, 5–12, 15, 20,
        23–27, 30–33, 38–39, 45–46, 239–40,
        344
    death of, 58–59
    death of wife Pauline and, 51–52, 56
    marries Pauline Reed, 9, 59, 239–40

Herring, Don Reed, 1, 10, 144, 210, 236, 241, 344
  death of father and, 58
  death of wife Nancy and, 31–32
Herring, Ethel, 143
Herring, Grant, 9
Herring, John, 1, 10, 31–32, 39, 52, 144, 210, 236, 241, 344
  death of father and, 58
Herring, Mark, 144
Herring, Melinda, 145, 269
Herring, Nancy, 31
Herring, Pauline Louise Reed "Polly", 1, 5–8, 11–12, 15, 20, 24–27, 30–32, 38–39, 45, 270
  death of, 51–52, 56, 59, 241
  marries Donald Jones Herring, 9–10, 59, 239
  Native American background of, 9, 143, 239–40
Hoffman, Matt, 335n
Home Affordable Modification Program (HAMP), 301n, 304–5n
home equity loans, 43, 76, 87, 279n, 293–94n
homes and homeownership. See also foreclosures; mortgages
  as asset, 41, 88, 294n
  bankruptcy and, 80, 86–87, 281n
  financial crisis and, 304n
  size of, 290n
Housing and Urban Development Department (HUD), 310n, 318n
housing bubble and crash, 72, 87–88, 91–93, 117, 290n, 294–96nn
Howard, Ron, 158
Huffington Post, 158, 232, 312n
Human Rights Campaign, 328n

IBM, 13–14, 18
Independent Community Bankers of America (ICBA), 319n, 321n
infrastructure, 2, 90, 215, 247, 295n
insider trading, 181, 316–17n
interest rates. See also mortgages
  car loans and, 130–31, 308n
  CFPB and, 137

  credit cards and, 128
  deregulation of, 40–41, 87, 283–84n
  military families and, 190, 317n
  payday lenders and, 131, 190, 290n, 308n
  student loans and, 274–76, 335–36n
  teaser, 86–87
Internal Revenue Service (IRS), 80, 291n
International Alliance of Theatrical Stage Employees, 308n
International Association of Bridge, Structural, Ornamental & Reinforcing Iron Workers, 308n
International Association of Fire Fighters, 308n
International Association of Heat & Frost Insulators and Asbestos Workers, 308n
International Association of Machinists & Aerospace Workers, 308n
International Brotherhood of Boilermakers, 309n
International Brotherhood of Electrical Workers, 309n
International Brotherhood of Teamsters, 309n
International Longshore and Warehouse Union, 309n
International Longshoremen's Association, 309n
International Union of Bricklayers & Allied Craftworkers, 309n
International Union of Elevator Constructors, 309n
International Union of Operating Engineers, 309n
International Union of Painters & Allied Trades, 309n
investment banks, 141, 297n
Iraq war, 189
Ivashina, Victoria, 303n

Jackson, Peter, 179, 340
Jacobs, Samuel P., 219–20, 327n
Jacoby, Melissa, 61–63, 280n, 335n, 338
Jarrett, Valerie, 166, 168
"Jason," 130–31

Jay Leno Show, The (TV show), 140
job loss
  bankruptcy and, 34, 44, 55, 57, 59, 62, 73, 129, 130, 281n, 286n
  financial crisis and, 96, 112
jobs, 96, 112, 129, 130, 226, 238. *See also* unemployment
Joint Base San Antonio, 188, 191
Jones, Edith Hollan, 55–57, 59, 284n, 285n, 286n
JPMorgan Chase, 176, 294n, 297n, 301n, 315n, 321n, 321n, 330n. *See also* Dimon, Jamie
  Bear Stearns and, 297n
  financial reform and, 146
  foreclosure scandal and, 197
  London Whale and, 241
Justice Department, 120–21, 293n, 331n

Kagan, Elena, 266–67
Kashkari, Neel, 89, 95, 295n, 299n
Kaufman, Ted, 305n
Kay, Liz F., 308n
Keating, Bill, 332n
Keenan, John, 219
Kelly, Ed, 258–59
Kennedy, Anthony, 266
Kennedy, Caroline, 333n
Kennedy, Edward M. "Ted," 208–9, 222, 246, 269, 274, 288n
  bankruptcy battle and, 61–67, 81, 246
  CFPB and, 138–39, 144, 162, 246
  death of, 152, 157
Kennedy, Edward M., Jr. "Ted," 335n
Kennedy, Ethel, 265, 335n
Kennedy, John F., 61, 152, 274
Kennedy, Joseph P., Sr., 178
Kennedy, Joseph P., III, 138–39
Kennedy, Patrick, 335n
Kennedy, Robert F. "Bobby," 138, 152
Kennedy, Rory, 265
Kennedy, Vicki, 62–63, 242
Kerry, John, 74–75, 245, 257, 332n
Kiley, Tom, 342
Kilroy, Mary Jo, 304n
Kineavy, Michael, 258
King, Angus, 295n

Knight, Thaya Brook, 340
Know Before You Owe project, 318–20nn
Kroll, Steve, 112, 340
Krugman, Paul, 294n, 314n

Laborers' International Union of North America, 309n
labor unions, 132, 162, 259–60, 271, 308–9n, 332–33n
  auto bailouts and, 301n
Latinos
  financial meltdown of 2008 and, 294n
  home foreclosure and, 293n
  predatory and deceptive lending and, 87, 284n, 324n
Lau, Roger, 236–37, 258–59, 267, 342, 343
Lawless, Robert M., 291n, 338
Lawyer's Committee for Civil Rights Under Law, 311n
Leadership Conference on Civil and Human Rights, 311n
Leadership Conference on Civil Rights, 287n
League of Conservation Voters, 232, 249, 329n, 334n
Legal Defense Fund, 287n
Legoland, 206, 262
Lehman Brothers, 92, 291n, 297n
Leno, Jay, 310n
Lerner, Alfred, 291n
Lerner, Norma, 291n
Levitin, Adam J., 310n
Lewis, John, 257
Lewis, Tracey, 217, 242, 267, 343
LGBT community, 271, 327n
Limbaugh, Rush, 216–17, 326n
Linehan, Joyce, 325n
Littwin, Angela K., 285n, 291n, 338
lobbyists, 2
  bankruptcy law and, 98, 60, 64–66, 286n
  CFPB and, 132, 135–36, 142–43, 146–52, 157–58, 161–62
  foreclosures and, 302n
  National Bankruptcy Review Commission and, 57
  spending and influence of, 54, 66, 149–51, 311–13nn, 315n

London Whale scandal, 241, 330n. *See also* JPMorgan Chase
LoPucki, Lynn, 44
low-income families, 82, 122, 238, 284n
Lucas, Deborah J., 299n
Lumas, Ryan Anthony, 314–15n
Lux, Mike, 313n, 340
Lynch, Steve, 332n

MacDonald, Elizabeth, 340
Maddow, Rachel, 201
Madigan, Lisa, 313n
Main Street Brigade, 315n
Maloney, Carolyn, 323n
Mandarini, Lou, 333n, 343
Mann, Bruce, 70, 107, 142, 157, 270, 345
  background of, 25–26
  CFPB and, 172–73, 176, 191, 205
  COP and, 84–85
  dog Otis and, 79, 234, 252–53, 268
  Harvard and, 44–47, 79
  marriage and family life and, 39–40, 102, 144, 180–81, 206, 210
  marries Warren, 25–27, 30–31
  parents and siblings of, 47, 59, 94
  Summer Shack dinners and, 114–15, 152, 159, 208
  tennis and, 25
  Tyagi wedding and, 159
  UPenn and, 38
  urges Warren do something about bankruptcy, 44, 46–47
  UT Austin and, 27–28, 30
  Warren's mother and, 51–52
  Warren's Senate campaign and, 213, 221–24, 233, 236, 242, 244, 246, 267, 269, 330n, 332n
  Washington University and, 30–31
Mann, Ronald, 286n
Mapes, Ina, 242
Marine Engineers Beneficial Association, 309n
Markey, Ed, 332n
Marquette National Bank v. First of Omaha Service Corp., 283n
Martin, Alyssa, 174, 178, 179, 341, 343

Massachusetts
  campaigning as woman in, 227–28
  election turnout of 2012, 271, 335n
  firefighters union and, 258–60
  Senate election of 2010, 157
  Senate election of 2012, 208–72, 335n
  voter registration and, 251, 331n
Massachusetts Citizens for Life, 335n
Massachusetts Credit Union League, 331n
Massachusetts Democratic Party
  nominating convention of 2012, 244–46
  Senate nomination campaign of 2012, 217–19, 330n
Masterson, Billy, 121
Mathews, Chris, 314n
MBNA, 75, 291n
McCain, John, 295n
McCollum, Bill, 286n, 288n
McConnell, Mitch, 323n
McCoy, Pat, 194–96
McGovern, Jim, 332n
McGraw, Dr. Phil, 75–77
McGreevy, Patrick, 340
McHenry, Patrick, 200–201, 322n
McIntosh, Jess, 327n
McKinsey consulting, 70
McWatters, Mark, 119, 305n, 339
media. *See also specific outlets*
  bank lobbyists and, 65
  CFPB and, 135, 139, 148, 158, 179, 203–4
  financial reform bill and, 146–47
  foreclosure scandal and, 321n
  interest rates and, 87
  Two-Income Trap and, 290n
medical problems. *See* health care; scientific and medical research
Medicare, 260
Meehan, Marty, 287n
Menino, Thomas, 257–58, 333n
Merrill Lynch, 92, 291n, 297n
Merton, Robert, 303n
MetLife Bank, 321n
middle class
  bankruptcy and, 34–36, 69, 81, 281n
  challenges ahead for, 276–77
  home as asset and, 41, 88, 294n

squeeze on, 3, 54, 70–82, 138, 212, 238, 289–91nn
  taxes and, 248
  unions and, 260
  Warren's Senate campaign and, 210, 212, 228, 236, 256
Mierzwinski, Ed, 162, 311n, 340
Mikulski, Barbara, 265, 334n
Military Lending Act (2006), 318n
military servicemembers, 188–91, 206, 317–18n, 324n
Miller, Brad, 138–39, 162, 323n
Miller, Lauren, 242, 343
Miller, Tom, 313n
minimum wage, 260
Montgomery Ward, 6–8, 10
Mooney, Beth, 307n
Moran, Jerry, 323n
Morgan Stanley, 291n
Morgenson, Gretchen, 305n, 307n
Morning Joe (TV show), 157
mortgage-backed securities, 91–93, 121, 295–97nn
mortgages, 41. *See also* foreclosures
  adjustable rate (ARM), 87, 195–96, 292–93n
  bankruptcy and, 34, 80, 86, 287n
  CFPB and, 133–34, 194–96
  COP and, 101–2
  cost of, and middle class, 72–73
  dishonest and dangerous, 3, 43, 76, 86–88, 128, 136, 170, 190, 192, 290n, 292–93n, 315n, 324n
  financial crisis and, 86–88, 91–93, 117, 194
  military families and, 190
  need for regulation of, 92, 121, 128–29, 134, 143, 310n
  one-page, 194–96
  racial discrimination and, 324n
  subprime, 86–88, 121, 284n, 293n, 296n, 297n, 304n
  TARP and, 92–93
  underwater, 88, 124, 294n, 307n
Moss, David, 311n
Mothers for Justice and Equality, 237–38

Motor Voter law. *See* National Voter Registration Act
Mourdock, Richard, 265
Moveon.org, 216, 249–50, 311n, 326n
MSPCA Angell Animal Medical Center, 234, 253, 268
Mullane, Mike, 258–59
Murkowski, Lisa, 322n
Murray, Patty, 227
Murray, Sara, 304n
Muslim, Adnaan, 335n, 342
Myers, Mindy, 217, 267, 335n, 342, 343

Nalder, Jerrold, 287n
NARAL, 334n
Nasiripour, Shahien, 314n, 315n, 321n, 335n
National Association for the Advancement of Colored People (NAACP), 81, 287n, 311n
  Legal Defense Fund, 311n
National Association of Consumer Bankruptcy Attorneys (NACBA), 287n
National Association of Federal Credit Unions, 319n
National Association of Government Employees, 309n
National Association of Letter Carriers, 309n
National Bankruptcy Review Commission (NBRC), 48–61, 65, 81, 84, 284n, 286n
  death of Synar and, 53–55
  hearings, 56–57, 100
  report of 1997, 57–59, 65
  Warren appointed to, 48–51
National Center for Injury Prevention and Control, 329n
National City Bank, 324n
National Community Reinvestment Coalition, 311n, 317n
National Consumer Law Center (NCLC), 287n, 293n, 311n, 313n
National Consumers League, 311n
National Council of La Raza, 311n
National Credit Union Administration (NCUA), 309n, 323n

National Economic Council, 106
National Education Association, 309n
National Fair Housing Alliance, 311n
National Guard, 209
National Nurses United, 309n
National Institutes of Health (NIH), 327n
National Organization for Women
	(NOW), 219, 326n, 334n
National Partnership for Women &
	Families, 60–61, 287n
National People's Action, 311n
National Postal Mail Handlers Union,
	309n
National Public Radio (NPR), 74, 291n
National Rifle Association, 49
National Science Foundation (NSF), 327n
National Treasury Employees Union, 309n
National Urban League, 311n
National Voter Registration Act (NVRA,
	"Motor Voter," 1993), 251, 331–32n
Native American ancestry, 239–42,
	262–63, 329n, 330n, 333n
Neal, Richie, 332n
Negron, Michael, 97–98, 340
Neiman, Richard, 88–89, 100–102, 339
Newsweek, 74, 290n
New York Times, 166, 295n, 307–7n, 314n
9/11 Commission, 99
Nocera, Joe, 314n
nonprofits, 92, 147, 151, 157, 162
Northwestern University, 11–13

Obama, Barack, 124, 132, 302n, 310n,
	321n
	CFPB and, 131, 139–40, 145–46, 158,
		164–73, 202–7, 322n, 323n
	Democratic National Convention and,
		253
	Dimon and, 177
	Dodd-Frank and, 145–46, 160–61
	recess appointments and, 203–4
	TARP and, 105
	Warren's Senate campaign and, 205
Occupy Boston, 220
Occupy Wall Street, 220–22, 230, 327n,
	328n
Octonion I, 296n

Odom, Kim, 237–38
Odom, Stephen, 237
Office & Professional Employees
	International Union, 309n
Office of Congressional Ethics, 316n
Office of the Comptroller of the Currency
	(OCC), 197–98, 309n, 310n, 321n,
	323n
Office of Thrift Supervision (OTS), 309n,
	310n, 322n
oil industry, 31, 246, 256, 263, 328n, 334n
Olver, John, 332n
O'Neill, Terry, 326n
OpenSecrets.org, 291n, 335n. *See also*
	Center for Responsive Politics
Operation Rescue, 288n
Operative Plasterer's & Cement Mason's
	International Association, 309n

PACs and Super PACs, 75, 229, 231, 232,
	271, 316n, 328n
Pandit, Vikram, 120, 306n
Panetta, Leon, 317n
Patrick, Deval, 222–23, 257, 331n, 333n
Patton, Matt, 331n, 343
Paulson, Henry M., 88–89, 92, 103–5,
	123–24, 295n, 298n, 300n, 302n, 316n
payday lenders, 73, 131, 133–34, 190, 238,
	290n, 292n, 308n, 310n, 318n
Pelosi, Nancy, 88, 327n
pensions, 34, 92
People's Pledge, 232, 250, 258, 271, 329n,
	333n
Petraeus, Holly, 189–92, 196, 206,
	324–25n, 341
Pew Research Center, 294n
PICO National Network, 311n
Planned Parenthood, 218, 334n
Plato, 283n
Pleasant Hill Baptist Church, 244
Plunkett, Travis, 162, 311n, 340
PNC, 302n, 321n, 324n
Politico, 232
Porter, Katherine M., 286n, 291n, 320n,
	335n, 338
Pottow, John A., 291n, 338
Powell, Hank, 326n

Powell, M J, 326n
P-PIP program, 108
Pratt, Michael, 249, 343
predatory lending, 41, 62, 86–87, 189–92, 290n, 293n, 304n, 308n, 317–18n. *See also* mortgages; payday lenders
preschool, 72, 90, 289n
Professional Aviation Safety Specialists, 309n
Progressive Change Campaign Committee, 249, 296n, 311n, 314n
Progressives United, 250
ProPublica, 294n
Public Citizen, 311n, 312n
Public Interest Research Group (PIRG), 147, 162, 287n, 311n, 313n, 316–17nn

Rachel Maddow Show, The (TV Show), 157
racial discrimination, 317n, 318n, 324n
Rakoff, Jeb, 307n
Ramalho, Art, 264, 334n
Reagan, Ronald, 158, 185, 329n
recession of early 1980s, 34–35
Reed, Bessie Amelia "Aunt Bee," 6–7, 14, 22–27, 30, 32, 38, 45–47, 52
death of, 58–59
Reed, Jack, 303n
Reid, Harry, 83–85, 88, 108–9, 125, 323n, 339
Republican Party
Affordable Care Act and, 264–65
AIG and, 105
bankruptcy law and, 66
banks vs. families and, 236
campaign contributions and, 291n
CFPB and, 149, 166, 169, 172, 181, 198–205, 322–23n
COP and, 93, 97–100, 103, 119–20, 305–6n
foreclosure scandal and, 198–202
House elections of 2010 and, 187–88
National Bankruptcy Review Commission and, 53
Senate elections of 2010 and, 157
Senate elections of 2012 and, 209–12, 221, 229–33, 239–42, 250–52, 257

spending cuts and, 215, 226
TARP and, 88
tax loopholes and, 263
voter registration and, 251–52
women's rights and, 264–67
Responsible Borrower Protection Bankruptcy bill (industry-backed bill, introduced 1997), 286–88nn. *See also* bankruptcy
Retail, the Wholesale and Department Store Union, 309n
Rhinesmith, Alan, 340
Rich, Andrew, 312n, 340
Riesenfeld, Stefan, 29–30
Ritchie, Donald A., 323n
Roberts, John G., Jr., 266
robo-signing, 320–21n, 324n
Romash, Marla, 327n, 342
Romney, Mitt, 256
Roosevelt, Franklin D., 143
Roosevelt Institute, 147, 311n
Rose, Charlie, 303n
Rouse, Pete, 166
Rove, Karl, 210, 229–32, 250, 258, 328n, 333n
Rowsey, Jan "Candy," 5
Rubin, Doug, 222, 342
Russell, David O., 334n
Rutgers Law School, 16, 18

Sanders, Bernie, 332n
Saturday Night Live (TV Show), 158
savings, 34, 72–73, 78, 290n
savings and loan (S&L) crisis, 121, 306n
Scalia, Antonin, 266
Schapiro, Mary, 122–23
Schor, Juliet, 288n
Schriock, Stephanie, 227
Schumer, Chuck, 64, 67, 81, 139, 162, 287n, 310n, 338
Schumer Amendment, 288n
Schweizer, Peter, 316n
scientific and medical research, 2, 90, 225–26, 236, 247, 295n, 327n
Seafarers International Union, 309n
Sealy, Will, 331n
Sears Roebuck, 7–8

Seay, Thomas, 340
Securities Act (1933), 283n
Securities and Exchange Act (1934), 283n
Securities and Exchange Commission
    (SEC), 122, 178
Segel, Jim, 142
self employed, 248
senior citizens, 87, 192, 215, 226, 293n
Service Employees International Union
    (SEIU), 309n, 311n
Shaheen, Jeanne, 332n
Shea, Dillon, 319n
Sheet Metal Workers International
    Association, 309n
Shelby, Richard, 166, 198–99, 202–3, 322n,
    324nn
Shepard, James I., 284n
Sierra Club, 334n
SIGTARP (Special Inspector General of
    TARP), 116, 295n, 301n, 303n.
    See also Barofsky, Neil
Silvers, Damon, 88–89, 100–102, 104, 113,
    123–24, 131–33, 135, 335n, 339
Silvers, Rosie, 335n
single parents, 60, 80–81, 287n. See also
    child support
Sitaraman, Ganesh
    COP and, 94–95, 337
    Senate race and, 212, 228, 254, 340
60 Minutes (TV show), 181, 316n
small banks, 318–19n, 320–21n. See also
    community banks
    CFPB and, 148, 195
    disadvantages of, vs. large banks, 283n
    failures of, 112, 124, 302n, 307n
    FDIC and, 122
    foreclosures and, 197
    Know Before You Owe and, 319–20nn
    TARP and, 89, 112, 124, 302–3nn
small business, 41, 301n
    bankruptcy and, 37, 81, 282n
    financial crisis and, 124, 298n, 302n
    TARP and, 93, 111–12, 124, 300n
    Warren's Senate campaign and, 247
Smith, Eugene, 19
Smith, Howard, 306n
Snowe, Olympia, 305n

Social Security, 86, 260, 333n
soft money, 315n
Sotomayor, Sonia, 266
Sovereign Bank, 321n
Spitzer, Eliot, 120, 306n
Standard & Poor's, 296n
Stanley, David, 280n
"State of Lending in America," 289n,
    290n, 292n, 294n
Stein, Eric, 147, 162, 174
Stephan, Jeffrey, 320n
Stewart, Jon, 106–9, 157
stress tests, 115, 302–3n
student loans, 41, 133, 218, 224, 274–76,
    317n, 324n, 327n. See also Bank on
    Students bill
    bankruptcy law and, 60, 80, 279n
    consumer complaints and, 324–25n
    interest rates and, 335–36n
Subprime Virus, The (McCoy), 194
Sullivan, Kyle, 219–20, 328n, 342
Sullivan, Teresa A., 33, 44, 69, 280–82nn,
    285n, 338
Summers, Larry, 105–6
Summer Shack, 114, 152, 159, 208
SunTrust, 321n
Sununu, John, 103, 119, 305n
Sweeney, John, 133, 145
Synar, Mike, 48–51, 57, 81, 84, 284, 284n,
    338
    death of, 51, 53–54

Talbott, Scott, 312n
Talley, Eric, 302n
taxes, 2, 65, 215, 226, 247–48, 260, 263,
    331n
Taylor, James, 257
Taylor, Kim, 257
Taylor, Stephanie, 314n
Teamsters Union, 245, 273
Tea Party, 117, 157, 184, 187–88, 252
Terry, Randall, 288n
Thorne, Deborah K., 285n, 291n, 338
Tierney, John, 332n
Time, 122, 304n
toaster analogy, 127–29, 138–40, 145,
    308n, 310n

Tobin Project, 141, 311n
Tocci, Lynda, 242, 343
Today (TV show), 74
Too Big to Fail (TBTF), 109–12, 124–25, 301n, 309n
Torres, Jess, 237, 267, 343
transgender people, 229, 276, 327n
Transport Workers Union, 309n
Travis, Adam, 234, 258, 267, 343
Treasury Department. *See also* Troubled Asset Relief Program; *and specific individuals and agencies*
  AIG and, 111, 299n
  auto bailouts and, 301n
  CFPB and, 166, 169–70, 173–76, 179–80
  Citibank and, 89–90, 98, 295n
  COP and, 83–85, 88–91, 94, 96, 102–3, 124–25, 292n, 298–99n
  financial reform and, 145, 147
  foreclosure crisis and, 112, 116–19, 124, 301n, 304–5n
  Geithner succeeds Paulson at, 105
  HAMP and, 304–5n
  small business and, 301n
  Summers and, 105–6
  TARP and, 294–95nn, 298–99nn, 301–5nn
  TARP warrants and, 104–5, 303n
Tribe, Laurence H., 329n
Troske, Ken, 119, 305n, 339
Troubled Asset Relief Program (TARP, bank bailouts), 3, 60, 197, 241, 294–95nn, 298–304nn. *See also* banks and banking; Congressional Oversight Panel; Treasury Department; *and specific individuals; financial institutions; and government agencies*
  AIG and, 105, 111, 299n
  alternatives to, 90–91, 295n, 300n
  Bear Stearns and, 105, 297n
  bank stocks or warrants and, 104–5, 115–16, 299n, 303–4n
  Barofsky and, 116
  Citi-weekend and, 90
  COP and, 83–105, 124
  costs of regulation vs., 314n

  creation and goals of, 84, 88–93, 99, 111–12
  Daily Show and, 107–8
  foreclosures and, 301n, 320n
  Geithner and, 166
  negotiated reorganization and, 300n
  no-strings-attached approach of, 93, 110–12, 120, 124, 132, 300–302nn
  Reid asks Warren to serve on oversight of, 83–84
  small business and, 301n
  stress tests and, 115
  Too Big to Fail and, 110–11, 301n
  Warren's Senate campaign of 2012 and, 230
True the Vote, 252
True Vine Church (Dorchester), 237
Trumka, Rich, 145–46
Tsongas, Niki, 332n
Twitter, 162, 223
Twohig, Peggy, 192, 193, 319n, 341
Two-Income Trap, The (Warren and Tyagi), 69–77, 81, 251, 280n, 281n, 284–91nn, 294n
Tyagi, Amelia Louise Warren, 39, 45–46, 56, 102, 210, 211, 236, 337
  All Your Worth and, 77–79
  birth and childhood of, 14–19, 21, 24–25, 30, 127–28, 135
  birth of Atticus and, 159, 164, 169, 173, 176, 180–81
  birth of Lavinia and, 77, 79
  birth of Octavia and, 69–70
  death of father and, 77
  Demos and, 251, 331n
  education and, 39–40, 45–46
  marriage and family life of, 69–70, 159
  marries Sushil Tyagi, 69–70
  Two-Income Trap and, 69–76, 81, 280n, 281n, 284–91nn
  Warren's Senate campaign of 2012 and, 245, 250–52
Tyagi, Atticus Mann, 180–81, 210, 235, 245, 246
Tyagi, Lavinia, 79, 102, 164, 180, 206, 235, 245, 246

Tyagi, Octavia, 70, 102, 164, 180, 235, 245–46
Tyagi, Sushil, 69–70, 79, 159, 164, 173, 176, 344

unemployment, 73, 119, 213, 226, 274, 276
United Association of Plumbers, Fitters, Welders and HVAC Service Techs, 309n
United Auto Workers (UAW), 287n
United Automobile, Aerospace and Agriculture Implement Workers of America, 309n
United Brotherhood of Carpenters, 309n
United Food and Commercial Workers International Union, 309n
United Mine Workers of America; the United Steelworkers, 309n
U.S. Army, 10
U.S. Army Air Forces, 9
U.S. Bancorp, 294n
US Chamber of Commerce, 323n
U.S. Congress, 49, 275
    bank bailout and, 91, 298n
    bank regulation and, 131–32
    bankruptcy bill and, 29–30, 48, 55, 59, 65, 66–67, 75, 79, 84, 282n
    car dealers and, 155
    CFPB and, 135, 139–44, 147–55, 181–82, 184, 203
    COP and, 93
    financial crisis and short-selling by, 181, 316n
    financial industry access and, 151, 177–78
    financial reform bill and, 147, 159–60
    government spending and, 215
    interest rates and, 41, 190, 283n
    lobbyists and, 2, 29, 282n, 312n
    National Bankruptcy Review Commission and, 48, 55
    repeal of Glass-Steagall and, 295n
    TARP and, 84
    TARP warrants and, 304n
U.S. Constitution, 59
U.S. House of Representatives, 49, 66, 67
    bankruptcy act and, 81

CFPB and, 139–40, 153–55, 165, 198–202, 314n
    elections of 2010 and, 187–88
    financial reform bill and, 147, 155, 159
    Financial Services Committee, 140–41, 151, 181, 199–202, 298n, 312–13n
    foreclosure scandal and, 198–202
    TARP and, 100, 299n
U.S. Marines, 187
U.S. Senate
    Banking Committee, 156–59, 198, 275, 282n, 298n, 314n, 322n
    bankruptcy act and, 62–65, 66–67, 81
    CFPB and, 139, 140, 155–59, 165–66, 169, 202, 204–5, 314n, 322–23n
    Cordray nomination and, 206, 275
    elections of 2010, 157, 187
    elections of 2012, 269–72
    filibusters in, 275
    financial reform and, 147, 155, 159–60
U.S. Senate campaign of 2012, 205, 208–72, 325–35nn
    debates and, 261–63, 266–67
    Democratic National Convention and, 253–56
    fundraising and, 248–50, 271
    gaffes and, 219–22
    GOP tracker and, 221–22
    investing in Americans' future and, 224–26
    Massachusetts state nomination convention and, 244–46
    Native American issue and, 239–42
    People's Pledge and, 229–32, 329n, 333n
    staff and, 227, 236–37, 249
    volunteers and, 222–24, 242–43, 270–71
    Warren's family and, 267–68
    women's issues and, 227–28
U.S. Supreme Court, 41, 53, 55, 266–67, 283n, 334n
    Warren's appearance before, 81–82
UNITE-HERE, 309n
United Transportation Union, 309n
United Union of Roofers, Waterproofers, and Allied Workers, 309n
University of Connecticut, 26

University of Houston, 14, 18–23, 26–27, 329n
University of Pennsylvania (UPenn), 38–39, 45–46, 79, 262, 329n
University of Texas, Austin (UT Austin), 27, 30, 33, 36–37, 329n
University of Virginia, 33
USAction, 311n
usury laws, 41, 283n
Utility Workers Union of America, 309n

Vale, Elizabeth, 176, 247, 331n, 341, 343
Veneck, Bessie. *See* Reed, Bessie Amelia
Veneck, Stanley, 6
Vietnam War, 1, 31
Violence Against Women Act (2013), 266
Virginia elections of 2012, 335n
Volcker, Paul, 161
voter registration, 251–52, 331n

Wahlberg, Mark, 334n
Walden, Johan, 302n
Wall Street Journal, 155, 157, 177
Wall Street. *See also* banks and banking; big banks; *and specific institutions*
    Brown and, 325n
    deregulation and, 296n
    lack of accountability, 220
    Obama and, 124
    "sheriffs" of, 122–24
    Warren's Senate campaign and, 209–11, 216–17, 241, 246, 250, 256
Walsh, John, 331–32n
Warren, Alex, 45–46, 56, 210–11, 345
    birth and childhood of, 17–19, 21–22, 24, 30, 40
    college and, 46
    death of father and, 77
    marriage of, 236
    Warren's teaching and, 37

Warren, Amelia Louise. *See* Tyagi, Amelia Louise Warren
Warren, Elise Hutcherson, 236
Warren, James
    marriage and family life and, 13–15, 18–19, 21
    death of, 77, 211
    divorce from, 23–24, 30
Washington Post, 230
Waters, Maxine, 312n
Weaver, Caleb, 96, 340
Wells Fargo, 158, 301n, 321n, 321n
Wellstone, Paul, 64, 66, 81, 287n, 338
Westbrook, Jay Lawrence, 33, 44, 69, 280n, 281n, 282n, 284n, 338
West End Gym (Lowell), 264, 334n
Whitehouse, Sheldon, 332n
Wilkerson, Tewana, 112, 340
Williamson, Brady C., 53–54, 57, 172, 284n, 285n, 338, 344
Willumstad, Robert, 306n
women
    as bank executives, 307n
    as candidates for office, 227–28, 265, 326n, 327n, 334n
    equal pay for, 260, 265–67, 333n
    incomes of, vs. men, 289n
    law firms and, 16–17, 20
    lending discrimination and, 318n
    married mothers working, 72, 290n
    reproductive rights and, 334n
    as "sheriffs" of Wall Street, 122–24
    Warren's Senate campaign and, 209, 219, 227–28, 264–67, 271, 334n
women's movement, 15–16
Wood, Carrie, 234–35
World War II, 9

YouTube, 96–97, 120, 201, 216

Zimmer, Hans, 158, 315n
Zopatti, Gretchen, 94
Zopatti, Steve, 94

About the Author

Elizabeth Warren is the senior senator from Massachusetts. A former Harvard Law School professor and an expert on economic issues, she is the author of nine books, including *All Your Worth: The Ultimate Lifetime Money Plan* and *The Two-Income Trap: Why Middle-Class Parents Are Going Broke*, both written with her daughter, Amelia Tyagi. She is widely credited with developing the idea for the Consumer Financial Protection Bureau, and she helped set up the new agency as an assistant to President Obama. She also served as chair of the TARP Congressional Oversight Panel and as the senior advisor to the National Bankruptcy Review Commission. The mother of two and grandmother of three, she lives in Cambridge, Massachusetts, with her husband, Bruce Mann.